❖

A LIBRARY OF PROTESTANT THOUGHT

❖

A LIBRARY OF PROTESTANT THOUGHT

✤ ✤ ✤

EDITORIAL BOARD

✤ ✤ ✤

✤ ✤ ✤

THE
CAMBRIDGE
PLATONISTS

Edited by

GERALD R. CRAGG

New York

OXFORD UNIVERSITY PRESS

1968

A Library of Protestant Thought

A LIBRARY OF PROTESTANT THOUGHT is a collection of writings intended to illumine and interpret the history of the Christian faith in its Protestant expression. It is as variegated in its literary forms and theological positions as is the movement it mirrors. Tracts, letters, sermons, monographs, and other types of literature comprising the heritage of Protestant thought find a place in this series. Works that were originally composed in English, whether in Great Britain or in the New World, and works that were originally written in other languages, many of them not previously translated into English, are included. But it is neither necessary nor desirable that every segment of Protestant theology, piety, and ethics receive equal space. The trite theology, the conventional piety, and the platitudinous ethics always bulk larger in any tradition, also in the Protestantism of the past four centuries, than does the creative output of the religious spirit. The latter is our primary interest in this Library. While we have not felt obligated to grant them equal attention, we have included works that are typical of the more commonplace literature of the Protestant tradition. On the other hand, some works which logically belong in this series have not been included because they are readily available elsewhere.

In keeping with the fundamental purpose of this Library, the voices of Protestantism are allowed to speak for themselves, with only as much introduction, commentary, and exposition as will in fact allow them to do so. Wherever feasible, documents are reproduced in their entirety. A few representative selections have been preferred to more numerous but shorter passages, for the Library tries to depict the structure of thought rather than the genetic development of a man or a movement. Nevertheless, the variety of Protestant forms precludes a uniform treatment throughout. Our aim has been to be representative rather than exhaustive and to employ the best available tools of critical historical scholarship. Despite its ambitious scope, A Library of Protestant Thought is not an encyclopedia of Protestantism. It is a series of volumes from which not only clergymen and theologians, but students of philosophy, history, literature, political science and other disciplines can gain a more balanced view of how the Protestant mind has thought and spoken since the Reformation.

The Board is grateful to the Hazen Foundation for an initial grant enabling it to begin its work; to the Sealantic Fund, Inc., for a grant making possible Board meetings, consultations, and editorial assistance in the preparation of specific volumes; and to the Oxford University Press for undertaking the publication of the Library.

THE EDITORIAL BOARD

Preface

The Cambridge Platonists have long suffered from an unmerited neglect. Most of the histories of philosophy written in English dismiss them with a few perfunctory and inexact remarks. Continental scholars, with the notable exception of Ernst Cassirer, have virtually ignored them. Even in their own age they received far less attention than they deserved.

This may be regretted; it is not entirely surprising. Their style has impeded their influence. They reflect some of the worst faults of seventeenth-century prose: they are often prolix and they are occasionally tedious. But there are other and more fundamental reasons for the neglect from which they have suffered. In a fiercely partisan era they refused to repeat the shibboleths of any party. They were critical of the Calvinism that was dominant before 1660; they were equally opposed to the type of Arminianism that triumphed at the Restoration. Their convictions cut across all the prevailing orthodoxies of a dogmatic age. They aggravated their divergence from accepted patterns by advocating a kind of religious freedom that few of their contemporaries were prepared to accept. They lived at a time when the "spiritually-minded" were suspicious of reason, and when the rationalists increasingly allowed scope for little except the powers of man's mind. By urging the claims of a spirituality that transcended the limits of reason but never repudiated its legitimate claims, the Cambridge Platonists antagonized all the dominant parties and forfeited the support of any appreciable group. Arminians and Calvinists, Anglicans and dissenters, rationalists and mystics, all rejected the cooperation of such dubious allies.

Actually the message of the Cambridge Platonists was peculiarly relevant to the needs of the seventeenth century. It can be argued that the problems of that age were not entirely dissimilar to those of the late twentieth century. Certainly the central concerns of the Platonists speak more persuasively to the modern temper than either the Puritanism or the Laudianism which originally combined to obscure what they had to say. More than providing a body of teaching, they represent a certain method of approaching perennial theological problems. An age like ours, which is groping amid the ruins of previous systems for a new way of dealing with theological issues, might profitably examine the spirit, the temper and the teachings of these men.

It is not, however, an easy task to make the works of the Cambridge Platonists more readily accessible. It is notoriously difficult to extract passages from most seventeenth-century writers, and the Cambridge Platonists are no exception. This is a result partly of their style, but to an even greater extent of their method. They relied neither on analysis nor on demonstration. When necessary they could argue cogently enough, but their aim was to foster insight, not to establish proof. Their works are not tightly knit or closely articulated. They do not marshal their arguments and march them like a phalanx through their opponents' position. It would be more appropriate to compare their dialectic to the movement of currents through an ocean inlet, shifting this way or that as the tide ebbs or flows. This method followed naturally from their Platonic outlook and their understanding of the soul. A good example may be found in Henry More's *Explanation of the Grand Mystery of Godliness*—a work that extends to nearly four hundred large folio pages. The distinctive quality of the book is in the leisurely, meandering course of the discussion, and this is something which no selection of extracts can hope to capture. My choice has often been determined by simple considerations of what could be included in an edition such as this. Those well acquainted with the Cambridge Platonists will miss many favorite passages. I cannot hope that my selection will satisfy all whose familiarity with these men qualifies them to judge it. I cannot even claim that I have satisfied myself. With many a regretful glance at sections which I could not use, I have attempted to select such passages as would, in combination, faithfully reflect the fundamental convictions of the Cambridge Platonists.

There are other difficulties inseparable from an undertaking of this kind; I must also explain my method with regard to them. The aim of this edition is to present a representative selection in a way that will be at once faithful to the intention of the authors and intelligible to the reader of today. I have modernized the spelling. Very occasionally, when the form of a word has changed slightly in the intervening centuries and when the original would be pointlessly archaic or even positively misleading, I have changed it to correspond to modern usage. I have tried to simplify the punctuation, though this is a process which, in view of the complexities of seventeenth-century style, cannot be pushed too far, nor even (I fear) be consistently applied.

The most baffling problems have been posed by the hundreds of classical quotations. The Cambridge Platonists were university teachers in an age when a parade of classical learning was a part of the idiom of scholarly discussion. For the modern reader, however, a page liberally spattered with Greek quotations is first a hindrance and then an exasperation. I was relieved to notice that I am not the first person who has been troubled by these quotations and who has tried to reduce the problem to manageable proportions. John Worthington, the friend and editor of John Smith, mentions his difficulties in a preface to the *Select Discourses:* "As for some short allusions and expressions borrowed out of ancient authors, serving rather for ornament than support of the matter in hand, there seemed to be less need of being solicitous about all of them." To judge from the problem that remains, Worthington exercised his editorial prerogative on a modest scale. I have dealt with this situation as follows: The Cambridge Platonists often quoted extensive passages from classical authors, and then immediately provided a translation. In such cases I have simply deleted the original text. Sometimes they cited a Greek or Latin phrase and immediately added its English equivalent. Here I have often, but by no means always, deleted the classical words. Where the removal of the original would require a revision, I have, of course, left the sentence as the author wrote it. The difficulty is obvious: the flavor of these works is due in part to the way the writers invoked the authority of the classical world, and the flavor is best conveyed by the recurrence of the languages in which the ancients wrote. I have tried to preserve the quality of the works without allowing the mannerisms to become too great an irritation to the modern reader. I am acutely aware that this somewhat flexible method is as difficult to justify as it has been to apply. The textual purist may well feel that I have gone too far; the advocate of intelligibility may complain that I have not gone far enough.

I have sometimes substituted a translation for a quotation which the author himself did not render into English. Where a classical expression is used and then paraphrased or freely interpreted, I have not offered a translation either in the text or in a note.

Many of the classical quotations are taken from relatively obscure authors. I have identified the sources where possible (and in this I have received much help from others). To my regret some of the quotations have baffled all my efforts to pin them down.

I am grateful to many people who have lightened my labors. Librarians generously placed their resources at my disposal. Professor Winthrop Hudson and Professor William Morris read the manuscript and offered helpful suggestions. Professor Albert Outler subjected the whole work to a most detailed and searching scrutiny and delivered the book and its editor from many a pitfall. Miss Amy Clampitt provided invaluable editorial assistance. My daughter Betty helped with the typing of initial drafts of various sections. My wife helped in innumerable ways—typing material, checking extracts, correcting proofs, compiling the index.

Table of Contents

Introduction

THE CAMBRIDGE PLATONISTS occupied a distinctive and significant place in the intellectual world of the seventeenth century. They were a small group, knit together by personal ties and united by certain basic concerns and convictions. They had no formal leader, though they all acknowledged their indebtedness to Benjamin Whichcote. They had a common point of view, though they can be described as a "school" only with certain reservations—the term usually implies a relationship more formal and explicit than that which actually bound them together. It is not a simple matter even to delimit the membership of the group. Though its center was at Cambridge—indeed, of the inner circle, all except one initially belonged to a single college, Emmanuel—a couple of Oxford men might be included, and on the fringes there were other writers who had attended neither university.

1. Who Were the Cambridge Platonists?

The senior member of the group, and the one with the strongest claim to be considered its founder, was Benjamin Whichcote. He came of a middle-class family of some means, but we know very little about his early life. He entered Emmanuel College, Cambridge, in 1628, and became, in due course, a fellow of the college and a very successful tutor. In 1642 the Long Parliament convened. The following year, Whichcote accepted a college living in Somerset, but in 1644 he returned to Cambridge to become Provost of King's College, succeeding a man who had been ejected during the recent parliamentary visitation of the university. This fact is significant of the political and social turmoil in which even retiring scholars were involved. Whichcote was not a man of pronounced party loyalties. He insisted on sharing his stipend with his predecessor, and he avoided taking the National Covenant—one of the oaths imposed by the triumphant parliamentary party. Though not a partisan, he lost his office at the Restoration of 1660. He took the oaths required by the Act of Uniformity (1662), and until his death in 1683 he officiated as an Anglican clergyman

3

in London. As a university teacher Whichcote had a profound influence on his pupils, but he made his chief permanent contribution through the pulpit; and (apart from some notable letters) his surviving works consist entirely of sermons.

The biographical details about Whichcote may be meager, but we can form a very clear picture of the man himself. His correspondence with Tuckney reveals him as a man of broad outlook, convinced of his own position but courteous in maintaining it against his critics. His sermons leave the impression of a person to whom his parishioners must have listened with profit and with whom his friends doubtless conversed with pleasure beside his hearth. The most vivid contemporary account of Whichcote, given us by Bishop Burnet in his *History of My Own Time*, confirms this impression, and deserves to be quoted in full.

> Whichcote was a man of a rare temper, very mild and obliging. He had great credit with some that had been eminent in the late times [i.e., during the Interregnum] and made all the use he could of it to protect good men of all persuasions. He was much for liberty of conscience: and being disgusted with the dry systematic way of those times, he studied to raise those that conversed with him to a nobler set of thoughts, and to consider religion as the seed of a deiform nature (to use one of his own phrases). In order to this he set young students much on reading Plato, Tully [Cicero] and Plotin[us], and on considering the Christian doctrine as a religion sent from God both to elevate and sweeten human nature; in which he was a great example, as well as a wise and kind instructor.[1]

Among Whichcote's pupils at Emmanuel were two young men, close contemporaries, both of whom should be classified as Cambridge Platonists. Of Nathanael Culverwel (1618–51) we know almost nothing except that he was under Whichcote's tuition at Emmanuel, was elected a fellow of the college, and died young. His most important work, *An Elegant and Learned Discourse of the Light of Nature*, was published posthumously in 1652. John Smith (1616–52) came from a humble background (his father was "a small farmer" in Northamptonshire), profited from his studies under Whichcote, and in due course was elected a fellow of Queens' College. Here he spent the remainder of his brief career. As dean and catechist he was responsible for certain kinds of religious instruction in the college; in discharging his duties he wrote the *Discourses* which constitute his principal claim to fame. Like Culverwel, he died young. We

---

1. G. Burnet, *History of My Own Time*, ed. O. Airy (Oxford, 1897), I, 331.

know considerably more about him than we do about Culverwel. His friend John Worthington included in the volume of *Discourses*, which he edited and published, the tribute delivered at Smith's funeral by Simon Patrick (also a fellow of Queens' and subsequently bishop of Chichester and of Ely). Even if one discounts the extravagant language of this eulogy, it is obvious that Smith commanded the affection as well as the respect of his colleagues. He was a young man of great promise, learned and devout.

Ralph Cudworth (1617–88) was successively a fellow and tutor of Emmanuel College, Master of Clare Hall, Regius Professor of Hebrew in the university, and Master of Christ's College. His father was a minister of pronounced Puritan sympathies. The son himself was consulted by the leaders of the parliamentary cause,[2] and was invited to preach before the House of Commons; but he was not a man of partisan spirit, and at the Restoration he was left in undisturbed possession of his mastership at Christ's. Cudworth was a scholar of vast but undisciplined learning. He was apparently unable to resist the temptation to pursue every inviting bypath, and his *True Intellectual System of the Universe* is a fragment (though on an enormous scale) of his projected work. Nor was he more successful with his treatise on ethics; he restated the principles of his thought, but he neither fully expounded his moral theory nor even finished the work. Yet Cudworth was obviously a thinker of unusual power; had he controlled his material with greater rigor and completed his projected writings, he would have made a major contribution to English philosophy.

Henry More (1614–87) was the only major member of the group not associated with Emmanuel College. We know that he came from a background where Puritan influences were strong. From Eton he went to Christ's College, Cambridge; he became a fellow, refused high preferment in the Church, and made the college his home for the rest of his life. Even by seventeenth-century standards, More was a prolific writer. Whereas Cudworth completed almost nothing, More poured forth an impressive stream of works—poems, dialogues, treatises on philosophy and theology, excursions into Cabbalistic literature, exercises in exegesis, and investigations of spiritualistic phenomena. Nor was More's range and versatility displayed only in the forms he used. There are two distinct tendencies in his thought. On the one hand he exalts the importance of intellectual effort;

2. Cf. Cudworth's letters to Thurloe (Cromwell's secretary of State) in *A Collection of the State Papers of John Thurloe, Esq.*, ed. Thomas Birch, 7 vols. (London, 1724).

on the other, he insists upon its limits.[3] He expresses more fully than any other of the Platonists the mystical element which is an intermittent but characteristic ingredient in their thought. He explores with delight the prophetic and apocalyptical strains in Scripture. In much of his writing we are conscious of an exhilaration of thought, sweeping him into a realm which many scholars never enter. A less attractive writer than John Smith, he has, like him, the elusive but unmistakable quality of spiritual genius.

John Norris of All Souls College, Oxford, represents the later developments of the "school." Though a considerably younger man, he made contact with More, corresponded with him at considerable length, and was obviously deeply influenced by him. Norris's work is clearly an extension of certain elements in the thought of the Cambridge men, but he also introduced novel elements. He was clearly indebted to Nicholas Malebranche, the French philosopher whose system combined the thought of both Augustine and Descartes. When John Locke published his *Essay Upon the Human Understanding*, Norris responded with a very perceptive critique—an event that brings into focus the relation of Locke to the Cambridge Platonists. There is no disputing their influence on his thought —he frankly admits his indebtedness to them—but there are significant differences between his system and theirs. Ultimately there can be no reconciliation between his "empiricism" and their "idealism." Norris was not content merely to complain that the whole temper of the *Essay* was at variance with the mode of thought in which he had been trained. He subjected Locke's treatment of ideas to a searching examination, and put his finger on many of the weaknesses inherent in Locke's system. Norris was more than a shrewd critic; in his *Essay Towards the Theory of the Ideal and Intelligible World* (Vol. I, 1701; Vol. II, 1704) he advanced his own theory about the world we know and its relation to our understanding.

Several other men have some claim to be included among the Cambridge Platonists. Joseph Glanvill (1638–80), an Oxford graduate who was rector of the Abbey Church at Bath, was an admirer and correspondent of Henry More. One of his chief contributions to the thought of the age was his claim that skepticism can be an adjunct rather than a threat to faith. His *Vanity of Dogmatizing* reflects the conviction, shared by all the Platonists, that there is a non-dogmatic way of exploring and expressing religious truths. This is so fundamental to the Cambridge Platonists, and so important an aspect of their contribution to Protestant thought, that Glanvill is properly associated with them. But his primary concerns were with

3. Cf. A. Lichtenstein, *Henry More* (Cambridge, Mass., 1962), passim.

science and its relation to religion, and though this too occupied the Platonists, his approach here was distinctive, and it is debatable whether he can be regarded as more than a marginal member of the group. Peter Sterry (1613–72), a graduate of Emmanuel, produced an interesting amalgam of Calvinism and Neo-Platonism. Both theologically and politically he remained more deeply committed than his friends to the Puritanism from which they all sprang, but he was united to them both by the main elements in his thought and by a strong belief in the necessity of tolerance grounded in Christian love. Richard Cumberland (1632–1718) had strong affinities with the Platonists, but his major work (*De Legibus Naturae*) really represents a transition to a different position. George Rust, Theophilus Gale and John Worthington might also be considered Platonists, but theologically they are more shadowy figures, and it is doubtful whether they should be included in the classification.

For this edition, I have drawn mainly on the works of Whichcote, Smith, Cudworth and More. I have included one extract from Culverwel and three from Norris. When much had to be excluded, these seemed to be the men whose claims could not be denied.

II. *The Intellectual Background of the Cambridge Platonists*

The historical context of the Cambridge Platonists is particularly important for an appreciation of their work.

Both politically and intellectually the seventeenth century was an age of fierce tensions and of revolutionary changes. It might be supposed that in the quiet refuge of their Cambridge courts, scholars were safely isolated from the turmoils of the time. Nothing could be farther from the truth. The issues at stake invaded every man's study and challenged the very foundations of his daily life. Emmanuel College must be thought of as a kind of portent. In the latter part of Elizabeth's reign, when Puritanism was struggling to promote the further reformation of the Church of England, Sir Walter Mildmay, the Queen's treasurer, founded the college as a nursery for godly ministers. When Elizabeth chided him for establishing a Puritan foundation, he neither admitted the charge nor denied it. "Madam," he said, "far be it from me to countenance anything contrary to your established laws, but I have set an acorn, which when it becomes an oak, God knows what will be the fruit thereof." Neither the nature nor the quantity of that fruit was to remain long in doubt. The first two masters of Emmanuel, Lawrence Chaderton and John Preston, were among the most distinguished Puritan divines of the early seventeenth century, and from its earliest days the college fulfilled the pious hopes of its founder by producing a mighty host of Puritan preachers. In the Old World and in the New, Emmanuel played a notable role: during the eleven years from 1629 to 1640, thirty-three of its graduates emigrated to Massachusetts Bay.[4]

Puritanism established itself in Cambridge in an atmosphere of intense debate. The struggle between Whitgift and Cartwright soon passed into history, but other controversies supervened. When Archbishop Bancroft moved against the Puritans, many men at Cambridge were affected. When Archbishop Laud was pressing for conformity, he silenced even so distinguished a Cambridge preacher as Richard Sibbes, lecturer at Holy Trinity Church. The atmosphere was one of eager discussion and incessant controversy. With the meeting of the Long Parliament and the outbreak of the Civil War, Cambridge was engulfed by the upheavals of the time. The town saw the coming and going of Cromwell and his troops; the university experienced the "visitations" designed to purge it of royalist sympathizers. It was perhaps inevitable that our earliest significant record of the Cambridge Platonists should be the products of a controversy in which one of their number was engaged. Whichcote's preaching had attracted notice. In his sermons a distinguished Puritan leader, Dr. Tuckney, Master of Emmanuel, had detected traces of unsound theology. In those days religious differences were not merely the subject matter of theoretical discussion; they were matters of passionate concern, inseparable from the great debates then raging in church and state.

With scarcely an exception, the Cambridge Platonists came out of a Puritan background. For the most part they were educated in the very citadel of Puritan zeal. But they cannot be classed as Puritans. They retained some of the finest qualities of Puritanism—its moral earnestness, for example—but they abandoned its theology. Nevertheless, it did not follow that, having shed their Calvinism, they accepted the principal alternative then available. They disliked the rigidity of Archbishop Laud as much as they did the dogmatism of the Puritans. In periods of intense debate, most people can recognize only two alternatives. The Cambridge Platonists were in the awkward position of advocating a third position, different from both the others then current, but likely to be confused by the careless with the one or the other. When the Restoration of 1660

4. S. E. Morison, *The Founding of Harvard College* (Cambridge, Mass., 1935), Appendix B.

brought back the House of Stuart and the Church of England, the Cambridge Platonists were still in an ambiguous position. They were not dissenters, though occasionally their Puritan background invited misunderstanding. They accepted the established church, but they had little sympathy with the resurgent Anglicanism of men like Archbishop Sheldon or Herbert Thorndike. They came to be designated "Latitudinarians," but the term led as much to confusion as it did to clarification. They were liberals, but of a distinctive kind. A new breed of thinkers was emerging—calmly reasonable in tone, strongly ethical in emphasis—and to these men the term "Latitudinarian" appropriately applies. But Tillotson, Stillingfleet, Burnet and Patrick, though they were deeply influenced by the Platonists, reflected a different mood. These younger men lacked the subtle sense of spiritual truth, the mystical awareness of an eternal order, which marked the older generation of Cambridge men. They walked in the light, but the light of the new day was hard and cold as well as clear. So once again the Platonists occupied an intermediate position, slightly apart from, and liable to misunderstanding by, all the contending parties. That they were often ignored is hardly surprising, but none the less tragic. They represented a position peculiarly relevant to the needs of that turbulent and distracted period. They were concerned with the problems of an age when mounting sectarianism seemed the only alternative to the impasse at which wrangling ideologies had arrived. Tragically enough, the strife and turmoil in which their contemporaries were embroiled largely obscured the fact.

In short, the Cambridge Platonists came from a Puritan background against which they found themselves in vigorous reaction. The doctrine of predestination—to thoughtful people the very essence of the dogmatic Calvinism so prevalent in Puritan circles—was especially repellent to them. Henry More early discovered that he could not "swallow down that hard doctrine concerning fate." In a fragment of autobiography he has left us a vivid picture of the inner struggles of a lad revolted by the prevailing orthodoxy. He tells us that even as a schoolboy he "did . . . very stoutly and earnestly for my years dispute against this fate or Calvinistic predestination as it is called." He had, he adds,

> such a deep aversion in my temper to this opinion, and so firm and
> unshaken a persuasion of the divine justice and goodness, that on a
> certain day, in a ground belonging to Eton College where the boys
> used to play and exercise themselves, musing concerning these things
> with myself and recalling to my mind this doctrine of Calvin, I did

thus seriously and deliberately conclude with myself, viz., "If I am one of those that are predestined unto Hell, where all things are full of nothing but cursing and blasphemy, yet will I behave myself there patiently and submissively towards God; and if there be any one thing more than another that is acceptable to him, that will I set myself to do with a sincere heart and to the utmost of my power"; being certainly persuaded that if I thus demeaned myself, he would hardly keep me long in that place.[5]

What began as an emotional revulsion from predestination became a considered attack on its intellectual implications. To Cudworth, predestination was chiefly abhorrent because it was one form of determinism. Admittedly, it was different from the variety expounded by Hobbes, but it was no less pernicious. Cudworth called the one "divine fatalism arbitrary," the other "divine fatalism natural," and vehemently attacked them both. In his sermon before the House of Commons, he defined with care and denounced with courage the doctrine of election. It had done, he declared, incalculable damage to the cause of true religion. Predestination, when argued theoretically, was likely to appear a rather abstruse doctrine; [6] other aspects of Calvinism had more immediately practical implications. The elect were summoned to "walk worthy of their calling;" therefore ethical theory was necessarily involved. What is "the right"—and how is it established? The Calvinists insisted that right is right because God wills it to be so. On the contrary, replied the Platonists, the distinction between right and wrong is eternal and immutable. The Cambridge Platonists valued the strain of high moral seriousness in Calvinism; what they attacked was the theoretical foundation on which it rested.

Another disconcerting aspect of Calvinism was its uncompromising denigration of man. Yet man had been made in the image of God. He had been endowed with reason. "The spirit of a man," as Whichcote delighted to repeat, "is the candle of the Lord, lighted by God and lighting us to God." [7] Even in its tarnished state the divine endowment must not be despised. Calvinism tended to obliterate reason in deference to faith; to Whichcote this seemed to jeopardize man's fairest prospect of appro-

5. Richard Ward, *The Life of the Learned and Pious Dr. Henry More* (London, 1710), 6–7. Professor William Morris has pointed out that More's attitude here is similar to the willingness to be damned for the glory of God which we find in some of the early New England theologians.

6. Many Puritans, who were perhaps unable to repeat all the arguments for or against predestination, were satisfied that they grasped its essential meaning, and from it they derived a strong sense of meaning and purpose in life.

7. Whichcote, *Moral and Religious Aphorisms* (London, 1753), No. 916. He is quoting Proverbs 20:27.

priating the truth. The Platonists, it is clear, opposed certain specific doctrines inculcated by Calvinism. They disliked even more intensely the
temper and spirit which dogmatism fostered. For a hundred years men
had been debating the abstruse refinements of theology, and the most
conspicuous result had been an increase of contention and bitterness.
Bad fruit implied a corrupt source. "The more false any one is in his religion, the more fierce and furious in maintaining it; the more mistaken,
the more imposing." [8]

Calvinism was not the only position which had recently been maintained in an inflexible spirit. The Cambridge Platonists had been deeply
influenced by the Dutch Arminians,[9] but in England those who were
popularly known as Arminians had shown no less exclusive a temper than
their opponents. The Laudians had been as much at fault as the Calvinists.
The Cambridge men were eager to show that there was a mediating position between the two extremes. According to a pamphleteer who signed
himself "S. P." (probably Simon Patrick), they advocated a "virtuous
mediocrity" between "the meretricious gaudiness of the Church of Rome
and the squalid sluttery of fanatic conventicles," [10] and they were anxious
to prove that in thought as well as in ritual and church order there was a
middle way. Against the Laudians they declared that morality was more
important than polity; against the Calvinists they insisted that reason must
not be fettered; against both they maintained that the legitimate seat of
authority in religion was the individual conscience, governed by reason
and illuminated by a revelation which could not be inconsistent with
reason itself.[11]

Other, more purely intellectual influences powerfully affected the Cambridge Platonists. These men were scholars, steeped in the comprehensive
(and sometimes undiscriminating) learning that was a heritage from the
Renaissance. But they were also well aware of what was happening around
them. The contents of Cudworth's personal library are revealing. Recent
scientists represented on his shelves were Harvey, Boyle, Tycho Brahe,
Copernicus, Galileo and Newton; modern philosophers included Bacon,
Descartes, Hobbes, Gassendi and Spinoza.[12] In his response to these men

8. Whichcote, *Aphorisms*, No. 499.
9. For the relations between the Dutch Arminians and the Cambridge Platonists,
cf. Rosalie L. Colie, *Light and Enlightenment* (Cambridge, England, 1957), passim.
10. "S. P.," *A Brief Account of the New Sect of Latitude Men* (London, 1662), 11.
11. Cf. G. R. Cragg, *From Puritanism to the Age of Reason* (Cambridge, England,
1950), 41 .
12. *Bibliotheca Cudworthiana*, a catalogue of the sale of books at Roll's Coffee-
House, London, 1690. Cf. J. A. Passmore, *Ralph Cudworth* (Cambridge, 1951), 3.

Cudworth was sometimes cautiously sympathetic, often critically hostile. Like Whichcote and Smith, he referred to Bacon's "idols" of the theater and of the cave, but he had serious doubts concerning Bacon's general position. The rejection of final causes seemed to him "the very spirit of atheism." The Platonists believed that philosophy should have a religious foundation; Bacon was careful to isolate theology from scientific and philosophical concerns.[13] This difference, more than any other, explains the reservations with which Cudworth and More regarded Bacon's program. Their aim was to unify all knowledge; his, to safeguard the autonomy of science by protecting it against the impact of theology.

Descartes' influence was at once stronger than Bacon's and more ambiguous. Initially the Cambridge men gave his thought a cordial welcome. John Smith, it was asserted, introduced the study of Descartes to Cambridge. Henry More corresponded with the French philosopher, and the deferential tone of his letters is unmistakable. Cartesianism seemed to provide exactly the kind of foundation which the intellectual life of the new age demanded. It saw the material world as subject to the strict rule of mechanical laws, yet at the same time it acknowledged the reality of the spiritual world. It was wide in the range of its interests yet explicit in its demand for exact observation and experiment; it provided a skillful synthesis in which science and religion both had an honored place. For twenty years More remained in some degree a disciple of Descartes. By 1665 (in his *Divine Dialogues*) his uneasiness was becoming apparent. Two years later (in *Enchiridion Ethicum*) his disenchantment with Descartes was shown to be complete. After a further lapse of four years he published his *Enchiridion Metaphysicum*—one of the most vigorous and searching attacks on Cartesianism that the age produced. The reasons for More's change of view are clear. Initially he was dazzled by the brilliance of Descartes' achievement and delighted with the new possibilities it opened up. The implications of Descartes' separation of the material and the spiritual, the body and the soul, became increasingly evident and seemed increasingly grave; and Descartes' definition of matter as extension appeared to More a philosophical aberration of the most dangerous consequence.

Cudworth's response to Descartes, though similar, was more complex than More's. He saw that Descartes was really reviving one of the ancient

13. Cf. F. Bacon, *The Advancement of Learning*, Bk II, xxv, 1, §§ 3–5. For a careful assessment of Bacon's intentions in separating theology and science, see Christopher Hill, *The Intellectual Origins of the English Revolution* (Oxford, 1965), esp. 91–96.

forms of atomic philosophy—a development not necessarily dangerous in itself, but one which in Descartes he regarded as a trend towards pure mechanism. He was disturbed at the inference that the universe could function independently of its Creator. In spite of Descartes' sincere protestations of orthodoxy, it was becoming clear that Cartesianism was thickly strewn with anti-Christian elements. The God who (or which?) occupied so important a place in the system of Descartes was not really the Christian God at all.[14] Dualism seemed to be inherent in Cartesianism; and Cudworth, who was not necessarily opposed to dualism as such, nevertheless believed that the pattern implicit in Descartes was dangerous. Cudworth, however, never denounced Descartes in such unmeasured terms as those finally employed by More. He was prepared to accept much of the French philosopher's method, and always spoke of him with obvious respect.

The Cambridge Platonists may have been slightly ambivalent in their response to Descartes; in their reaction to Spinoza and Hobbes they were explicit and emphatic. They detected the influence of Descartes in both men, and this confirmed their suspicions about the former's system. Both Cudworth and More regarded Spinoza as a modern manifestation of ancient forms of atheism and materialism. More, in particular, was well acquainted with Spinoza's works; he attacked them repeatedly and with vigor.[15]

In Hobbes the Cambridge Platonists found the most convincing proof of the dangers lurking in contemporary trends of thought. He was a threat precisely because he epitomized so much that was already current. Though Smith's work antedated the recognition that Hobbes menaced much that had been valued as true, and though Whichcote showed no explicit concern with Hobbes, both men attacked exactly the tendencies in contemporary thought which Cudworth and More regarded as the distinguishing features of Hobbes's system. In certain respects, it is true, Hobbes and his critics seemed to occupy common ground. They defended the use of reason in the life of faith; so did he. "In religion," he wrote, "we are not to renounce our senses and experience; nor (that which is the undoubted word of God) our natural reason. For they are the talents which he hath put into our hands to negotiate till the coming again of our blessed Savior; and therefore not to be folded up in the napkin

14. See Cudworth, *A Treatise of Free Will* (London, 1838), 49.
15. See R. L. Colie, *Light and Enlightenment,* Chapter v, for a valuable study of More's attitude to Spinoza.

of an implicit faith, but employed in the purchase of justice, peace and true religion." [16] But Hobbes, it appeared, intended to use reason for ends abhorrent to the Cambridge scholars. Moreover, his view of man and of society threatened almost all the values which the Platonists were anxious to conserve. To them he seemed to be the aggressive advocate of modern atheism.[17] His occasional professions of belief in God had all the appearance of calculated hypocrisy, since the main ingredients of his thought threatened the very foundations of theism. His materialism was particularly offensive to thinkers who asserted the priority and supremacy of spiritual realities. Hobbes denied the freedom of the will; thus he opened the door to determinism. Combined with this was an ethical relativism which presupposed that right and wrong could be determined by political expediency and imposed by political power: nothing, that is, was inherently good or bad, and in the final analysis, might was right. Hobbes's view of man seemed to imply a pronounced individualism, whereas the Platonists believed that man was to find his fulfillment in community, and that society could be understood only in organic terms. Their account of Hobbes's teaching may appear extreme and one-sided. Certainly Cudworth and More reacted violently to his methodology and to the content of his thought.[18] But contrary to appearances, he did not inspire in them a purely negative response. Rather, he served as a kind of catalyst, and at one point after another he helped to crystallize the distinctive doctrines of the Cambridge Platonists.

These men were alert to movements of thought in their own day. They were also scholars, steeped in classical learning, and they drew heavily on Greek philosophy. It was natural to call them Platonists, but the term is not entirely exact. They were, of course, intimately acquainted with Plato's dialogues, and their deep indebtedness to his thought is obvious. The role of ideas, the nature of the soul, the place of reason, the eternity of moral concepts—all of these came to them from Plato. Cudworth's theory of knowledge was derived from the *Theaetetus;* the germ of his moral

16. Hobbes, *Leviathan,* Part III, Ch. XLIII.

17. For a helpful discussion of the reaction of the Cambridge Platonists to Hobbes, see S. I. Mintz, *The Hunting of Leviathan* (Cambridge, 1962), especially chapters v and vi.

18. Though Hobbes's style is clear and vigorous, there has been a good deal of disagreement about his actual beliefs. For a rather different interpretation, cf. F. C. Hood, *The Divine Politics of Thomas Hobbes* (Oxford, 1964). But Professor Mintz has shown that by seventeenth-century standards the reaction of the Cambridge Platonists was neither extreme nor exceptional.

theory can be found in the *Euthyphro*. But the Cambridge men drew upon
other classical sources as well. They quoted Plotinus even more freely
than Plato. It is true that they lived before the advent of modern literary
criticism, at a time when scholarship did not accurately distinguish between Plato's thought and the modifications it had received at the hands
of his successors. It is now sometimes assumed that Plotinus was responsible
for a confused and corrupt version of Platonism. But the Cambridge men
believed that Plotinus had carried Plato's thought forward and had sharp-
ened its implications in a particularly valuable way. This attitude was not
due to a failure of critical acumen but to their primary intellectual aims.
Their attitude towards their sources was closely related to their concern
for a spiritual interpretation of reality. To them Platonism was the entire
tradition of metaphysics inaugurated by Plato, and continued and expanded by his successors. This "Platonism," of course, had reached them
through interpreters who had modified its character. The Renaissance
scholars, particularly Marsilio Ficino and Pico della Mirandola, put their
own imprint on the subsequent understanding of Greek thought.[19] Nor
must we forget that in the pages of the Schoolmen the Cambridge men
first encountered much that affected their interpretation of Plato.[20] But
from whatever sources they drew their material, the Cambridge Platonists
were certainly not content merely to repeat the concepts of ancient Greek
philosophy. Plato's debate with Pythagoras, they believed, had first exposed the very issues which were involved in their own controversy with
Hobbes. If the problems were identical, were not the same insights required to solve those problems? For this reason, Platonism seemed to them
totally contemporary with the major struggle of their own day.

To a modern classical scholar, it might appear that the Cambridge
Platonists treated their sources with considerable freedom. No one can
suggest that they allowed their eclectic tendencies to confuse or obscure
their primary emphasis. They welcomed Plato as a partner because the
Church had always treated him as a valuable ally in its task of interpreting
the faith. A sympathetic contemporary observer remarked that it was the
purpose of the Cambridge men to bring the Church back to "her old
loving nurse, the Platonic philosophy." [21] The Cambridge Platonists knew
the patristic surmise that Plato had drawn upon the wisdom of Moses.

19. Concerning the influence of Renaissance Platonism on the Cambridge Platonists,
see P. O. Kristeller, *The Philosophy of Marsilio Ficino* (New York, 1943), 19.
20. Smith, More and Cudworth all acknowledged their debt to Aquinas.
21. "S. P.," *A Brief Account of the New Sect of Latitude Men*, 9.

They delighted in setting forth the parallels between the Platonic and the Christian Trinities.[22] They quoted Clement of Alexandria and Origen because these Fathers represented an alliance between Greek philosophy and Christian theology such as they were eager to perpetuate. But there was never a trace of uncertainty in their minds as to which was the senior partner in this association.

> I cannot, [said More] conceal from whence I am, viz., of Christ; but yet acknowledging that God hath not left the heathen, Plato especially, without witness of himself. Whose doctrine might strike our adulterate Christian professors with shame and astonishment; their lives falling so exceeding short of the better heathen. How far short are they of that admirable and transcendent high mystery of true Christianism? To which Plato is a very good subservient minister; whose philosophy, I singing here in a full heat, why may it not be free for me to break out into a higher strain, and under it to touch upon some points of Christianity? [23]

As Professor Willey has aptly said, "The Alexandrian Fathers grafted Christianity on to a recognized philosophy; the Cambridge Platonists grafted philosophy on to a recognized Christianity." [24] In the Scriptures the Platonists found their primary source, and it is obvious that the Johannine strain proved particularly congenial to them. A glance at the biblical passages cited in the sermons of Whichcote, Smith and Cudworth establishes two things: the catholicity of their references and the indubitably Christian character of their writings.

III. *The Basic Teachings of the Cambridge Platonists*

The relation of faith to reason was an exceptionally important issue in the seventeenth century. As we have already seen, there were forces at work in the intellectual world which insisted that the two be kept apart. The Cambridge Platonists, on the other hand, were determined that they should be kept together. This was not an attitude inspired by a desire to find a theoretical answer to an important intellectual problem. These

22. Cudworth, *The True Intellectual System*, Ch. IV; More, "To the Reader, upon this second edition"; and "Psychozoia, or the first part of the Song of the Soul, containing a Christiano-Platonical display of LIFE; To the Reader," in *Philosophical Poems* (Cambridge, 1647).

23. More, "Psychozoia; To the Reader."

24. B. Willey, *The English Moralists* (London, 1964), 172.

scholars were men of deep religious experience. They were convinced that the wholeness of the abundant life could be preserved only if its essential unity were maintained. But to set faith and reason in opposition—even to allow them to drift apart—would be to destroy the only basis on which harmony could be established. "Sir," Whichcote wrote to his friend Tuckney, "I oppose not rational to spiritual, for spiritual is most rational." [25] The faith that religion evokes is not the repudiation of our intellectual faculties, but their highest fulfillment. A blind faith, which will not submit to examination by the mind nor accept justification by it, becomes a contradiction in terms. This is not to suggest that our unaided reason can attain to divine truth without the assistance of grace. But the Platonists refused to divorce natural theology from revealed religion; this, they insisted, would be to divorce what God had joined together.

Their awareness of the unity of the different kinds of truth was not a novel discovery. Even pre-Christian thinkers had seen that it is dangerous to let knowledge and insight drift apart. "It was," said John Smith, "a degenerate and unworthy spirit in that philosophy which first separated and made such distances between metaphysical truths and the truths of nature, whereas the first and most ancient wisdom amongst the heathens was indeed a philosophical divinity or a divine philosophy." [26] Men arrange their thought in various patterns; behind all these partial systems lies an eternal truth, as perfect in its unity as in its comprehensiveness and beauty. To reach *that* truth is the goal of man's intellectual quest, and what he seeks is what God gives. Truth, said Whichcote,

> is so near to the soul, so much the very image and form of it, that it may be said of truth, that as the soul is by derivation from God, so truth is by communication. No sooner doth the truth of God come into the soul's sight but the soul knows her to be her first and old acquaintance. Though they have been by some accident unhappily parted a great while, yet having now through the divine Providence happily met, they greet one another and renew their acquaintance as those that were first and ancient friends. . . . Nothing is more natural to man's soul than to receive truth. [27]

Natural and revealed religion differed only "in the way of descent to us"; they were "equally connatural" to man, and appealed to his complete and

25. Whichcote, Letters to Tuckney, No. 3. See infra, 46.
26. J. Smith, "The Excellency and Necessity of True Religion," *Select Discourses*, Discourse IX, Ch. VIII.
27. Whichcote, *Works* (Aberdeen, 1753), III, 17f.

indivisible being in ways which, though diverse, were not irreconcilable.[28]

God had equipped man both to receive the truth and to find his deepest satisfaction in it. "If God had not made man to know there is a God, there is nothing that God could have demanded of him, nothing wherein he might have challenged him, nothing that he could have expected man should have received of him."[29] Therefore men might rightfully affirm that religion neither denies reason nor represses it. Faith was not "a bird of prey that comes to peck out the eyes of men, . . . no extinguisher to put out the candle of the Lord."[30] In religion, reason played a very necessary role; it provided the measure by which any system of belief must be judged. "What has not reason in it or for it," said Whichcote, "if held out for religion, is man's superstition. It was not religion of God's making."[31] Indeed, when reason was suppressed the very possibility of religion was destroyed. Our reason "is not laid aside nor discharged, much less is it confounded, by any of the materials of religion; but awakened, excited, employed, directed and improved by it; for the . . . understanding is that faculty whereby man is made capable of God and apprehensive of him, receptive from him and able to make returns unto him."[32] It could therefore be confidently assumed that the power of reason would lead men of sincere and teachable spirit to a sufficient knowledge of religious truth. What faith demanded could never endanger, still less destroy, the dignity of the human mind. "They are greatly mistaken who in religion oppose points of reason and matters of faith; as if nature went one way and the author of nature went another."[33] To deny our reason was to be guilty of treason against him who gave it to be our instrument of judgment in our search for the truth. "To go against reason is to go against God; it is the selfsame thing to do that which the reason of the case doth require and that which God himself doth appoint. Reason is the divine governor of man's life; it is the very voice of God."[34]

A faculty invested with such dignity and possessed of such powers could not be restricted to simple and elementary functions. As a first step towards understanding its role, the Cambridge Platonists distinguished

28. Whichcote, *Works*, III, 20.
29. Whichcote, *Works*, III, 144.
30. Culverwel, *The Light of Nature* (London, 1652), Chapter I.
31. Whichcote, *Aphorisms*, No. 102.
32. Whichcote, *Select Discourses*, IV, 139f.
33. Whichcote, *Aphorisms*, No. 878.
34. Whichcote, *Aphorisms*, No. 76.

between two different activities of reason. On the one hand they were convinced that it embraced the strenuous discipline of exact philosophical thought. The rigorous pursuit of truth stood in clear opposition to the unthinking repetition of words or phrases dictated by tradition or authority. Part of the fundamental religious problem of their age, they believed, was the wide currency of slogans which were fortified by unction but not by understanding. "I contradistinguish rational to conceited, impotent, affected CANTING," wrote Whichcote to Tuckney.[35] On the other hand, however, the Cambridge Platonists interpreted reason as the means whereby the soul is inwardly enlightened. When reason was operating at the purely natural level, it dealt with the impressions of sense; similarly, at the supernatural level it received the communications of revelation and appropriated them. Reason could therefore appropriately be defined as "the organ of supersenuous." It indicated the means by which spiritual truths are apprehended. Man's reason was a feeble and distorted replica of the divine reason; behind all phenomena was the "Reason of things," and human reason was a finite and imperfect copy of it. Here, then, were two levels (human and divine) at which this kind of reason operates; was not the chasm between them so vast that the testimony of man's mind had little value? This inference, seemingly so logical, was modified by a further consideration. A gulf unquestionably existed; moral obedience bridged it. Those who did the will of God were able to judge the truth of religious doctrine (cf. Jn. 7:17). Christian discipleship produced the inward illumination by which the soul was enlightened. "It is," said John Smith, "but a thin, airy knowledge that is got by mere speculation, which is ushered in by syllogism and demonstrations; but that which springs forth from true goodness is θειότερον τί πάσης ἀποδείξεως, as Origen speaks —it brings such a divine light into the soul, as is more clear and convincing than any demonstration." [36]

For the Cambridge Platonists the pursuit of reason thus became a moral discipline. The relation between thought and action was by nature intimate; it was decisive in its results. "When the doctrine of the Gospel becomes the reason of our mind, it will be the principle of our life." [37] Without a sincere attempt to live a moral life, there was no possibility of obtaining any insight into divine truth. For Whichcote the basis of

35. Whichcote, Letters to Tuckney, see infra, 46; in *Aphorisms*, 108. Cf. S. I. Mintz, *The Hunting of Leviathan*, 82.
36. J. Smith, *Select Discourses* (London, 1660), 4.
37. Whichcote, *Aphorisms*, No. 94.

morality lay in the fact that God made man to know him and to become like him. Those who relaxed the great requirements of godliness, righteousness and sobriety did not emancipate man from primitive tutelage; they merely robbed him of his essential nature. "Holiness in angels and men," said Whichcote, "is their dei-formity: likeness to God in goodness, righteousness and truth. Such real holiness sanctifies the subject by its presence; and where that is, the person is made pure, good and righteous." [38] Whichcote, it is clear, regarded the moral element in the Gospel as supremely important. When he examined great theological concepts like judgment and forgiveness, he always approached them from an ethical standpoint. He constantly emphasized the relation between faith and conduct. Both the institutions and the prescriptions of organized religion must, he believed, serve moral ends or they would cease to be religious instruments.

From their view of the relation of faith to reason, and of theology to ethics, it naturally followed that the Cambridge Platonists believed in liberty of conscience. In few areas was their contribution more important. In his sermons Whichcote repeatedly reverted to our need of freedom to follow the leading of truth, and he firmly established the plea for toleration as a distinguishing mark of the little group that looked to him for leadership. He was, said Tillotson, of "a most profound and well-poised judgment; yet he was, of all men I ever knew, the most patient to hear others differ from him, and the most easy to be convinced, when good reason was offered." [39] Both Culverwel and Smith appealed frequently for the freedom without which our quest of the truth is stultified. Cudworth's famous sermon before the House of Commons is a courageous appeal against fettering the mind in its search for truth. Henry More discussed at even greater length than his colleagues the claims of toleration and the limitations to which it must submit.

The Platonists were unanimous about the need for toleration; naturally they were agreed about the inferences to be drawn from their position. They believed that every man is entitled to complete freedom in forming his own judgment, and complete freedom to abide by his convictions. They saw religion as resting on a few firm principles which man's reason would help him to discover; what Christianity really asked men to accept, they believed, was simple in its character and well within the reach of human capacities. It was as foolish as it was wrong to insist on uniformity

38. Whichcote, *Aphorisms*, No. 262.
39. *The Works of the Most Reverend Dr. John Tillotson*, 10th ed (London, 1735), I, 220.

in belief and worship. The measure of agreement which persecution presupposed had never existed. The arguments used in favor of repression were neither convincing nor Christian. Intellectual arrogance tempted men to make God responsible for their own dogmatic assurance. Actually, the human grasp of the truth was so imperfect that one dared not dictate to others the frontiers within which their thoughts must stay. Men ought to be diffident in advancing their own claims and respectful in observing those of others. The plea for toleration rested in part on the inviolability of reason. Any external coercion of the understanding violated one of the most sacred elements in man's spiritual nature. Reason and faith must both be left unfettered; persecution tried to put them both in chains. Consequently the Christian was committed to toleration, so long as he was convinced of the spiritual character of religion. He was also persuaded that truth would ultimately triumph; having gained the victory in his own life, it would extend its dominion over all mankind. Reason could not defend persecution; religion should be ashamed to try. Neither natural nor revealed theology, neither public policy nor the legitimate claims of the church, provided any valid arguments against religious toleration. When restrictions were removed and when liberty at last prevailed, "then the truth of God [will] be like an unsheathed sword, bright and glittering, sharp and cutting and irresistibly convincing the rational spirit of a man. Whenas now our religion is wrapped up in so many wreaths of hay and straw that no man can see nor feel the edge of it." [40]

The earlier Platonists—Whichcote and Smith in particular—were acutely aware of tendencies in the world which threatened the essentials of true religion. For this reason, they resisted the alienation of faith from reason, the fanatical spirit, the bitterness which seemed to be the chief result of most religious controversy. As an alternative to these forces they advocated a general interpretation of Christianity which even now is attractive and of great persuasive power. It was the task of the later Cambridge Platonists to advance beyond this somewhat vaguely defined position and to fashion a "philosophy of religion." [41] As we have already noticed, the incentive to embark upon this undertaking came principally from Hobbes. Even the positive doctrines of the Cambridge Platonists were developed in conscious antipathy to Hobbes's position.

Materialism was the primary challenge which Hobbes posed. It was a

40. H. More, "The Mystery of Godliness," Bk. X, Ch. xii (in *Theological Works*, London, 1708, 368).

41. Apparently Cudworth coined this phrase. See J. H. Muirhead, *The Platonic Tradition in Anglo-Saxon Philosophy* (London, 1931), 28.

method of interpreting the universe which excluded most of the values which religious men had traditionally been taught to cherish. Once you had denied the validity of non-material realities, you had to

> admit that it is impossible there should be any God or soul or angel, good or bad, or any immortality of life to come. That there is no piety nor impiety, no virtue nor vice, justice nor injustice, but what it pleases him that has the longest sword to call so. That there is no freedom of will, nor consequently any rational remorse of conscience in any being whatsoever, but that all that is, is nothing but matter and corporeal motion; and therefore that every trace of man's life is as necessary as the tracts of lightning and the falling of thunder, the blind impulse of the matter breaking through or being stopped everywhere, with as certain and determinate necessity as the course of a torrent after mighty storms and showers of rain.[42]

Materialism was synonymous with atheism. Whichever word you happened to choose, you were merely defining what is a "false system" of the universe. The fundamental error of atheism, said Cudworth, was that it dethroned mind as the originating principle behind all things, and replaced it with unthinking matter or arbitrary chance. The Cambridge Platonists were convinced that divine intelligence is the ultimate reality. From this it followed that the spiritual world was "senior" to the material world, and that mind was prior to matter. This was the point, they believed, at which philosophy had so often gone astray. "Why bodies only should engross and monopolize natural philosophy and why a soul cannot be admitted into it . . . is a thing altogether unaccountable. . . . Yet herein Plato was defective that he did not correct and reform the abuse of this word nature, that he did not screw it up to an higher and more spiritual notion. For 'tis very agreeable to the choicest and supremest being." [43] More was scandalized by the lifelessness to which materialism condemned the universe. "The primordials of the world," he wrote, "are not mechanical but spermatical or vital, . . . which some moderns call the spirit of nature." [44]

The error of materialism was serious. Its cause, however, was relatively simple: Hobbes had misconceived the nature of matter and spirit.[45] More

---

42. H. More, *The Immortality of the Soul* (London, 1659), Bk. I, Ch. IX, §1.
43. Culverwel, *The Light of Nature*, Ch. III.
44. H. More, *Divine Dialogues* (London, 1665), Third Series.
45. Cf. More's treatment of this in his *Antidote Against Atheism* and in *The Immortality of the Soul*.

argued at length against the assumption that "universe [is] nothing else but an aggregate of bodies." [46] Hobbes's error could be exposed by a careful examination both of the findings of science and of the way we appropriate knowledge. Basically, More believed that we must acknowledge the existence of two distinct kinds of substance: matter and spirit. The former was impenetrable; the latter was penetrable but "indiscerptible." [47] More criticized Hobbes's doctrine of space with imagination and insight. Cudworth attacked Hobbes's doctrine of sensation. The first raised the question of the existence of God, the second the problem of a theory of knowledge.

In the first part of his *Antidote Against Atheism*, More offered a carefully developed argument for belief in God. His basic presupposition was the reality of spirit. Hobbes regarded extension as exclusively an attribute of matter; but this, according to More, was a wholly unwarranted assumption, and he advanced the rather novel claim that one could just as legitimately regard it as characteristic of God. This is one of More's distinctive views. For the most part he was content with much more traditional arguments. By precise logical steps he built up the case for the existence of God, and showed that the concept of a Supreme Being was not only reasonable but necessary and inescapable. More relied heavily on the ontological argument for the existence of God. At this point Descartes provided the immediate background of his thought, and More repeated the familiar proof in the form that his contemporaries would have considered most cogent. Here Cudworth agreed with him, but was also concerned to show the hollowness of the arguments with which the atheists attacked belief in God. Their view of Providence, he declared, was distorted and misconceived. He insisted that God's wise direction of all things was perfectly congruous with an enlightened understanding of nature and of human history. Equally false, he argued, was the atheists' suggestion that belief in God was merely a theological cloak with which men disguised their ignorance and fear. Theology could not simply be dismissed as a mythological interpretation of phenomena for which primitive man could find no other explanation. Nor was it an expedient by which unscrupulous rulers could more readily control their subjects. Cudworth did not deny that fear was an ancient shadow which fell across the human soul; its more sinister forms, he conceded, could be manipulated

46. H. More, *The Immortality of the Soul*, Bk. I, Ch. x, §1.
47. I.e., indissoluble. From the early eighteenth century, the word was spelled "indiscerptible." Cf. O.E.D.

by wicked men for evil ends. But there was also a godly reverence which played a necessary part in the experience of finite beings. When life was stripped of awe it lacked the essential safeguards against arrogance and pride. The fear of God was not a servile dread of the incomprehensible; it was the proper creaturely response to the wisdom, love and power that control the universe.

Cudworth was also confronted with the argument that because God is incomprehensible he must be inconceivable, and that what is inconceivable must be non-existent. He denied that the incomprehensible could thus be equated with the inconceivable. There were some things which the finite human intelligence could not fully grasp, but it did not necessarily follow that they lacked reality. This incapacity said more about the limitations of the intelligence than it did about the truths after which man groped. Men's comprehension of themselves was limited enough, but this did not make mankind inconceivable, still less unreal. Because God's nature was vaster than theirs, Cudworth argued, men knew less about him than they did about themselves, but this was not sufficient ground for denying that he exists.

The atheists' attack upon our knowledge of God brought into question the source of our knowledge about anything. Hobbes believed that what we know is the result of what we experience, and is in fact "nothing else but a tumult in the mind, raised by external things that press the organical parts of man's body." [48] To Cudworth this was a gross oversimplification of our intellectual processes.[49] Admittedly sensation might begin with what Hobbes called "local motion," but it must be perceived and interpreted before it could become the most elementary kind of knowledge. Beyond this knowledge lay the much more significant stage during which reason regulated and ordered the impressions of sense; then, as our standards were more clearly defined, it would become possible for us to assess the nature of reality and judge the character of truth. Since even sensation could not be a wholly passive process, it was wrong to assume that "mutual conception" was due to the pressures of external stimuli. Ideas and concepts presupposed something beyond impressions from the outer world. But how could we account for them? More, influenced by Descartes, was inclined to postulate the existence of innate ideas. Cudworth was more cautious. He explained the conceptual element in knowledge by appealing to the nature of mind itself. By its ability to take and unify the materials

48. Hobbes, *Leviathan*, Bk. III, Ch. xxxi.
49. Cf. Cudworth, *The True Intellectual System* (London, 1845), III, 62ff.

which sense perception supplies, he argued, the mind builds up the body of ideas without which we cannot judge the significance of immediate experience. Cudworth provided an interesting excursion into a region as yet imperfectly explored. It was characteristic of his outlook that he found in the principles of human knowledge a significant confirmation of the existence of the ultimate object of all knowledge, God himself.

Materialism was one of the principal threats posed by Hobbes. Determinism was the other. Hobbes's treatise *Of Liberty and Necessity* (1654) and his *Questions Concerning Liberty, Necessity and Chance* (1656) were his contributions to the vigorous debate which he carried on with Bishop Bramhall. Bramhall was an able and resourceful controversialist, a worthy though not an equal opponent. Cudworth, however, was not satisfied with the way Bramhall treated Hobbes's position. To rectify matters, he himself produced *A Discourse of Liberty and Necessity*—a vast unfinished work, of which a fragment was published in the nineteenth century. What remains of the manuscript is in the British Museum. Much of the original has been lost.[50] Cudworth's position rested on the assumption that spirit is a reality. If you conceded this—and he believed that its reality could be proved—Hobbes's particular kind of determinism was virtually overthrown. Cudworth recognized other threats to free will, on the one hand from the Calvinists, on the other from Descartes. Like his fellow Platonists, he believed that the "power in ourselves" to do what is right is a distinctively human capacity. If we investigate the precise character of this unique endowment, said Cudworth, we find that it cannot be regarded as a function of reason. It was not simply the final act of intelligence as it reached a decisive judgment. Cudworth believed that reason and will are neither "separate substances" nor distinct faculties of the soul. Both represented the whole soul; will was the soul "redoubled" upon itself. But was the will, then, entirely free to choose as it pleased? No, said Cudworth; if it were, the moral law would be seriously jeopardized. There was a natural inclination in the will which disposed it to select the right and reject the wrong. But he realized how narrow and slippery was the path between determinism and indifference.

50. The published portion was *A Treatise of Freewill*, ed. John Allen (London, 1838). This was printed from B. M. Add. MS. 4978, and may have been written as a summary of the longer work. The fragments of "A Discourse of Liberty and Necessity" are Add. MSS. 4979-82. Cf. J. A. Passmore, *Ralph Cudworth* (Cambridge, 1951), Appendix, 110-12. With the possible exception of a summary of Cudworth's views on free will (at the end of MS. 4981), the material is too formless and fragmentary to be of much use.

Cudworth's exploration of free will was admittedly tentative and incomplete. The same is true of the Cambridge Platonists' contribution to the much larger field of moral theory in general. Cudworth's *Treatise Concerning Eternal and Immutable Morality* has a brave title, but in reality it is less a system of ethics than a recapitulation of the essential principles of his *True Intellectual System*. More's *Enchiridion Ethicum* is more complete, but it explores the subject less profoundly than we might reasonably expect. We have already noted, however, that certain basic assumptions are common to the moral theory of all the Platonists. Among these is the conviction that right and wrong are not derivative principles —that they are not established by human law or by divine fiat, but exist by virtue of an eternal autonomy. Equally important is the belief that character is gradually molded by conduct, especially when that conduct is governed by knowledge. This followed naturally from what the Cambridge Platonists regarded as an inevitable law. By the operation of that same law, actions which might seem to be purely secular in character became spiritual when transformed by the intention of the actor. "Motion in our particular calling hinders not religion. For begin with God, acknowledge God, refer to God, and thy whole conversation becomes religious. That which is worldly, in respect of the matter, is made spiritual and religious through the principles and intention of the agent." [51] Thus, the moral integrity and the unity of character so indispensable to the abundant life were gradually fashioned as religious faith is transformed into character. "Religion," said Whichcote, "doth possess and affect the *whole* man; in the understanding, it is knowledge; in the life, it is obedience; in the affections, it is delight in God; in our carriage and behavior, it is modesty, calmness, gentleness, candor, ingenuity; in our dealings, it is uprightness, integrity, correspondence with the rule of righteousness." [52] The Platonists insisted that faith is consistent with reason; that both are in harmony with the moral law; and that when all three act in concert, the true life of religious obedience, in all its freedom, joy and power, is the result.

It is possible for us, here and now, the Cambridge Platonists believed, to achieve in some measure this integration of the various aspects of our life. But for them this present experience implied a further and future fulfillment. The moral law which fused mind and body, reason and spirit into a single harmonious whole confirmed man's most persistent intuition about

51. Whichcote, *Aphorisms*, No. 520.
52. Whichcote, *Aphorisms*, No. 956.

his final destiny. The Cambridge Platonists advanced, of course, the customary arguments to prove the immortality of the soul, but they also had their own distinctive approach to the question. In our present state, they argued, we come to know the powers of our souls through the contemplation of God. He was the proper object of our highest and most serious attention. He awakened our souls to their true and proper activity. In response to him our spirits unfolded as the flowers open to the sun. What began under temporal conditions could not be restricted to this mortal life. We venture to harbor this hope, they argued, because what God gives us now assures us of what he will grant hereafter.

At many points the views of the Cambridge Platonists are predictable enough. If we know the assumptions with which they began, and the problems they faced, we can anticipate much of the teaching we encounter in their works. This is not true of the doctrine of "plastic nature," which nevertheless is one of their most distinctive contributions. It is not original, since it is clearly derived from classical and Renaissance sources. The Cambridge Platonists refashioned the doctrine to fit their own needs, and it proved extremely useful to them in their controversies with both materialists and Calvinists. They were convinced that "the primordials of the world are not mechanical but vital"; natural phenomena could be explained, they contended, only by "some inward principle of life and motion." [53] Consequently, they challenged Hobbes's contention that the world is controlled by purely mechanical forces. They were equally opposed to the view (widely accepted in Puritan circles) that God continually intervenes in the regular functioning of the universe. The Cambridge Platonists insisted that there was an intermediate position between theories based either on continual divine manipulation or on the interaction of mechanical impulses. They argued for the existence of what More called "particular plastic spirits" or "seminal forms." "A seminal form," he said, "is a created spirit organizing duly prepared matter into life and vegetation. . . . This is the first degree of particular life in the world." [54] He believed that at the Creation God had endowed matter with its own form of spiritual nature, the lowest manifestation of spiritual vitality in existence. As a result, according to More, we are justified in speaking of the "soul of the world." "The spirit of nature," he wrote, "is . . . a substance incorporeal but without sense and animadversion, pervading the whole matter of the universe and exercising a plastical power

53. H. More, *Divine Dialogues*, Series I.
54. H. More, *The Immortality of the Soul*, Bk I, Ch. VIII, §3.

therein, . . . raising such phenomena in the world . . . as cannot be re-solved into mere mechanical powers." [55] Plastic nature did not represent a conscious manifestation of spiritual energy. It worked blindly to accom-plish God's purposes in creation, since it was not aware of what those purposes are. It was the means by which God allowed a participation in the realm of ends to that part of nature which does not rise to the level of conscious life. Once you have conceded a principle of vitality underlying all phenomena, nature cannot be treated as dead matter. It must be re-garded as spirit which is asleep.

The theory of plastic nature had certain obvious advantages. By refuting the mechanistic views of Hobbes, it preserved the dignity and the religious significance of the created order. At the same time it relieved God of the mechanical responsibility of constantly adjusting the operation of the world. It helped to interpret the Creation story in Genesis, and it appealed to men like Robert Boyle as a means of reconciling science and religion. It enabled thoughtful religious leaders honestly to meet the challenge of empirical discoveries. Scientists like John Ray found it an invaluable aid in avoiding the hazards latent in materialism. As developed by the Plato-nists the theory had certain obvious defects, but even in its imperfect form it proved a useful concept. In particular it was able to allow for aspects of biological science which other theories ignored or suppressed. In a variety of ways it anticipated later developments. It can be regarded as a fore-runner of such hypotheses as Bergson's *élan vital* and Smuts's holistic principle; it has affinities with certain emphases in modern physics and in molecular biology.

The Cambridge Platonists were not experimental scientists, but they were sympathetically disposed towards those who were. Boyle and More read each other's works with interest. John Worthington was deeply interested in the development of natural history. John Smith believed that science and theology shared certain basic presuppositions. Cudworth kept abreast of scientific literature. He was interested in microscopes and "looking-glasses." He made the first major attempt in England to bring the new science into harmony with the older traditions of philosophy and religion. More referred frequently to medical developments, and discussed current theories in physiology. He regarded natural science as providing a vast array of knowledge to support and confirm religious truth. Because he was persuaded of the essential unity of reality, he was convinced that two such aspects of that reality as science and religion could not be in

55. H. More, *The Immortality of the Soul*, Bk. III, Ch. XII, §1.

conflict. This interest in nature, although it is so prevalent throughout the Platonists' works, is not easily represented in a collection such as the present volume; but if its presence is ignored, there will be difficulty in explaining the immense influence of these men on their successors. John Ray's celebrated work, *The Wisdom of God Manifested in the Works of Creation*, clearly reflects the wise and reverent attitude to nature that he had learned from his mentors—an outlook very different from that traditionally fostered by theology. The Platonists refused to put grace in opposition to nature. "God," said Whichcote, "hath set up two lights to enlighten us in our way: the light of reason, which is the light of his creation, and the light of Scripture, which is after-revelation from him. Let us make use of these two lights and suffer neither to be put out." [56] If this wise admonition had been heeded, the subsequent relations of the two disciplines might have been very different.

The influence of the Cambridge Platonists extended far beyond this particular sphere. These men were university teachers—unusually effective ones, it would appear—and in various ways they fashioned the outlook of the succeeding generation. Tillotson's generous tribute to Whichcote stressed the cumulative influence of the latter's sermons at Cambridge: "Every Lord's Day afternoon for almost twenty years together he preached at Trinity Church, . . . and contributed more to the forming of the students to a sober sense of religion than any man of that age." [57] Tillotson himself clearly bore the imprint of that influence. So did all the other leading members of the Latitudinarian school.[58] These younger men repeated many of the emphases characteristic of their teachers. We find in them the same desire to keep faith and reason in proper equipoise, the same conviction that the moral life is the true manifestation of Christian belief. We encounter the same determination to maintain a charitable outlook, as well as the moderate spirit which repudiates fanaticism—the "enthusiasm" the age so deeply deplored. The reasonableness of the Platonists became the rationalism of the next generation, and the Cambridge men were in part to blame. "If you would be religious," wrote Whichcote, "be rational in your religion." [59] This might be regarded as the major

56. Whichcote, *Aphorisms*, No. 109.

57. *The Works of the Most Reverend John Tillotson*, I, 221.

58. Cf. Burnet, *History of My Own Time*, I, 335: "The most eminent of those who were formed under these great men were Tillotson, Stillingfleet and Patrick." Cf. also Burnet, *A Sermon Preached at the Funeral of . . . John . . . Lord Archbishop of Canterbury* (1695), 11, 12.

59. Whichcote, *Aphorisms*, No. 339.

thesis of all early eighteenth-century theology, and the Cambridge Platonists doubtless encouraged the rising deistical trend. But it is important to keep clearly in mind the important differences which divide the Platonists from the deists. We have already noticed that Whichcote and his followers used reason in a twofold way. The deists amplified only one element in this delicately balanced system, and consequently both their general temper and their specific doctrines are conspicuously different.

Because the Cambridge Platonists embraced elements of thought not always held in balance, their influence can be detected in directions where its presence is usually overlooked. They asserted the essential congruity of Christianity and Platonism, and so re-established an association between the two which was to have far-reaching effects. They represent, indeed, a very important stage in the establishment of an idealist tradition in Anglo-Saxon thought.[60] Another unexpected area in which the influence of the Platonists can be traced is the Evangelical movement of the eighteenth century, which was profoundly affected by Henry Scougal's popular devotional work, *The Life of God in the Soul of Man*. George Whitefield attributed his conversion to this work; its most characteristic phrases were constantly on the lips of Whitefield and the Wesleys. For anyone who compares their works, the indebtedness of Scougal to John Smith can hardly be doubted. The Cambridge Platonists also had an influence on the thought of English Independency. During the years when Whichcote was a tutor at Emmanuel College, he came in contact with many of the men who were to become important figures among the Dissenting Brethren. The Platonists and the Independents had certain objectives in common. Between the contending dogmatisms of the time, they sought a mediating position which presupposed the acknowledgment of human fallibility. Both groups were much in favor of liberty of conscience; they believed that toleration would be possible if men of differing views realized that the true experience of God united those who differed in opinion.[61]

In many respects the spirit which inspired the work of the Cambridge Platonists was as significant as the content of their teaching. In an age addicted to controversy, they refused to wrangle or dispute. "There is nothing more unnatural to religion," said Whichcote, "than contentions

60. Cf. J. A. Passmore, *Ralph Cudworth*, 18, 90–106; J. H. Muirhead, *The Platonic Tradition*, 28, 69–70.

61. For the contents of the above paragraph I am indebted to a comment of Professor Winthrop Hudson. See also the evidence advanced in his article, "Denominationalism as a Basis for Ecumenicity: A Seventeenth Century Conception," *Church History*, March 1955.

about it." [62] Much argument about faith had done little to foster the Christian life. "It is to be feared," said John Smith, "that our nice speculations about what concerns us in theology have tended more to exercise men's wits than to reform their lives." [63] According to their belief, those who insist that religion is primarily concerned with dogma are wrong: humility and charity bring us much nearer to its essential nature. Certain qualities, they argued, establish within us the right disposition of spirit, the proper attitude of mind, and so the appropriate orientation of our lives. "Nothing is the true improvement of our rational faculties but the exercise of the several virtues of sobriety, modesty, gentleness, humility, obedience to God, and charity to men." [64] Their writings are marked by a quality which is humane and devout, one as refreshing as it is rare. They had as little doubt about the only true source of the abundant life as they had concerning its essential character. The true Christian, said Cudworth, is "he that hath the spirit of Christ within him." It was the truth from God and about God which delivered men from the deadening effect of a conventional faith, for "the Gospel . . . is a quickening spirit within us."

Cudworth spoke of "the secret mysteries of a divine life, of a new nature, of Christ formed in our hearts"; [65] but he and his colleagues never forgot that the life they commended was a life lived among men. The one convincing evidence of Christianity was the power of the Christian life. The experience which men shared with others, in this present world, at the present time, witnessed to the truth and confirmed it.

> I give much to the Spirit of God breathing in good men with whom I converse in the present world . . . and think that, if I may learn much by the writings of good men in former ages . . . I may learn more by the actings of the Divine Spirit in the minds of good men now alive; and I must not shut my eyes against any manifestations of God in the times in which I live. The times wherein I live are more to me than any else; the works of God in them which I am to discern, direct in me both principle, affection and action; and I dare not blaspheme free and noble spirits in religion who seek after truth with indifference and ingenuity.[66]

62. Whichcote, *Aphorisms*, No. 756.
63. J. Smith, *Select Discourses* (Cambridge, England, 1859), 456.
64. Whichcote, *Aphorisms*, No. 541. Cf. No. 434: "Modesty and humility are the sobriety of the mind."
65. This quotation, like the two preceding, is from Cudworth, *Sermon before the House of Commons* (Cambridge, 1647), 4–5.
66. Whichcote, Letters to Tuckney, in *Aphorisms*, p. 115.

PART ONE

❖

Anticipatory: A Pattern of Thought Emerges

✤ ✤ ✤ ✤ ✤ ✤ ✤ ✤

Letters of Benjamin Whichcote to Antony Tuckney

Editor's Introduction. Benjamin Whichcote (1609–83) can reasonably be regarded as the man more responsible than any other for molding the pattern of thought generally characteristic of the Cambridge Platonists.

He entered Emmanuel College, Cambridge, in 1626. We know virtually nothing about his earlier life, but since he came to the great Puritan college we may surmise that he came from a Puritan household. At Emmanuel he was successively the pupil of two distinguished Puritans, Antony Tuckney and Thomas Hill (later Master of Trinity). They left their mark on his mind; they certainly did not cramp its development.

With Tuckney, in particular, Whichcote was united by a sympathy which diverging views did not efface. In due course both men left Cambridge to engage in parish work. Both returned to positions of influence in the university—Tuckney as Master of Emmanuel, Whichcote as Provost of King's. Whichcote also instituted a Sunday afternoon "lecture" at Holy Trinity Church. In doing so he followed a popular Puritan tradition, but in what he preached he diverged from Puritan patterns. Samuel Salter, his eighteenth-century editor, says his purpose was "to preserve a spirit of sober piety and rational religion in the university and town of Cambridge, in opposition to the fanatic enthusiasm and senseless canting then in vogue"—but this is a characteristically eighteenth-century assessment. Bishop Burnet, a near contemporary and a more reliable witness, tells us that Whichcote "was much for liberty of conscience, and, being disgusted with the dry systematical way of those times, he studied to raise those who conversed with him to a nobler set of thoughts and to consider religion as a seed of deiform nature (to use one of his own phrases)."[1]

In 1650–51, Whichcote was vice-chancellor of the university, and the office lent added weight to his words, especially when he preached in Great St. Mary's Church. Tuckney and his friends became increasingly alarmed at the tendency which they detected in his public utterances. They suspected that they were witnessing the emergence, among some of the younger men, of a more liberal and flexible theology. It is to this

1. G. Burnet, *History of My Own Time*, ed. by O. Airy (Oxford, 1900), I, 331.

concern that we owe the correspondence between Tuckney and Which-cote. The letters belong to the earliest period of the Platonist school. We can see clearly enough what disturbed the Puritan leaders in the university. "I have seldom heard you preach," wrote Tuckney, "but that something hath been delivered by you, and that so authoritatively, and with the big words, sometimes of 'divinest reason,' and sometimes of 'more than mathematical demonstration,' that hath very much grieved me, and I believe others with me" (p. 2). These younger men ("whom you head, as some think") were exalting reason at the expense of faith (p. 19), and in this they were apparently influenced by the pernicious works of Socinians and Arminians (p. 26). They seemed to rely on the ancient philosophers, not on the Holy Scriptures; they offered "a kind of moral divinity . . . , only with a tincture of Christ added; nay a Platonic faith united to God" (p. 38). Matters might have aroused less alarm if Whichcote and his friends had been willing "to forbear the insisting on these arguments of the power of nature and reason, . . . which in Scripture are rather abased than exalted" (p. 75).

In reply to these strictures, Whichcote not only stood his ground but firmly and courteously pressed the claims of his position. Tuckney ultimately realized that the discussion had gone as far as it profitably could. He had made his own views clear; obviously he was not changing Whichcote's. "I believe," he said, "you seek and love the truth, and yet think you may in some things mistake" (p. 82). The whole correspondence is an interesting reflection of two sincere and high-minded men, debating questions of the utmost religious importance. They were friends of long standing; they remained friends after discovering that they no longer agreed.

The correspondence was published in 1753. *Eight Letters which Passed between Dr Whichcote Provost of King's College and Dr Tuckney Master of Emmanuel College in Cambridge* were annexed to the edition by Samuel Salter of Whichcote's *Moral and Religious Aphorisms*. Salter had tried to trace the original documents and had failed. With the rest of Whichcote's papers they had come into the possession of a Dr. Jeffery (who published a couple of volumes of *Discourses* and made the initial selection of the *Aphorisms*); but Whichcote wrote an illegible hand, Jeffery may have deciphered some passages incorrectly, and Jeffery's brother had then transcribed the surviving copy—how accurately no one can say. It is surprising that the letters survived at all.

❖   ❖   ❖   ❖

Whichcote's First Letter

. . . Now, Sir, to deal clearly with you, the matter of your letter meets
with no guilt in my conscience. I am not self-convinced, not self-condemned. Either you have mistaken me, or, in my understanding, it is God's
truth you do reprove. . . . [To vindicate himself, Whichcote quotes from
his notes for the sermon to which Tuckney particularly took exception:]

> ɪ. I persuade myself, that all truly good men among us do substan-
> tially agree in all things saving. ɪɪ. That some things, wherein we
> differ, are not certainly determined in Scripture; but that which both
> parties say, seems to have countenance somewhere or other. Yea, I
> think, God may have reserved somewhat from us, as not "of these
> times"; or his secret, and that he would not have us know. "Do not
> desire to know sublime things," in this case. ɪɪɪ. The proposal for
> peace: that all be looked upon as fallible, which goes beyond Scrip-
> ture or falls short of it.

(And, Sir, is there on earth power to add, alter or change? Is not the
foundation of Protestancy, "Holy Scripture is a sufficient rule of faith"?
Are not Scripture forms of words sufficient, yea aptest, to convey and
carry all saving truth to the minds and understandings of men? Farther I
argue thus for peace among good Christians.)

> "Good men, differing in *their own* expressions, yet agree in *Scripture*
> forms of words; acknowledging, the meaning of the Holy Ghost in
> them is true; and they endeavor to understand and find it out, as well
> as they can. Therefore they should continue friends; and think they
> agree, rather than think they do not agree (because they *do* agree in
> what is God's and infallible) and upon this consideration forbear one
> another, and not impose their own, either sense or phrase. . . ."

(And truly, Sir, I think I should give a great deal too little to the wisdom
of God in Scripture, if should not think it, without any human supplement, sufficient to convince Popery, to assert the divinity of Christ, and
to declare the notion of his death, and to secure the minds of men from
whatsoever supposed heresy or blasphemy. And I persuade myself, that
good men have light enough and direction plain and full enough, from
Scripture, to enable them to discover and decline such wicked company as
your letter supposeth. And, Sir, whereas you say you discern in whose

footsteps I tread: if you mean any late author, I can assure you I can show you all these matters in a "position" in Emmanuel College chapel at Problems [2] made by me fourteen years ago, "Concerning the authority and government of the Church," which I wonder that those times should bear and not these. So that it is true, that you say, my heart was full; for indeed my head hath been possessed with this truth these many years; and I have long since freely reasoned and disputed it with some of the ancientest and in chief place in the university. So that I am not late or new in that persuasion concerning Scripture sufficiency and non-imposing.)

> iv. The proposal for progress and growth in knowledge: that an ingenuous-spirited Christian, after application to God and diligent use of means to find out truth, might fairly propose, without offense taken, what upon search he finds cause to believe; and whereon he will venture his own soul.

This (I said) might be converse to mutual edification, and without disturbance to the world; and so I have long thought; and do continue to think so still. And if herein I be in an error, I should be glad to be shown it.

For the point of Reconciliation, I shall write you out a copy of my notes in that point, whereby you will easily understand how you wrong both my words and meaning.

> Christ doth not save us by only doing for us, *without* us. Yea, we come at that which Christ hath done for us with God by what he doth for us *within* us. For, in order of execution, it is, as the words are placed in the text [evidently Acts 5:31], repentance before forgiveness of sins. Christ is to be acknowledged as a principle of grace *in* us, as well as an advocate *for* us. For the Scripture holds forth Christ to us under a double notion: 1. To be felt in us, as the new man, in contradiction to the old man; as a divine nature in contradistinction to the degenerate and apostate nature; and as a principle of heavenly life, contrary to the life of sin and spirit of the world; 2. To be believed on by us as a sacrifice for the expiation and atonement of sin, as an advocate and means of reconciliation between God and man. And Christ doth not dividedly perform these offices, one and not the other. For reconciliation between God and us is not wrought, as sometimes it is said and pretended to be in the world, between

2. [ED.] Disputations in the college chapels at Cambridge were called "Problems." A "position" was the statement of a thesis or proposition.

parties mutually incensed and exasperated one against another, when
the urgency of a case makes them to forbear hostility and acting one
against the other, their inward antipathy and enmity in the mean-
while rather increased, inflamed; because they take not up the difference fairly, nor come to agree in the cause; but the reason for
enmity still continues, so that, though an amnesty be consented to,
yet are they not friends, but in heart enemies. Wherefore our Savior,
to distinguish, saith "If ye from your hearts forgive not, &c." (Mt.
18:35). But with God there cannot be reconciliation without our
becoming God-like, for God's acts are not false, overly, imperfect.
God cannot make a vain show; God, being perfectly under the
power of goodness, cannot deny himself; because, if he should, he
would depart from goodness, which is impossible to God. Therefore
we must yield, be subdued to the rules of goodness, receive stamps
and impressions from God; and God cannot be farther pleased, than
goodness takes place. They therefore deceive and flatter themselves
extremely, who think of reconciliation with God by means of a
Savior acting upon God in their behalf, and not also working in or
upon them, to make them God-like. Nothing is more impossible than
this, as being against the nature of God; which is in perfect agreement with goodness, and hath an absolute antipathy against iniquity,
unrighteousness and sin. And we cannot imagine, that God by his
will and pleasure can go against his nature and being.

(The phrase, "divinity minted or taught in Hell" I find not in my notes;
but it was suddenly spoken, upon this abuse of God and cheat of ourselves.)

To put this upon a Savior to do and impotently to flatter ourselves in
the conceit of such a thing, . . . were instead of reconciling heaven
and earth, to divide God against himself. And this is a demonstration
in divinity, beyond which no demonstration in astronomy is more
certain. If we would be true to ourselves, let our faith have no contradiction from within us; let not our sense give our conceits the lie;
"let us taste and see, &c." [cf. Ps. 34:8].

Now, whether there be anything in all this contrary to "free grace,
freely justifying the ungodly," as you seem to infer, I leave to yourself
upon second thoughts to judge. Or whether this whole discourse be not,
as was by me intended, wholly pointed against those that "turn the grace
of God into wantonness," and pretend to be reconciled to God through
Justification, whereas they continue enemies to God through want of
Sanctification and the renewing of the spirit by Christ.

Whichcote's Second Letter

... I endeavored to make it appear that the truth declared by God concerning our relief by Christ was amiable, grateful, acceptable to mind and understanding, and such as spake itself from God; as our Savior spake himself to be Christ to the inward sense of the Samaritans. And to this purpose reason was made use of, as a receiver, as a discerner, as a principle to be instructed and taught; not as an author or inventor or controller of what God speaks, divine truth always carrying its own light and evidence, so as that the mind receiving it is illuminated, edified, satisfied. . . . [Sacred Scripture] speaks for itself, it recommends itself to its subject, it satisfies the reason of the mind; procures its own entertainment, by its own excellency. I add also that the persuasion of the Holy Spirit contributes to the mind's assurance and satisfaction. I receive the truth of Christian religion in a way of illumination, affection and choice; I myself am taken with it, as understanding and knowing it; I retain it, as a welcome guest; it is not forced into me, but I let it in, yet so as taught by God; and I see cause for my continuance to embrace it. Do I dishonor my faith, or do any wrong to it, to tell the world that my mind and understanding are satisfied in it? I have no reason against it; yea, the highest and purest reason is for it! What doth God speak to, but my reason? And should not that which is spoken to hear? Should it not judge, discern, conceive what is God's meaning? . . .

These five Protestant principles have led me into all the conclusions I lay out, about the rule of faith:

1. *Sacra scriptura est* ἀυτόπιστος [Holy Scripture is credible in itself].

2. *Sacra scriptura est adaequata regula fidei* [Holy Scripture is a sufficient rule of faith].

3. *Omnia ad salutem necessaria perspicue traduntur in scripturis* [All things necessary to salvation are clearly taught in the Scriptures].

4. *Cuilibet Christiano conceditur judicium discretionis* [Freedom of judgment is conceded to every Christian].

5. *Quilibet abundet in suo sensu*: and *Fides non est cogenda* [Any one is rich in his own mind: and, Faith must not be forced].

I understand them all in a real and full sense, according to the import of the words and what necessarily follows from them; and so, I verily persuade myself, they will patronize my four next conclusions.

You say, it may be you and I may differ in the number of things saving.

I hope we do not differ in the entertaining of anything saving, because of "Omnia perspicue traduntur," one of the five principles; and it is not equally necessary to determine the number, as to entertain the saving principles. I do entertain the whole Scripture, and in the sense my understanding tells me the Holy Ghost meant, using all means and helps I hear of in the world, so far as I have opportunity, viz., Fathers, Councils, expositors, comments, confessions, systems. And what many convened have agreed, I have considered (wherein they have agreed) with greater reverence, because "the judgment of many men" is the best in the world, especially if they have been free from the suspicion of faction and partiality—which, you know, very many councils were not. You mistake me, therefore, if you think I mean to lay aside the endeavors of Fathers, Councils, or any good men, to clear up Scripture truth against error; but I abate of the degree of certainty, in what is so done, of what I find in Scripture.

Is there not also an imperfection in the understandings of those who make interpretations?—so that though we thank them for their good will and make use of their pains, yet everyone for himself is to discern "whether the gloss corrupts or illuminates the text." A laudable endeavor of them I acknowledge; and I am beholden to them for their help; and I will duly consider what they say. But I am not sure because they so resolve. I must see with my own eyes. My own understanding must be satisfied. Otherwise I equalize them to the penmen of Scripture.

And I persuade myself, because of "Omnia perspicue" &c., that he who with an honest intention of finding out the will of God, in order to conformity therewith and obedience thereto, seeking to God to teach him, searcheth carefully the Holy Scripture, will miss of nothing saving. Notwithstanding the greatest difference that ever I heard of, yet I believe no good man leaves out any fundamental. Yea, I am apt to think that many who have been exasperated one against another are far nearer to one another in sense than in words. In respect of God, who searcheth hearts, they agree more than in the view of the world, which only sees outward expressions. I believe for one *real* difference in matters of consequence between persons considerable there are mistakes of meanings, and could they see one another's hearts, they would think better one of another. But opposites too often study to represent each other in the worst sense. I perceive it in men alive, therefore suspect it of the dead. If once disaffected to each other, they never after deal fairly with one another.

I agree with you that things revealed in Scripture are to be matters of our enquiry, and that we are not curiously to pry into God's secrets (Rom. 12:3); but still, I say, fundaments are so clear that there is little danger of good men differing about them.

What is added of Socinians, Arminians, &c, in respect of me,[3] is groundless. I have given no cause nor occasion. I rather approve him who said, "I am not a Christian of any other designation." . . . And truly, Sir, you are wholly mistaken in the whole course of my studies. . . . Truly I shame myself to tell you how little I have been acquainted with books, but for your satisfaction I do. While fellow of Emmanuel College, employment with pupils took my time from me. I have not read many books, but I have studied a few. Meditation and invention hath been rather my life than reading, and truly I have read more Calvin and Perkins and Beza [4] than all the books, authors or names you mention. I have always expected reason for what men say, less valuing persons or authority in the stating and resolving of truth. And therefore I have read them most where I have found it. I have not looked at anything as more than an opinion which hath not been underpropt by convincing reason or plain and satisfactory Scripture. Had I given less to Scripture than I have done, I believe I had better avoided than I have done those offences against me, whereof you advertise me that many have taken them. If I know my own heart, nothing of worldly design or respect to aught less than the honor of God and the safety of my soul rules in me, to the balancing of my judgment in the discerning of truth. I keep myself free to follow reason and Scripture, and I am never against them whosoever shows them me. . . .

Whereas you suggest that "fundamentals may be shaken and endangered by such a free proposal, &c.," truly, I think this cannot worthily be conceived of such truths. "Great is the truth, and it will prevail; the truth does

---

3. [ED.] Cf. this, from Tuckney's second letter: "Sir, those whose footsteps I observed were the Socinians and Arminians, the latter whereof, I conceive, you have been everywhere reading." In particular, Tuckney thought he could detect the influence of John Goodwin, the Puritan liberal who was regarded as a deviationist in theology, in ecclesiology and in social theory.

4. [ED.] These are the great authorities to whom the Puritans normally appealed. Theodore Beza (1519–1605) was Calvin's successor at Geneva. He published a critical edition of his own translation into Latin, and subsequently issued what can be called the first genuinely critical text, of the Greek New Testament. His theological position represents a hardening of Calvinism in the direction of rigid determinism. William Perkins, fellow of Christ's College, Cambridge, was the most influential of English Puritan writers. He was a strong controversialist, against both Catholics and Arminians. More than any other man he was responsible for crystallizing English Puritan thought.

not seek out corners." The foundations of truths necessary to salvation are so immovably laid by God that no power, either of the devil or of the degenerate world can overcome them; and the light of them is so full, so clear, so satisfactory that no ingenuous unengaged teachable mind, as every good man's mind should be, can be mistaken about them.

In the next place you brand those who have pleaded for such a liberty "Socinians, Arminians, *colluries* of sectaries &c." May we temper and qualify Divinity with prudential considerations? May we do God's work for him, taking it out of his hands? Or is it not better to leave the case to "God will provide" [Gen. 22:8]? "Cuilibet Christiano est judicium discretionis" is the foundation of Protestancy. Therefore every Christian must think and believe as he finds cause. And shall he speak in religion otherwise than he thinks, or if he be asked, shall he answer false? The great engagement upon me, to hold them to truth is, that at a man's peril it is to run away with a lie. Truth is truth, whoever hath spoken it or howsoever it hath been abused. But if this liberty may not be allowed to the university, wherefore do we study? We should have nothing to do but to get good memories and to learn by heart. . . .

That precept of wisdom, "Acknowledge him in all thy ways" [Prov. 3:6], I am sure overrules me, head, heart, hand; it is the inward sense of my soul, digested into a temper, complexion, constitution. I never leave God out. I ever give him the principal place: "All things from God, all things under God, all things with the good God." In the sense of my mind I was very far from taking from God, to give to myself. God is really all in all to me. I hold of him, derive from him, live by him, enjoy myself under him, hope in him, expect from him. There is nothing more written in my heart than the sense of my dependency upon him. There is nothing that I am more free to acknowledge than his influence, operation and presence. So far was it from me to understand what you fetch out of the words, that nothing seems to me more horrid, monstrous, violent, contranatural. My heart riseth with indignation against such a thing; I have a perfect antipathy in my soul against it. I should sin against all the experience I have of God my life if I should say or think such a thing. . . .

In the next place, you advise me "not to affect school phrases and learning, in preaching, nor the use of philosophy and metaphysics." Truly, Sir, understanding that I ought not to "do the work of the Lord negligently" (Jer. 48:10), but to serve him in the utmost use and improvement of myself and what God hath given me, I have, to my best, endeavored to confirm truth and convince the understandings of men therein. And to that purpose, as I have been able, have made use of all those principles that derive from God and speak him in the world, thinking that the efficacy of the application depended upon the solid confirmation of the doctrine.

The time I have spent in philosophers I have no cause to repent of, and the use I have made of them I dare not disown. I heartily thank God for what I have found in them; neither have I, upon this occasion, one jot less loved the Scriptures. I find the philosophers that I have read good, so far as they go; and it makes me secretly blush before God when I find either my head, heart or life challenged by them, which I must confess I have often found. I have sometimes publicly declared what points of religion I have found excellently held forth by them; and I have never found them enemies to the faith of the Gospel. I think St. Augustine saith of St. Paul, "He does not tear down the truth which he finds among the pagans." I have thought it profitable to provoke to jealousy lazy or loose Christians by philosophers, as Paul did the Jews by the Gentiles entertaining the faith of Christ. . . .

Whichcote's Third Letter

. . . Did you ever find me leaving God out, and not acknowledging him principal, original; and the creature mere vanity, divided from him; a lie, in contradiction to him? I have declared the quality and fitness of the principle, as from God, in the hand of God: "the candle of the Lord," *res illuminata illuminans* [a thing that gives light because it is lighted]. With all my heart and soul I acknowledge and assert (and wholly depend thereon), the Holy Spirit's superintendency, conduct, presence, influence, guidance, government of men's mind, in the discerning of the things of God. There is nothing that I have more insisted upon and more carefully endeavored to demonstrate *de industria*, upon texts purposely chosen, occasionally still interposing clauses to this purpose. Yet it had a large place in my speech at which, you say, so much offence was taken. I am not clearer, fuller, in any point. I experimentally know it, I thank God, to be true. I have witness of it within me. It is my sufficiency, it is my strength, it is my security. God with me is all in all. . . .

But I think a man may truly say of the grand articles of Christian faith (expiation, remission of sins) that to one acquainted with his own state and condition, and considerative of God's goodness, the matter of those articles revealed is rather a matter expected as becoming God, godlike, than either contrary to reason or unworthy of God. I believe, in the true use of understanding, a serious and considerative mind would be apt to think that either God would pardon sin to penitents who reform *absolutely*, or else would propose a way in which, and terms on and conditions on which, he would forgive and be reconciled, God being duly looked upon as the fountain and original of goodness. So that, when the revelation of faith comes, the inward sense, awakened to the entertainment thereof, saith, EUREKA, it is as I imagined; the thing expected proves; Christ the desire of all nations: sc. the desire of their state—at least, the necessity of their state.

So far am I from quarrelling with any of the revelations of God. My reason is nowhere so satisfied as in matter of Christian faith. . . .

Sir, you will pardon me; upon this third provocation from you, I must not be wanting to my own innocency, at least not to God's truth. I think I did myself right, where I did God service; and in this respect I appeal from you to God. I well know, that the love of truth ruled in my heart; and I then had, and still have, such evidence and assurance of being in the truth that I cannot but think I never spent an hour in my life upon a better account. Sir, I had well considered the matter of the speech before I came there; had resolved myself, upon many thoughts, of the certainty, of the truth, of the importance and usefulness to the auditory. When I understood your taking offence, and some others, I gave so much to your authority and judgment, that I re-examined all over again, and am fully settled in my thoughts that the matter is unexceptionable and that which must be stood to, highly tending to God's honor and worthy the Gospel. And there is nothing of reality against it but mistakes, misapprehensions, jealousies and misprisions. Sir, this I would not write to you, did I not think the honor of God and truth engaged and the interest of souls concerned; and were not I myself so assured, as that thereto, if called to it, I must give attestation with my life. Therefore, Sir, though I dearly love you, in my relation to you, and highly honor you for your own worth, yet cannot I, out of respect to you, give up so noble, so choice a truth, so antidotical against temptation, so satisfactory, so convictive, so quietive, in so full confirmation, to my mind, of the truth of Christian religion. Sir, this knowledge, God being merciful to me, I will keep till I die, not out of worldly design but out of love to my soul.

[Certain truths, Whichcote argues, can be neglected only at our peril.] Such points are the creature's due observance of God, compliance with his will, surrender of self up to him, dependence upon him, acknowledgment of him, affection settled on him, reference to him; good self-government and moderation in worldly desires and affections; and composure in a still, quiet, calm, serene apprehension of God; the mind discharged of passion, undue affection and molestation from sense, justice, righteousness, equal and fair dealing with men; no insolency, usurpation, arrogancy, oppression, and a multitude of such excellent doctrines; which, if settled in the hearts and lives of men would make this world resemble Heaven, whereas now the contrary speak Hell broken loose. And "too much" and "too often" on these points! [5] The Scriptures full of such truths, and I handle them too much and too often! And not discourse of them rationally! Sir, I oppose not rational to spiritual, for spiritual is most rational. But I contradistinguish rational to conceited,[6] impotent, affected CANTING (as I may call it, when the ear receives words which offer no matter to the understanding, make no impression on the inward sense). And I think where the demonstration of the Spirit is, there is the highest, purest reason; so as to satisfy, convince, command the mind; things are most thoroughly seen into, most clearly understood; the mind not so much amused with the form of words, as made acquainted with the inwards of things, the reason of them and the necessary connexion of terms clearly laid open to the mind and discovered. I have no skill at all in the Bible, if the prophets and apostles and our Savior himself are not frequent in rational arguments and argumentations.

I always thought that *that* doth most affect and command the heart which doth most fully satisfy and convince the mind; and what reacheth the mind but reason, the reason of the thing? . . .

I give much to the Spirit of God, breathing in good men, with whom I converse in the present world, in the university and otherwhere; and think that if I may learn much by the writings of good men in former ages (which you advise me to, and I hope I do not neglect), that by the actings of the divine Spirit in the minds of good men now alive I may learn more; and I must not shut my eyes against any manifestations of God in the times in which I live. The times wherein I live are more to me than any else; the works of God in them, which I am to discern, direct in me both

5. [ED.] Tuckney had charged Whichcote with preaching too often on moral rather than theological subjects, on philosophical themes rather than the great biblical doctrines.

6. [ED.] I.e., having a conceit or fanciful notion; based on an idea or opinion. Cf. *Oxford English Dictionary.*

principle, affection and action. And I dare not blaspheme free and noble spirits in religion who search after truth with indifference and ingenuity,[7] lest in so doing I should degenerate into a spirit of persecution, in the reality of the thing, though in another guise. For a mistaken spirit may conceit itself to be acted by the zeal of God. And I have observed that in former times some, whose names and memories I otherwise honor and value their writings, have been sharp and censorious, severe and keen, even to the persecution of such whom I doubt not but God had received. And I greatly fear that also in *our* times do so too. And I believe that the destroying this spirit out of the Church is a piece of reformation which God, in these times of changes, aims at; and I fear to be under the power of anti-character to the work that God is about, and to stand disaffected to what God is doing in the world. . . .

Sir, you have now an account of the secret sense of my soul, and I have told you what God hath whispered in my ear,—or else I am under such a delusion as I think God never delivers such up to as with honest hearts seek to him. And I pray you, Sir, so far as you value me in religion, consider this thing with freedom, laying aside awhile presupposition and prepossessions. They who differ from me in some apprehensions (though I may conceive the things as I apprehend them, weighty; and so, in respect of my own person, I am bound), may be as honest-hearted towards God and as well lovers of truth as I myself am. In this case I must leave them to run their hazard of being right or wrong as I must do mine. Every one stands or falls to his own master.

But, to return to what I was saying before, I am out of doubt, that truly good men, dear to God, fell under the persecution of the tongue, the pen, the misreport of persons of eminency, whom, save in this, I do not condemn, but think them among the number of the better of their times in causes, wherein they were not only honest-hearted and meant well, but were little, if at all mistaken. And I pray God our zeal in these times may be so kindled with pure fire from God's altar, that it may rather warm than burn, enliven rather than inflame, and that the spirits of good men may truly be qualified with Gospel principles, true fruits of the divine Spirit. And truly, I think that the members of the Church, if not the leaders (notwithstanding all the perfections of the times before us, so much pretended or applauded), in this point have very much yet to learn. For I am persuaded that Christian love and affection among all partakers of the

---

7. [ED.] "Indifference," impartiality, objectivity; "ingenuity," candor, frankness, openness. Cf. O.E.D.

Gospel grace is a point of such importance and certain foundation, so pressed upon us by our Savior and his apostles, that it is not to be prejudiced by *supposals* of differences in points of religion anyways disputable, though thought weighty, as determined by the parties on either side, nor yet by the *truly* different persuasions of those who cannot be satisfied either in our conceited forms of expression; or particular determinations beyond Scripture; which, as some have observed, have indeed enlarged Divinity, but have lessened charity and multiplied divisions. For the maintenance of truth is rather God's charge (Jn. 16:13), and the continuance of charity ours (Heb. 13:1) . . . I think I may suppose, without offence, that the cunning devil, who is always vigilant to do mischief, may lay a snare in the notion of orthodoxy against charity. And, as I said before, persons valuable for their love and desire of truth, differing from us, generally mean better than our prejudice, occasioned upon this difference, admits us to conceive of them. For I make account that Scripture is so clear and satisfactory in matters of weight ("Omnia necessaria perspicue traduntur") that none, but they who unworthily practice and design upon truth, can be mistaken; and these in religion are not considerable, as not being under the power of it but serving ends. But, sure enough, where the love of truth rules in the heart, the light of truth will guide the mind. I believe it is not to be found in Scripture or otherwhere, that honesty, uprightness, integrity, are in conjunction with heresy; and the Scripture way is to rectify simple misapprehensions with tenderness. . . .

I think their excellence [i.e., of Phil. 3 and Gal. 3] lies in a real and effectual participation of Christ and of his spirit. I profess myself as full and clear as any one in the world in that grand point of our acceptance with God, in and through Christ. Yet I confess, I cannot but marvel to see you balance matters of knowledge against principles of goodness, and seem to insist on Christ less as a principle of divine nature in us than as a sacrifice for us. I acknowledge they both speak the rich grace of God in Christ to man: I mean, expiation of sin in the blood of Christ, and true participation of the divine nature, to the making of us truly God-like or conform to God, through Christ being formed in us. And I know not well (or rather dare not) compare them, both being the provision of Heaven, to make us capable of happiness, and fundamentally necessary to our safety. . . .

Now that Christ is more known and freely professed [than in the apostles' time], let him also be inwardly felt and secretly understood, as a principle of divine life within us as well as a Savior without us. Christ is the leaven of Heaven, sent into the world and given to us to leaven us into the nature of God. And this, I conceive, is worthy of Gospel preachers (as your phrase is) to do; in this progress and proficiency of Gospel knowledge and grace and farther advance of the kingdom of Messiah, I am very free to acknowledge Christ the only foundation since the apostasy and sin of man. He alone gave the stop to God's just displeasure; his interposing prevailed with God, not to take the forfeiture, or, if taken, he procured the restoration and recovery. Upon this account I acknowledge Christ, in parts of nature, reason, and understanding, as well as in gifts of grace. So that Christ is not by men anywhere left out nor faith neglected; no, nor not advanced to a superiority and super-eminency everywhere, for I believe that I hold and enjoy my reason and understanding by and under Christ. And what I have meant, expressed and endeavored all along hath been to call men to the due and careful use and employment of what they hold by and under Christ. You have no cause to suspect me for scant and narrow apprehensions of free grace, Christ's merits and divine goodness. Yet I confess my shallowness, but that is my grievance and burthen. And I would have my apprehensions raised, and my thoughts of the Gospel enlarged. I attribute to the creature, upon its own account, nothing but unworthiness, inability and insufficiency, and look at Christ as the only ground of acceptance, and his spirit as the only principle of enablement, power and sufficiency.

"We walk by *faith*," till we be comprehensors, till we be possessed of all that blessedness, which is promised and expected. A true complacential *love* signifies something of fruition, in what degree soever; and whether, and how far a man may enter into this state in this life, let him determine who hath acted to the utmost extent permissible of a truly divine, free and unrestrained faith. . . .

PART TWO

❖

The Place of Reason in the
Realm of Faith

NATHANAEL CULVERWEL

An Elegant and Learned Discourse of the Light of Nature

Editor's Introduction. Culverwel is one of the most shadowy and indistinct of the Cambridge Platonists. He entered Emmanuel College in 1633; nine years later he became a fellow of the college. His *Light of Nature* was published in 1652. Beyond these few facts we know almost nothing about his life.

The Light of Nature is one of the most remarkable works produced by the English Platonic movement. It reflects the wide readings of a very learned young man. Culverwel was deeply versed in classical literature (the stock-in-trade of a seventeenth-century scholar); he was also alert to contemporary movements of thought. He had read Bacon, Descartes, Lord Brooke and Lord Herbert of Cherbury. He was a writer of considerable philosophical promise. He developed a theory of knowledge similar to Lord Herbert's; at certain points he anticipated John Locke.

His book is primarily concerned with the place of reason and with the special nobility of its function in the search for truth. To Culverwel this was a congenial theme; it was also one particularly relevant to the contemporary scene. William Dillingham, the first editor of the work, points out that part of the author's aim was "to vindicate the use of reason in matters of religion from the aspersions and prejudices of some weaker ones in those times. . . ." This explains the care with which Culverwel expounds a favorite text of the Platonists. He finds that the description of the "spirit of man" as the "candle of the Lord" is "a brief commendation of natural light, or the light of reason." So he proceeds to raise three questions: "1. What nature is? 2. What the law of nature is? 3. What the light of nature is?" Having answered these questions, he is free to show that the light of reason ("a derivative light") is "directive" and "calm and peaceable." In developing his theme, Culverwell is clearly defending his position both against those who unduly depreciate reason and against those who exalt it excessively—against Calvinists and against Socinians.

The Light of Nature is a vigorous attempt to reconcile two aspects of man's life which are too often allowed to drift apart. More impressive than the quality of the argument is the radiant religious confidence which pervades the work.*

❖   ❖   ❖   ❖

Proverbs 20:27: "The understanding of a man is the candle of the Lord."[1]

CHAPTER I. THE PORCH, OR INTRODUCTION

It is a work that requires our choicest thought and the exactest discussion that can be, a thing very material and desirable, to give unto reason the things that are reason's and unto faith the things that are faith's, to give faith her full scope and latitude, and to give reason also her just bounds and limits; this is the first-born, but the other has the blessing [cf. Gen. 27]. And yet there is no such a vast hiatus neither, such a μέγα χάσμα [great chasm] between them as some would imagine. There is no such implacable antipathy, no such irreconcilable jarring between them as some do fancy to themselves. They may very well salute one another ἁγίῳ φιλήματι, osculo pacis [with a kiss of peace]; reason and faith may kiss each other [cf. Ps. 85:10]. There is a twin-light springing from both, and they both spring from the same fountain of light, and they both sweetly conspire in the same end, the glory of that being from which they shine and the welfare and happiness of that being upon which they shine. So that to blaspheme reason, 'tis to reproach Heaven itself and to dishonor the God of reason, to question the beauty of his image and by a strange ingratitude to slight this great and royal gift of our Creator. For 'tis he that set up these two great luminaries in every heavenly soul, "the sun to rule the day and the moon to rule the night" [cf. Gen. 1:16], and though there be some kind of creatures that will bark at this lesser light, and others so severely critical as that they make mountains of those spots and freckles which they see in her face, yet others know how to be thankful for her weaker beams, and will follow the least light of God's setting up, though it be but "the candle of the Lord."

* The first edition of *The Light of Nature* (prepared by William Dillingham) was published in 1652; a second edition (essentially a reprint) appeared in Oxford in 1669. In 1857 a third edition (prepared by John Brown) was published in Edinburgh. A large part of the work was included in E. T. Campagnac, *The Cambridge Platonists* (Oxford, 1901).

1. [ED.] The AV reads, "The spirit of man . . ." Culverwel quotes both the Hebrew text and the Septuagint, and translates as above.

But some are so strangely prejudiced against reason (and that upon sufficient reason too, as they think, which yet involves a flat contradiction) as that they look upon it not as "the candle of the Lord," but as on some blazing comet that portends ruin to the church and to the soul and carries a fatal and venomous influence along with it. And because the unruly head of Socinus [2] and his followers, by their mere pretences to reason, have made shipwreck of faith and have been very injurious to the Gospel, therefore these weak and staggering apprehensions are afraid of understanding anything; and think that the very name of reason, especially in a pulpit, in matters of religion must needs have at least a thousand heresies couched in it. If you do but offer to make a syllogism, they'll straightway cry it down for carnal reasoning. What would these men have? Would they be banished from their own essences? Would they forfeit and renounce their understandings? Or have they any to forfeit or disclaim? Would they put out this "candle of the Lord," intellectuals [3] of his lighting? Or have they any to put out? Would they creep into some lower species and go a-grazing with Nebuchadnezzar among the beasts of the field? [Dan. 4:33] or are they not there already? Or, if they themselves can be willing to be so shamefully degraded, do they think that all others too are bound to follow their example? Oh, what hard thoughts have these of religion? Do they look upon it only as on a bird of prey, that comes to peck out the eyes of men? Is this all the nobility that it gives, that men by virtue of it must be beheaded presently? Does it chop off the intellectuals at one blow? Let's hear awhile what are the offences of reason. Are they so heinous and capital? What has it done? What laws has it violated? Whose commands has it broken? What did it ever do against the crown and dignity of Heaven, or against the peace and tranquility of men? Why are a weak and perverse generation so angry and displeased with it? Is it because this "daughter of the morning" is fallen from her primitive glory, from her original vigor and perfection? Far be it from me to extenuate that great and fatal overthrow which the sons of men had in their first and original apostasy from their God—that under which the whole creation sighs and groans [cf. Rom. 8:22]. But this we are sure, it did not

2. [ED.] Socinus (F. P. Sozzini, 1539–1604), an Italian reformer, who moved from Siena to Basel, to Transylvania, and thence to Poland. His views became progressively more and more liberal, and he was regarded as the chief initiator of modern Unitarianism. His appeal to reason made him, both then and later, anathema to the champions of orthodoxy. Rigid Calvinists cited him as an example of the results of relying too exclusively on reason.

3. [ED.] In the seventeenth century, "intellectuals" meant "intellect."

annihilate the soul, it did not destroy the essence, the powers and faculties, nor the operations of the soul, though it did defile them and disorder them and every way indispose them.

Well, then, because the eye of reason is weakened and vitiated, will they therefore pluck it out immediately? And must Leah be hated upon no other account but because she is blear-eyed? The whole head is wounded and aches, and is there no other way but to cut it off? "The candle of the Lord" does not shine so clearly as it was wont; must it therefore be extinguished presently? Is it not better to enjoy the faint and languishing light of this "candle of the Lord" rather than to be in palpable and disconsolate darkness? There are indeed but a few seminal sparks left in the ashes, and must there be whole floods of water cast on them to quench them? 'Tis but an old imperfect manuscript, with some broken periods, some letters worn out; must they therefore with an unmerciful indignation rend it and tear it asunder? 'Tis granted that the picture has lost its gloss and beauty, the oriency of its colors, the elegancy of its lineaments, the comeliness of its proportion; must it therefore be totally defaced? Must it be made one great blot?—and must the very frame of it be broken in pieces? Would you persuade the lutanist to cut all his strings in sunder because they are out of tune? And will you break the bow upon no other account but because it is unbended? Because men have not so much reason as they should, will they therefore resolve to have none at all? Will you throw away your gold because it's mixed with dross? Thy very being, that's imperfect too; thy graces, they are imperfect; wilt thou refuse these also? And then consider that the very apprehending the weakness of reason, even this in some measure comes from reason. Reason, when awakened, it feels her own wounds, it hears her own jarrings, she sees the dimness of her own sight. 'Tis a glass that discovers its own spots; and must it therefore be broke in pieces? Reason herself has made many sad complaints unto you. She has told you often, and that with tears in her eyes, what a great shipwreck she has suffered, what goods she has lost, how hardly she escaped with a poor decayed being. She has shown you often some broken relics, as the sad remembrancers of her former ruins. She told you that when she swam for her life, she had nothing but two or three jewels about her, two or three common notions; and would you rob her of them also? Is this all your tenderness and compassion? Is this your kindness to your friend? Will you trample upon her now she is so low? Is this a sufficient cause to give her a Bill of Divorcement, because she has lost her former beauty and fruitfulness?

Or is reason thus offensive to them because she cannot grasp and comprehend the things of God? Vain men, will they pluck out their eyes because they cannot look upon the sun in his brightness and glory? What though reason cannot reach to the depths, to the bottoms of the ocean, may it not therefore swim and hold up the head as well as it can? What though it cannot enter into the *sanctum sanctorum* [holy of holies] and pierce within the veil, may it not, notwithstanding, lie in the porch, "at the gate of the temple called Beautiful" and "be a door-keeper in the house of its God" [Acts 3:2; Ps. 84:10]? Its wings are clipt indeed; it cannot fly so high as it might have done; it cannot fly so swiftly, so strongly, as once it could. Will they not therefore allow it to move, to stir, to flutter up and down, as well as it can? The turrets and pinnacles of the stately structure are fallen: will they therefore demolish the whole fabric, and shake the very foundations of it and down with it to the ground? Though it be not a Jacob's ladder to climb to heaven by [Gen. 28:12], yet may they not use it as a staff to walk upon earth withal? And then reason itself knows this also and acknowledges that 'tis dazzled with the majesty and glory of God; that it cannot pierce into his mysterious and unsearchable ways; it never was so vain as to go about to measure immensity by its own infinite compass, or to span out absolute eternity by its own more imperfect duration. True reason did never go about to comprise the Bible in its own nutshell. And if reason be content with its own sphere, why should it not have the liberty of its proper motion?

Is it because it opposes the things of God and wrangles against the mysteries of salvation, is it therefore excluded? An heinous and frequent accusation indeed; but nothing more false and injurious. And if it had been an open enemy that had done her this wrong, why then she could have borne it. But it's thou, her friend and companion, ye have "took sweet counsel together" [Ps. 55:14], and have entered into the house of God as friends, 'tis you, that have your dependence upon her, that cannot speak one word of purpose against her without her help and assistance. What mean you thus to revile your most intimate and inseparable self? Why do you thus slander your own being? Would you have all this to be true, which you say? Name but the time, if you can, whenever right reason did oppose one jot or apex of the work of God. Certainly these men speak of distorted reason all this while. Surely they do not speak of the "candle of the Lord," but of some shadow and appearance of it. But if they tell us that all reason is distorted, whether then is theirs so in telling us so? If they say that they do not know this by reason, but by the Word of God,

whether then is that their reason, when it acknowledges the Word of
God? Whether is it then distorted, or no? Besides, if there were no right
reason in the world, what difference between sobriety and madness,
between these men and wiser ones? How then were the "heathen left
without excuse" [cf. Rom. 1:20], who had nothing to see by but this
"candle of the Lord"? And how does this thrust men below sensitive
creatures?—for better have no reason at all than such as does perpetually
deceive them and delude them.

Or does reason thus displease them, because the blackest errors sometimes come under the fair disguise of so beautiful a name and have some
tincture of reason in them? But truly this is so far from being a disparagement to reason, as that 'tis no small commendation of it, for men love to
put a plausible title, a winning frontispiece upon the foulest errors. Thus
licentiousness would fain be called by the name of liberty, and all dis-
soluteness would fain be countenanced and secured under the patronage
and protection of free grace. Thus wickedness would willingly forget its
own name and adopt itself into the family of goodness. Thus Arminianism [4] pleads for itself under the specious notion of "God's love to mankind." Thus that silly error of Antinomianism [5] will needs style itself an
"evangelical honeycomb." Thus all irregularities and anomalies in church
affairs must pride themselves in these glittering titles of a "new light," "a
Gospel way," "an Heaven upon earth." No wonder then that some also
pretend to reason, who yet run out of it and beyond it and besides it; but
must none therefore come near it? Because Socinus has burnt his wings at
this "candle of the Lord," must none therefore make use of it?

May he not be conquered with his own weapons and beat out of his
own strongholds, and may not the head of an "uncircumcised Philistine"
be cut off with his own sword [cf. 1 Sam. 17:26,51]?

Or lastly, are they thus afraid of reason because, by virtue of this, men

4. [ED.] The theological system initiated by the Dutch theologian Jacob Arminius
(ob. 1609) and set forth in the Remonstrance of 1610. Its doctrines were a reaction
against the rigidities of Calvinism. So God's sovereignty does not obliterate man's free
will; Christ died for all men, not for the elect alone; predestination is an unbiblical
doctrine. The echoes of Culverwel's Puritan background can be detected in the terms
in which he speaks of Arminianism. For the general attitude of the Cambridge
Platonists, cf. R. L. Colie, *Light and Enlightenment* (Cambridge, 1957), passim.

5. [ED.] The belief that grace liberates us from the restraints of the moral law. Paul's
critics accused him, unjustly, of this view; it was held by various heretical sects in the
patristic period. After the Reformation it was revived by certain groups as an inference drawn from the Lutheran doctrine of justification by faith. During the Commonwealth in England, certain short-lived Antinomian sects emerged.

of wit and subtlety will presently argue and dispute them into an error, so as that they shall not be able to disentangle a truth, though in itself it be never so plain and unquestionable? But first reason itself tells them that it may be thus, and so prepares and fortifies them against such a trial; and then this only shows that some men's reason is not so well advanced and improved, either as it might be, or as others' is; a sharper edge would quickly cut such difficulties asunder. Some have more refined and clarified intellectuals, more vigorous and sparkling eyes than others, and one soul differs from another in glory; and that reason, which can make some shift to maintain error, might with a great deal less sweat and pains maintain a truth.

There's no question but that Bellarmine [6] and the rest of the learned Papists could have, if they had pleased, far more easily defended the Protestant religion than that of their own. Besides, the vigor and triumph of reason is principally to be seen in those first-born beams, those pure and unspotted irradiations, that shine from it; I mean those first bubblings up of common principles that are owned and acknowledged by all, and those evident and kindly derivations that flow from them. Reason shows her face more amiably and pleasantly in a pure and clear stream than in those mudded and troubled waters in which the Schoolmen (that have leisure enough) are always fishing.[7] Nay, some of their works are like so many raging seas, full of perpetual tossings, and disquietings, and foamings, and sometimes casting up mire and dirt; and yet these vast and voluminous Leviathans love to sport therein [cf. Ps. 104:26], and that, which is most intolerable, these grand σοφοί ["wise men"—but actually Sophists], that seemed so zealous for reason, at length in express terms disclaim it, and in a most blindfold and confused manner, cry up their great Diana [Acts 19:34], their idol of Transubstantiation; and the Lutherans are very fierce against reason too, much upon the same account, because it would never allow of that their monstrous and misshapen lump of Consubstantiation.

6. [ED.] Cardinal Robert Bellarmine (1542–1621) was one of the greatest of Roman Catholic controversialists. An Italian Jesuit, famous for his learning, he was a strong opponent of Protestantism. He tried to meet its case by reason and argument, not by the dogmatism and abuse so common in that age. He intervened in the controversy regarding the oath of allegiance demanded of English Catholics. He took a rather moderate view of the Pope's temporal power. His most famous work was *Disputationes de Controversiis Christianae Fidei adversus hujus temporis Haereticos*, 3 vols. (Ingolstadt, 1586–93).

7. [ED.] To the seventeenth century, the Schoolmen (i.e., the medieval scholastic philosophers and theologians) seemed the epitome of interminable and utterly unprofitable speculation.

But why I have all this while beaten the air and spilt words upon the ground? Why do I speak to such as are incurable and incapable?—for if we speak reason to them, that's that which they so much disclaim; if we do not speak reason to them, that were to disclaim it too.

But I speak to men, to Christians, to the friends of learning, to the professors of reason, to such as put this "candle of the Lord" into a golden candlestick and pour continual oil into it [cf. Rev. 1:20]. Yet lest any among you, Athenians,[8] should erect an altar "to an unknown God," lest you should ignorantly worship him, we will declare him to you [Acts 17:23].

And that, which we have now said, may serve as porch and preamble to what we shall speak hereafter out of those words; where we shall see, first, how "the understanding of a man is the candle of the Lord"; secondly, what this "candle of the Lord" discovers; where we shall find, first, that all the moral law is founded in natural, and common light of reason; secondly, that there's nothing in the mysteries of the Gospel contrary to the light of reason, nothing repugnant to this light, that shines from "the candle of the Lord."

8. [ED.] Almost nothing is known about the circumstances governing the composition of this work. Presumably it was addressed to a university audience, and by "Athenians" Culverwel meant the Cambridge dons and undergraduates.

❖ ❖ ❖ ❖ ❖ ❖ ❖ ❖

BENJAMIN WHICHCOTE

The Work of Reason

Editor's Introduction. The sermon was Whichcote's great instrument of teaching. Week by week, year after year, he used it with telling effect as the afternoon lecturer at Holy Trinity Church, Cambridge. By its means he profoundly influenced the outlook of the rising generation of religious leaders. Later in life, as a London preacher, he attracted a large and discriminating following. Apparently a series of sermons was a favorite device for probing a theme or a passage more thoroughly than a single discourse would permit. One of the longest of these series, and certainly one of the ablest, was his careful examination of Philippians 4:8. This is the final sermon in the series; the first one ("Whatsoever Things Are True") is also included in this volume.

Fundamental to Whichcote's approach to all religious questions is his conviction that we cannot possibly understand such questions if we begin by repudiating the use of our reason. God gave us our minds; he expects us to use them. If we stifle reason, we destroy even the possibility of true religion. "What has not reason in it or for it, if held out for religion, is man's superstition. It is not religion of God's making" (*Moral and Religious Aphorisms*, No. 102). Whichcote had no patience with those who tried to exalt faith by depreciating reason—a tendency that not only had disastrous practical results, but also ran counter to the principles underlying God's creative purpose. "A man has as much right to use his understanding in judging of truth as he has a right to use his own eyes to see his way" (*Aphorisms*, No. 40). To this theme he reverted again and again. "To go against reason," he said, "is to go against God; it is the selfsame thing to do that which the reason of the case doth require and that which God himself doth appoint. Reason is the divine governor of man's life; it is the very voice of God" (*Aphorisms*, No. 76).

Whichcote's sermons were almost all published posthumously. They were largely based on his notes, amplified by the stenographic reports of listeners. No MSS. now survive. They were published as follows: *Select Sermons* (with a preface by the Third Earl of Shaftesbury, London, 1689);

Select Discourses, 4 vols. (ed. J. Jeffery, London, 1701); *The Sermons of Benjamin Whichcote,* 4 vols. (ed. William Wishart, Edinburgh, 1742); *The Works of the learned Benjamin Whichcote, D.D.,* 4 vols. (Aberdeen, 1751).

❖ ❖ ❖ ❖

Philippians 4:8: "Think on these things."

I have treated (as you know) of the several perfections and accomplishments that are charged upon us here by the Apostle upon account of religion, and have given you an account what those things are that the Apostle doth recommend as the necessary qualifications and due endowments of a Christian spirit.

In the first place we had "Whatsoever things are true." Religion requires simplicity, ingenuity, sincerity, integrity, uprightness in our profession.

2. "Whatsoever things are grave, venerable, seemly, comely, honorable" unto the person. Religion requires good behavior, fair deportment of ourselves, such demeanor and carriage as may gain reverence and esteem, and bear off all contempt and disrespect.

3. "Whatsoever things are just or equal." Religion holds us to rules of right; and if equity require that which is better and exceeds right, we are to do the thing that is equal, to consider all compassionable cases as God does, to make allowance as far as reason may require.

4. "Whatsoever things are pure or holy." A person of religion is truly devout; affected towards God, and the things wherein he may observe him and show his regard towards him. He is no trifler nor dallier with God, nor a profaner of holy things.

5. "Whatsoever things are lovely." A person of religion is for the nobler and worthier part, in all competition of things and actions.

6. "Whatsoever things are of good report." A person of religion approves himself to all rules and laws of reason and of righteousness, is irreprovable in the judgment of sober and impartial men.

7. "If there be any virtue." Whatsoever virtue there is in account or esteem amongst men; a person of religion is prepared to all good offices, he is for all good purposes, he is a person exercised in all the several virtues and accomplishments of human nature; he is baptised into and sanctified by the virtues, as the moralist speaks.

8. And lastly, "If there be any praise." A person of religion employs himself in things that are commendable and praiseworthy. Of all these I have given you some account.

And now here, upon the whole matter he doth enjoin them all together by superadding these words, "Think on these things." The English translation abates of the emphasis that is in the Greek; for if you read them according to the Greek, it is, "In the use of your reason and understanding think these things to be reasonable"; use your own faculties; use mind and understanding, and you will be satisfied that all these things are worthy of you and becoming you; they will be suitable to your reason.

A person of religion is, first, all this in his judgment and internal sense.

2dly, he is all this in his temper and the disposition of his mind, the settled complexion and constitution of his soul.

3dly, he is so in his life and practice, and in his whole conversation with men; he is not only so now and then, and as we say, by fits and starts, on occasion, when he is specially engaged; but the very reason of his mind is reconciled to the rule and measure of things and actions.

Now this is that which I am to recommend to you, not only that these things should have an obligation upon you at some times (for that is but dull), but that you should be reconciled to all these things in the reason of your minds, that these things should become natural to you, a frame and temper, a complexion and constitution of soul. Apply these things to the reason of your minds and you cannot but be convinced of the reasonableness of them; for the materials of religion do exercise, teach, and satisfy.

That which is the height and excellency of human nature, viz., our reason, is not laid aside nor discharged, much less is it confounded by any of the materials of religion; but awakened, excited, employed, directed and improved by it. For the mind and understanding of man is that faculty whereby man is made capable of God and apprehensive of him, receptive from him and able to make returns upon him and acknowledgments to him. Bring that with you, or else you are not capable receivers. Unless you drink in these moral principles, unless you do receive them by reason, the reason of things by the reason of your mind, your religion is but shallow and superficial. For this you are to understand, that man is a compound of different things, hath several sorts of faculties, above any creature in this visible world. He hath an immortal spirit, as well as a bodily substance. And though the spirit of man in this state be joined to a body and made a member of this material visible world, yet itself doth belong to another country. I say, a man is a compound of different and several things; he hath several sorts of faculties, which we are wont in our philosophy to call his upper and his lower powers, and by these he doth converse with things of a very different order. By the higher powers he is able to converse both with God and things spiritual and celestial, and by the lower powers with terrene and earthly. As to instance: by mind and understanding and will he hath intercourse and communion with God and things invisible, and by these he is fitted to the improving all the lower objects to heavenly ends and purposes. But then by sense, imagination and brutish affection we can only maintain acquaintance with this outward and lower world. But by this principle of reason and understanding we are made capable of religion. So that man's peculiar object and proper business is in things of the mind; and therefore he ought to use those high faculties of his soul to enquire after God, and find out truth and the reason of things; and consequently after such enquiry to determine himself in his resolution and choice, to things according to their intrinsic worth and value.

Two things here I say: 1st, no man is born to be idle in the world. For though it is the privilege of some particular persons that they who were born before them have provided for all comforts, necessities and conveniences of life, so that they have enough to enjoy, with a superfluity and abundance, yet this I will say of all men, and indifferently of all our ancestors, that though they might acquire inheritances and worldly conveniencies, yet they could not acquire for, or leave to any of us, mental endowments, no habitual dispositions. But in respect of these 'tis true that everybody is master of his own fortune under God. Every man hath himself as he useth himself. He that by motion upwards contemplates God converses with angels and separate souls, but he that through brutishness and sensuality sinks into this lower world and lives to grow less, he will finally shrivel up and come to nothing.

Now here is that which I recommend to you all: work for the mind, and this is that which is most peculiar and proper to human nature. No one is born to this, more than another. But if you will be intellectually improved, if you will be refined in your spirits, refined in your morals, if you will be more than the *vulgus hominum*, you must set yourselves in the ways of reading, meditation and conference and self-reflection, and awaken your intellectuals; or else you shall come to nothing.

2. That which in the second place I superadd is this: that the first operation in religion is mental and intellectual, (viz.) consideration, discussion, examination, self-reflection, approving the reason of things to the reason of our minds as the proper rule. This is a notion worthy of your consideration. In all things of weight, in the great points of conscience, in the great materials of religion, there is a reason in the things that doth enforce them and enjoin them upon us and require them of us—as, if I be God's creature, stand in relation to him, am capable of him, I am naturally and unavoidably

under an obligation of duty and affection to him, and I am bound to serve him, honor and live in regard of him. Here is the reason of the thing. And the reason of your mind is to find it out, which a beast cannot do, therefore is uncapable of religion. But this is that which you are to do, and there is no religion but in this. I say, if so be a man doth not admit what he receives, with satisfaction to the reason of his mind, he doth not receive it as an intelligent agent, but he receives it as a vessel receives water; he is *continens* rather than *recipiens*. But this is the peculiarity of human nature, that through the reason of his mind he may come to understand the reason of things. And this is that you are to do, and there is no coming to religion but this way. Wherefore they begin at the wrong end, who do not set themselves at first thus to work, and so are not likely to hold out or go on; or if they do continue to retain a certain mode or way of religion, they are not likely to bring anything in religion to perfection. For the mind's satisfaction and resolution is the first and principal. And if we leap over this and jump into a profession of religion without this consideration, discussion, examination, self-reflection and approving the reason of our minds to the reason of things as the proper rule, we shall be ever lame in our way and slight in our business. We shall not build upon a rock; we shall not lay a solid foundation. Our Savior therefore bids us, before we engage to build a tower, to sit down, consider and recount whether we shall be able to finish it, Luke 14, 26 to the 32. For assure yourselves, whatsoever is rashly begun, it uncertainly goes on and foolishly deceives, either in religion or anything else.

Of all impotencies in the world, credulity in religion is the greatest. This Solomon hath observed, that simple, weak, shallow heads are foolish and believe that which any one saith; sail with every wind that blows. Proverbs 14:15: "The simple believeth every word; but the prudent man looketh well about him." When a man hath made a deliberate act of judgment in a case, upon consideration of reason, grounds and principles, he hath always ever after within him, whereby to encourage him to go on and answer all objections as they shall arise. Whereas he that begins not thus, upon all contrary appearances he will be unsettled and unstable in all his ways. But the person of examination and consideration, that begins upon discussion, &c., and so comes to well-grounded resolution, he is encouraged from the memory of the motives that made him begin, the motives that set him at work, and the prospect of the end at which he did aim and which he did design and which he hath also constantly in his eye. But he that begins inconsiderately, he is so weak in his way that there is little expectation of his holding out. And truly this is a just account of all the shameful and horrid apostasy of all formal professors; they did never weigh and examine, they did never reconcile their religion to the reason of their minds, so that really they have but an external denomination from their profession.

Man is not at all settled or confirmed in his religion until his religion is the self-same with the reason of his mind, that when he thinks he speaks reason, he speaks religion, or when he speaks religiously he speaks reasonably. And his religion and reason is mingled together. They pass into one principle. They are no longer two but one. Just as the light in the air makes one illuminated sphere, so reason and religion in the subject are one principle.

To hold this forth more fully, I will lay it out in four propositions.

First, it is lowness and imperfection in religion to drudge in it. And every man drudges in religion that takes up religion as a task, carries it as a burden; and doth it because he must do it, or because his superiors require it of him, or because time and place and custom calls for it, because the day requires it, or because it is such an hour, because he is now up, or because he must now go to bed. If this be the best motive a man hath, his religion is but a burthen. But they who are come to any growth in religion are free-spirited in it, and do it with inward satisfaction, pleasure and content. They harmonize with it. They understand it is in itself best and fit so to do, and that it is also good in itself and good for them; worthy in respect of God and becoming them in the relation they stand in to him; tends to their perfection and will bring them to happiness.

A man hath this at least by his religion, that if by accident he admits of sin, he never does it with pleasure. He doth not, like the ox, drink iniquity like water, as Eliphas elegantly expresses it [cf. Job 15:16]. But this is his temper and he hath Joseph's resolution, "How can I do this great wickedness and sin against God?" (Gen. 39:9) I say again, he hath this advantage by his religion, that if by temptation, by surprise, or by violent assault, he happens to admit any evil, he doth it with displacency, he offends himself as well as God. And he hath a principle within him of self-recovery, viz., that which St Paul speaks of Romans 7:23, "the law of his mind." So that, as water, if it chance to be sullied, hath in it a principle to work the dregs to the bottom, so will this man by repentance and ingenuity recover himself to his innocency. And this is that which our Savior means by "pure in heart"; and in this he hath a convinced, satisfied judgment, because he hath an internal principle. The reason of his mind is taught and illuminated;

he is in this condemned in his own conscience, and he will hasten to make his peace with himself as well as with God.

And indeed I tell you by the way, it is a harder matter for a truly good man of honest principles to forgive himself than to obtain forgiveness of God; though I make no question but that God, according to his promise, doth presently forgive every true penitent, if he go to God according to his direction.

I say in this case he is condemned of himself, and therefore he will hasten to set all things right and straight within himself and be at peace with his own mind; and this by the revocation of what was done amiss; by deprecating God's displeasure, by asking God forgiveness, by crying him mercy, by double diligence and watchfulness and resolution never to do the like again.

Secondly, the seat of religion is the inward man; it is first the sense of a man's soul, the temper of his mind, the pulse of his heart. You have always in intellectual nature the elicit acts, as we call them; that is, mental and internal acts; and they always precede and go before imperate acts, that is, external acts. The elicit acts of the mind, they are first. It lies first within the mind; after that, it doth appear externally in speeches, gestures, actions and the effects of all good self-government.

In rational and in all intellectual nature, you have first that which we call the speech of a man's mind with itself; the mind doth parley with itself, debates the thing throughly. Then you have the overt acts, and afterwards you have the mind's sense put into language. This is the way of operation in intellectual natures, to speak with ourselves before we speak with others; and it doth not become us to make too much haste with the latter before the former be over. It is just as Solomon hath observed it, Ecclesiastes 10:14: "The fool is full of words, but the wise man is not so"; at least he thinks before he speaks.

My third proposition is this, that in the state of religion, spirituals and naturals join and mingle in their subjects, so that if a man be once in a true state of religion he cannot distinguish between religion and the reason of his mind; so that his religion is the reason of his mind, and the reason of his mind is his religion. They are not two things now. They do not go two several ways, but concur and agree. They both run into one principle, they make one spirit, make one stream. The effects and products of his reason and religion are the same in a person that is truly religious. His reason is sanctified by his religion, and his religion helps and makes use of his reason. So that in the subject it is but one thing; you may call it, if you will, religious reason and reason made religious. They are not divided or separated, but the union is more intimate and near as these principles are more immaterial and spiritual, whereas gross and material things keep at a distance, because of the impossibility of penetration.

Fourthly and lastly: religion doth us great service, great pleasure both for mind and body.

1. For our mind, immediately by its formal presence and residence.

2. For our body, by the good consequences that follow upon the mind's good government.

In particular, your religion is the mind's health and good temper, and it doth help to conserve the body's strength. As for instance, sobriety, gentleness, temperance, meekness, modesty, humility, which are the materials of religion; all these do spare and favor the body. On the contrary, pride, arrogance, haughtiness, presumption, fierceness, intemperance, which are things contrary to religion, these waste and spoil the body. Also faith and affiance in God, love of God, goodness and complacence with God, harmony with him, delight in him; these do maintain and keep up men's spirits; and you know men's spirits do strongly resist all manner of disease. On the contrary, malcontent, distrust, despair, diffidence, sourness, peevishness, wrathfulness, anger, displeasure, these do hurt our minds, spoil all our mettle and abate our courage. Wherefore you see God hath given us religion altogether for our advantage, not only for the future estate, but also for the present: the soul's safety, the body's better security.

To go on further: how doth malice, envy and purpose of revenge prey upon the body, spend men's spirits?—whereas they who live in love and good will are of gentle and quiet spirits, they favor their bodies. The body is wasted under the former, but bodily strength is maintained under these. Psalm 55:23: "The bloody and deceitful men do not live out half their days." And it is observed by Solomon, Proverbs 3:13: "Happy is the man that findeth wisdom." Wisdom is religion in his sense. And verse 16, "Length of days are in her right hand, and in her left hand riches and honor. Her ways are ways of pleasantness, and all her paths are peace." Farther, in ways of temperance there is health, strength and long life, whereas the licentious and exorbitant livers, they do load themselves with distempers and often die before the time. Wherefore Solomon advises, Ecclesiastes 7:17: "Be not overmuch wicked, neither be thou foolish; why shouldest thou die before thy time?" Wherefore you see religion is good for the purposes of this life, as well as for the state of eternity.

I hasten now to a conclusion, and will conclude with a double exhortation.

1st. If you love yourselves, either bodies or souls, acquaint yourselves with religion.

2dly. If you would be religious, be intelligent and rational in your religion, or else your religion may be only a denomination and not sovereign to you.

1st. If you love yourselves, either in respect of the present or future state, acquaint yourselves with religion.

2dly. If you meddle with religion, be intelligent and rational in your religion. Study religion till the reason of your minds receives satisfaction, for till then you cannot account it your own, neither call it your own; neither hath it security and settlement in its subject.

And till this be, men will not be friendly to their religion, they will not make it their choice, but rather look upon it as their exactor, their tormentor, the controller of their liberty. It will be a taskmaster, they will carry it as their burthen, which a man will throw off as soon as he hath opportunity.

Now I dare undertake to show, that all true reason is for religion, and nothing of truth against it; and this I will show thus. There are but two things that are sincere and solid, real and substantial in the world, the reason of the thing, or the rule; and the reason of the subject for the discerning faculty. Now the reason of the thing, that is certainly for religion; and the reason of the thing is as infallible a rule and as certain as the law of Heaven. For the reason of the thing, if it be in Institutes, it is according to the revelation of the Divine Will. In things that are in themselves necessary, it is according to the nature of God. Therefore the reason of the thing, that is certainly for religion. Now the reason of the subject, either it is blind or biased, prepossessed or corrupted, if it be against it; that for certain. Now if it be so, here is our great challenge. The reason of the thing, that is made to our hands; the use of our faculties, that is to find it out. The reason of the thing, it is a rule to the reason of the subject; if it varies, it is to be rectified, corrected by the rule. The reason of the thing is always for religion; if the reason of the subject is to comply with the rule, then a man's reason and his religion will accord and meet. If we be in the true use of reason, we may see cause for what we do in the way of religion; but if we be ignorant we are neither rational nor religious.

Where a man hath not weighed and considered, searched and examined, he is nobody. If he be rational, then he discerns the reason of the thing; and the reason of the thing, if he comply with it, is religion. Blind presumption and suspicion are very sorry things, and have no place anywhere; for prepossession and anticipation shew men to be of a party but no true discerners of truth.

In the close of all, let me advise you to clear understanding, true perception and right apprehensions of things, that you charge yourselves with upon account of religion. I would never advise a man to be light of faith in matters of religion, or to run away with suppositions, or dully to refer himself or compromise with any party; but so far as he thinks religion concerns him, let him take to himself leisure and opportunity; let him weigh and consider, and let him use his faculties, as he may do. This is the direction in religion; use your reason so far as you may have perception of these things and such a sensation of them that you may receive satisfaction. If you do not do so, really you do not come within the compass of religion. A man may not admit that which is a true principle upon account of religion; yet because he doth not receive it upon account of its own evidence, light and truth, he doth not entertain that of religion as a point of religion; but he believes it as he believes a story that he hears a man tell but never considers it whether it be true or false.

Religion is not a thing that can be made up of ignorant well-meanings, or of fond or slight imaginations, credulous suspicion, or fond conceit; such are the suppositions of all superstition; but of deliberate resolutions and diligent searches into the reason of things and into the rational sense of Holy Scripture.

We have cause to give God thanks, that so far as revelation is necessary to convey anything by way of superaddition to the light of God's creation, to the principles whereof, God made us in the moment of his creation, God hath not left us to vain supposition, not to the ungrounded guesses of fond minds; but you have it clearly, plainly, fully, satisfactorily laid down in Holy Scripture; so that religion is the clearest and most self-evident thing in the world. But if a man do not enquire into the reason and grounds of his persuasion, if he gives himself up to drudge in the world, and refer himself in his religion to other men's sense, delivering himself to a party, I will assure him he is not religious, not in that which he receives, though it may be materially true in religion. For he doth not receive it as becomes a disciple of reason, much less of religion; for it might have been false, or the contrary, for anything he knows. And for the selfsame reason that he admitted this as truth, he might have admitted the contrary if so be the party, with which he doth compromise, had offered it.

The truly religious are not idle bodies, but they do exercise themselves in the highest and noblest employment and their work is to affect the inward man. And we are wont to say that in competition the body is nothing, it is but the soul's mansion-house. Every man's mind is the man.

I will conclude all in a few words, to recommend religion to the reason of your minds.

1st. It doth relieve us in the case of the greatest evils that we are in danger of; and the greatest evils we are exposed to are the guiltiness of our consciences and the malignity in our minds.

2ndly. Religion doth possess us of the truest inward good.

3rdly. It restores us to the object of our happiness, and to our ultimate end.

First. Religion doth relieve us in respect of the greatest inward evils that we are liable to, viz., guiltiness in our conscience and malignity in our minds; which, if not removed, we must of necessity be miserable as a man must be miserable though he lie upon a bed of down if he be sick and distempered and cannot be cured of internal malady. Now these two are internal evils that are greater than any other internal evils in the world: a wound in the conscience, guiltiness in the mind; the worm of conscience, the sting of sin; these two are the life of Hell. And then the other great evil is malignity, rancor, malice and poison in the mind. And this mars our nature, spoils our dispositions and tempers and puts us at a distance and abhorrence of God and goodness and makes us harmonize with the Devil and sin. Now there is no way to be relieved in respect of these internal evils but in the way of religion and by the blood of sprinkling, for the cleansing our consciences by way of atonement and by the operation of the Spirit for the renewing, repairing and restoring our natures. That's the *first*.

Secondly. It possesses us of the truest inward good, and that in three particulars.

1. Satisfaction to a man's mind and content, all the world will say, is one of the greatest goods. What is better to a man than his mind's satisfaction? And in the way of religion, a man's mind is satisfied, for he understands upon what grounds and in what way, and he sees before him and knows what he is to trust to.

2. Religion is restorative to the nature of man. And what is more to any man than to be internally whole? If a man hath an internal disease, an internal wound or any inward ulcer in his mind, to restore him to perfect health and strength, this is done in the way of religion.

3. It is pacifying to a man's conscience. For what is more dreadful than

the torments of a man's own breast? When a man's heart aches, though he be applauded and adored by by-standers, yet his heart aches because of his guilt, he finds internal wounds. He may fly from the world but he cannot fly from himself: "The wicked flies when no man pursues." [1] And it is observed that guilt in a man's breast is a prophet that foretells future evil: "Art thou come to call my sins to remembrance?" [I Kings 17:18] But innocency is stout, rises up in its own defence. But when a man is faulty, his heart will not serve him.

Thirdly and lastly. Religion restores us to the object of our happiness, to our ultimate end. So saith the Psalmist, Psalm 17:15, "I will behold thy face in righteousness: I will be satisfied when I awake with thy likeness." We must be reconciled in temper and disposition to the nature, mind and will of God and the law of everlasting goodness, righteousness and truth. Or else it will come to what Solomon saith, "Can two walk together that are not agreed?" [Amos 3:3].

Thus have I given you an account of this full and pregnant Scripture that doth contract and epitomize our religion, comprehends the moral part of religion, that which in part will make us like God; and if these things be received into a temper, complexion and constitution of soul, we shall become God-like and partakers of the very nature of God.

1. [ED.] The words Whichcote quotes are from Proverbs 28:1, but the sense suggests that he was already thinking of Amos 3:3, which he cites in the next paragraph but incorrectly attributes to Solomon.

❖ ❖ ❖ ❖ ❖ ❖ ❖ ❖

BENJAMIN WHICHCOTE

Whatsoever Things are True[1]
(FROM DISCOURSE II)

Editor's Introduction. This brief passage is one of the most condensed and illuminating expositions of what the Cambridge Platonists mean by "truth." It occurs in Discourse LXVIII, one of the great series of sermons which Whichcote preached on Philippians 4:8.

But now, that I may the more encourage you in your endeavors after truth, I will show you how many are the advantages that attend men's abiding therein. 1. Truth hath always God to maintain it; so that none need fear he shall perish in the way. If a man be in the truth, he need do no more than his part; for God is primarily concerned to defend truth. 2. Truth hath defence in itself; for great is truth, and it will prevail. Truth may be overborne for a while, but it will recover. 3. Truth hath goodness to accompany it; therefore none need fear shame or cause to repent. 4. Truth hath liberty consequent upon it; "the truth shall make you free" (Jn. 8:32). He that is in the truth is not thoughtful; but a liar had need carry about with him a good memory. He that confines himself to speak truth, if his memory fails him, he never varies from himself nor from the truth; but a liar if his memory fails him, betrays himself. 5. Truth is connatural to our principles; for a man forceth himself when he departs from the truth. We force ourselves when we tell a lie. 6. Truth is the foundation of order. All things will be in a hurlyburly and confusion if not ordered and united and governed by truth; for falsehood puts everything out of its place. 7. Truth is the ground of human converse; no man is sure of another, neither knows where to have him, if he abides not in the truth. 8. Truth is the bond of union. Where men agree in the truth, they meet friendly and harmonize one with another, and great sympathy is between them. But out of the ways of truth men run counter and cross and contradict one another everywhere. Where there is perfect truth, there is motion without contradiction. And further, God's government in the

1. [ED.] From *The Works of the learned Benjamin Whichcote, D.D.* (Aberdeen, 1751), III, 387–89.

world is brought to nothing; the rules and measures thereof are destroyed if men depart from truth and righteousness. In the ways of truth and righteousness there is settlement and security. This we are to know, that God's superintendence over human affairs aims at this; this is the effect of it, that truth and righteousness may obtain an universal empire in the world. And this is an explication of that great phrase, "God's doing all for his own glory," for it is else an inexplicable form of words to say that "God doth all for himself particularly," as if God were a particular agent and sought his own particular interest. But the sense is, that which God superintends the world for, is, that truth, righteousness and goodness should take place everywhere in the world, and for the advancement of this, every man in the sphere of his activity and within his compass ought to endeavor; and this is for us "to act to the glory of God."

❖ ❖ ❖ ❖ ❖ ❖ ❖ ❖

JOHN SMITH

Discourses

Editor's Introduction. The *Discourses* of John Smith are one of the most characteristic and certainly one of the most attractive statements of the general position adopted by the Cambridge Platonists. Among the offices which Smith held as a Fellow of Queens' College, Cambridge, were those of dean and catechist. In fulfilling his duties, he delivered a series of addresses which were intended to instruct as well as to edify. The *Discourses*, therefore, had their origin in a program of careful teaching, and in the first half of the work at least they developed a connected theme. They were an attempt to establish "the main heads and principles of religion." With "The True Way or Method of Attaining to Divine Knowledge," Smith laid the groundwork for his system of thought. The next two discourses ("Of Superstition" and "Of Atheism") deal with counterfeit forms of religious knowledge. Smith was now ready to expound the central truths of the Christian faith, and he turned first to "The Immortality of the Soul." He then examined "The Existence and Nature of God," and this led him, under the title "Of Prophecy," to the way in which God's revelation of himself at length culminated in Christ. At this point death interrupted Smith's work; his friend John Worthington, who edited and published his works, added four further discourses to round out the volume and to illustrate other aspects of Smith's thought. Among these is the notable study "Of the Excellency and Nobleness of True Religion" (No. 9 in the published volume).

The late Dean Inge of St. Paul's placed these *Discourses* in the highest rank of that demanding category, the university sermon.[1] The praise is justified, but the designation is not entirely exact. Queens' College Chapel was a less formal setting than Great St. Mary's Church, and the audience was much smaller. But Smith did address himself to a congregation of students. This explains certain features of his work. He appealed to concepts and he quoted from writings which undergraduates might be expected to know. He was able to take for granted a knowledge of the

---

1. [ED.] W. R. Inge, *The Platonic Tradition in English Religious Thought* (London, 1926), 62.

ancient languages and used them generously, though he usually took the precaution of translating or paraphrasing the original.

Of the two discourses here reproduced (No. 1 and No. 9), the first ("The True Way or Method of Attaining to Divine Knowledge") sets forth the principles underlying Smith's thought; the second ("Of the Excellency and Nobleness of True Religion") amplifies and illustrates them. Ultimately, Smith asserted, all knowledge springs from the soul within. In the debate then current between materialism and idealism, there is no doubt as to which position he embraced. For him, sensation could not account for the emergence and apprehension of divine truth. The material world could tell us some things, but Smith believed that the knowledge of God belonged to a different order and consequently had a different origin. There is, he argued, a vital sense within us which is able to grasp the truths appropriate to it, a power resident in the soul which explains our response to divine truth: "Theology involves in its very nature the supposition of a power within us answering to and apprehensive of a power above us." Divine truth, for him, was the counterpart of the divine spirit in man; and there was a divine intuition which authenticated the things it grasped. This approach to reality neither eliminated the role of reason nor minimized the place of moral effort. The immediate illumination which is God's gift, the use of the reason with which he has endowed us, the performance of the duties to which he summons us—these are always near the forefront of Smith's thought.

❖ ❖ ❖ ❖ ❖ ❖ ❖ ❖

A Discourse Concerning the True Way or Method of Attaining Divine Knowledge [1]

SECTION I

That divine things are to be understood rather by a spiritual sensation than a verbal description, or mere speculation. Sin and wickedness prejudicial to true knowledge. That purity of heart and life, as also an ingenuous freedom of judgment, are the best grounds and preparations for the entertainment of truth.

It hath been long since well observed that every art and science hath some certain principles upon which the whole frame and body of it must

1. [ED.] On the title page of this work, Smith placed a series of texts: Ps. 111:10, Jn. 7:17, and three from Clement of Alexandria's *Stromateis* III:5.

depend; and he that will fully acquaint himself with the mysteries thereof must come furnished with some *praecognita*, or προλήψεις [preconceptions], that I may speak in the language of the Stoics. Were I indeed to define divinity, I should rather call it a *divine life* than a *divine science;* it being something rather to be understood by a spiritual sensation than by any verbal description, as all things of sense and life are best known by sentient and vital faculties; γνῶσις ἑκάστων δι' ὁμοιότητος γίνεται, as the Greek philosopher hath well observed [2]—everything is best known by that which bears a just resemblance and analogy with it. And therefore the Scripture is wont to set forth a good life as the prolepsis and fundamental principle of divine science: "Wisdom hath builded her house and hewn out her seven pillars," but "the fear of the Lord is the beginning of wisdom"—the foundation of the whole fabric [Prov. 9:1,10].

We shall therefore, as a prolegomenon or preface to what we shall afterward discourse upon the heads of divinity, speak something of this *true method of knowing*, which is not so much by notions as actions; as religion itself consists not so much in words as in things. They are not always the best skilled in divinity that are the most studied in those pandects, into which it is sometimes digested, or that have erected the greatest monopolies of art and science. He that is most practical in divine things hath the purest and sincerest knowledge of them, and not he that is most dogmatical. Divinity indeed is a true efflux from the eternal light, which, like the sunbeams, does not only enlighten but heat and enliven; therefore our Savior hath, in his beatitudes, connected purity of heart with the beatifical vision [Mt. 5:8]. And as the eye cannot behold the sun, ἡλιοειδὴς μὴ γινόμενος—unless it be sunlike, and hath the form and resemblance of the sun drawn in it; so neither can the soul of man behold God, θεοειδὴς μὴ γινομένη—unless it be Godlike and hath God formed in it, and be made partaker of the divine nature.[3] And the apostle St. Paul, when he would lay open the right way of attaining to divine truth, saith that "knowledge puffeth," but it is "love that edifieth" [1 Cor. 8:1]. The knowledge of divinity that appears in systems and models is but a poor wan light; but the powerful energy of divine knowledge displays itself in purified souls. Here we shall find the true πεδίον ἀληθείας, as the ancient philosophy speaks—"the land of truth." [4]

To seek our divinity merely in books and writings is to seek the living among the dead [cf. Lk. 24:5]. We do but in vain seek God many times in

2. [ED.] Plotinus, *The Enneads*, 1.8.1.
3. [ED.] Plotinus, *The Enneads*, 1.6.1.
4. [ED.] Plotinus, *The Enneads*, 1.3.4., VI.7.13.

these, where his truth too often is not so much enshrined as entombed. No, *intra te quaere Deum*, seek for God within thine own soul. He is best discerned νοερᾷ ἐπαφῇ, as Plotinus phraseth it—by an intellectual touch of him.[5] We must "see with our eyes and hear with our ears and our hands must handle the word of life," that I may express it in St. John's words [1 Jn. 1:1]. The soul itself hath its sense as well as the body. And therefore David, when he would teach us how to know what the divine goodness is, calls not for speculation but sensation: "Taste and see how good the Lord is" [Ps. 34:8]. That is not the best and truest knowledge of God which is wrought out by the labor and sweat of the brain, but that which is kindled within us by a heavenly warmth in our hearts. As, in the natural body, it is the heart that sends up good blood and warm spirits into the head, whereby it is best enabled to perform its several functions, so that which enables us to know and understand aright in the things of God must be a living principle of holiness within us. When the tree of knowledge is not planted by the tree of life, and sucks not up sap from thence, it may as well be fruitful with evil as with good and bring forth bitter fruit as well as sweet. If we would indeed have our knowledge thrive and flourish, we must water the tender plants of it with holiness. When Zoroaster's scholars asked him what they should do to get winged souls, such as might soar aloft in the bright beams of divine truth, he bids them bathe themselves in the waters of life; they asking what they were, he tells them, the four cardinal virtues, which are the four rivers of Paradise. It is but a thin, airy knowledge that is got by mere speculation, which is ushered in by syllogisms and demonstrations; but that which springs forth from true goodness is θειότερόν τι πάσης ἀποδείξεως, as Origen speaks—it brings such a divine light into the soul, as is more clear and convincing than any demonstration. The reason why, notwithstanding all our acute reasons and subtle disputes, truth prevails no more in the world, is, we so often disjoin truth and true goodness, which in themselves can never be disunited; they grow both from the same root and live in one another. We may, like those in Plato's deep pit,[6] with their faces bended downwards, converse with sounds and shadows, but not with the life and substance of truth, while our souls remain defiled with any vice or lusts. These are the black Lethe Lake which drench the souls of men; he that wants [lacks] true virtue, in Heaven's logic, "is blind and cannot see afar off" [2 Pet. 1:9]. Those filthy mists that perpetually arise from impure and terrene minds, like an

5. [ED.] The thought, though not the words, comes from Plotinus (*Enn.* 1.2.6).
6. [ED.] Plato, *The Republic*, Book VII, 514A.

atmosphere, perpetually encompass them, that they cannot see that sun of divine truth that shines about them, but never shines into any unpurged souls; the darkness comprehends it not, the foolish man understands it not [cf. Jn. 1:5]. All the light and knowledge that may seem sometimes to rise up in unhallowed minds is but like those fuliginous flames that rise up from our culinary fire, that are soon quenched in their own smoke; or like those foolish fires that fetch their birth from terrene exudations, that do but hop up and down and flit to and fro upon the surface of this earth, where they were first brought forth; and serve not so much to enlighten as to delude us; not to direct the wandering traveller into his way, but to lead him farther out of it. While we lodge any filthy vice in us, this will be perpetually twisting up itself into the thread of our finest-spun speculations; it will be continually climbing up into the hegemonical powers of the soul, into the bed of reason and defile it; like the wanton ivy twisting itself about the oak, it will twine about our judgments and understandings, till it hath sucked out the life and spirit of them. I cannot think such black oblivion should possess the minds of some, as to make them question that truth which to good men shines as bright as the sun at noonday, had they not foully defiled their own souls with some hellish vice or other, how fairly soever it may be they may dissemble it. There is a benumbing spirit, a congealing vapor that ariseth from sin and vice that will stupefy the senses of the soul; as the naturalists say there is from the torpedo [7] that smites the senses of those that approach it. This is that venomous solanum,[8] that deadly nightshade, that infuses its cold poison into the understandings of men.

Such as men themselves are, such will God himself seem to be. It is the maxim of most wicked men that the Deity is some way or other like themselves; their souls do more than whisper it, though their lips speak it not; and though their tongues be silent, yet their lives cry it upon the housetops and in the public streets. That idea which men generally have of God is nothing else but the picture of their own complexions; that archetypal notion of him which hath the supremacy in their minds is none else but such a one as hath been shaped out according to some pattern of themselves; though they may so clothe and disguise this idol of their own, when they carry it about in a pompous procession to expose it to the view of the world, that it may seem very beautiful, and indeed anything else rather

7. [ED.] A flatfish of the family *Torpedinidae*, having the faculty of emitting electric charges.
8. [ED.] A plant of the nightshade family.

than what it is. Most men (though it may be they themselves take no great notice of it) like that dissembling monk—"alitere sentire in scholis, aliter in musaeis"—are of a different judgment in the schools from what they are in the retirements of their private closets. There is a double head as well as a double heart. Men's corrupt hearts will not suffer their notions and conceptions of divine things to be cast into that form, into which a higher reason, which may sometimes work within them, would put them.

I would not be thought, all this while, to banish the belief of all innate notions of divine truth, but these are too often smothered or tainted with a deep dye of men's filthy lusts. It is but *lux sepulta in opaca materia*—light buried and stifled in some dark body, from whence all those colored, or rather discolored, notions and apprehensions of divine things are begotten. Though these common notions may be very busy sometimes in the vegetation of divine knowledge, yet the corrupt vices of men may so clog, disturb and overrule them (as the naturalists say this unruly and masterless matter doth the natural forms in the formation of living creatures) that they may produce nothing but monsters, miserably distorted and misshapen. This kind of science, as Plotinus speaks, "associating too familiarly with matter, and receiving and imbibing it into itself, changeth its shape by this incestuous mixture." [9] At best, while any inward lust is harbored in the minds of men, it will so weaken them that they can never bring forth any masculine or generous knowledge; as Ælian observes of the stork, that if the night-owl chanceth to sit upon her eggs, they become presently as it were ὑπηνέμια [full of wind, so unfertilized], and all incubation is rendered impotent and ineffectual.[10] Sin and lust are always of a hungry nature, and suck up all those vital affections of men's souls which should feed and nourish their understandings.

What are all our most sublime speculations of the Deity, that are not impregnated with true goodness, but insipid things that have no taste nor life in them, that do but swell, like empty froth, in the souls of men! They do not feed men's souls, but only puff them up, and fill them with pride and arrogance, contempt and tyranny towards those that cannot well understand their subtle curiosities; as those philosophers that Cicero complains of in his times, who made their knowledge only matter of ostentation, to venditate and set off themselves, but never caring to square and govern their lives by it.[11] Such as these do but, spider-like, take a great

9. [ED.] Plotinus, *The Enneads*, 1.6.5.

10. [ED.] Ælian, *De natura animalium* (Leipzig, 1864), Bk. 1.37. The term Ælian uses is ἀνεμιαῖα.

11. [ED.] Cicero, *Tusculan Disputations*, Bk. 11.4.

deal of pains to spin a worthless web out of their own bowels, which will
not keep them warm. These indeed are those silly souls that are "ever
learning, but never come to the knowledge of the truth" [2 Tim. 3:7].
They may, with Pharaoh's lean kine [Gen. 41:3], eat up and devour all
tongues and sciences, and yet, when they have done, still remain lean and
ill-favored as they were at first. Jejune and barren speculations may be
hovering and fluttering up and down about divinity, but they cannot
settle or fix themselves upon it. They unfold the plicatures of truth's
garment, but they cannot behold the lovely face of it. There are hidden
mysteries in divine truth, wrapt up one within another, which cannot be
discerned but by divine "Epoptists." [12]

We must not think we have then attained to the right knowledge of
truth, when we have broken through the outward shell of words and
phrases that house it up; or when, by a logical analysis, we have found out
the dependencies and coherencies of them one with another; or when, like
stout champions of it, having well guarded it with the invincible strength
of our demonstration, we dare stand out in the face of the world, and
challenge the field of all those that would pretend to be our rivals.

We have many grave and reverend idolaters that worship truth only in
the image of their own wits; that could never adore it so much as they may
seem to do, were it anything else but such a form of belief as their own
wandering speculations had at last met together in; were it not that they
find their own image and superscription upon it.

There is a knowing of "the truth as it is in Jesus"—as it is in a Christ-
like nature, as it is in that sweet, mild, humble and loving spirit of Jesus,
which spreads itself, like a morning sun, upon the souls of good men, full
of light and life. It profits little to know Christ himself after the flesh
[cf. 2 Cor. 5:16]; but he gives his Spirit to good men, that searcheth the
deep things of God. There is an inward beauty, life and loveliness in divine
truth, which cannot be known but then when it is digested into life and
practice. The Greek philosopher could tell those high-soaring Gnostics
that thought themselves no less than *Jovis alites;* that could (as he speaks
in the comedy) ἀεροβατεῖν καὶ περιφρονεῖν τὸν ἥλιον,[13] and cried out so much,
"Look upon God," that "without virtue and real goodness God is but a
name," a dry and empty notion.[14] The profane sort of men, like those old

---

12. [ED.] "Epoptist," a beholder, especially one enlightened by a burst of light in
darkness; hence, one initiated into the Eleusinian mysteries.

13. [ED.] Aristophanes, *The Clouds,* 225: "Soc.: I tread the air and look down on the
sun."

14. [ED.] Plotinus, *The Enneads,* II.9.15.

Gentile Greeks, may make many ruptures in the walls of God's temple, and break into the holy ground, but yet may find God no more there than they did.

Divine truth is better understood, as it unfolds itself in the purity of men's hearts and lives, than in all those subtle niceties into which curious wits may lay it forth. And therefore our Savior, who is the great master of it, would not, while he was here on earth, draw it up into any system or body, nor would his disciples after him. He would not lay it out to us in any canons or articles of belief, not being indeed so careful to stock and enrich the world with opinions and notions, as with true piety and a God-like pattern of purity, as the best way to thrive in all spiritual understanding. His main scope [15] was to promote a holy life as the best and most compendious way to a right belief. He hangs all true acquaintance with divinity upon the doing God's will: "If any man will do his will, he shall know of the doctrine, whether it be of God" [Jn. 7:17]. This is that alone which will make us, as St. Peter tells us, "that we shall not be barren nor unfruitful in the knowledge of our Lord and Savior" [2 Pet. 1:18]. There is an inward sweetness and deliciousness in divine truth which no sensual mind can taste or relish: this is that ψυκικὸς ἀνέρ—that natural man that savors not the things of God. Corrupt passions and terrene affections are apt, of their own nature, to disturb all serene thoughts, to precipitate our judgments, and warp our understandings. It was a good maxim of the old Jewish writers: "The Holy Spirit dwells not in terrene and earthly passions." Divinity is not so well perceived by a subtle wit "as by a purified sense," as Plotinus phraseth it.

Neither was the ancient philosophy unacquainted with this way and method of attaining to the knowledge of divine things; and therefore Aristotle himself thought a young man unfit to meddle with the grave precepts of morality till the heat and violent precipitancy of his youthful affections were cooled and moderated.[16] And it is observed of Pythagoras that he had several ways to try the capacity of his scholars, and to prove the sedateness and moral temper of their minds before he would entrust them with the sublimer mysteries of his philosophy. The Platonists were herein so wary and solicitous that they thought the minds of men could never be purged enough from those earthly dregs of sense and passion in which they were so much steeped, before they could be capable of their divine metaphysics.[17] And therefore they so much solicit a χωρισμὸς ἀπὸ

15. [ED.] I.e., something aimed at, or desired; an object, purpose, aim. Cf. O.E.D.
16. [ED.] Aristotle, *Nicomachean Ethics*, Bk. 1.3.
17. [ED.] Plato, *Sophist*, 253E.

τοῦ σώματος, as they are wont to phrase it—"a separation from the body,"
in all those that would καθαρῶς φιλοσοφεῖν, as Socrates speaks, that is indeed,
"sincerely understand divine truth"; for that was the scope of their philosophy. This was also intimated by them in their defining philosophy to be
"a meditation of death"; [18] aiming herein at only a moral way of dying,
by loosening the soul from the body and this sensitive life; which they
thought was necessary to a right contemplation of intelligible things. And
therefore, besides those ἀρεταὶ καθαρτικαί [things fit to cleanse] by which
the souls of men were to be separated from sensuality and purged from
fleshly filth, they devised a farther way of separation more accommodated
to the condition of philosophers, which was their *mathemata*, or mathematical contemplations, whereby the souls of men might farther shake off
their dependency upon sense and learn to go as it were alone, without the
crutch of any sensible or material thing to support them; and so being a
little inured, being once got up above the body, to converse freely with
immaterial natures, without looking down again and falling back into
sense. Besides, many other ways they had, whereby to rise out of this dark
body—ἀναβάσεις ἐκ τοῦ σπηλαίου, as they are wont to call them [19]—several
steps and scents out of this miry cave of mortality, before they could set
any sure footing with their intellectual part in the land of light and
immortal being.

And thus we should pass from this topic of our discourse, upon which
we have dwelt too long already, but that before we quite let it go, I hope
we may fairly make this use of it farther (besides what we have openly
aimed at all this while), which is, to learn not to devote or give up ourselves to any private opinions or dictates of men in matters of religion, nor
too zealously to propugn the dogmas of any sect. As we should not, like
rigid censurers, arraign and condemn the creeds of other men which we
comply not with, before a full and mature understanding of them, ripened
not only by the natural sagacity of our own reason, but by the benign
influence of holy and mortified affection; so neither should we over-hastily
credere in fidem alienam—subscribe to the symbols and articles of other
men. They are not always the best men that blot most paper. Truth is
not, I fear, so voluminous nor swells into such a mighty bulk as our books
do. Those minds are not always the most chaste that are most parturient
with these learned discourses, which too often bear upon them a foul
stain of their unlawful propagation. A bitter juice of corrupt affections

18. [ED.] Plato, *Phaedrus*, 80E.
19. [ED.] Plotinus, *The Enneads*, II.9.6: "The ancient Greek philosophy which
taught . . . the ascent from the cave . . ."

may sometimes be strained into the ink of our greatest scholars; their doctrines may taste too sour of the cask they come through. We are not always happy in meeting with that wholesome food (as some are wont to call the doctrinal part of religion) which hath been dressed out by the cleanest hands. Some men have too bad hearts to have good heads: they cannot be good at theory who have been so bad at practice, as we may justly fear too many of those, from whom we are apt to take the articles of our belief, have been. Whilst we plead so much our right to the patrimony of our fathers, we may take too fast a possession of their errors, as well as of their sober opinions. There are *idola specus* [idols of the cave] [20] —innate prejudices and deceitful hypotheses that many times wander up and down in the minds of good men, that may fly out from them with their graver determinations. We can never be well assured what our traditional divinity is; nor can we securely enough addict ourselves to any sect of men. That which was the philosopher's motto, Ἐλεύθερον εἶναι δεῖ τῇ γνώμῃ τὸν μέλλοντα φιλοσοφεῖν, we may a little enlarge and so fit it for an ingenuous pursuer after divine truth: "He that will find truth, must seek it with a free judgment and a sanctified mind." He that thus seeks shall find; he shall live in truth, and that shall live in him; it shall be like a stream of living waters issuing out of his own soul; he shall drink of the waters of his own cistern, and be satisfied; he shall every morning find this heavenly manna lying upon the top of his own soul, and be fed with it to eternal life; he will find satisfaction within, feeling himself in conjunction with truth, though all the world should dispute against him.

SECTION II

An objection against the method of knowing laid down in the former section, answered. That men generally, notwithstanding their apostasy, are furnished with the radical principles of true knowledge. Men want not so much means of knowing what they ought to do, as wills to do what they know. Practical knowledge differs from all other knowledge, and excels it.

And thus I should again leave this argument, but that perhaps we may, all this while, have seemed to undermine what we intend to build up. For if divine truth spring up only from the root of true goodness, how shall

20. [ED.] Bacon had made current the concept of the "idols" of the mind—of the tribe, of the cave, of the market place and of the theater. Cf. *Novum Organum*, Bk. I, XXXIX–LXVI.

we endeavor to be good, before we know what it is to be so?—or how shall we convince the gainsaying world of truth, unless we could also inspire virtue into it?

To both which we shall make this reply: that there are some radical principles of knowledge that are so deeply sunk in the souls of men as that the impression cannot easily be obliterated, though it may be much darkened. Sensual baseness doth not so grossly sully and bemire the souls of all wicked men at first as to make them, with Diagoras, deny the Deity, or, with Protagoras, doubt of, or, with Diodorus, to question the immortality of rational souls. Neither are the common principles of virtue so pulled up by the roots in all as to make them so dubious in stating the bounds of virtue and vice as Epicurus was, though he could not but sometimes take notice of them.[21] Neither is the retentive power of truth so weak and loose in all skeptics as it was in him, who being well scourged in the streets till the blood ran about him, questioned when he came home whether he had been beaten or not. Arrian hath well observed that the common notions of God and virtue impressed upon the souls of men are more clear and perspicuous than any else; and that if they have not more certainty, yet they have more evidence, and display themselves with less difficulty to our reflective faculty than any geometrical demonstrations. And these are both available to prescribe out ways of virtue to men's own souls and to force an acknowledgement of truth from those that oppose, when they are well guided by a skillful hand. Truth needs not at any time fly from reason, there being an eternal amity between them. They are only some private dogmas that may well be suspected as spurious and adulterate, that dare not abide the trial thereof. And this reason is not everywhere so extinguished as that we may not, by that, enter into the souls of men. What the magnetical virtue is in these earthly bodies, that reason is in men's minds, which, when it is put forth, draws them one to another. Besides, in wicked men there are sometimes distastes of vice and flashes of love to virtue; which are the motions which spring from a true intellect, and the faint strugglings of a higher life within them, which they crucify again by

21. [ED.] Smith is citing literary and philosophical writers whose works were assumed to have an atheistic, agnostic or materialistic tendency. Diodorus (fl. c. 300 B.C.) was famous for the argument against the possibility of that which is not actual. Protagoras, a Sophist of the fifth century B.C., was best known for the saying, "Man is the measure of all things"; was regarded as an agnostic as to belief in the gods; and was a complete skeptic as to the claims of any science to universal validity. Diagoras (fifth century B.C.) was renowned for his atheism, and for his disparagement of the mysteries.

their wicked sensuality. As truth doth not always act in good men, so neither doth sense always act in wicked men; they may sometimes have their sober fits; and a divine spirit blowing and breathing upon them may then blow up some live sparks of true understanding within them; though they may soon endeavor to quench them again and to rake them up in the ashes of their own earthly thoughts.

All this and more that might be said upon this argument may serve to point out the way of virtue. We want not so much means of knowing what we ought to do as will to do that which we may know. But yet all that knowledge which is separated from an inward acquaintance with virtue and goodness is of a far different nature from that which ariseth out of a true living sense of them, which is the best discerner thereof, and by which alone we know the true perfection, sweetness, energy and loveliness of them, and all that which is ὄντε ῥητὸν, οὔτε γραπτόν [neither spoken nor written]—that which can no more be known by a naked demonstration than colors can be perceived by a blind man and by any definition or description which he can hear of them.

And, further, the clearest and most distinct notions of truth that shine in the souls of the common sort of men may be extremely clouded, if they be not accompanied with that answerable practice that might preserve their integrity. These tender plants may soon be spoiled by the continual droppings of our corrupt affections upon them; they are but of a weak and feminine nature, and so may be sooner deceived by that wily serpent of sensuality that harbors within us.

While the soul is "full of the body," while we suffer those notions and common principles of religion to lie asleep within us, that "power of an animal life" will be apt to incorporate and mingle itself with them; and that reason that is within us, as Plotinus hath well expressed it, becomes more and more σύμφυτος κακαῖς ταῖς ἐπιγινομέναις δόξαις—it will be infected with those evil opinions that arise from our corporeal life.[22] The more deeply our souls dive into our bodies, the more will reason and sensuality run one into another, and make up a most dilute, unsavory and muddy kind of knowledge. We must therefore endeavor more and more to withdraw ourselves from these bodily things, to set our soul as free as may be from its miserable slavery to this base flesh. We must shut the eyes of sense, and open that brighter eye of our understandings, that other eye of

22. [ED.] Plotinus, The Enneads, III.5.7; but the passage hardly bears the sense attributed to it here. Smith usually made his own translations, and they do not always agree with those in modern critical editions.

the soul, (as the philosopher calls our intellectual faculty,) "which indeed all have, but few make use of." [23] This is the way to see clearly; the light of the divine world will then begin to fall upon us, and those sacred ἐλλάμψεις [a shining in of]—those pure coruscations of immortal and ever-living truth will shine into us, and in God's own light shall we behold him. The fruit of this knowledge will be sweet to our taste and pleasant to our palates, "sweeter than honey or the honeycomb" [Ps. 19:10]. The priests of Mercury, as Plutarch tells us, in the eating of their holy things, were wont to cry out, "Sweet is truth." [24] But how sweet and delicious that truth is which holy and Heaven-born souls feed upon in their mysterious converse with God, it is turned into sense: that which before was only faith well built upon sure principles (for such our science may be) now becomes vision. We shall then converse with God τῷ νῷ [with the mind], whereas before we conversed with him only τῇ διανοίᾳ—with our discursive faculty—as the Platonists were wont to distinguish. Before, we laid hold on him only with a struggling, agonistical and contentious reason, hotly combating with difficulties and sharp contests of diverse opinions, and laboring in itself, in its deductions of one thing from another; we shall then fasten our minds upon him with such a "serene understanding," such an intellectual calmness and serenity as will present us with a blissful, steady and invariable sight of him.

SECTION III

Men may be considered in a fourfold capacity in order to the perfection of divine things. That the best and most excellent knowledge of divine things belongs only to the true and sober Christian; and that it is but in its infancy while he is in this earthly body.

And now, if you please, setting aside the Epicurean herd of brutish men, who have drowned all their own sober reason in the deepest Lethe of sensuality, we shall divide the rest of men into these four ranks, according to that method which Simplicius upon Epictetus hath already laid out to us, with respect to a fourfold kind of knowledge, which we have all this while glanced at.

The first whereof is "that complex and multifarious man that is made up of soul and body," as it were by a just equality and arithmetical proportion

23. [ED.] Plotinus, *The Enneads*, 1.6.8.
24. [ED.] Plutarch, *De Iside et Osiride*, 378B.

of parts and powers in each of them.[25] The knowledge of these men I should call ἀμυδρὸν δόξαν, in Plutarch's phrase; "a knowledge wherein sense and reason are so twisted up together," that it cannot easily be unravelled and laid out into its first principles. Their highest reason is "complying with their senses," and both conspire together in vulgar opinion. To these that motto which the the Stoics have made for them may very well agree, βίος ὑπόληψις [a life based on prejudice or hasty assumption], their life being steered by nothing else but opinion and imagination. Their higher notions of God and religion are so entangled with the birdlime of fleshly passions and mundane vanity, that they cannot rise up above the surface of this dark earth, or easily entertain any but earthly conceptions of heavenly things. Such souls as are here lodged, as Plato speaks, are "heavy behind," [26] and are continually pressing down to this world's center. And though like the spider, they may appear sometime moving up and down aloft in the air, yet they do but sit in the loom and move in that web of their own gross fancies, which they fasten and pin to some earthly thing or other.

The second is the man that looks at himself as being what he is rather by his soul than by his body; that thinks not fit to view his own face in any other glass but that of reason and understanding; that reckons upon his soul as that which was made to rule, his body as that which was born to obey, and like a handmaid perpetually to wait upon his higher and nobler part.[27] And in such a one the common principles of virtue and goodness are more clear and steady. To such a one we may allow "more clear and distinct opinions," as being already "in a method or course of purgation," or at least fit to be initiated into "the lesser mysteries of religion." For though these innate notions of truth may be but poor, empty and hungry things of themselves, before they be fed and filled with the practice of true virtue; yet they are capable of being impregnated and exalted with the rules and precepts of it. And therefore the Stoics supposed that the doctrine of political and moral virtues was fit to be delivered to such as these; and though they may not be so well prepared for divine virtue (which is of a higher emanation), yet they are not immature for human, as having the seeds of it already within themselves, which, being watered by answerable practice, may sprout up within them.

25. [ED.] Simplicius, *Commentary on the Enchiridion of Epictetus*, Preface.

26. [ED.] Plotinus, *The Enneads*, VI.9.4, is quoted by Simplicius, and this, rather than any passage in Plato, seems to be Smith's source.

27. [ED.] Simplicius, *Commentary on Epictetus*, Preface.

The third is he whose soul is already purged by this lower sort of virtue, and so is continually flying off from the body and bodily passion, and returning into himself.[28] Such, in St. Peter's language, are those "who have escaped the pollutions which are in the world through lust" [2 Pet. 2:20]. To these we may attribute a lower degree of science—their inward sense of virtue and moral goodness being far transcendent to all mere speculative opinions of it. But if this knowledge settle here, it may be quickly apt to corrupt. Many of our most refined moralists may be, in a worse sense than Plotinus means, "full with their own pregnancy";[29] their souls may have too much heave and swell with the sense of their own virtue and knowledge. There may be an ill ferment of self-love lying at the bottom, which may puff it up the more with pride, arrogance and self-conceit. Those forces with which the divine bounty supplies us to keep a stronger guard against the evil spirit may be abused by our own rebellious pride, enticing them from their allegiance to God, to Heaven: like that supercilious Stoic who, when he thought his mind well armed and appointed with wisdom and virtue, cried out, "Sapiens contendet cum ipso Jove de felicitate."[30] They may make an airy heaven of these, and wall it about with their own self-flattery, and then sit in it as gods, as Cosroes the Persian king was sometimes laughed at for enshrining himself in a temple of his own. And therefore, if this knowledge be not attended with humility and a deep sense of self-penury and self-emptiness, we may easily fall short of that true knowledge of God after which we aspire. We may carry such an image and species of ourselves constantly before us, as will make us lose the clear sight of the Divinity, and be too apt to rest in a mere "logical life" (an expression of Simplicius) without any true participation of the divine life, if we do not (as many do, if not all, who rise no higher) relapse and slide back by vain-glory, popularity, or such like vices, into some mundane and external vanity or other.

The fourth is the true metaphysical and contemplative man, who, running and shooting up above his own logical or self-rational life, pierceth into the highest life;[31] such a one who, by universal love and holy affection, abstracting himself from himself, endeavors to attain the nearest

28. [ED.] Simplicius, as in note 25.

29. [ED.] Plotinus, *The Enneads*, iii.5.7.

30. [ED.] Seneca, *Moral Epistles*, xxv, 4: "Nemo ad haec pauper est intra quae quisquis desiderium suum dusit, cum ipso Iove de felicitate contendat (No one is poor according to this standard: when a man has limited his desires within these bounds, he can challenge the happiness of Jove himself)."

31. [ED.] Simplicius, *Commentary on Epictetus*, Preface.

union with the divine essence that may be, κέντρον κέντρῳ συνάψας [uniting the center to the center], as Plotinus speaks; [32] knitting his own center, if he have any, unto the center of divine being. To such a one the Platonists are wont to attribute "a true divine wisdom," powerfully displaying itself "in an intellectual life," as they phrase it. Such a knowledge, they say, is always pregnant with divine virtue, which ariseth out of a happy union of souls with God, and is nothing else but a living imitation of a god-like perfection drawn out by a strong fervent love of it. This divine knowledge, as Plotinus speaks, makes us amorous of divine beauty, beautiful and lovely; [33] and this divine love and purity reciprocally exalts divine knowledge; both of them growing up together, like that Ἔρως and Ἀντέρως that Pausanias sometimes speaks of. [34] Though, by the Platonists' leave, such a life and knowledge as this is peculiarly belongs to the true and sober Christian, who lives in him who is life itself and is enlightened by him who is the truth itself and is made partaker of the divine unction, "and knoweth all things," as St. John speaks [1 Jn. 3:20]. This life is nothing else but God's own breath within him, and an infant-Christ (if I may use the expression) formed in his soul, who is in a sense "the shining forth of the Father's glory" [Heb. 1:3]. But yet we must not mistake; this knowledge is but here in its infancy; there is a higher knowledge, or a higher degree of this knowledge, that doth not, that cannot, descend upon us in these earthly habitations. We cannot here see *in speculo lucido* [in a bright mirror]; here we can see but in a glass, and that darkly too [1 Cor. 13:12]. Our own imaginative powers, which are perpetually attending the highest acts of our souls, will be breathing a gross dew upon the pure glass of our understandings, and so sully and besmear it, that we cannot see the image of the Divinity sincerely in it. But yet this knowledge, being a true, heavenly fire kindled from God's own altar, begets an undaunted courage in the souls of good men, and enables them to cast a holy scorn upon the poor, petty trash of this life, in comparison with divine things, and to pity those poor, brutish Epicureans that have nothing but the mere husks of fleshly pleasure to feed themselves with. This sign of God makes pious souls breathe after that blessed time when mortality shall be swallowed up of life, when they shall no more behold the Divinity through the dark mediums that eclipse the blessed sight of it.

32. [ED.] Plotinus, *The Enneads*, VI.9.10.
33. [ED.] Plotinus, *The Enneads*, I.6.7.
34. [ED.] Pausanias, *Itinerary of Greece*, Bk. 1.30.1: the god of love, and the god who avenged slighted love.

❖ ❖ ❖ ❖ ❖ ❖ ❖ ❖

JOHN SMITH

The Excellency and Nobleness of True Religion

1. In its Rise and Original.
2. In its Nature and Essence.
3. In its Properties and Operations.
4. In its Progress.
5. In its Term and End.

To the saints that are in the earth, and to the excellent, in whom is all my delight.—Psalm 16:3 [1]

❖ ❖ ❖ ❖

Introduction

The way of life is above to the wise, that he may depart from hell beneath.—Proverbs 15:24

In this whole book of the Proverbs we find Solomon, one of the eldest sons of Wisdöm, always standing up and calling her blessed; his heart was both enlarged and filled with the pure influences of her beams, and, therefore, was perpetually adoring that sun which gave him light. "Wisdom is justified of all her children" [Lk. 7:35]; though the offspring of darkness and the children of folly see no beauty nor comeliness in her, that they should desire her, as they said of Christ [cf. Is. 53:2]. That mind which is not touched with an inward sense of divine wisdom cannot estimate the true worth of it.[2] But when Wisdom once displays her own excellences and glories in a purified soul, she is entertained there with the greatest love and delight, and receives her own image, reflected back to herself in

---

1. [ED.] On the title page of this discourse, Smith links with the text from Psalm 16 three quotations from the Fathers—two from Gregory Nazianzen, one from Paulinus. This yoking of Scripture and the Fathers is highly characteristic of the Cambridge Platonists.

2. [ED.] Plotinus, *The Enneads*, III.7.6.

91

sweetest returns of love and praise. We have a clear manifestation of this sacred sympathy in Solomon, whom we may not unfitly call *sapientiae organum*—an instrument Wisdom herself had tuned on which to play her divine lessons; his words were everywhere full of divine sweetness, matched with strength and beauty, πολὺν νοῦν ἔχοντες ἔνδον, or, as himself phraseth it, "like apples of gold in pictures of silver" [Prov. 25:11]. The mind of a proverb is to utter wisdom in a mystery—as the apostle sometimes speaks [cf. 1 Cor. 2:7]—and to wrap up divine truth in a kind of enigmatical way, though in vulgar expressions. This method of delivering divine doctrine (not to mention the writings of the ancient philosophers) we find frequently pursued in the Holy Scripture, thereby both opening and hiding, at once, the truth which is offered to us. A proverb or parable being once unfolded, by reason of its affinity with the fancy, the more sweetly insinuates itself into that, and is from thence, with the greater advantage, transmitted to the understanding. In this state, we are not able to behold truth in its own native beauty and luster; but, while we are veiled with mortality, truth must veil itself too, that it may the more freely converse with us. St. Austin hath well assigned the reason why we are so much delighted with metaphors, allegories, etc., because they are so much proportioned to our senses, with which our reason hath contracted an intimacy and familiarity.[3] And therefore God, to accommodate his truth to our weak capacities, does, as it were, embody it in earthly expressions; according to that ancient maxim of the Cabbalists, "Lumen supernum nunquam descendit sine indumento";[4] agreeable to which is that of Dionysius not seldom quoted by the Schoolmen: "Impossibile est nobis aliter lucere radium divinum, nisi varietate sacrorum velaminum circumvelatum."[5]

Thus much by way of preface or introduction to these words, being one of Solomon's excellent proverbs, viz., "The way of life is above to the wise." Without any mincing or mangling of the words, or running out into any critical curiosities about them, I shall, from these words, take occasion to set forth the nobleness and generous spirit of true religion,

3. [ED.] St. Augustine, *Ep.* LV, §XI, Par. 21.

4. [ED.] "The light from above never comes down without mask (or covering)." This was a common Cabbalistic saying which emphasized the way in which the divine presence is mediated through forms which shield men from its immediate impact.

5. [ED.] "It is impossible for the divine light to shine upon us in any other way except enveloped by a kind of sacred veil." Dionysius the Areopagite, *Of the Heavenly Hierarchy*, Ch. I, §2.

which I suppose to be meant here by "the way of life." The word לְמַעְלָה here rendered "above," may signify that which is divine and heavenly, high and excellent, as the word ἄνω does in the New Testament —τῆς ἄνω κλήσεως; τὰ ἄνω φρονεῖτε.[6] St. Austin supposeth the things of religion to be meant by the τὰ ἄνω, "superna," for this reason, "quod merito excellentiae longe superant res terrenas."[7] And in this sense I shall consider it, my purpose being from hence to discourse of the excellent and noble spirit of true religion, whether it be taken *in abstracto*—as it is in itself; or *in concreto*—as it becomes an inward form and soul to the minds and spirits of good men; and this in opposition to that low and base-born spirit of irreligion, which is perpetually sinking from God, till it couches to the very center of misery, "the lowermost Hell."

In discoursing upon this argument, I shall observe this method; viz., I shall consider the excellency and nobleness of true religion: 1. In its rise and original. 2. In its nature and essence. 3. In its properties and operations. 4. In its progress. 5. In its term and end.

Chapter 1

1. The nobleness of religion in regard of its original and fountain: it comes from Heaven and moves towards Heaven again. God the first excellency and primitive perfection. All perfections and excellences in any kind are to be measured by their approach to, and participation of, the first perfection. Religion the greatest participation of God: none capable of this divine communication but the highest created beings: and consequently religion the greatest excellency. A twofold fountain in God whence religion flows, viz.: 1. His nature. 2. His will. Of truth, natural and revealed. Of an outward and an inward revelation of God's will.

We begin with the *first, viz., True religion is a noble thing in its rise and original, and in regard of its descent.* True religion derives its pedigree from Heaven; it comes from Heaven, and constantly moves toward Heaven again. It is a beam from God, as "every good gift and every perfect gift is from above, and cometh down from the Father of lights, with whom is no variableness, neither shadow of turning," as St. James speaks [Jas. 1:17]. God is the first truth and primitive goodness; true religion is a vigorous efflux and emanation of both upon the spirits of men,

---

6. [ED.] Phil. 3:14; Col. 3:2.

7. [ED.] "Heavenly things because by virtue of excellence they far surpass earthly things."

and, therefore, is called "a participation of the divine nature." [8] Indeed, God hath copied out himself in all created being, having no other pattern to frame anything by, than his own essence; so that all created being is *umbratilis similitudo entis increati,*[9] and is, by some stamp or other of God upon it, at least remotely allied to him. But true religion is such a communication of the Divinity, as none but the highest of created beings are capable of. On the other side, sin and wickedness is of the basest and lowest original, as being nothing else but a perfect degeneration from God, and those eternal rules of goodness which are derived from him. Religion is a Heaven-born thing, the seed of God in the spirits of men, whereby they are formed to a similitude and likeness of himself. A true Christian is every way of a most noble extraction, of a heavenly and divine pedigree, being born ἄνωθεν, "from above," as St. John expresseth it [Jn. 3:31]. The line of all earthly nobility, if it were followed to the beginning, would lead to Adam, where all the lines of descent meet in one; and the root of all extractions would be found planted in nothing else but Adamah, "red earth" [cf. Gen. 2:7]. But a Christian derives his line from Christ, who is the only-begotten Son of God, "the shining forth of his glory, and the character of his person," as he is styled [cf. Heb. 1:3]. We may truly say of Christ and Christians, as Zebah and Zalmunna said of Gideon's brothers, "As he is, so are they (according to their capacity), each one resembling the children of a king" [Judg. 8:18]. Titles of worldly honor in Heaven's heraldry are only *tituli nominales* [titles in name]; but titles of divine dignity signify some real thing, some real and divine communications to the spirits and minds of men. All perfections and excellences, in any kind, are to be measured by their approach to that primitive perfection of all, God himself; and, therefore, participation of the divine nature cannot but entitle a Christian to the highest degree of dignity: "Behold what manner of love the Father hath bestowed upon us, that we should be called the sons of God" [1 Jn. 3:1].

Thus much for a more general discovery of the nobleness of religion, as to its fountain and original. We may further and more particularly take notice of this in reference to that twofold fountain in God, from whence all true religion flows and issues forth, viz.: 1. *His immutable nature.* 2. *His will.*

8. [ED.] Cf. 2 Peter 1:4: " . . . that by these ye might be partakers of the divine nature . . ."

9. [ED.] "A shadowy likeness of uncreated being."

1. *The immutable nature of God.* From thence arise all those eternal rules of truth and goodness, which are the foundation of all religion, and which God at the first creation folded up in the soul of man. These we may call the truths of natural inscription; understanding, hereby, either those fundamental principles of truth which reason, by a naked intuition, may behold in God, or those necessary corollaries and deductions that may be drawn from thence. I cannot think it as proper to say, that God ought infinitely to be loved because he commands it, as because he is, indeed, an infinite and unchangeable goodness. God hath stamped a copy of his own archetypal loveliness upon the soul, that man, by reflecting into himself, might behold there the glory of God, see within his soul all those ideas of truth which concern the nature and essence of God, by reason of its own resemblance to God; and, so, beget within himself the most free and generous motions of love to God. Reason in man being *lumen de lumine*—a light flowing from the Fountain and Father of lights [cf. Jas. 1:17]—and being, as Cicero phraseth it, *participata similitudo rationis aeternae:* [10] (as the law of nature—the νόμος γραπτός—the law written in man's heart is *participatio legis in rationali creatura*): [11] it was to enable man to work out of himself all those notions of God, which are the true groundwork of love and obedience to God, and conformity to him: and in molding the inward man into the greatest conformity to the nature of God was the perfection and efficacy of the religion of nature. But since man's fall from God, the inward virtue and vigor of reason is much abated, the soul having suffered a πτερορρύησις, as Plato speaks—a *defluvium pennarum.* [12] Those principles of divine truth, which were first engraven upon man's heart with the finger of God, are now, as the characters of some ancient monuments, less clear and legible than at first. And, therefore, besides the truth of natural inscription,

2. God hath provided the truth of divine revelation, which issues forth from his own free will, and clearly discovers the way of our return to God, from whom we are fallen. And this truth, with the effects and productions of it in the minds of men, the Scripture is wont to set forth

10. [ED.] "Made a partaker of the likeness of eternal reason." The thought is characteristic of Cicero, but the quotation is probably from Thomas Aquinas, *Summa Theologica,* Pt. I, Q. LXXXIV, 5.

11. [ED.] "The participation of the law in the rational creature." Thomas Aquinas, *Summa Theol.,* Pt. I, Q. XCI, 2.

12. [ED.] Plato, *Phaedrus,* 246C, 248C. Both the Greek and Latin mean "molting [of feathers]."

under the name of *grace*, as proceeding merely from the free bounty and overflowings of the divine love. Of this revealed will is that of the apostle to be understood—τὰ τοῦ θεοῦ οὐδεὶς οἶδεν, "The things of God knoweth no man" [1 Cor. 2:11]; οὐδεὶς, none, neither angel nor man, could know the mind of God, could unlock the breast of God, or search out the counsels of his will. But God, out of the infinite riches of his compassions towards mankind, is pleased to unbosom his secrets, and most clearly to manifest "the way into the holiest of all" [Heb. 9:3] and "bring to light life and immortality" [2 Tim. 1:10], and, in these last ages, to send his Son, who lay in his bosom from all eternity, to teach us his will, and declare his mind to us. When we "look unto the earth, then behold darkness and dimness of anguish," that I may use those words of the prophet Isaiah [8:22]. But when we look towards Heaven, then behold light breaking forth upon us, like the eyelids of the morning, and spreading its wings over the horizon of mankind, sitting in darkness and the shadow of death, "to guide our feet into the way of peace" [Lk. 1:79].

But besides this outward revelation of God's will to men, there is also an inward impression of it on their minds and spirits, which is in a more special manner attributed to God. We cannot see divine things but in a divine light; God only, who is the true light, and in whom there is no darkness at all, can so shine out of himself upon our glassy understandings, as to beget in them a picture of himself, his own will and pleasure, and turn the soul, as the phrase is, like wax or "clay to the seal" [Job 38:14] of his own light and love. He that made our souls in his own image and likeness can easily find a way into them. The word that God speaks, having found a way into the soul, imprints itself there, as with the point of a diamond, and becomes λόγος ἐγγεγραμμένος ἐν τῇ τοῦ μανθάνοντος ψυκῇ, that I may borrow Plato's expression.[13] Men may teach the grammar and rhetoric, but God teaches the divinity. Thus it is God alone that acquaints the soul with the truth of revelation. And he it is also that does strengthen and raise the soul to better apprehensions even of natural truth; "God being that in the intellectual world, which the sun is in the sensible," [14] as some of the ancient Fathers love to speak, and the ancient philosophers too, who meant God by their *intellectus agens*, whose proper work they supposed to be, not so much to enlighten the object, as the faculty.

13. [ED.] Probably a quotation from memory of *Phaedrus*, 276A: "a word graven in the soul of the learner."

14. [ED.] Philo Judaeus, *On Who Is the Heir of Divine Things*, Ch. LIII.

Chapter II

2. The nobleness of religion in respect of its nature, briefly dis-
covered in some particulars. How a man actuated by religion, 1.
Lives above the world; 2. Converses with himself, and knows how
to love, value, and reverence himself, in the best sense; 3. Lives above
himself, not being content to enjoy himself, except he may enjoy
God too, and himself in God. How he denies himself for God. To
deny a man's self, is not to deny right reason, for that were to deny
God, instead of denying himself for God. Self-love the only prin-
ciple that actuates wicked men. The happy privileges of a soul united
to God.

2. We have done with the first head, and come now to discourse, with
the like brevity, on another (our purpose being to insist most upon the
third particular, viz., *the nobleness of religion in its properties*, after we
have handled the second) which is *the excellency and nobleness of religion*
in regard of its nature, whether it be taken *in abstracto* or *in concreto;*
which we shall treat of promiscuously, without any rigid tying of ourselves to exact rules of art. And so we shall glance at it in these following
notions, rising as it were step by step.

1. *A good man, that is actuated by religion, lives above the world and all*
mundane delights and excellences. The soul is too vigorous and puissant a
thing, when it is once restored to the possession of its own being, than to
be bounded within the narrow sphere of mortality, or to be straitened
within the narrow prison of sensual and corporeal delights; but it will
break forth with the greatest vehemency, and ascend upwards towards
immortality. And, when it converses more intimately with religion, it can
scarce look back upon its own converses, though in a lawful way, with
earthly things, without being touched with a holy shamefacedness and
modest blushing; and, as Porphyry speaks of Plotinus, "It seems to be
ashamed that it should be in the body." [15] It is true religion only that
teaches and enables men to die to this world and to all earthly things, and
to rise above that vaporous sphere of sensual and earthly pleasures, which
darken the mind, and hinder it from enjoying the brightness of divine light. The proper motion of religion is still upwards to its first
original. Whereas, on the contrary, the souls of wicked men ὑποβρύχιαι
συμπεριφέρονται, as Plato somewhere speaks, "being moistened with the
exudations of their sensual parts, become heavy and sink down into

15. [ED.] Cf. Porphyry, *On the Life of Plotinus*, §1.

earthly things, and couch, as near as may be, to the center." [16] Wicked
men bury their souls in their bodies; all their objects and designs are
bounded within the compass of this earth which they tread upon. The
fleshly mind regards nothing but flesh, and never rises above the outward
matter, but always creeps up and down, like shadows, upon the surface of
the earth; and if it begins, at any time, to make any faint essays upwards,
it presently finds itself laden with a weight of sensuality which draws it
down again. It was the opinion of the Academics that the souls of wicked
men, after their death, could not, of a long season, depart from the graves
and sepulchers where their mates were buried; but there wandered up
and down in a desolate manner, as not being able to leave those bodies to
which they were so much wedded in this life.[17]

2. *A good man, one that is actuated by religion, lives in converse with
his own reason;* he lives at the height of his own being. This a great
philosopher makes the property of a good man: "He knows how to converse with himself, and truly love and value himself" [18]—he measures not
himself, like the epicure,[19] by his inferior and earthly part, but by an
immortal essence, and that of him which is from above; and so does
"climb up to the height of that immortal principle which is within him." [20]
The Stoics thought no man a fit auditor of their ethics till he were dispossessed of that opinion, that man was nothing but συμπλοκὴ ψυχῆς καὶ
σώματος [an interweaving of soul and body], as professing to teach men
how to live only κατὰ λόγον [according to reason], as they speak.[21] Perhaps
their divinity was in some things too rigid; but I am sure a good man acts
the best of this their doctrine in the best sense, and knows better how to
reverence himself, without any self-flattery or admiration, than any Stoic
did. He principally looks upon himself as being what he is rather by his
soul than by his body. He values himself by his soul, that being which hath
the greatest affinity with God; and so does not seek himself in the fading
vanities of this life, nor in those poor and low delights of his senses, as
wicked men do; but as the philosopher doth well express it, ὅση δύναμις
φεύγειν ἀπὸ τοῦ σώματος βούλεται καὶ ἀπὸ σωματικῶν παθῶν εἰς ἑαυτὸν συννεύειν,[22]

16. [ED.] Plato, *Phaedrus,* 248A.
17. [ED.] Cf. Plato, *Phaedrus,* 81B.
18. [ED.] Proclus, *On the Timaeus of Plato,* 173C.
19. [ED.] "Epicure," in this context, is obviously intended to refer to Epicurus and
his general philosophical position.
20. [ED.] Plotinus, *The Enneads,* VI.9.3
21. [ED.] Simplicius, *On the Enchiridion of Epictetus,* Preface.
22. [ED.] *Ibid.:* "Whatever power wills to flee from the body and from the physical emotions to converge upon itself."

and when the soul thus retires into itself, and views its own worth and excellency, it presently finds a chaste and virgin love stirred up within itself towards itself, and is from within the more excited and obliged as Simplicius speaks, "to mind the preserving of its own dignity and glory." [23] To conclude this particular: a good man endeavors to walk by eternal and unchangeable rules of reason: reason, in a good man, sits in the throne, and governs all the powers of his soul in a sweet harmony and agreement with itself: whereas wicked men live only "a life of illusion," being led up and down by the foolish fires of their own sensual apprehensions. In wicked men there is a democracy of wild lusts and passions, which violently hurry the soul up and down with restless motions. All sin and wickedness is "a sedition stirred up in the soul by the sensitive powers against reason." It is one of the great evils that Solomon saw under the sun: "Servants on horseback, and princes going as servants upon the ground" [Eccles. 10:7]. We may find the moral of it in all wicked men, whose souls are only as servants to wait upon their senses. In all such men, the cardinal points of motion in this little world are changed to contrary positions; but the motions of a good man are methodical, regular and concentrical to reason. It is a fond imagination that religion should extinguish reason; whereas religion makes it more illustrious and vigorous; and they that live most in the exercise of religion shall find their reason most enlarged. I might add that reason, in relation to the capacitating of man for converse with God, was thought by some to be the formal difference of man. Plutarch, after a large debate whether brutes had not reason in them as well as man, concludes it negatively upon this ground—"because they had no knowledge and sense of the Deity." [24] In Cicero's account, this capableness of religion seemed to be nothing different from rationality, and, therefore, he doubts not to give this for the most proper characteristic of reason, that it is *vinculum Dei et hominis* [the bond between God and man]. And, so, with them (not to name others of the same apprehensions) *animal rationale* and *animal capax religionis* [25] seemed to be of the like importance; reason, as enabling and fitting man to converse with God by knowing him and loving him, being a character most unquestionably differencing man from brute creatures.

3. *A good man, one that is informed by true religion, lives above himself, and is raised to an intimate converse with the Divinity.* He moves in a

23. [ED.] *Ibid.*
24. [ED.] Plutarch, *Gryllus.*
25. [ED.] "A rational animal" and "an animal capable of (or susceptible to) religion."

larger sphere than his own being, and cannot be content to enjoy himself, except he may enjoy God also, and himself in God.

This we shall consider two ways.

1. In the self-denial of good men: they are content and ready to deny themselves for God. I mean not that they should deny their own reason, as some would have it; for that were to deny a beam of divine light, and to deny God, instead of denying ourselves for him.... But by self-denial I mean the soul's quitting all its own interest in itself, and an entire resignation of itself to him, as to all points of service and duty. And thus the soul loves itself in God, and lives in the possession, not so much of its own being, as of the Divinity; desiring only to be great in God, to glory in his light, and spread itself in his fullness; to be filled always by him, and to empty itself again into him; to receive all from him, and to expend all for him; and so to live, not as its own, but as God's. The highest ambition of a good man is to serve the will of God. He takes no pleasure in himself, nor in any thing within himself, further than he sees a stamp of God upon it. Whereas wicked men are imprisoned within the narrow circumference of their own beings, and perpetually frozen into cold self-love, which binds up all the innate vigor of their souls, that it cannot break forth or express itself in any noble way. The soul in which religion rules says, as St. Paul did, "I live; and yet not I, but Christ liveth in me" [Gal. 2:20]. On the contrary, a wicked man swells in his own thoughts, and pleaseth himself more or less with the imagination of a self-sufficiency. The Stoics, seeing they could not raise themselves up to God, endeavored to bring down God to their own model, imagining the Deity to be nothing else but some greater kind of animal, and a wise man to be almost one of his peers.[26] And this is more or less the genius of wicked men; they will be something in themselves, they wrap up themselves in their own being, move up and down in a sphere of self-love, live a professed independency of God, and maintain a *meum et tuum* [mine and thine] between God and themselves. It is the character only of a good man to deny and disown himself, and to make a full surrender of himself unto God; forgetting himself and minding nothing but the will of his Creator; triumphing in nothing more than in his own nothingness and in the allness of the Divinity. But indeed, this, his being nothing, is the only way to be all things; this, his having nothing, the truest way of possessing all things.

2. As a good man lives above himself in a way of self-denial, so he lives also above himself in the enjoyment of God. And this is the very soul

26. [ED.] Cf. Seneca, *Letters*, No. 52.

and essence of true religion, to unite the soul in the nearest intimacy and conjunction with God, who is "the wellspring of life, the wellspring also of intellect, the beginning of being," as Plotinus speaks.[27] Then, indeed, the soul lives most nobly, when it feels itself to "live, and move, and have its being in God" [Acts 17:28]; which though the law of nature makes the common condition of all created being, yet is it only true religion that can give us a more feeling and comfortable sense of it. God is not present to wicked men, when his almighty essence supports them and maintains them in being; "but he is present to him that can touch him," hath an inward feeling knowledge of God, and is intimately united to him: "but to him that cannot thus touch him he is not present." [28]

Religion is life and spirit, which, flowing out from God, who is that underived existence that hath life in himself, returns to him again as into its own original, carrying the souls of good men up with it. The spirit of religion is always ascending upwards, and, spreading itself through the whole essence of the soul, loosens it from a self-confinement and narrowness, and so renders it more capacious of divine enjoyment. God envies not his people any good; but, being infinitely bountiful, is pleased to impart himself to them in this life, so far as they are capable of his communications; they stay not for all their happiness till they come to Heaven. Religion always carries its reward along with it, and when it acts most vigorously upon the mind and spirit of man, it then, most of all, fills it with an inward sense of divine sweetness. To conclude: to walk with God is, in Scripture, made the character of a good man, and it is the highest perfection and privilege of created nature to converse with the Divinity. Whereas, on the contrary, wicked men converse with nothing but their lusts and the vanities of this fading life, which here flatter them, for a while, with unhallowed delights, and a mere shadow of contentment; and when these are gone, they find both substance and shadow to be lost eternally. But true goodness brings in a constant revenue of solid and substantial satisfaction to the spirit of a good man, delighting always to sit by those eternal springs that feed and maintain it. The spirit of a good man, as it is well expressed by the philosopher, "is unalterably settled in the being of the divine goodness," [29] and is always drinking in fountain-goodness, and fills itself more and more, till it is filled with all the fullness of God.

27. [ED.] Plotinus, *The Enneads*, VI.9.9.
28. [ED.] Plotinus, *The Enneads*, VI.9.7.
29. [ED.] Simplicius, *On the Enchiridion of Epictetus*, Ch. I, §1.

Chapter III

3. *The nobleness of religion in regard of its properties, &c., of*
which this is one, viz., religion enlarges all the faculties of the soul,
and begets a true ingenuousness, liberty, and amplitude, the most
free and generous spirit in the minds of good men. The nearer any
being comes to God, the more large and free; the further it slides
from God, the more straitened. Sin is the sinking of man's soul from
God into sensual selfishness. An account when the most generous
freedom of the soul is to be taken in its just proportions. How me-
chanical and formal Christians make an art of religion, set it such
bounds as may not exceed the scant measure of their principles; and
then fit their own notions as so many examples to it. A good man
finds not his religion without him, but as a living principle within
him. God's immutable and external goodness the unchangeable rule of
his will. Peevish, self-willed, and imperious men shape out such
notions of God as are agreeable to this pattern of themselves. The
truly religious have better apprehensions of God.

Having discoursed of the nobleness of religion in its original and nature,
we come now to consider the excellency of religion in its properties, its
proper effects, and vital operations. In treating of this third particular we
shall, as we have formerly done, without tying ourselves precisely to any
strict rules of art and method, confound the notions of religion *in abstracto*
and *in concreto* together, handling them promiscuously. As religion is a
noble thing, (1) in respect of its *original;* (2) in respect of its *nature;* so
also, (3) in respect of its *properties* and *effects.*

1. The *first* property and effect of true religion whereby it expresseth
its own nobleness is this: *that it widens and enlarges all the faculties of the*
soul, and begets a true ingenuousness, liberty and amplitude, the most free
and generous spirit, in the minds of good men. Those in whom religion
rules are בני תנדים [the sons of the free, or of the noble], there is a true
generous spirit within them, which shows the nobleness of their extraction.
The Jews have a good maxim to this purpose: "None truly noble, but he
that applies himself to religion, and a faithful observance of the divine
law." [30] Cicero could see so much in his natural philosophy as made him
say, "Scientia naturae ampliat animum, et ad divina attolit." [31] But this is

30. [ED.] *The Mishnah,* Fourth Division, Aboth, Ch. VI, §2 (ed. H. C. Danby,
Oxford, 1933, 459).
31. [ED.] "The knowledge of nature enlarges the rational soul and elevates it to
divine things."

most true of religion, that, in a higher sense, it does work the soul into a true and divine amplitude. There is a living soul of religion in good men which, spreading itself through all their faculties, spirits all the wheels of motion, and enables them to dilate and extend themselves more fully upon God and all divine things, without being pinched or straitened within themselves. Whereas wicked men are of most narrow and confined spirits; they are so contracted by the pinching particularities of earthly and created things, so imprisoned in a dark dungeon of sensuality and selfishness, so straitened through their carnal designs and ends, that they cannot stretch themselves, nor look beyond the horizon of time and sense.

The nearer any being comes to God, who is that infinite fullness that fills all in all, the more vast and large and unbounded it is; as the further it slides from him, the more it is straitened and confined; as Plato hath long since concluded concerning the condition of sensual men, that they live "like a shellfish" [32]—and can never move up and down but in their own prison, which they ever carry about with them. Were I to define sin, I would call it, *the sinking of a man's soul from God into a sensual selfishness*. All the freedom that wicked men have is but like that of banished men—to wander up and down in the wilderness of this world from one den and cave to another.

The more high and noble any being is, the deeper radication have all its innate virtues and properties within it, and are by so much the more universal in their issues and actings upon other things; and such an inward, living principle of virtue and activity, further heightened, and united, and informed with light and truth, we may call liberty. Of this truly noble and divine liberty, religion is the mother and nurse, leading the soul to God, and so impregnating that inward, vital principle of activity and vigor that is embosomed in it, that it is able, without any inward disturbance and resistance from any controlling lusts, to exercise itself, and act with the greatest complacency, in the most full and ample manner, upon that first, universal and unbounded essence which is God himself. The most generous freedom can never be taken in its full and just dimensions and proportion, but then, when all powers of the soul exercise and spend themselves, in the most large and ample manner, upon the infinite essential goodness, as upon their own most proper object. If we should ask a good man, when he finds himself best at ease, when he finds himself most free, his answer would be, when he is under the most powerful constraints of divine love. There is a sort of mechanical Christians in the

32. [ED.] Plato, *Phaedrus*, 250c.

world, who, not finding religion acting like a living form within them, satisfy themselves only to make an art of it, and rather inform and actuate it, than to be informed by it; and setting it such bounds and limits as may not exceed the short and scant measures of their own homeborn principles, then they endeavor to fit the notions of their own minds as so many examples to it; and, it being a circle of their own making, they can force their own minds and dispositions to agree and suit with it. But true religion, indeed, is no art, but an inward nature that contains all the laws and measures of its motion within itself. A good man finds not his religion without him, but as a living principle within him; and all his faculties are still endeavoring to unite themselves more and more in the nearest intimacy with it, as with their proper perfection. There is that amiableness in religion, that strong sympathy between the soul and it, that it needs carry no testimonials or commendations along with it. If it could be supposed that God should plant a religion in the soul that had no affinity or alliance with it, it would grow there but as a strange slip. But God, when he gives his laws to men, does not, by virtue of his absolute dominion, dictate anything at random, and in such an arbitrary way, as some imagine; but he measures all by his own eternal goodness. Had God himself been anything else than the first and greatest good of man, then to have loved him with the full strength of all our faculties should have not have been "the first and greatest commandment" [Mt. 22:38], as our Savior tells us it is. Some are apt to look upon God as some peevish and self-willed being, because themselves are such; and, seeing that their own absolute and naked wills are for the most part the rules of all their actions and the impositions which they lay upon others, they think that Heaven's monarchy is such an arbitrary thing too, as being governed by nothing else but by an almighty absolute will. But the soul that is most intimately acquainted with the divine will would more certainly resolve us that God's unchangeable goodness (which makes the Divinity to be a uniform thing, and to settle together upon its own center, as I may speak with reverence) is also the unchangeable rule of his will; neither can he any more swerve from it, than he can swerve from himself. Nor does he charge any duty upon man, without consulting first of all with his goodness; which being the original and adequate object of a good man's will and affections, it must needs be that all the issues and effluxes of it be entertained with an answerable complacency and cheerfulness. This is the hinge upon which all true religion turns, the proper center about which it moves; which, taking a fast and sure hold of an innate and correspondent principle in the soul of man, raiseth it up above the confines of mortality, and, in the day of its mighty power, makes it become a free-will offering unto God.

Chapter IV

The second property discovering the nobleness of religion, viz., that it restores man to a just power and dominion over himself, and enables him to overcome his self-will and passions. Of self-will, and the many evils that flow from it. That religion does nowhere discover its power and prowess so much, as in subduing this dangerous and potent enemy. The highest and noblest victories are those over our wills; the happiness and the privileges of such a state. How that magnanimity and puissance, which religion begets in holy souls, differ from and excel that gallantry and puissance, which the great Nimrods of this world boast of.

2. The second property or effect of religion, whereby it discovers its own nobleness (and it is somewhat akin to the former particular, and will help further to illustrate and enforce it), is this, *that it restores a good man to a just power and dominion over himself and his own will, and enables him to overcome himself, his own self-will and passions, and to command himself and all his powers for God.* It is only religion that restores that αὐτεξούσιν [intrinsic authority] to which the Stoical philosophy so impotently pretended; it is this only that enthrones man's deposed reason, and establishes within him a just empire over all those blind powers and passions, which so impetuously rend a man from the possession and enjoyment of himself. Those turbulent and unruly, uncertain and unconstant motions of passion and self-will, that dwell in degenerate minds, divide them perpetually from themselves, and are always molding several factions and tumultuous combinations within them against the dominion of reason. And the only way to unite man firmly to himself is by uniting him to God, and establishing in him a firm amity and agreement with the first and primitive Being.

There is nothing in the world so boisterous as a man's own self-will, which is never guided by any fixed or steady rules, but is perpetually hurried to and fro by a blind *impetus* of pride and passions issuing from within itself. This is the true source and spring of all that envy, malice, bitterness of spirit, malecontentedness and impatience, of all those black and dark passions, those inordinate desires and lusts, that reign in the hearts and lives of wicked men. A man's own self-will throws him out of all true enjoyment of his own being; therefore, it is our Savior's counsel to his disciples, "In patience possess ye your souls" [Lk. 21:19]. We may say of that self-will which is lodged in the heart of a wicked man, as the Jews speak of the evil image so often mentioned in their writings, that it is the prince of death and darkness, which is at continual enmity with Heaven, and the filthiness and poison of the serpent. This is the seed of the evil spirit, which is perpetually at enmity with the seed of God and the Heaven-born nature: its design and scope is, with a giant-like pride, to climb up into the throne of the Almighty, and to establish an unbounded tyranny in contradiction to the will of God, which is nothing else but the issue and efflux of his eternal and unbounded goodness. This is the very heart of the old Adam that is within men. This is the hellish spirit of self-will: it would solely prescribe laws to all things; it would fain be the source and fountain of all affairs and events; it would judge all things at its own tribunal. They, in whose spirits this principle rules, would have their own fancies and opinions, their perverse and boisterous wills to be the just square and measure of all good and evil; these are the plumb-lines they apply to all things, to find out their rectitude or obliquity. He that will not submit himself to, nor comply with, the eternal and uncreated will, but instead of it endeavors to set up his own will, makes himself the most real idol in the world, and exalts himself against all that is called God and ought to be worshipped. To worship a graven image, or to make cakes and burn incense to the queen of heaven, is not a worse idolatry than it is for a man to set up self-will, to devote himself to the serving of it, and to give up himself to a compliance with his own will, as contrary to the divine and eternal will. When God made the world, he did not make it merely for the exercise of his almighty power, and then throw it out of his hands, and leave it alone, to subsist by itself, as a thing that had no further relation to him. But he derived himself through the whole creation, so gathering and knitting up all the several pieces of it again; that, as the first production and continued subsistence of all things are from himself, so the ultimate resolution and tendency of all things might be to him. Now that which first endeavored after a divorce between God and his creation and to make a conquest of it was that diabolical arrogancy and self-will, that crept up and wound itself, serpent-like, into apostate minds and spirits. This is the true strain of that hellish nature, to live independently of God, and to derive the principles from another beginning, and carry on the line of all motions and operations to another end than God himself, by whom, and to whom, and for whom, all things subsist.

From what hath been said concerning this powerful and dangerous enemy, that wars against our souls and against the divine will, may the excellency and noble spirit of true religion appear, in that it tames the impetuousness and turbulency of this self-will. Then, indeed, does religion perform the highest and bravest conquests; then does it display the greatness of its strength and the excellency of its power, when it overcomes this great Arimanius, that hath so firmly seated himself in the very center of the soul. "Who is the man of courage and valor? It is he that subdues his concupiscence, his own will," [33] is a Jewish maxim attributed to Ben Zoma, and a most undoubted truth. This was the grand lesson that our great Lord and Master came to teach us, viz., to deny our own wills; neither was there anything that he endeavored more to promote by his own example, as he tells us of himself, "I came down from Heaven, not to do mine own will, but the will of him that sent me" [Jn. 6:38] and, again, "Lo, I come (in the volume of the book it is written of me) to do thy will, O God, yea thy law is within my heart" [Ps. 40:7–8; Heb. 10:7]; and in his greatest agonies, with a clear and cheerful submission to the divine will, he often repeats; "Not my will, but thine be done" [Mk. 14:36]; and so he hath taught us to pray, and so to live. This, indeed, is the true life and spirit of religion; this is religion in its meridian altitude, its just dimensions. A true Christian that hath power over his own will may live nobly and happily, and enjoy a clear heaven within the serenity of his own mind perpetually. When the sea of this world is most rough and tempestuous about him, then can he ride safely at anchor within the haven, by a sweet compliance of his will with God's will. He can look about him, and, with an even and indifferent mind, behold the world either smile or frown upon him; neither will he abate the least of his contentment for all the ill and unkind usage he meets withal in this life. He that hath got the mastery over his own will feels no violence from without, finds no contest within; and, like a strong man keeping his house, he preserves all his goods in safety [Lk. 11:21] and when God calls for him out of this state of mortality, he finds in himself a power to lay down his own life; neither is it so much taken from him, as quietly and freely surrendered up by him [cf. Jn. 10:15,17]. This is the highest piece of prowess, the noblest achievement, by which a man becomes lord over himself, and the master of his own thoughts, motions and purposes. This is the royal prerogative, the high dignity conferred upon good men by our Lord and Savior, whereby they, overcoming this both his and their enemy, their self-will

33. [ED.] *The Mishnah*, Fourth Division, Aboth, Ch. 4, §1, ed. H. C. Danby (Oxford, 1933), 453.

and passions, are enabled to sit down with him in his throne, as he, over-coming in another way, "is set down with his Father in his throne" [Rev. 3:21], as the phrase is.

Religion begets the most heroic, free and generous motions in the minds of good men. There is nowhere so much of a truly magnanimous and raised spirit, as in those who are best acquainted with the power of religion. Other men are slaves and captives to one vanity or other, but the truly religious is above them all, and able to command himself and all his powers for God. That bravery and gallantness, which seem to be in the great Nimrods of this world, are nothing less but the swelling of their own unbounded pride and vain-glory. It hath been observed of the greatest monarchs of the world, that, in the midst of their triumphs, they themselves have been led captives to one vice or another. All the gallantry and puissance of which the bravest spirits of the world boast, is but a poor, confined thing, and extends itself only to some particular cases and circumstances: but the valor and puissance of a soul impregnated by religion hath, in a sort, a universal extent, as St. Paul speaks of himself: "I can do all things through Christ which strengtheneth me" [Phil. 4:13]; it is not determined to this or that particular object, or time, or place, but πάντα— all things whatsoever belong to a creature—fall under the level thereof. Religion is by St. Paul described to be πνεῦμα δυνάμεως—"the spirit of power"—in opposition to the spirit of fear [2 Tim. 1:7], as all sin is by Simplicius well described to be ἀδυναμία—"impotency and weakness." [34] Sin, by its deadly infusions into the soul of man, wastes and eats out the innate vigor of the soul, and casts it into such a deep lethargy, as that it is not able to recover itself. But religion, like that *balsamum vitae* [balm of life], being once conveyed into the soul, awakens and enlivens it, and makes it renew its strength like an eagle, and mount strongly upwards towards heaven; and so, uniting the soul to God, the center of life and strength, it renders it undaunted and invincible. Who can tell the inward life and vigor that the soul may be filled with, when once it is in conjunction with an almighty essence? There is a latent and hidden virtue in the soul of man, which then begins to discover itself when the Divine Spirit spreads forth its influences upon it. The more spiritual anything is, and the higher and nobler it is in its being, the more active and vigorous it is; as the more anything falls and sinks into matter, the more dull, and sluggish, and unwieldy it is. Now, nothing doth more purify, more sublimate and exalt the soul, than religion, when the soul suffers God to sit within it "as

34. [ED.] Simplicius, *On the Enchiridion of Epictetus*, Ch. 1, 1.

a refiner and purifier of silver," and when it "abides the day of his coming; for he is like a refiner's fire, and like fuller's soap" [Mal. 3:2,3]. Thus the soul, being purified and spiritualized, and changed more and more into the glorious image of God, is able to do all things, "out of weakness is made strong" [cf. Heb. 11:34], gives proof of its divine vigor and activity, and shows itself to be a noble and puissant spirit, such as God did at first create it.

Chapter v

The third property or effect discovering the nobleness of religion, viz., that it directs and enables a man to propound to himself the best end, viz., the glory of God, and his own becoming like unto God. Low and particular ends and interests both debase and straiten a man's spirit; the universal, highest and last end both ennobles and enlarges it. A man is such as the end is he aims at. The great power the end hath to mold and fashion man into its likeness. Religion obliges a man, not to seek himself, nor to drive a trade for himself; but to seek the glory of God, to live wholly to him; and guides him steadily and uniformly to the one chief good and last end. Men are prone to flatter themselves with a pretended aiming at the glory of God. A more full and distinct explication of what is meant by a man's directing all his actions to the glory of God. What it is truly and really to glorify God. God's seeking his glory in respect of us is the flowing forth of his goodness upon us; our seeking the glory of God is our endeavoring to partake more of God, and to resemble him as much as we can, in true holiness and every divine virtue. That we are not nicely to distinguish between the glory of God and our own salvation. That salvation is nothing else, for the main, but a true participation of the divine nature. To love God above ourselves is not to love him above the salvation of our souls, but above our particular beings and above our sinful affections, &c. The difference between things that are good relatively and those that are good absolutely and essentially; that, in our conforming to these, God is most glorified, and we are made most happy.

3. The *third* property or effect whereby religion discovers its own excellency, is this: *that it directs and enables a man to propound to himself the best end and scope of life, viz., the glory of God, the highest Being, and his own assimilation, or becoming like unto God.*

That Christian in whom religion rules powerfully is not so low in his ambitions as to pursue any of the things of this world as his ultimate end. His soul is too big for earthly designs and interests, but, understanding himself to come from God, he is continually returning to him again. It is not worthy of the mind of man to pursue any perfection lower than its own, or to aim at any end more ignoble than itself. There is nothing that more straitens and confines the freeborn soul than the particularity, indigency and penury of that end which it pursues, when it complies most of all with this lower world, as is well observed by an excellent philosopher: "The true nobleness and freedom of it is then most disputable," and the title it holds to true liberty becomes most litigious.[35] It never more slides and degenerates from itself than when it becomes enthralled to some particular interest; as, on the other side, it never acts more freely or fully than when it extends itself upon the most universal end. Everything is so much the more noble as it has wider limits, as was well observed by Cicero. As low ends debase a man's spirit, supplant and rob it of its birthright, so the highest and last end raises and ennobles it, and enlarges it into a more universal and comprehensive capacity of enjoying that one unbounded goodness, which is God himself. It makes it spread and dilate itself in the infinite sphere of the divine being and blessedness; it makes it live in the fullness of him that fills all in all [Eph. 1:23].

Everything is most properly such as the end is which is aimed at. The mind of man is always shaping itself into a conformity, as much as may be, to that which is his end, and the nearer it draws to it in the achievement thereof, the greater likeness it bears to it. There is a plastic virtue, a secret energy, issuing forth from that which the mind propounds to itself as its end, to mold and fashion it according to its own model. The soul is always stamped with the same characters as are engraven upon the end it aims at; and, while it converses with it, and sets itself before it, "it is turned as wax to the seal," to use that phrase in Job [38:14].[36] Man's soul conceives all its thoughts and imaginations before his end, as Laban's ewes did their young, before the rods in the watering-troughs [Gen. 30:38–39]. He that pursues any worldly interest of earthly thing as his end becomes himself also γεώδης—"earthly"; and the more the soul directs itself to God, the more it becomes θεοειδής—"god-like," deriving a print of that glory and beauty upon itself with which it converseth, as it is excellently set forth by the apostle: "But we all, with open face, beholding, as in a glass, the glory of the Lord, are changed into the same image, from glory to glory" [2 Cor. 3:18]. That spirit of ambition and popularity, that so violently

35. [ED.] Simplicius, *On the Enchiridion of Epictetus*, Ch. 1, §1.
36. [ED.] Cf. supra 96, where Smith speaks of "clay or wax." The KJV has "clay."

transports the minds of men into a pursuit of vain-glory, makes them as vain as that popular air they live upon. The spirit of this world, that draws forth a man's designs after worldly interests, makes him as unstable, inconstant, tumultuous, and perplexed a thing as the world is. On the contrary, the spirit of true religion, steering and directing the mind and life to God, makes it a uniform, stable and quiet thing, as God himself is. It is only true goodness in the soul of man, guiding it steadily and uniformly towards God, directing it and all its actions to the one last end and chief good, that can give it a true consistency and composedness within itself. All self-seeking and self-love do but imprison the soul and confine it to its own home. The mind of a good man is too noble, too big for such a particular life; he hath learned to despise his own being, in comparison of that uncreated beauty and goodness, which is so infinitely transcendent to himself or any created thing. He reckons upon his choice and best affections and designs, as too choice and precious a treasure to be spent upon such a poor sorry thing as himself, or upon anything else but God himself.

This was the life of Christ, and is, in some degree, the life of every one that partakes of the Spirit of Christ. Such Christians seek not their own glory, but the glory of him that sent them into this world. They know they were brought forth into this world, not to set up or drive a trade for themselves, but to serve the will and pleasure of him that made them, and to finish that work he hath appointed them. It were not worth the while to have been born or to live, had it been only for such a penurious end as ourselves are. It is most god-like, and best suits with the spirit of religion, for a Christian to live wholly to God, to live the life of God, "having his own life hid with Christ in God" [Col. 3:3]; and thus, in a sober sense, he becomes deified. This indeed is such a θέωσις—"deification"—as is not transacted merely upon the stage of fancy, by arrogance and presumption, but in the highest powers of the soul, by a living and quickening spirit of true religion there, uniting God and the soul together in unity of affections, will and end.

I should now pass from this to another particular; but, because many are apt to misapprehend the notion of God's glory, and flatter themselves with their pretended and imaginary aiming at the glory of God, I think it may be of good use a little further and more distinctly to unfold the design that a religious mind pursues in directing itself and all its actions to God. We are, therefore, to consider, that this doth not consist in some transient thoughts of God and his glory, as the end we propound to ourselves in any undertakings. A man does not direct all his actions to the glory of God by forming a conception in his mind, or stirring up a strong imagination upon any action, that that must be for the glory of God. It is not the thinking of God's glory that is glorifying of him. As all other parts of religion may be apishly acted over by fancy and imagination, so also may the internal parts of religion be acted over with much seeming grace by our fancy and passions; these often love to be drawing pictures of religion, and use their best arts to render them more beautiful and pleasing. But though true practical religion derives its force and beauty through all the lower powers of a man's soul, yet hath it not its rise nor throne there. As religion consists not in a form of words which signify nothing, so neither doth it consist in a set of fancies or internal apprehensions. Our Savior hath best taught what it is to live to God's glory, or to glorify God, viz., to be fruitful in all holiness, and to live so as that our lives may shine with his grace spreading itself through our whole man.

We rather glorify God by entertaining the impressions of his glory upon us, than by communicating any kind of glory to him. Then does a good man become the tabernacle of God, wherein the divine Shechinah does rest, and which the divine glory fills, when the frame of his mind and life is wholly according to that idea and pattern which he receives from the mount [cf. Ex. 25:40]. We best glorify him when we grow most like to him; and we then act most for his glory, when a true spirit of sanctity, justice, meekness, &c., runs through all our actions; when we so live in the world as becomes those that converse with the great Mind and Wisdom of the whole world; with that Almighty Spirit that made, supports and governs all things; with that Being from whence all good flows, and in which there is no spot, stain or shadow of evil; and so, being captivated and overcome by the sense of the divine loveliness and goodness, we endeavor to be like him, and conform ourselves, as much as may be, to him.

When God seeks his own glory, he does not so much endeavor after anything without himself. He did not bring this stately fabric of the universe into being, that he might, for such a monument of his mighty power and beneficence, gain some panegyrics or applause from a little of that fading breath which he had made. Neither was that gracious contrivance of restoring lapsed men to himself a plot to get himself some eternal hallelujahs, as if he had so ardently thirsted after the lays of glorified spirits, or desired a choir of souls to sing forth his praises. Neither was it to let the world see how magnificent he was. No: it is his own internal glory that he most loves, and the communication thereof which he seeks. As Plato sometimes speaks of the divine love, it arises not out of indigency, as created love does, but out of fullness and redundancy. It is an overflowing fountain, and that love which descends upon created being is a free efflux from the almighty source of love; and it is well-pleasing to him that those creatures which he hath made should partake of it. Though God cannot seek his own glory so as if he might acquire any addition to himself, yet he may seek it so as to communicate it out of himself. It was a good maxim of Plato—τῷ θεῷ οὐδεὶς φθόνος,[37] which is better stated by St. James, "God giveth to all men liberally, and upbraideth not" [Jas. 1:5]. And by that glory of his, which he loves to impart to his creatures, I understand those stamps and impressions of wisdom, justice, patience, mercy, love, peace, joy and other divine gifts, which he bestows freely upon the minds of men. And thus God triumphs in his own glory, and takes pleasure in the communication of it.

As God's seeking his own glory in respect of us is most properly the flowing forth of his goodness upon us, so our seeking the glory of God is most properly our endeavoring after a participation of his goodness, and an earnest incessant pursuing after divine perfection. When God becomes so great in our eyes, and all created things so little, that we reckon upon nothing as worthy of our aims or ambitions, but a serious participation of the divine nature, and the exercise of divine virtues, love, joy, peace, longsuffering, kindness, goodness, and the like [cf. Gal. 5:22]; when the soul, beholding the infinite beauty and loveliness of the Divinity, and then looking down and beholding all created perfection mantled over with darkness, is ravished into love and admiration of that never-setting brightness, and endeavors after the greatest resemblance of God in justice, love, and goodness; when, conversing with him ἐν ἡσύχω ἐπαφῇ [38]—by a secret feeling of the virtue, sweetness, and power of his goodness, we endeavor to assimilate ourselves to him; then we may be said to glorify him indeed. God seeks no glory but his own; and we have none of our own to give him. God in all things seeks himself and his own glory, as finding nothing better than himself; and when we love him above all things, and endeavor to be most like him, we declare plainly that we count nothing better than he is.

I doubt we are too nice logicians sometimes, in distinguishing between the glory of God and our own salvation. We cannot, in a true sense, seek our own salvation more than the glory of God, which triumphs most and

---

37. [ED.] Cf. Plato, *Timaeus*, 29E: "He was good, and none that is good is ever subject to any motion of grudging."

38. [ED.] Plotinus, *The Enneads*, VI.9.9.

discovers itself most effectually in the salvation of souls; for, indeed, this salvation is nothing else but a true participation of the divine nature. Heaven is not a thing without us, nor is happiness anything distinct from a true conjunction of the mind with God in a secret feeling of his goodness, and reciprocation of affection to him, wherein the divine glory most unfolds itself. And there is nothing that a soul, touched with any serious sense of God, can more earnestly thirst after or seek with more strength of affection than this. Then shall we be happy, when God comes to be all in us. To love God above ourselves is not, indeed, so properly to love him above the salvation of our souls, as if these were distinct things; but it is to love him above all our own sinful affections, and above our particular beings, and to conform ourselves to him. And as that which is good relatively, and in order to us, is so much the better by how much the more it is commensurate and conformed to us, so, on the other side, that which is good absolutely and essentially requires that our minds and affections should, as far as may be, be commensurate and conformed to it. And herein is God most glorified, and we made happy. As we cannot truly love the first and highest good while we serve a design upon it, and subordinate it to ourselves; so neither is our own salvation consistent with any such sordid, pinching and particular love. We cannot be completely blessed till the *idea boni*, or the *ipsum bonum*, which is God, exercise its sovereignty over all the faculties of our souls, rendering them as like to itself as may consist with their proper capacity.

Chapter VI

The fourth property or effect discovering the excellency of religion, viz., that it begets the greatest serenity and composedness of mind, and brings the truest contentment, the purest and most satisfying joy and pleasure to every holy soul. God, as being that uniform chief good, and the one last end, does attract and fix the soul. Wicked men distracted through a multiplicity of objects and ends. How the restless appetites of our wills after some supreme good leads to the knowledge, as of a Deity, so of the unity of a Deity. How the joys and delights of good men differ from, and far excel, those of the wicked. The constancy and tranquility of the spirits of good men in reference to external troubles. All perturbations of the mind arise from an inward, rather than an outward cause. The method of the Stoics for attaining ἀταραξία [tranquility] and true rest examined, and the insufficiency of it discovered. A further illustration of what has been said concerning the peaceful and happy state of good men, from the contrary state of the wicked.

4. The *fourth* property and effect of true religion, wherein it expresseth its own nobleness, is this: *that it begets the greatest serenity, constancy and composedness of mind, and brings the truest contentment, the most satisfying joy and pleasure, the purest and most divine sweetness and pleasure to the spirits of good men.* Every good man, in whom religion rules, is at peace and unity with himself, is as a city compacted together [cf. Ps. 122:3]. Grace doth more and more reduce all the faculties of the soul into a perfect subjection and subordination to itself. The union and conjunction of the soul with God, that primitive Unity, is that which is the alone original and fountain of all peace, and the center of rest; as the further any being slides from God, the more it breaks into discords within itself, as not having any center within itself, which might collect and unite all the faculties thereof to itself, and so knit them up together in a sweet confederacy amongst themselves. God only is such an almighty goodness as can attract all the powers in man's soul to itself, as being an object transcendently adequate to the largest capacities of any created being, and so unite men perfectly to himself in the true enjoyment of one uniform and simple good.

It must be one last end and supreme good that can fix man's mind, which otherwise will be tossed up and down in perpetual uncertainties and become as many several things as those poor particularities are which it meets with. A wicked man's life is so distracted by a multiplicity of ends and objects that it never is, nor can be, consistent with itself, nor continue in any composed, settled frame. It is the most intricate, irregular and confused thing in the world, no one part of it agreeing with another, because the whole is not firmly knit together, by the power of some one last end running through all. Whereas the life of a good man is under the sweet command of one supreme goodness and last end. This alone is that living form and soul which, running through all the powers of the mind and actions of life, collects all together into one fair and beautiful system, making all that variety conspire into perfect unity; whereas else, all would fall asunder like the members of a dead body, when once the soul is gone, all the little particles flitting each from the rest. It was a good maxim of Pythagoras quoted by Clemens Alexandrinus, "Oportet etiam hominem unum fieri." [39] A divided mind and a multiform life speak the greatest disparagement that may be; it is only the intermediation of one last end, that can reconcile a man perfectly to himself and his own happiness. This is the best temper and composedness of the soul, ὅταν εἰς ἓν καὶ εἰς μίαν

39. [ED.] Clement of Alexandria, *Stromateis*, Bk. IV, 23: "Man ought indeed to become one."

ὁμολογίαν ἐνωθῇ, as Plotinus speaks—when by a conjunction with one chief good and last end it is drawn up in a unity and consent with itself; when all the faculties of the soul, with their several issues and motions, though never so many in themselves, like so many lines, meet together in one and the same center.[40] It is not one and the same goodness that always actuates the faculties of a wicked man; but as many several images and pictures of goodness as a quick and working fancy can represent to him; which so divide his affections, that he is no one thing within himself, but tossed hither and thither by the most independent principles and imaginations that may be. But a good man hath singled out the supreme goodness, which, by an omnipotent sweetness, draws all his affections after it, and so makes them all, with the greatest complacency, conspire together in the pursuit and embraces of it. Were there not some infinite and self-sufficient goodness, and that perfectly one ("a sovereign unit," as Simplicius doth phrase it), man would be a most miserably distracted creature. As the restless appetite within man after some infinite and sovereign good (without the enjoyment of which it could never be satisfied), does commend unto us the notion of a deity, so the perpetual distractions and divisions that would arise in the soul upon a plurality of deities may seem no less to evince the unity of that deity. Were not this chief good perfectly one, were there any other equal to it, man's soul would hang *in aequilibrio*, equally poised, equally desiring the enjoyment of both, but moving to neither, like a piece of iron between two loadstones of equal virtue. But when religion enters into the soul, it charms all its restless rage and violent appetite, by discovering to it the universal fountain-fullness of one supreme almighty goodness; and, leading it out of itself into a conjunction therewith, it lulls it into the most undisturbed rest and quietness in the lap of divine enjoyment; where it meets with full contentment, and rests adequately satisfied in the fruition of the infinite, uniform and essential goodness and loveliness, the true "form of the admirable" that is not πῇ μὲν καλὸν πῇ δὲ οὐ καλὸν ἀλλ' ὅλον δι' ὅλον καλὸν,[41] as a noble philosopher doth well express it.

The peace which a religious soul is possessed of, is such a "peace as passeth all understanding"; the joy that it meets with in the ways of holiness is "unspeakable and full of glory" [Phil. 4:7; 1 Pet. 1:8]. The delights and sweetness that accompany a religious life are of a purer and

---

40. [ED.] Plotinus, *The Enneads*, VI.9.1.

41. [ED.] Simplicius, *On the Enchiridion of Epictetus*, Ch. XXXI: "Partly good on the one hand, partly evil on the other, but absolutely good—."

more excellent nature than the pleasures of worldly men. The spirit of a good man is too pure and refined a thing than to delight itself in the thick mire of earthly and sensual pleasures, in which carnal men roll and tumble themselves with so much greediness: "The rapacious man is not permitted a refuge in the dusty earth," as the Arabic proverb hath it. It speaks the degeneration of any soul whatsoever that it should desire to incorporate itself with any of the gross, dreggy, sensual delights here below. But a soul purified by religion from earthly dregs delights to mingle itself only with things that are most divine and spiritual. There is nothing that can beget any pleasure or sweetness, but in some harmonical faculty which hath some kindred and acquaintance with it. As it is in the senses, so in every other faculty, there is a natural kind of science whereby it can single out its own proper object from everything else, and is better able to define it to itself than the most exact artist in the world can; and when once it hath found it out, it presently feels itself so perfectly fitted and matched by it, that it dissolves into secret joy and pleasure in the entertainment of it. True delight and joy is begotten by the conjunction of some discerning faculty with its proper object. The proper objects for a mind and spirit are divine and immaterial things, with which it hath the greatest affinity, and therefore triumphs most in its converse with them; as it is well observed by Seneca; [42] and when it converseth most with these high and noble objects, it behaves itself most gracefully and lives most becoming itself; and it lives also most deliciously, nor can it anywhere else be better provided for, or, indeed, fare so well. A good man disdains to be beholden to the wit, art or industry of any creature to find him out, and bring him in a constant revenue and maintenance for his joy and pleasure; the language of his heart is that of the Psalmist: "Lord, lift thou up the light of thy countenance upon me" [Ps. 4:6]. Religion always carries a sufficient provision of joy and sweetness along with it to maintain itself withal: "The ways of wisdom are ways of pleasantness, and all her paths are peace" [cf. Prov. 3:17]. Religion is no sullen stoicism or oppressing melancholy; it is no enthralling tyranny exercised over those noble and vivacious affections of love and delight, as those men that were never acquainted with the life of it may imagine; but it is full of a vigorous and masculine delight and joy, and such as advances and ennobles the soul, and does not weaken or dispirit the life and power of it, as sensual and earthly joys do, when the soul, unacquainted with religion, is enforced to give entertainment to those gross and earthly things, for the want of enjoyment

42. [ED.] Seneca, *Physical Investigations*, Preface.

of some better good. The spirit of a good man may justly behave itself with a noble disdain to all terrene pleasures, because it knows where to mend its fare: it is the almighty and eternal goodness which is the happiness of God and of all good men. The truly religious soul affects nothing primarily and fundamentally but God himself; his contentment, even in the midst of his worldly employments, is in the sun of the divine favor that shines upon him. This is as the manna that lies upon the top of all outward blessings, which his spirit gathers up and feeds upon with delight. Religion consists not in a toilsome drudgery about some bodily exercises and external performances; nor is it only the spending of ourselves in such attendances upon God and services to him as are only accommodated to this life, though every employment for God is both amiable and honorable. But there is something of our religion that interests us in a present possession of that "joy which is unspeakable and full of glory" [1 Pet. 1:8], which leads us into the porch of Heaven and to the confines of eternity. It sometimes carries up the soul into a mount of transfiguration or to the top of Pisgah, where it may take a prospect of the promised land, and gives it a map or scheme of its future inheritance; it gives it sometimes some anticipations of blessedness, some foretastes of those joys, those rivers of pleasure which run at God's right hand for evermore [cf. Mk. 9:2; Deut. 3:27; Ps. 16:11].

I might further add, as a *mantissa* [43] to this present argument, the tranquility and composedness of a good man's spirit in reference to all external molestations. Religion, having made a thorough pacification of the soul within itself, renders it impregnable to all outward assaults; so that it is at rest, and lives securely in the midst of all those boisterous storms and tempests which make such violent impressions upon the spirits of wicked men. Here, the Stoics have stated the case aright, that all perturbations of the mind arise not properly from an outward but an inward cause: it is not an outward evil, but an inward imagination, bred in the womb of the soul itself, that molests and grieves it. The more the soul is restored to itself and lives at the height of its own being, the more easily may it disdain and despise any design or combination against it by the most blustering giants in the world. A Christian that enjoys himself in God will not be beholden to the world's fair and gentle usage, for the composedness of his mind; no: he enjoys that peace and tranquility within himself, which no creature can bestow upon him, or take from him.

43. [ED.] An addition of trivial importance.

But the Stoics were not so happy in their notions about the way to true rest and composedness of spirit. It is not (by their leave) the soul's collecting and gathering up itself within the circumference of its own essence; nor is it a rigid restraining and keeping in its own issues and motions within the confines of its own natural endowments, which is able to confer upon it that ἀταραξία [calmness] and composedness of mind, which they so much idolize, as the supreme and only bliss of man, and render it free from all kinds of perturbations: for, by what we find in Seneca and others, it appears that the Stoics, seeking an autarchy within themselves, and being loath to be beholden to God for their happiness, but that each of them might be as God, self-sufficient, and happy in the enjoyment of himself, endeavored, by their sour doctrine and a rigid discipline over their souls, their severities against passions and all those restless motions in the soul after some higher good, to attain a complete and a full contentment within themselves.[44] But herein they missed the true method of finding rest to themselves, it being the union of the soul with God, that uniform, simple and unbounded good, which is the sole original of all true inward peace. Neither were it a happiness worth the having, for a mind, like a hermit sequestered from all things else by a recession into itself, to spend an eternity in self-converse and the enjoyment of such a diminutive, superficial nothing as itself is and must necessarily be to itself. It is only peculiar to God to be happy in himself alone; and God, who has been more liberal in his provisions for man, hath created in man such a spring of restless motion, that, with the greatest impatience, forceth him out of himself and violently tosseth him to and fro, till he come to fix himself upon some solid and self-subsistent goodness. Could a man find himself withdrawn from all terrene and material things and perfectly retired into himself; were the whole world so quiet and calm about him as not to offer to make the least attempt upon the composedness and constancy of his mind; might he be so well entertained at his own home as to find no frowns, no sour looks from his own conscience; might he have that security from Heaven, that God would not disquiet his fancied tranquility by embittering his thoughts with any dreadful apprehensions; yet he should find something within him that would not let him be at rest, but would rend him from himself and toss him from his own foundation and consistency. There is an insatiable appetite in the soul of man, like a greedy lion hunting after his prey, that would render him impatient of his own pinching penury,

44. [ED.] Cf. Seneca, *Moral Epistles*, xcii, cxvi; *Moral Essays* (esp. "De Tranquillitate Animi" and "De Beneficiis").

and could never satisfy itself with such a thin and spare diet as he finds at home. There are two principal faculties in the soul which, like two daughters of the horseleach, are always crying, Give, Give [Prov. 30:15]; these are those hungry vultures which, if they cannot find their prey abroad, return and gnaw the soul itself: "Where the carcase is, there will the eagles be gathered together" [Mt. 24:28]. By this we may see how unavailable to the attaining of true rest and peace that conceit of the Stoics was, who supposed the only way and method hereto was this, to confine the soul thus monastically to its own home. We read in the Gospel of such a question of our Savior's: "What went ye out into the wilderness to see?" [Mt. 11:7]; we may invert it: "What do you return within to see? A soul confined within the private and narrow cell of its own particular being?" Such a soul deprives itself of all that almighty and essential glory and goodness which shines round about it, which spreads itself through the whole universe—I say, it deprives itself of all this, for the enjoying of such a poor, petty and diminutive thing as itself is, which yet it can never enjoy truly in such a retiredness.

We have seen the peaceful and happy state of the truly religious. But it is otherwise with wicked and irreligious men. "There is no peace to the wicked; but they are like the troubled sea, when it cannot rest, whose waters cast up mire and dirt" [cf. Is. 57:20], as it is expressed by the prophet Isaiah. The mind of a wicked man is like the sea, when it roars and rages through the striving of several contrary winds upon it. Furious lusts and wild passions within, as they war against Heaven and the more noble and divine part of the soul, so do they war amongst themselves, maintaining perpetual contests, and contending which shall be the greatest: "Scelera dissident [The wicked are at variance]." These, indeed, are the Cadmus-brood rising out of the serpent's teeth, ready armed one against another; [45] whence it is that the soul of a wicked man becomes a very uninhabitable and incommodious place to itself, full of disquietude and trouble, through the many contests and civil commotions maintained within it. The minds of wicked men are like those disconsolate and desolate spirits which our Savior speaks of, which, being cast out of their habitations, wander up and down through dry and desert places, seeking rest but finding none [Mt. 12:43]. The soul that finds not some solid and self-

45. [ED.] By the advice of Athena, Cadmus (son of Agenor, king of Tyre) sowed the teeth of a dragon he had killed, and there sprang up a harvest of armed men. Cadmus set them fighting one against another. Five survived and became the ancestors of the nobility of Thebes.

sufficient good to center itself upon is a boisterous and restless thing; and, being without God, it wanders up and down the world, destitute, afflicted, tormented with vehement hunger and thirst after some satisfying good; and, as any one shall bring it tidings, "Lo here, or, Lo there is good" [cf. Mt. 24:23], it presently goes out towards it, and, with a swift and speedy flight, hastens after it. The sense of an inward indigency doth stimulate and enforce it to seek its contentment without itself, and so it wanders up and down from one creature to another; and thus becomes distracted by a multiplicity of objects. And while it cannot find some one and only object upon which, as being perfectly adequate to its capacities, it may wholly bestow itself; while it is tossed with restless and vehement motions of desire and love, through a world of painted beauties, false, glozing [46] excellencies; courting all, but matching nowhere; violently hurried everywhere, but finding nowhere "the object corresponding to the desire"; while it converseth only with these pinching particularities here below, and is not yet acquainted with the universal goodness; it is certainly far from true rest and satisfaction, from a fixed, composed temper of spirit; but being distracted by multiplicity of objects and ends, there can never be any firm and stable peace or friendship at home, among all its powers and faculties; nor can there be a firm amity and friendship abroad betwixt wicked men themselves, as Aristotle concludes in his Ethics,[47] because all vice is so multiform and inconsistent a thing; and so there can be no true concatenation of affections and ends between them. Whereas, in all good men, virtue and goodness is one form and soul to them all, that unites them together; and there is the one, simple, uniform good, that guides and governs them all. They are not as a ship, tossed in the tumultuous ocean of this world, without any compass at all to steer by, but they direct their course by certain guidance of the one last end, as the true polestar of all their motion. But while the soul lies benighted in a thick ignorance, as it is with wicked men, and beholds not some stable and eternal good towards which it may move; though it may, by the strength of that principle of activeness within itself, spend itself perpetually with swift and giddy motions; yet will it be always contesting with secret disturbances, and cannot act but with many reluctancies, as not finding an object equal to the force and strength of its vast affections to act upon.

By what hath been said, may appear the vast difference between the ways of sin and of holiness. Inward distractions and disturbances, "tribula-

46. [ED.] I.e., speciously deceitful. Cf. O.E.D.
47. [ED.] Aristotle, Nicomachean Ethics, Bk. VIII.

tion and anguish upon every soul that doth evil: but to every man that
worketh good, glory, honor and peace" [Rom. 2:9,10], inward composedness and tranquility of spirit, and full satisfaction in God, whom the
pious soul loves above all things and longs still after a nearer enjoyment of
him. I shall conclude this particular with that which Plotinus concludes
his book—that the life of holy and divine men is "a life not touched with
these vanishing delights of time, but a flight of the soul alone to God." [48]

Chapter VII

*The fifth property or effect discovering the excellency of religion,
viz., that it advanceth the soul to a holy boldness and humble familiarity with God and to a comfortable confidence concerning the
love of God toward it and its own salvation. Fearfulness, consternation of mind and frightful passions are consequent upon sin and guilt.
These, together with the most dismal deportments of trembling and
amazement, are agreeable to the nature of the devil, who delights to
be served in this manner by his worshippers. Love, joy, and hope are
most agreeable to the nature of God and most pleasing to him. The
right apprehensions of God are such as are apt to beget love to God,
delight and confidence in him. A true Christian is more for a solid
and well-grounded peace, than for high raptures and feelings of joy.
How a Christian should endeavor after the assurance of his salvation.
That he should not importunately expect or desire some extraordinary manifestations of God to him, but rather look after the manifestation of the life of God within him, the foundation or beginning of
heaven and salvation in his own soul. That self-resignation, and the
subduing of our own wills, are greatly available to obtain assurance.
The vanity and absurdity of that opinion, viz., that in a perfect
resignation of our wills to God's will, a man should be content with
his own damnation, and to be the subject of eternal wrath in Hell, if
it should so please God.*

5. The *fifth* property or effect whereby true religion discovers its
own nobleness and excellency is this: *that it advanceth the soul to a holy
boldness and humble familiarity with God, as also a well-grounded hope
and comfortable confidence concerning the love of God toward it and its
own salvation.* The truly religious soul maintains a humble and sweet
familiarity with God; and, with great alacrity of spirit, without consternation and servility of spirit, is enabled to look upon the glory and majesty
of the Most High; but sin and wickedness is pregnant with fearfulness and

48. [ED.] Plotinus, *The Enneads*, VI.9.11.

horror. That trembling and consternation of mind which possesses wicked men is nothing else but the offspring of darkness, an ῍Εμπουσα [a hobgoblin] begotten in corrupt and irreligious hearts. While men "walk in darkness," and "are of the night" [1 Jn. 1:6; 1 Thess. 5:5], as the apostle speaks, then only is it that they are vexed with those ugly and ghastly μορμόνες [bugbears] that terrify and torment them. But when once the day breaks and true religion opens herself upon the soul, like the eyelids of the morning, then all light, and love and joy descend from above, from the Father of lights [Jas. 1:17]. So all darkness and fearfulness and despair are from below; they arise from corrupt and earthly minds, and are like those gross vapors arising from this earthly globe, that, not being able to get up towards Heaven, spread themselves about the circumference of that body where they were first begotten, infesting it with darkness, and generating into thunder and lightning, clouds and tempests. But the higher a Christian ascends ἐκ τοῦ σπηλαίου [out of the cavern]—above this dark dungeon of the body; the more that religion prevails within him, the more then shall he find himself, as it were, in a clear heaven, in a region that is calm and serene; and the more will those black and dark affections of fear and despair vanish away, and those clear and bright affections of love, and joy, and hope break forth in their strength and luster.

The devil, who is the prince of darkness and the great tyrant, delights to be served with ghastly affections and the most dismal deportments of trembling and astonishment; as having nothing at all of amiableness or excellency in him to commend himself to his worshippers. Slavery and servility (that "coffin of the spirit," as Longinus truly calls it) [49] is the badge and livery of the devil's religion; hence those "horrible mysteries" of the heavens, performed with much trembling and horror. But God, who is the supreme goodness and both essential love and loveliness, takes most pleasure in those sweet and delightful affections of the soul, viz., love, joy and hope, which are most correspondent to his own nature. The ancient superstition of the heathens was always very nice and curious in honoring every one of their gods with sacrifices and rites most agreeable to their natures: I am sure there is no incense, no offering which we can present to God so sweet, so acceptable to him as our love and delight and confidence in him; and when he comes into the souls of men, he makes these his throne, his place of rest, as finding the greatest agreeableness therein to his own essence. A good man that finds himself made partaker

49. [ED.] Pseudo-Longinus, *On the Sublime*, XLIV.5.

of the divine nature and transformed into the image of God, infinitely takes pleasure in God as being "altogether lovely," according to that in Canticles, "Totus ipse est desideria"; and his "meditation of God is sweet unto him" [Song 5:16; Ps. 104:34]. St. John, that lay in the bosom of Christ, who came from the bosom of the Father and perfectly understood his eternal essence, hath given us the fullest description that he could make of him, when he tells us that "God is love; and he that dwelleth in God, dwelleth in love" [1 Jn. 4:16]; and, reposing himself in the bosom of an almighty goodness, where he finds nothing but love and loveliness, he now displays all the strength and beauty of those his choicest and the most precious affections of love and joy and confidence. His soul is now at ease and rests in peace, neither is there anything to make afraid. He is got beyond all those powers of darkness which give continual alarms in this lower world, and are always troubling the earth. He is got above all fears and despairs; he is in a bright, clear region, above clouds and tempests— "Infra se despicit nubes [He looks down on the clouds beneath him]." There is no frightful terribleness in the supreme majesty. That we apprehend God at any time in such a dismal manner must not at all be made an argument of his nature but of our sinfulness and weakness. The sun in the heavens always was, and always will be, a globe of light and brightness, however a purblind eye is rather dazzled than enlightened by it. There is an inward sense in man's soul, which, were it once awakened and excited with an inward taste and relish of the Divinity, could better define God to him than all the world else. It is the sincere Christian that so tastes and sees how good and sweet the Lord is, as none else does; "the God of hope fills him with all joy and peace in believing," so that he "abounds in hope," as the apostle speaks [Rom. 15:13]. He quietly reposes himself in God; "his heart is fixed, trusting in the Lord" [Ps. 112:7]. He is more for a solid peace and settled calm of spirit than for high raptures and feelings of joy or extraordinary manifestations of God to him. He does not passionately desire nor importunately expect such things; he rather looks after the manifestations of the goodness and power of God within him, in subduing all in his soul that is unlike and contrary to God, and forming him into his image and likeness.

Though I think it worthy of a Christian to endeavor after the assurance of his own salvation, yet perhaps it might be the safest way to moderate his curiosity of prying into God's book of life and to stay a while until he sees himself within the confines of salvation itself. Should a man hear a voice from Heaven or see a vision from the Almighty to testify unto him the love of God towards him, yet, methinks, it were more desirable to find a revelation of all from within, arising up from the bottom and center of a man's soul, in the real and internal impressions of a godlike nature upon his own spirit; and thus to find the foundation and beginning of Heaven and happiness within himself. It were more desirable to see the crucifying of our own will, the mortifying of the mere animal life, and to see a divine life rising up in the room of it, as a sure pledge and inchoation of immortality and happiness, the very essence of which consists in a perfect conformity and cheerful compliance of all the powers of our souls with the will of God.

The best way of gaining a well-grounded assurance of the divine love is this—for a man to overcome himself and his own will: "To him that overcometh shall be given that white stone, and in it the new name written, which no man knoweth but he that receiveth it" [Rev. 2:17]. He that beholds the Sun of Righteousness arising in the horizon of his soul with healing in its wings [cf. Mal. 4:2], and chasing away all that misty darkness of his own self-will and passions: such a one desires not now the star-light to know whether it be day or not, nor cares he to pry into Heaven's secrets and to search into the hidden rolls of eternity, there to see the whole plot of his salvation; for he views it transacted upon the inward stage of his own soul, and, reflecting upon himself, he may behold a Heaven opened from within, and a throne set up in his soul, and an almighty Savior sitting upon it, and reigning within him, and sees that it is not a thing merely reserved for him without him, being already made a partaker of the sweetness and efficacy of it. What the Jews say of the Spirit of Prophecy may not unfitly be applied to the Holy Ghost, the true Comforter, dwelling in the minds of good men, as a sure earnest of their eternal inheritance; "The Spirit resides not but upon a man of fortitude" [50]—one that gives proof of this fortitude in subduing his own self-will and his affections. We read of Elisha, that he was fain to call for a musical instrument, and one to play before him, to allay the heat of his passions, before he could converse with the prophetical spirit [cf. 2 Kings 3:15]. The Holy Spirit is too pure and gentle a thing to dwell in a mind muddled and disturbed by those impure dregs, those thick fogs and mists that arise from our self-will and passions. Our prevailing over these is the best way to cherish the Holy Spirit, by which we may be sealed unto the day of redemption.

50. [ED.] Cf. The Talmud, Sanhedrin III, 10.

To conclude this particular: it is a venturous and rugged guess and conceit which some men have, that in a perfect resignation of our wills to the divine will, a man should be content with his own damnation and to be the subject of eternal wrath in Hell, if it should so please God; which is as impossible as it is for him that infinitely thirsts after a true participation of the divine nature, and most earnestly endeavors after a most inward union with God in spirit, by a denial of himself and his own will, to swell up in self-love, pride and arrogancy against God; the one whereof is the most substantial Heaven, the other the most real Hell; whereas, indeed, by conquering ourselves, we are translated from death to life, and the kingdom of God and Heaven is already come into us.

Chapter VIII

> *The sixth property or effect discovering the excellency of religion, viz., that it spiritualizes material things and carries up the souls of good men from sensible and earthly things to things intellectual and divine. There are lesser and fuller representations of God in the creatures. To converse with God in the creation and to pass out of the sensible world into the intellectual is most effectually taught by religion. Wicked men converse not with God, as shining out in the creatures; they converse with them in a sensual and unspiritual manner. Religion does spiritualize the creation to good men; it teaches them to look at any perfections or excellencies in themselves and others, not so much as theirs or others, but as so many beams flowing from one and the same fountain of light; to love them all in God, and God in all—the universal goodness in a particular being. A good man enjoys and delights in whatsoever good he sees otherwhere, as if it were his own: he does not fondly love and esteem either himself or others. The divine temper and strain of the ancient philosophy.*

6. The *sixth* property or effect, wherein religion discovers its own excellency, is this, *that it spiritualizes material things, and so carries up the souls of good men from earthly things to things divine, from this sensible world to the intellectual.*

God made the universe and all the creatures contained therein, as so many glasses wherein he might reflect his own glory. He hath copied forth himself in the creation; and, in this outward world, we may read the lovely characters of the divine goodness, power and wisdom. In some creatures, there are darker representations of God; there are the prints and footsteps of God; but in others, there are clearer and fuller repre-

sentations of the Divinity, the face and image of God; according to that
known saying of the Schoolmen, "The more remote likenesses of the
creature to God are called a token; the closer ones truly a likeness." But
how to find God here, and feelingly converse with him, and, being
affected with the sense of the divine glory shining out upon the creation,
how to pass out of the sensible world into the intellectual, is not so effectually taught by that philosophy which professed it most, as by true
religion; that which knits and unites God and the soul together, can best
teach it how to ascend and descend upon those golden links that unite,
as it were, the world to God. That divine wisdom that contrived and
beautified this glorious structure can best explain her own art and carry
up the soul back again, in these reflected beams, to him who is the fountain
of them. Though good men, all of them, are not acquainted with all
those philosophical notions touching the relation between created and
uncreated being, yet may they easily find every creature pointing out to
that Being, whose image and superscription it bears, and climb up from
those darker resemblances of the divine wisdom and goodness, shining out
in different degrees upon several creatures, ὥσπερ ἀναβάθμος τισί [as a flight
of stairs to certain ones], as the ancients speak, till they sweetly repose
themselves in the bosom of the Divinity; and while they are thus conversing with this lower world, and are viewing "the invisible things of
God in the things that are made" [cf. Rom. 1:20], in this visible and
outward creation they find God, many times, secretly flowing into their
souls, and leading them silently out of the court of the temple into the
holy place. But it is otherwise with wicked men. They dwell perpetually
upon the dark side of the creatures, and converse with these things only
in a gross, sensual, earthly, and unspiritual manner. They are so encom-
passed with the thick and foggy mist of their own corruptions that they
cannot see God there, where he is most visible: "The light shineth in darkness, but the darkness comprehendeth it not" [Jn. 1:5]. Their souls are so
deeply sunk into that house of clay which they carry about with them,
that were there nothing of body or bulky matter before them, they could
find nothing to exercise themselves about.

But religion, where it is in truth and in power, renews the very spirit of
our minds, and doth, in a manner, spiritualize this outward creation to us,
and doth, in a more excellent way, perform that which the Peripatetics
are wont to affirm of their *intellectus agens* [active understanding], in
purging bodily and material things from the feculency and dregs of
matter, and separating them from those circumstantiating and straitening

conditions of time and place, and the like; and teaches the soul to look at those perfections which it finds here below, not so much as the perfections of this or that body, as they adorn this or that particular being, but as they are so many rays issuing forth from that first and essential perfection, in which they all meet, and embrace one another in the most close friendship. Every particular good is a blossom of the first goodness; every created excellency is a beam descending from the Father of lights [Jas. 1:17]. And should we separate all these particularities from God, all affection spent upon them would be unchaste and their embraces adulterous. We should love all things in God and God in all things, because he is all in all, the beginning and original of being, the perfect idea of their goodness and the end of their motion. It is nothing but a thick mist of pride and self-love that hinders men's eyes from beholding that sun which both enlightens them and all things else. But when true religion begins once to dawn upon men's souls, and, with its shining light, chases away their black night of ignorance, then they behold themselves and all things else enlightened, though in a different way, by one and the same sun, and all the powers of their souls fall down before God and ascribe all glory to him. Now it is that a good man is no more solicitous "whether this or that good thing be *mine*, or whether *my* perfections exceed the measure of *this* or *that* particular creature"; for whatsoever good he beholds anywhere, he enjoys and delights in it as much as if it were his own, and whatever he beholds in himself, he looks not upon it as his property, but as a common good; for all these beams come from one and the same fountain and ocean of light, in whom he loves them all with a universal love. When his affections run along the stream of any created excellencies, whether his own or any one's else, yet they stay not here, but run on till they fall into the ocean. They do not settle into a fond love and admiration, either of his own or any other's excellencies, but he regards them as so many pure effluxes and emanations from God, and, in a particular being, loves the universal goodness.

Thus may a good man walk up and down the world as in a garden of spices, and suck a divine sweetness out of every flower. There is a twofold meaning in every creature, as the Jews speak of their law—a literal and a mystical—and the one is but the ground of the other; and, as they say of divers pieces of their law, so a good man says of everything that his senses offer to him—"it speaks to his lower part, but it points out something above to his mind and spirit." It is the drowsy and muddy spirit of superstition which, being lulled asleep in the lap of worldly delights, is fain to set some idol at its elbow, something that may jog it and put it in mind of God. Whereas true religion never finds itself out of the infinite sphere of the Divinity, and wherever it finds beauty, harmony, goodness, love, ingenuousness, wisdom, holiness, justice and the like, it is ready to say, here, and there is God. Wheresoever any such perfections shine out, a holy mind climbs up by these sunbeams and raises itself up to God.

And seeing God hath never thrown the world from himself, but runs through all created essence, containing the archetypal ideas of all things in himself, and from thence deriving and imparting several prints of beauty and excellency all the world over; a soul that is truly θεοειδής, "god-like"— a mind that is enlightened from the same fountain, and hath its inward senses affected with the sweet relishes of divine goodness, cannot but everywhere behold itself in the midst of that glorious, unbounded Being who is indivisibly everywhere. A good man finds every place he treads upon holy ground; to him the world is God's temple; he is ready to say with Jacob, "How dreadful is this place! This is none other but the house of God" [Gen. 28:17].

To conclude: it was a degenerate and unworthy spirit in that philosophy which first separated and made such distances between metaphysical truths and the truths of nature; whereas, the first and most ancient wisdom amongst the heathens was indeed a philosophical divinity, or a divine philosophy, which continued for divers ages. But, as men grow worse, their queasy stomachs began to loathe it; which made the truly wise Socrates complain of the Sophists of that age, who began now to corrupt and debase it; whereas heretofore the spirit of philosophy was more generous and divine, and did more purify and ennoble the souls of men, commending intellectual things to them, and taking them off from settling upon sensible and material things here below, and still exciting them to endeavor after the nearest resemblance to God, the supreme goodness and loveliness, and an intimate conjunction with him; which, according to the strain of that philosophy, was the true happiness of immortal souls.

Chapter IX

The seventh and last property or effect discovering the excellency of religion, viz., that it raiseth the minds of good men to a due observance of and attendance upon divine Providence, and enables them to serve the will of God and to acquiesce in it. For a man to serve Providence and the will of God entirely, to work with God, and to

bring himself, and all his actions, into a compliance with God's will,
his ends and designs, is an argument of the truest nobleness of spirit;
it is the most excellent and divine life; and it is most for man's ad-
vantage. How the consideration of divine Providence is the way to
inward quietness and establishment of spirit. How wicked men carry
themselves unbecomingly through their impatience and fretfulness
under the disposals of Providence. The beauty and harmony of the
various methods of Providence.

7. The *seventh* and last property or effect wherein true religion expresseth its own nobleness and excellency, is this, *that it raiseth the minds*
of good men to a due observance of, and attendance upon, divine Provi-
dence, and enables them to serve the will of God, and to acquiesce in it.
Wheresoever God hath a tongue to speak, there they have ears to hear;
and, being attentive to God in the soft and still motions of Providence,
they are ready to obey his call, and to say with Isaiah, "Behold, here am I;
send me" [Is. 6:8]. They endeavor to copy forth that lesson which Christ
hath set Christians, seriously considering how that they came into this
world by God's appointment, not to do their own wills, but the will of
him that sent them.

As this consideration quiets the spirit of a good man, who is no idle
spectator of Providence, and keeps him in a calm and sober temper in the
midst of all storms and tempests, so it makes him most freely to engage
himself in the service of Providence, without any inward reluctancy or
disturbance. He cannot be content that Providence should make use of
him, as it doth even of those things that understand it least; but it is his
holy ambition to serve it. It is nothing but hellish pride and self-love that
makes men serve themselves, and so set up themselves as idols against God;
but it is, indeed, an argument of true nobleness of spirit for a man to view
himself, not in the narrow point of his own being, but in the unbounded
essence of the First Cause, so as to be ὅλως τῶν κρειττόνων,[51] and to live only
as an instrument in the hands of God, who worketh all things after the
counsel of his own will [Eph. 1:11]. "I would wish to be to God what my
hand is to me," was the expression of a holy soul.

To a good man, to serve the will of God is in the truest and best sense
to serve himself, who knows himself to be nothing without or in opposition to God. This is the most divine life that can be, for a man to act in
the world upon eternal designs, and to be so wholly devoted to the will of
God, as to serve it faithfully and entirely. This, indeed, bestows a kind of

51. [ED.] Cf. Simplicius, *On the Enchiridion of Epictetus*, Preface: " . . . wholly
of the things which are best."

immortality upon these flitting and transient acts of ours which in themselves are but the offspring of a moment. A pillar or a verse is a poor
sorry monument of any exploit, which yet may well enough become the
highest of the world's bravery. But good men, while they work with God
and endeavor to bring themselves and all their actions to a unity with God,
his ends and designs, enroll themselves in eternity. This is the proper
character of holy souls: their wills are so fully resolved into the divine will,
that they in all things subscribe to it without any murmurings or debates.
They rest well satisfied with and take complacency in any passages of
divine dispensation, as being ordered and disposed by a mind and wisdom
above, according to the highest rules of goodness.

The best way for a man rightly to enjoy himself is to maintain a universal, ready and cheerful compliance with the divine and uncreated will
in all things, as knowing that nothing can issue and flow forth from the
fountain of goodness but that which is good. And therefore a good man
is never offended with any piece of divine dispensation, nor hath he any
reluctancy against that will that dictates and determines all things by an
eternal rule of goodness; as knowing that there is an unbounded and almighty love that, without any disdain or envy, freely communicates itself
to everything he made; that makes his sun to shine and his rain to fall both
upon the just and unjust; that always infolds those in his everlasting arms,
who are made partakers of his own image, perpetually nourishing and
cherishing them with the fresh and vital influences of his grace; as knowing
also, that there is an all-seeing eye, an unbounded mind and understanding,
that derives itself through the whole universe, and, sitting in all the wheels
of motion, guides them all and powerfully governs the most eccentrical
motions [52] of creatures and carries them all most harmoniously in their
several orbs to one last end. Who then shall give law to God? "Where is
the wise? Where is the scribe? Where is the disputer of this world?"
[1 Cor. 1:20] Where is he that would climb up into that great consistory
in Heaven, and, sitting in consultation with the Almighty, instruct the
infinite and incomprehensible Wisdom? Shall vain man be wiser than his
Maker? This is the hellish temper of wicked men: they examine and judge
of all things by the line and measure of their own self-will, their own
opinions and designs; and, measuring all things by a crooked rule, they
think nothing to be straight; and, therefore, they fall out with God, and
with restless impatience fret and vex themselves; and this fretfulness and

52. [ED.] I.e., those of a circle.

impatiency in wicked men argues a breach in the just and due constitution of their minds and spirits.

But a good man, whose soul is restored to that frame and constitution in which it should be, has better apprehensions of the ways and works of God, and is better affected under the various disposals of Providence. Indeed, to a superficial observer of divine Providence, many things there are that seem to be nothing else but digressions from the main end of all, and to come to pass by a fortuitous concourse of circumstances, that come in so abruptly and without any concatenation or dependence one upon another, as if they were without any mind or understanding to guide them. But a wise man that looks from the beginning to the end of things, beholds them all in their due place and method, acting that part which the supreme Mind and Wisdom, that governs all things, hath appointed them; and carrying on one and the same eternal design, while they move according to their own proper inclinations and measures, and aim at their own particular ends. It were not worth the while to live in a world κενῷ θεοῦ καὶ προνοίας—"devoid of God and Providence"—as it was well observed by the Stoic.[53] And to be subservient unto Providence, is the holy ambition and great endeavor of a good man, who is so perfectly overpowered with the love of the universal and infinite goodness, that he would not serve any particular good whatsoever; no, not himself, so as to set up in the world and trade for himself, as the men of this world do, who are "lovers of their own selves, and lovers of pleasures more than lovers of God" [2 Tim. 3:2,4].

Chapter x

4. The excellency of religion in regard of its progress, as it is perpetually carrying on the soul towards perfection. Every nature hath its proper center to which it hastens. Sin and wickedness is within the attractive power of Hell, and hastens thither. It is not the speculation of Heaven, as a thing to come, that satisfies the desires of religious souls, but the real possession of it, even in this life. Men are apt to seek after assurance of Heaven as a thing to come, rather than after Heaven itself, and the inward possession of it here. How the assurance of Heaven rises from the growth of holiness, and the powerful progress of religion in our souls. That we are not hastily to believe that we are Christ's, or that Christ is in us. That the works which Christ does in holy souls testify of him, and the best evidence Christ's spiritual appearance in them.

53. [ED.] Cf. Marcus Antoninus, *De Seipso*, Bk. II, 8.

We have considered the excellency of true religion, 1. In regard of its descent and original; 2. In regard of its nature; 3. In regard of its properties and effects. We now proceed to a fourth particular, and shall show,

4. That religion is a generous and noble thing in regard of its progress; it is perpetually carrying on that mind, in which it is once seated, towards perfection. Though the first appearance of it, upon the souls of good men, may be but as the wings of the morning spreading themselves upon the mountains, yet is it still rising higher and higher upon them, chasing away all the filthy mists and vapors of sin and wickedness before it, till it arrives at its meridian altitude. There is the strength and force of the Divinity in it; and though, when it first enters into the minds of men, it may seem to be "sown in weakness," yet will it raise itself in power [cf. 1 Cor. 15:42–44]. As Christ was in his bodily appearance still increasing in wisdom and knowledge and favor with God and man [Lk. 2:52] until he was perfected in glory, so is he also in his spiritual appearance in the souls of men; and accordingly the New Testament does more than once distinguish between Christ in his several ages and degrees of growth in the souls of all true Christians. Good men are always "walking on from strength to strength, till at last they see God in Zion" [cf. Ps. 84:7]. Religion, though it hath its infancy, yet hath it no old age: while it is in its minority, it is always *in motu* [in motion]; but when it comes to its maturity and full age, it will always be *in quiete* [in repose]—it is then "always the same, and its years fail not, but it shall endure for ever" [cf. Heb. 1:12]. Holy and religious souls, being once touched with an inward sense of divine beauty and goodness, by a strong impress upon them are moved swiftly after God, and, as the apostle expresses himself, "forgetting those things which are behind, and reaching forth unto those things which are before, they press toward the mark for the prize of the high calling of God in Christ Jesus"; that so they may "attain to the resurrection of the dead" [Phil. 3:11,13,14].

Where a spirit of religion is, there is the central force of Heaven itself, quickening and enlivening those that are informed by it, in their motions towards Heaven. As, on the other side, all unhallowed and defiled minds are within the attractive power of Hell, and are continually hastening their course thither, being strongly pressed down by the weight of their wickedness. Ἀεί τινάς ἔχει κινήσες ἡ φύσις, as Plutarch hath well observed— "Every nature in this world hath some proper center to which it is always hastening." Sin and wickedness do not hover a little over the bottomless pit of Hell, and only flutter about it; but it is continually sinking lower and lower into it. Neither does true grace make some feeble assays towards

Heaven, but, by a mighty energy within itself, it is always soaring up higher and higher into Heaven. A good Christian does not only court his happiness, and cast now and then a smile upon it, or satisfy himself merely to be contracted to it; but, with the greatest ardors of love and desire, he pursues the solemnity of the just nuptials, that he may be wedded to it and made one with it. It is not an airy speculation of Heaven as a thing (though never so undoubtedly) to come, that can satisfy his hungry desires, but the real possession of it even in this life. Such a happiness would be less in the esteem of good men, that were only good to be enjoyed at the end of this life, when all other enjoyments fail him.

I wish there be not, among some, such a light and poor esteem of Heaven, as makes them more to seek after assurance of Heaven only in the idea of it as a thing to come, than after Heaven itself; which, indeed, we can never well be assured of, until we find it rising up within ourselves and glorifying our own souls. When true assurance comes, Heaven itself will appear upon the horizon of our souls like a morning light, chasing away all our dark and gloomy doubtings before it. We shall not need then to light up our candles to seek for it in corners. No, it will display its own luster and brightness so before us, that we may see it in its own light, and ourselves the true possessors of it. We may be too nice and vain in seeking for signs and tokens of Christ's spiritual appearances in the souls of men, as well as the Scribes and Pharisees were in seeking for them at his first appearance in the world. When he comes into us, let us expect till the works that he shall do within us may testify of him, and be not overcredulous, till we find that he doth those works there which none other could do. As for a true well-grounded assurance, say not so much, "Who shall ascend up into heaven," to fetch it down from thence? or, "Who shall descend into the deep" [cf. Rom. 10:6,7], to fetch it up from beneath? For in the growth of true internal goodness and in the progress of true religion it will freely unfold itself within us. Stay till the grain of mustard seed itself breaks forth from among the clods that buried it; till, through the descent of the heavenly dew, it sprouts up, and discovers itself openly. This holy assurance is, indeed, the budding and blossoming of felicity in our own souls; it is the inward sense and feeling of the true life, spirit, sweetness and beauty of grace, powerfully expressing its own energy within us.

Briefly: true religion, in the progress of it, transforms those minds in which it reigns, from glory to glory. It goes on and prospers in bringing all enemies in subjection under their feet, in reconciling the minds of men fully to God; and it instates them in a firm possession of the supreme good. This is the seed of God within holy souls, which is always warring against the seed of the serpent, till it prevail over it, through the divine strength and influence. Though Hell may open her mouth wide and without measure, yet a true Christian, in whom the seed of God remaineth, is in a good and safe condition: he finds himself borne up by an almighty arm, and carried upwards as upon eagles' wings; and the evil one hath no power over him; or, as St. John expresseth it, "The evil one toucheth him not" [1 Jn. 5:18].

Chapter XI

5. The excellency of religion in regard of its term and end, viz., perfect blessedness. How unable we are, in this state, to comprehend and describe the full and perfect state of happiness and glory to come. The more godlike a Christian is, the better may he understand that state. Holiness and happiness not two distinct things, but two several notions of one and the same thing. Heaven cannot so well be defined by anything without us, as by something within us. The great nearness and affinity between sin and Hell. The conclusion of this treatise, containing a serious exhortation to a diligent minding of religion, with a discovery of the vanity of those pretences which keep men off from minding religion.

5. We come now to the *fifth* and last particular, *viz., the excellency of religion in the term and end of it, which is nothing else but blessedness itself in its full maturity*. Which yet I may not here undertake to explain, for it is altogether "inexpressible," nor can it descend so low as to accommodate itself to any human style. Accordingly, St. John tells us, "it does not yet appear what we shall be"; and yet, that he may give us some glimpse of it, he directs us to God, and tells us, "We shall be like him, for we shall see him as he is" [1 Jn. 3:2]. Indeed, the best way to get a discovery of it is to endeavor, as much as may be, to be god-like, to live in a feeling converse with God, and in a powerful exercise and expression of all god-like dispositions. So shall our inner man be best enabled "to know the breadth and length, the depth and height, of that love and goodness which yet passeth all knowledge" [cf. Rom. 11:33; Eph. 3:18–19]. There is a state of perfection in the life to come, so far transcendent to any in this life, as that we are not able, from hence, to take the just proportions of it, or to form a full and comprehensive notion of it. We are unable to comprehend the vastness and fullness of that happiness to

which the most purified souls may be raised, or to apprehend how far the mighty power and strength of the Divinity, deriving itself into created being, may communicate a more transcendent life and blessedness to it. We know not what latent powers our souls may here contain within themselves, to let in the full streams of the divine goodness, when they come nearly and intimately to converse with it; or how blessedness may act upon those faculties of our minds which we now have. We know not what illapses and irradiations there may be from God upon souls in glory, that may raise them into a state of perfection surpassing all our imaginations.

As for corporeal happiness, there cannot be anything further added to the pleasure of our bodies or animal part, than a restoring of it from disturbing passion and pain, to its just and natural constitution; and, therefore, some philosophers have well disputed against the opinion of the Epicureans, who make happiness to consist in bodily pleasure, "seeing that the antecedent pain is many times more intense," [54] and when the molestation is gone, and the just constitution of nature recovered, pleasure ceaseth. But the highest pleasure of minds and spirits does not only consist in the relieving of them from any antecedent pains or grief, or in a relaxation from some former molesting passion; neither is their happiness a mere Stoical ἀταραξία [tranquility], as the happiness of the Deity is not a mere negative thing, rendering it free from all disturbance or molestation, so that it may eternally rest quiet within itself. It does not so much consist *in quiete*, as *in actu et vigore*. A mind and spirit is too full of activity and energy, is too quick and potent a thing, to enjoy a full and complete happiness in a mere cessation; this were to make happiness a heavy, spiritless thing. The philosopher hath well observed that there is infinite power and strength in divine joy, pleasure and happiness, commensurate with that Almighty Being and Goodness who is the eternal source of it.[55]

As created beings that are capable of conversing with God stand nearer to God or further off from him, and as they partake more or less of his likeness, so they partake more or less of that happiness which flows forth from him, and God communicates himself in different degrees to them. There may be as many degrees of sanctity and perfection as there are of states and conditions of creatures. And that is properly sanctity, which guides and orders all the faculties and actions of any creature in a way suitable and correspondent to that rank and state in which God hath

54. [ED.] Simplicius, *On the Enchiridion of Epictetus*, Ch. I, §1.
55. [ED.] Simplicius, *On the Enchiridion of Epictetus*, Ch. I, §1.

placed it; and while it doth so, it admits no sin or defilement to itself, though yet it may be elevated and advanced higher. And accordingly true positive sanctity comes to be advanced higher and higher, as any creature comes more to partake of the life of God and to be brought into a nearer conjunction with God; and so, the sanctity and happiness of innocency itself might have been perfected.

Thus we see how true religion carries up the souls of good men above the black regions of Hell and death. This, indeed, is the great ἀποκατάστασις [complete restoration] of souls. It is religion itself, or a real participation of God and his holiness, which is their true restitution and advancement. All that happiness which good men shall be made partakers of, as it cannot be borne up upon any other foundation than true goodness and a god-like nature within them, so neither is it distinct from it. Sin and Hell are so twined and twisted up together that if the power of sin be once dissolved, the bonds of death and Hell will also fall asunder. Sin and Hell are of the same kind, of the same lineage and descent; as, on the other side, true holiness or religion and true happiness are but two several notions of one thing, rather than distinct in themselves. Religion delivers us from Hell by instating us in a possession of true life and bliss. Hell is rather a nature than a place; and Heaven cannot be so truly defined by anything without us, as by something that is within us.

Thus have we done with those particulars, wherein we considered the excellency and nobleness of religion, which is here expressed by "the way of life" and elsewhere is styled by Solomon "a tree of life" [Prov. 15:4; 3:18], true religion being an inward principle of life, of a divine life, the best life, that which is life, most properly so called. Accordingly, in the Holy Scripture, a life of religion is styled life, as a life of sin and wickedness is styled death. In the ancient academical philosophy it was much disputed whether that corporeal and animal life, which was always drawing down the soul into terrene and material things, was not more properly to be styled death than life. What sense hereof the Pythagoreans had may appear by this practice of theirs: they were wont to set up empty coffins in the places of those that had forsaken their school and degenerated from their philosophy and good precepts, as being apostates from life itself and dead to virtue and a good life, which is the true life, and therefore fit only to be reckoned among the dead.[56]

For a conclusion of this discourse: the use which we shall make of all shall be this—to awaken and exhort every one to a serious minding of

56. [ED.] Iamblichus, *Life of Pythagoras*, Ch. 17.

religion; as Solomon doth earnestly exhort every one to seek after true wisdom, which is the same with religion and holiness, as sin is with folly: "Get wisdom, get understanding"; and "Get wisdom, and with all thy getting get understanding. Wisdom is the principal thing" [Prov. 4:5,7]. This is the sum of all, "the conclusion of the whole matter, Fear God, and keep his commandments; for this is the whole duty," business and concernment "of man" [Eccl. 12:13]. Let us not trifle away our time and opportunities which God hath given us, wherein we may lay hold upon life and immortality, in doing nothing or else pursuing Hell and death. Let us awake out of our vain dreams. Wisdom calls upon us, and offers us the hidden treasures of life and blessedness; let us not perpetually deliver ourselves over to laziness and slumbering. Say not, "There is a lion in the way" [Prov. 22:13]; say not, though religion be good, yet it is unattainable. No—but let us unite all our powers in a serious, resolved pursuance of it, and depend upon the assistance of Heaven which never fails those that soberly seek for it. It is, indeed, the levity of men's spirits, their heedlessness and regardlessness of their own lives, that betrays them to sin and death. It is the general practice of men "to extemporize in their handling of life," as the satirist speaks. They ordinarily ponder and deliberate upon everything more than how it becomes them to live. They so live as if their bodies had swallowed up their souls. Their lives are but a kind of lottery. The principles by which they are guided are nothing else but a confused multitude of fancies rudely jumbled together. Such is the life of most men: it is but a mere casual thing acted over at peradventure, without any fair and calm debates held either with religion or with reason, which in itself, as it is not distorted and depraved by corrupt men, is a true friend to religion, and directs men to God, and to things good and just, pure, lovely and praiseworthy; and the directions of this inward guide we are not to neglect. Unreasonableness, or the smothering and extinguishing the candle of the Lord within us, is no piece of religion, nor advantageous to it. That, certainly, will not raise men up to God which sinks them below men. There had never been such an apostasy from religion, nor had such a mystery of iniquity, full of deceivableness and imposture, been revealed and wrought so powerfully in the souls of some men, had there not first come an apostasy from sober reason, had there not first been a falling away and departure from natural truth.

It is to be feared our nice speculations about what concerns us in theology have tended more to exercise men's wits than to reform their lives, and that they have too much descended into their practice, and have tended rather to take men off from minding religion than to quicken them up to a diligent seeking after it. Though the powers of nature may now be weakened, and though we cannot produce a living form of religion in our own souls; yet we are not surely so resolved into a sluggish passiveness as that we cannot, or were not, in any kind or manner of way, to seek after it. Certainly a man may as well read the Scriptures as study a piece of Aristotle or of natural philosophy or mathematics. He that can observe anything comely and commendable, or unworthy and base, in another man, may also reflect upon himself, and see how "face answereth to face," as Solomon speaks [Prov. 27:19]. If men would seriously commune with their hearts, their own consciences would tell them plainly that they might avoid and omit more evil than they do, and that they might do more good than they do; and that they do not put forth that power which God hath given them, nor faithfully use those talents, nor improve the advantages and means afforded them.

I fear the ground of most men's misery will prove to be a second fall, and a lapse upon a lapse. I doubt God will not allow that proverb, "The fathers have eaten sour grapes, and the children's teeth are set on edge" [Ezek. 18:2], as not in respect of temporal misery, much less will he allow it in respect of eternal. It will not be so much because our first parents incurred God's displeasure, as because we have neglected what might have been done by us afterwards, in order to the seeking of God's face and favor while he might be found.

Up then and be doing, and the Lord will be with us. He will not leave us nor forsake us if we seriously set ourselves about the work. Let us endeavor to acquaint ourselves with our own lives, and the true rules of life, with this which Solomon here calls "the way of life." Let us inform our minds, as much as may be, in the excellency and loveliness of practical religion, that, beholding it in its own beauty and amiableness, we may the more sincerely close with it. As there would need nothing else to deter and affright men from sin but its own ugliness and deformity, were it presented to a naked view and seen as it is, so nothing would more effectually commend religion to the minds of men than displaying and unfolding the excellencies of its nature, than the true native beauty and inward luster of religion itself. "Neither the evening, nor the morning star" [57] could so sensibly commend itself to our bodily eyes, and delight them with its shining beauties, as true religion (which is an undefiled beam of the

57. [ED.] Smith is quoting from Aristotle (*Nicomachean Ethics*, Bk. V, Ch. 1), who in turn was quoting from Euripides (*Melanippe*, 486).

uncreated light) would to a mind capable of conversing with it. Religion, which is the true wisdom, is, as the author of the Book of Wisdom speaks of wisdom, "a pure influence flowing from the glory of the Almighty, . . . the brightness of the everlasting light, the unspotted mirror of the power of God, and the image of his goodness. . . . She is more beautiful than the sun, and above all the order of the stars; being compared with the light she is found before it" [Wisd. 7:25,26,29].

Religion is no such austere, sour and rigid thing, as to affright men away from it. No, but those that are acquainted with the power of it find it to be altogether sweet and amiable. A holy soul sees so much of the glory of religion in the lively impressions which it bears upon itself, as both woos and wins it. We may truly say concerning religion, to such souls, as St. Paul spake to the Corinthians, "Needs it any epistle of commendation to you?" Needs it anything to court your affections? "Ye are indeed its epistle, written, not with ink, but with the Spirit of the living God" [2 Cor. 3:1–3].

Religion is not like the prophet's roll, sweet as honey when it was in his mouth, but bitter as gall in his belly [Ezek. 3:3]. Religion is no sullen Stoicism, no sour Pharisaism. It does not consist in a few melancholy passions, in some dejected looks or depressions of mind, but it consists in freedom, love, peace, life and power. The more it comes to be digested into our lives, the more sweet and lovely we shall find it to be. Those spots and wrinkles which corrupt minds think they see in the face of religion are, indeed, nowhere else but in their own deformed and misshapen apprehensions. It is no wonder when a defiled fancy comes to be the glass, if you have an unlovely reflection. Let us therefore labor to purge our own souls from all worldly pollutions; let us breathe after the aid and assistance of the divine Spirit, that it may irradiate and enlighten our minds, that we may be able to see divine things in a divine light. Let us endeavor to live more in a real practice of those rules of religious and holy living, commended to us by our ever-blessed Lord and Savior. So we shall know religion better, and knowing it, love it; and, loving it, be still more and more ambitiously pursuing after it, till we come to a full attainment of it, and, therein, of our own perfection and everlasting bliss.

HENRY MORE

A Brief Discourse of the True Grounds of the Certainty of Faith in Points of Religion

Editor's Introduction. More's works are seldom terse or condensed. Many of them reach an inordinate length. This *Brief Discourse* is a conspicuous exception to the rule, and it is virtually the only one of his writings to which the designation "brief" can appropriately be applied. It is, as well, a valuable summary of many of the Platonists' most characteristic teachings. At the outset More explicitly repudiates, as a ground of confidence, the dogmatism which was so conspicuous in a great deal of seventeenth-century debate, and in his plea for a charitable spirit he reflects the generous outlook of the whole Cambridge school. He stresses the necessary role of reason in religious enquiry, and here again he brings into sharp focus one of the distinctive emphases of his associates. This leads to another point of vital importance to the Platonists: that spiritual understanding is clarified and confirmed by moral experience. More is also explicit about the importance of revelation and the place that must be assigned to Scripture. There are few aspects of the thought of the Cambridge Platonists that are not clarified by one or other of More's thirty-three points.

✤　✤　✤　✤

Faith and belief, though they be usually appropriated to matters of religion, yet those words in themselves signify nothing else but *a persuasion touching the truth of a thing arising from some ground or other.* Which persuasion may be undoubted or certain to us, that is to say, we may be certainly persuaded without any staggering, though the grounds be false and the thing itself false that we are thus firmly persuaded of. So that the being firmly persuaded is no sure sign to others, nor ought to be to ourselves, that either the grounds or the belief itself is true. . . .

But the true grounds of the certainty of faith are such as do not only beget a certain and firm faith, but a true one, and this in virtue of their own truth and solidity, as being such as will appear true and solid to all impartial and unprejudiced examiners, that is to say, to all such as neither complexion, nor education, nor passion, nor interest does pervert their judgment, but have their "kindling" clear as the eye to discriminate colors. Whence it is plain that the first and most necessary preparation to the discovery of the true grounds of the certainty of faith is moral prudence, in such a sense as the nature of it is described in a late moral discourse entitled *Enchiridion Ethicum*.[1] This ought to be antecedaneous to our judgment touching either authority or reason. But for a man of a polluted spirit to take upon him to dissent from the constitutions of the Church he is born under, is a very rash and insolent attempt. As if God were more bound to assist a single wicked man for the finding out of truth, than a multitude; or as if a man could more safely or more creditably err alone, than with a company that has the stamp of authority upon them. But if thy endeavor be to perfect holiness in the fear of God, and to walk in all humility before him and before men, thou mayest by such rational grounds as these examine the fidelity of thy teachers, and the truth of their doctrines of religion.

First then, it is plain that certainty of faith presupposeth certainty of both reason and sense rightly circumstantiated. For, forasmuch as faith properly so called is nothing but an unwavering assent to some doctrine proposed upon the ground of infallible testimony, there must be some reason to persuade us that that testimony is infallible; that is to say, that they that testify are neither obnoxious to error in the things they witness of, nor have a mind to make others to err or to think what is false, or else that they never had any opportunity of falsifying in the points they propound to our belief.[2] Certainty of sense is also required. For if the sense be not certain, there could be no infallible testimony of matter of fact, and Moses' conversing with God in the Mount may be but a dream; nor could there be any certain eye-witness of our Savior's resurrection and ascension, if God will delude our senses. Wherefore to take away the certainty of sense rightly circumstantiated, is to take away all certainty of belief in the main points of our religion.

1. [ED.] This work was one of More's chief contributions to ethics and was published in 1667. Its full title was *Enchiridion Ethicum, Praecipua Moralis Philosophiae Rudimenta complectens*. By 1711 the fourth Latin edition had appeared. An English translation by Edward Southwell was published under the title *An Account of Virtue: or, Dr. Henry More's Abridgment of Morals, Put into English* (London, 1690).

2. [ED.] This formal definition of faith is in direct line with those of Thomas Aquinas (*Summa Theol.*, Pt. II (II), Q.4) and Trent (cf. H. Denzinger, *Enchiridion Symbolorum* (28th ed., Freiburg-im-Breisgau, 1952), 798, 822.

Secondly, sense and reason are rightly circumstantiated, the one, when the organ is sound, the medium fitly qualified, and the distance of the object duly proportionated, and the like; the other, when it is accompanied with moral prudence rightly so called, such as it is defined in the above-said *Enchiridion*, that is to say, that this reason be lodged either in a perfectly unprejudiced mind, or at least unprejudiced touching the point propounded. For there are some truths so clear, that immorality itself (provided it do not besot a man or make him quite mad) puts no bar to the assenting to them, that is, puts no bar to their appearing to be true, no more than it does to the eye unhurt to the discerning of colors; which the wicked and godly do alike upon this supposition. Wherefore,

The third conclusion shall be, that there be natural truths, whether logical, physical, or mathematical, that are so palpably true, that they constantly and perpetually appear so as well to the wicked as the good, if they be *compotes mentis*, and do not manifest violence to their faculties.

The fourth, that these natural truths, whether common notions or scientifical conclusions, that are so palpably true that they perpetually appear so as well to the evil as the good, are at least as certain and indubitable as anything that the reason and understanding of a man can give assent to; that is to say, there is at least as great a certainty of these axioms that are true, as there can be of any. And therefore, because there is acknowledged a certainty in some points that our understanding and reason closeth with, let us set down for

The fifth conclusion, that these natural truths that constantly appear such as well to the evil as the good (if they be not crack-brained nor do violence to their faculties) are in themselves most certainly true.

The sixth, that what is a contradiction to a certain truth is not only uncertain, but necessarily false, forasmuch as both the parts of a contradiction cannot be true.

The seventh, that no revelation which either itself, or the revealing thereof, or its manner of revealing, is repugnant to the divine attributes, can be from God.

The eighth, that no tradition of any such revelation can be true, forasmuch as the revelation itself is impossible.

The ninth, that no revelation is from God that is repugnant to sense rightly circumstantiated. This is manifest from the first ground, that certainty of faith presupposeth certainty of sense duly circumstantiated. For if our senses may be mistaken when they act in due circumstances, we cannot be assured that they are at any time true. Which necessarily destroys the certainty of all revelation *ab extra* and all tradition, and consequently of our Christian religion. Wherefore God cannot be the author of any such revelation, by conclusion the seventh: for it were repugnant to his wisdom and goodness.

The tenth, that no revelation is from God that contradicts plain natural truths such as were above described. This is abundantly clear from conclusion the first, second, third, fourth, fifth, sixth, seventh. For if reason where it is clearest is false, we have no assurance it is ever true and therefore no certainty of faith, which presupposes reason, by conclusion the first. Besides, by conclusion the sixth, that which is contradictory to a certain truth is certainly false. But divine revelation is true. Therefore there can be no revelation from God that bears with it such a contradiction. Nay, we may add that if there were any truth that would constantly appear to reason rightly circumstantiated contradictory to any constant natural truth, God would not communicate any such truth to men, by conclusion the seventh. For the revealing of such a truth were repugnant to his attribute of wisdom, it making thereby true religion as obnoxious to suspicion and exception as false. For there is no greater exception against the truth of any religion than that it proposes articles that are repugnant to common notions or indubitable science. Besides that one such pretence of true revelation would enable a false priesthood to fill the world with figments and lies. Wherefore God will never be the author of so much mischief to mankind. And lastly, since the first revelation must be handed down by tradition, and tradition being but human testimony, and infinitely more lubricous and fallible than natural science, how will it be possible for any but sots or fools to believe tradition against solid science or common notion? So that the result must needs be either blind superstition, gross irreligion, or universal skepticism.

The eleventh, that no revelation that enforces, countenances, or abets immorality or dishonesty can be from God. This is manifested from the seventh conclusion. For it is repugnant to God's attributes, his justice, fidelity, goodness, and purity or sanctity. The image of God is righteousness and true holiness; wherefore no doctrine that tends to injustice, unrighteousness and impurity can be a revelation from God.

The twelfth, that no interpretation of any divine revelation that is repugnant to sense or reason rightly circumstantiated, or to plain and indubitable morality, whether it be made by a private or public hand, can be any inspiration from God. There needs no new confirmation of this conclusion. For the same arguments that prove that no divine revelation can be in this sort repugnant, do prove also that no interpretation of any revelation in this sort repugnant to sense, reason or sound morality, can be divine.

The thirteenth, that no interpretation of divine writ that justifies sedition, rebellion or tyranny, can be any inspiration from God. This is easily evinced from the foregoing conclusion. For sedition and rebellion are gross and ponderous species of injustice against the magistrate, as tyranny is also against the people; both such high strains of immorality, that no interpretation of Scripture that justifies these can be true, much less divinely inspired.

The fourteenth, no church that propounds as articles of belief such things as are repugnant to rightly-circumstantiated sense and reason, or sound morality, can rightly be deemed infallible. The reason is plain, for it appears out of what has hitherto been said, that they are already actually deceived, or at least intend to deceive others.

The fifteenth, that the certainty of faith cannot be grounded upon the infallibility of any church, particular or universal, as infallibly inspired, that is deprehended to be actually deceived in any points she proposes to be believed as necessary articles of faith. This is so plain, that it wants no farther proof.

The sixteenth, that the moral and human certainty of faith grounded upon the certainty of universal tradition, prophecy, history, and the nature of things delivered, reason and sense assisting the mind in her disquisitions touching these matters. That certainty of faith I call moral or human that is compatible[2] even to a carnal man or a man unregenerate; as it is said of the devils, that they believe and tremble [Jas. 2:19]. By universal tradition I understand such a tradition as has been from the apostles, that is to say, has been always (since the completion of their apostleships,) as well as in every place of the Church. For since there was to be so general and so early a degeneracy of the Church as is witnessed of in the Holy Scriptures, the generality of the votes of the Church was not always a sufficient warrant of the truth of tradition. But those truths that have been constantly held and unalterably from the apostles' times till now, it is a sign that they were very sacred, unquestionable and assured truths, and so vulgarly and universally known and acknowledged, that it was not in man's power to alter them. By prophecy I understand as well those divine predictions of the coming of Christ, as those touching the Church after he had come. By history I mean not only that of the Bible, and particularly the New Testament, but other history as well ecclesiastic as profane. And what I mean by the nature of the things delivered is best to be understood out of such treatises as write of the reasonableness of Christianity, such as Dr. Ham-

2. [ED.] I.e., appropriate, suitable, fitting. Cf. O.E.D.

mond's and Mr. Baxter's late book.[3] See also Dr. More's *Mystery of Godliness*, where the reasonableness of our Christian faith is more fully represented, and plainly demonstrated, that it has not been in the power of the Church to deceive us as touching the main points of our belief, though they would.

The seventeenth, that no tradition is more universal and certain than the tradition of the authenticness of such books of the Bible as all churches are agreed upon to be canonical. There can be no more certain nor universal tradition than this; in that it has the testimony of the whole Church and all the parts thereof with one consent, though in other things they do so vehemently disagree. Wherefore no tradition can be of any comparable authority to this. And therefore we may set down for conclusion

The eighteenth, that the Bible is the truest ground of the certainty of faith that can be offered to our understanding to rest in. The reason is, because it is the most universal both for time and place, the most unexceptionable and universally acknowledged tradition that is; and that upon account of peculiar and most solid reasons.

The nineteenth, that the Bible or Holy Writ dictated by the Spirit of God, that is, written by holy and inspired men, is sufficiently plain to an unprejudiced capacity in all points necessary to salvation. This must of necessity be true by conclusion the seventh. Otherwise the manner of God's revealing his truth in the Holy Scriptures would be repugnant to the divine attributes, and, which were blasphemy to utter, he would seem unskillfully to have inspired the holy penmen, that is to say, in such a way as were not at all accommodate to the end of the Scriptures, which is the salvation of men's souls; not to have provided for the recovering of the Church out of those gross errors he both foresaw and foretold she would fall into.

The twentieth, that the true and primary sense of Holy Scripture is literal or historical, unless in such parts or passages thereof as are intimated to be parables or visions writ in the prophetic style, or the literal meaning be repugnant to rightly circumstantiated sense or natural science, etc. For then it is a sign that the place is to be understood figuratively or parabolically, not literally. The truth of this appears out of the immediately foregoing conclusion. For else the Scripture would not be suffi-

3. [ED.] Henry Hammond and Richard Baxter were moderates in their respective schools of thought—Laudian on the one hand, Puritan on the other. More probably refers to Hammond's *Of the Reasonableness of the Christian Religion* (1650) and Baxter's *The Unreasonableness of Infidelity* (1655).

ciently plain in all points necessary to salvation; indeed in no points at all; but all the articles of our faith that respect the history of Christ might be most frivolously and whiffingly allegorized into mere romance or fable. But that the history of Christ is literally to be understood, is manifest both from the text itself, and from perpetual and universal tradition. Which if it were not the right sense, it were a sign that it is writ exceedingly obscure even in the chief points of faith; which is contrary to the foregoing conclusion. But that those places or passages that are repugnant to rightly circumstantiated sense or natural science are to be interpreted figuratively, is plain from the general consent of all men, in that they universally agree, when Christ says, "I am the door, I am the true vine," &c. [Jn. 10:7; 15:1], that these things cannot be literally true. And there is the same reason of "Hoc est corpus meum, This is my body."

The twenty-first, that no point of faith professed from the apostles' time to this very day, and acknowledged by all churches in Christendom, but is plainly revealed in the Scripture. This may be partly argued out of the nineteenth and twentieth conclusions, and also further approved by comparing these points of faith with texts of Scripture touching the same matter.

The twenty-second, that the comprehension of these points of faith always and everywhere held by all Christian churches from the apostles' time till now, and so plain by testimony of Scripture, is most rightfully termed the common or catholic and apostolic faith.

The twenty-third, that there is a divine certainty of faith, which, besides the grounds that the moral or human certainty hath, is supported and corroborated by the spirit of life in the new birth, and by illuminated reason. This is not to be argued, but by an internal sense to be felt. In the meantime no more is asserted than this, that this divine certainty has an higher degree of firmness and assurance of the truth of the Holy Scriptures, as having partaken of the same spirit with our Savior and the apostles, but does not vary in the truths held in the common faith.

The twenty-fourth, whatever pretended inspiration or interpretation of the divine oracles is repugnant to the above-described common or catholic and apostolic faith, is imposture or falsehood, be it from a private hand or public. The reason is apparent, because the articles of this common faith were the doctrines of men truly inspired from above, and the spirit of God cannot contradict itself.

The twenty-fifth, none of the Holy Writ is of itself unintelligible, but accordingly as men's spirits shall be prepared, and the time suitable; as

God has already, so he may (as seasons shall require) still impart farther and farther light to the souls of the faithful, for a fuller and a more general understanding the obscurest passages in the divine oracles. The truth of this assertion is so clear, that it seems little better than blasphemy to contradict it. For to say the Holy Writ is itself unintelligible is equivalent to the pronouncing it nonsense, or to aver that such and such books or passages of it were never to be understood by men, is to insinuate as if the wisdom of God did not only delight itself with the children of men, but even fool with them. This is but a subterfuge of that conscious Church, that is afraid of the fulgor of that light, that shines against her out of such places of Scripture as have for a long time seemed obscure.

The twenty-sixth, that there are innumerable passages of Scripture, as well preceptive as historical, that are as plainly to be understood as the very articles of the common faith, and which therefore may be very useful for clearing those that may seem more obscure. This wants no proof but appeal to experience and the twentieth conclusion.

The twenty-seventh, that no miracle, though done by such as may seem of an unexceptionable life and of more singular sanctity, can in reason ratify any doctrine or practice that is repugnant to rightly circumstantiated sense, or natural truths or science, or the common Christian faith, or any plain doctrine or assertion in Scripture. The truth of this is manifest from hence, that no man can be so certain that such a man is not a crafty and cautious hypocrite, and his miracle either a juggle or delusion of the devil, or (if he was not an eye-witness of it) a false report of a miracle, as he is certain of the truth of rightly circumstantiated sense, of common notions and natural science, of the articles of the apostolic faith, or of any plain assertion in the Scripture. And therefore that which is most certain in this case ought in all reason to be our guide.

The twenty-eighth, that it is not only the right but the duty of private men to converse with the Scriptures, being once but precautioned not to presume to interpret anything against rightly circumstantiated sense, natural truth, common honesty, the analogy of the catholic faith, or against other plain testimonies of Holy Writ. The truth of this appears from the conclusion immediately preceding. For why should they be kept from having recourse to so many and so profitable and powerful instructions from an infallible spirit, when they are so well forearmed against all mistake, and are so laid at by so many not only fallible but fallacious and deceitful persons to seduce them? And why is there not more danger of being led into error by such as are not only fallible, but false and deceitful, than by those inspired men that wrote the Scripture, who were neither fallible in what they wrote, nor had any design to deceive any man? Wherefore there being no such safe guide as the Scripture itself, which speaks without any passion, fraud, or interest, it is not only the right but the duty of every one to consult with the Scripture, and observe his times of conversing with it, as he tenders the salvation of his own soul.

The twenty-ninth, that even a private man assisted by the spirit of life in the new birth, and rightly circumstantiated reason, being also sufficiently furnished with the knowledge of tongues, history, and antiquity, and sound philosophy, may by the help of these, and the blessing of God upon his industry, clear up some of the more obscure places of Scripture to full satisfaction and certainty both to himself, and any unprejudiced peruser of his interpretations. That this assertion is true may be proved by manifold experience, there having been sundry persons that have cleared such places of Scripture as had for a time seemed obscure and intricate, with abundant satisfaction and conviction. But it is to be evinced also *a priori*, viz., from the seventeenth and eighteenth conclusions, which avouch the Scripture to be the most authentic tradition that is; as also from the twenty-fifth, that concludes it not unintelligible in itself nor to mankind; and lastly out of the first, that asserts that certainty of faith presupposes certainty of reason. For thus the object of our understanding being here certain, and we not spending our labor upon a fiction or mockery, and our reason rightly circumstantiated, not blinded by prejudice, nor precipitated into assent before due deliberation and clear comprehension of the matter; if after so cautious a disquisition she be fully satisfied, she is certainly satisfied, or else there is no certainty in rightly circumstantiated reason, which yet is presupposed in the certainty of faith, by the first conclusion. So that the certainty of faith itself seems ruinous, if no private man have any certainty of any interpretation of Scripture that has once been reputed obscure. Not to add, that all the Scripture that has been once obscure, and the interpretation thereof not yet declared by the Church universal, has been hitherto, and will be, God knows how long, utterly useless. Which is a very wild supposition, and such as none would willingly admit, unless those that would rather admit anything, than that light of the Scripture that discovers who they are, and what unworthy impostures they use in their dealings with the children of men.

The thirtieth, that no tradition can be true that is repugnant to any plain text of Scripture. The reason is, because the Scripture is the most true and the most authentic tradition that is, and such as the universal Church is agreed in.

The thirty-first, that if one point grounded upon the authority of tradition, that has been held by the Church time out of mind, prove false, there is no certainty that any tradition is true, unless such as it has not been in the power of the Church to forge, corrupt, deprave or else their interest not at all concerned so to do. The reason is, because the certainty of tradition as tradition is placed in this by those that contend so much for it, that nothing can be brought into the church as an apostolic practice or doctrine but whatever was so from the apostles. Wherefore if once a point be brought into the Church, and professed and practiced as apostolical, that may be clearly proved not to be so, this ground for tradition as tradition is utterly ruined, and, considering the falseness and imposture that has been so long practiced in Christendom, can be held no ground of certainty at all. As not reason *qua* reason, nor sense *qua* sense, but *quatenus* [how far, to what extent] rightly circumstantiated can be any ground of certainty of knowledge, so not tradition *qua* tradition can be the ground of the certainty of faith, but only such a tradition as it were not in the power of the degenerate Church to either forge or adulterate. And such were the records of the Holy Bible only.

The thirty-second, that rightly circumstantiated sense and reason and Holy Writ are the truest grounds of the certainty of faith. This is the common Protestant doctrine, and a great and undeniable truth, and will amount to the greatest certainty desirable, if the Spirit of life and of God assist. For that will seal all firm and close, and shut out all doubts and waverings. In the meantime, even in mere moral men, but yet such as use their sense and reason rightly circumstantiated in their dijudications [4] touching the truth of Holy Writ and religion, it is plain they are upon the truest grounds of faith they can go or apply themselves to, forasmuch as the Holy Writ is the truest and most certain tradition, and no tradition to be discerned true but upon the certainty of rightly circumstantiated sense and reason, as appears by the first conclusion.

These advertisements, though something numerous, are yet brief enough, but very effectual, I hope, if strictly followed, to make thee so wise, as neither to impose upon thyself, nor be imposed upon by others, in matters of religion; and so orthodox, as to become neither enthusiast nor Romanist, but a true catholic and primitive apostolic Christian.

4. [ED.] "Dijudication," a judgment, a decision. Wrongly spelled "disjudication" in many dictionaries. Cf. O.E.D.

JOHN NORRIS

On Faith and Reason

Editor's Introduction. John Norris, the youngest of the men represented in this collection, stands slightly apart from the others. He was a fellow of All Souls College, Oxford, and became rector of Bemerton, the Wiltshire parish once served by George Herbert. As a young man at Oxford he read, and was profoundly influenced by, the works of Cudworth and More. He wrote to More in rather stilted academic Latin—to which More replied in very straightforward English. The ensuing correspondence was ultimately published as an appendix to Norris's *The Theory and Regulation of Love* (1688).[1] The extent of Norris's debt to the Platonists is apparent in all his works, but that he was influenced by others is equally obvious. He learned both from Descartes and from Nicholas Malebranche, the French philosopher. Indeed, part of his importance lay in his having made the thought of Malebranche much more widely known in England. Malebranche asserted that matter cannot act upon mind. Sensation, he said, is the result of a new creative act in the mental order, parallel to what takes place in the physical realm. Echoes of this thinking can be found in Norris; but he did not merely develop a synthesis of Malebranche and the Platonists. He was an exceptionally perceptive critic of contemporary English thinkers. He was one of the first to expose certain inconsistencies in Locke's *Essay* (e.g., in *Cursory Reflections*, and especially in *An Essay Towards the Theory of the Ideal or Intelligible World*, 1701 and 1704) and he brought the same acumen to bear on John Toland's *Christianity not Mysterious* (1696). Toland's work marked the beginning of the intensive phase of the deistic controversy, and Norris's *An Account of Reason and Faith* (1697) is one of the earliest and ablest replies to Toland. Toland argued that neither God nor his revelation is above human reason; the mysteries which beclog Christianity, he believed, were the result of pagan corruptions. Norris relied on the distinction between things contrary to reason and things above reason. The human mind, he argued, is

---

1. Cf. infra 294, 306–7.

not the measure of truth, and the fact that we cannot understand something does not prove that it cannot be true. The passage here reproduced (Chapter VIII) leads to a concluding section on the true relation between reason and "the mysteries of Christianity."

The other excerpt from Norris is from the first of a number of short works published under the title, *Treatises upon Several Subjects* (1698). In form, "Reason and Religion" is a series of "Contemplations," each leading to "the use of this devotion," and followed by an "Aspiration." What Norris provides is a practical devotional treatise, written, as he tells us in the preface, "for the use of the learned reader, who, perhaps, needs as much to be assisted in his devotion as the more ignorant." It is nevertheless a book which demands the close attention of its readers, as the titles of some of the Contemplations will suggest: "Of the general idea of God; That God is a being absolutely perfect, proved from the preceding general idea of God; That therefore all the perfections of particular beings exist in God, and that after a more excellent manner than they do in particular beings themselves; Of the attributes of God in general: Particularly of the unity of God; Of the omniscience and omnipresence of God; Of the omnipotence of God; Of the divine goodness and philanthropy."

❖ ❖ ❖ ❖

An Account of Reason and Faith:
IN RELATION TO THE MYSTERIES OF CHRISTIANITY

Chapter VIII. Wherein is Shewn What is the
True Use of Reason in Believing

Reason being the great character and principle of man, that makes him like to the angels above him, and distinguishes him from the beasts that are below him, and which therefore only are below him for want of the rational power (being many of them in regard of their bodily endowments upon a level with him, and some beyond him), 'tis but just and natural it should appear in all that he does, and preside and govern in all his actions. For as the conduct of the infinitely wise and all-knowing God does always carry in it the characters of his essential and consubstantial reason, even of him who is the wisdom of the Father, the true intelligible light, so should also the conduct of man express in proportion the signatures of *his* reason, and though he cannot act by such exact and unerring measures as his

glorious Maker, nor yet with all that perfection of wisdom that even some
created intelligences express, yet at least he should act like himself, and not
by doing anything absurd or unaccountable deny his reasonable nature.

This has served for a principle to some scholastic and moral writers
whereon to build a very high and (as some think) very severe conclusion,
viz., that there is no individual action of man purely indifferent. Which I
suppose may be true enough of those actions of his which are properly
human, I mean that are done deliberately, with forethought and consideration, every one of which must, as far as I can see, be either good or bad
according to the circumstances wherewith they are clothed; however,
specifically considered in relation to their objects only, and as abstracted
from those circumstances, some of them may be indifferent. And certainly
we cannot suppose any action of a more neutral and adiaphorous nature
than an unprofitable word, and yet of such he that is to be our judge tells
us we shall render an account in the day of judgment [cf. Mt. 12:36].
Which plainly shows that there is no such thing as indifferency in the
actions of man as individually and concretely considered, but that all of
them are either good or bad according to the principle, manner, end and
other circumstances are that attend the doing of them. And that because
man being a rational creature, the order of reason is due at least to all his
deliberate actions, which accordingly ought to carry the characters of a
rational nature in them, the want of which will be enough to render any
of them evil and imperfect.

But then if reason ought to preside and direct in all the deliberate
actions of man, much more ought it in things of the greatest moment and
consequence, wherein his interest and welfare is more nearly concerned,
and which accordingly require his greatest consideration and the use of
the best light that he has. And because there cannot be a thing of greater
consequence and concernment to him than religion, upon which both his
present and his future, his temporal and his eternal happiness does entirely
depend, hence it follows that the principal use he ought to make of his
rational faculty is in religion, that here if anywhere he ought to think,
consider, advise, deliberate, reason and argue, consult both his own light
and that of others, neglect no advantage that may be had from nature or
art, from books or men, from the living or the dead, but employ all possible means for his direction and information, and not be as "the horse and
mule which have no understanding" (Ps. 32:9). For 'twas for this great
end and purpose that his reason was given him, and this is the best use he
can make of it. As for the study of nature, that turns to too little an

account, and as for the affairs of civil life they in themselves and without relation to another world are too little and inconsiderable for us to suppose that our reason was given us for the management of *them*. Religion only bears proportion to so noble a faculty, is most worthy of its application, and can also best reward the due exercise and use of it, and accordingly 'tis upon religion that it will be best bestowed.

Nor is there anything in religion that may justly fear to be brought before the bar of human reason, or to undergo the test of its severest discussion. The heathen religion indeed might, for which cause those that drew its picture cast a shade upon a great part of it and would not venture to expose it to common view. And the too much heathenized religion of some Christians may also very deservedly retire behind the curtain and decline coming to the light, for fear the absurdities and monstrous inconsistencies of it should be laid open. But certainly there is not anything, neither doctrine nor precept, in that true religion that is revealed by God, in evangelical Christianity, that need fly the light of reason or refuse to be tried by it. Christian religion is all over a "reasonable service" [Rom. 12:1], and the author of it is too reasonable a master to impose any other, or to require (whatever his vicar may do) that men should follow him blindfold and pull out their eyes to become his disciples. No, he that miraculously gave sight to so many has no need of, nor pleasure in the blind, nor has his divine religion any occasion for such judges or professors. For it is the religion of the eternal and uncreated wisdom, the divine Word, the true light of the world, and the universal reason of all spirits, and 'tis impossible that he should reveal anything that contradicts the measures of sound discourse, or the immutable laws of truth, as it is that any divine revelation should be truly opposite to right reason (however it may sometimes be *above* it) or that anything should be *theologically* true, which is *philosophically* false, as some with profoundness are pleased to distinguish. For the light of reason is as truly from God as the light of revelation is, and therefore though the latter of these lights may exceed and outshine the former, it can never be contrary to it. God as the sovereign truth cannot reveal anything against reason, and as the sovereign goodness he cannot require us to believe any such thing. Nay to descend some degrees below this, he cannot require us to believe not only what is *against* reason, but even what is *without* it. For to believe anything without reason is an unreasonable act, and 'tis impossible that God should ever require an unreasonable act, especially from a reasonable creature.

We therefore not only acknowledge the use of reason in religion, but also that 'tis in religion that 'tis chiefly to be used, so far are we from denying the use of it there. And it is a little unfairly done of our adversaries so much to insinuate the contrary as they do. For I cannot take it for less than such an insinuation, when they are arguing with us against the belief of the Christian mysteries to run out as they usually do into harangues and flourishes (whereof, by the way, I know none more guilty than the author of *Christianity not Mysterious*) about the reasonableness of the Christian religion and the rational nature of faith, what a reasonable act the one is, and what a reasonable service the other is, &c., as if we were against the use of reason in religion or were for a blind, groundless and unaccountable faith, or as if because we hold the belief of things above reason, therefore we are for having no reason for our belief. This, I say, is an unfair insinuation, and such as argues some want either of judgment or sincerity (I don't know which) in those that suggest it. For they seem plainly by running so much upon this vein to imply as if it were part of the question between us, whether there be any use of reason in religion, or whether faith is to be founded upon reason or no. But now this is no part of the controversy that lies between us; we acknowledge the use of reason in religion as well as they, and are as little for a senseless and irrational faith as they can be. This therefore being common to us both is no part of the question, and they do ill to insinuate that it is by so many popular declamatory strains upon the reasonableness of religion, and in particular of faith, whereas they do, or should know, that the thing in question between us is not whether there be any use of reason to be made in believing, but only what it is, or wherein the true use of it does consist.

Now this we may determine in a few words, having already laid the grounds of it. For since the incomprehensibility of a thing is no concluding argument against the belief of it . . . it is plain that the proper office and business of a believer's reason is to examine and inquire, not whether the thing proposed be comprehensible or not, but only whether it be revealed by God or no, since if it be, the incomprehensibleness of it will be no objection against it. That therefore ought to be no part of its question or deliberation, because indeed it is not to the purpose to consider whether such a thing be, when if it were it would be no just objection. The only considerable thing then here is whether such a proposition be indeed from God, and has him for its author or no. And here reason is to clear her eyes, put the matter in the best light, call in all the assistance that may be had both from the heart and the head, and determine of the thing with all the judgment and all the sincerity that she can. But as to the comprehensibility or incomprehensibility of the article, this is quite besides the question, and ought therefore to be no part of her scrutiny or debate, since if it were never so much above her comprehension, it would be never the less proper object for her belief.

The sum is, the incomprehensibility of a thing is no argument against the belief of it, therefore in the believing of a thing, the proper work of my reason is not to consider whether it be incomprehensible. But when a thing is proposed to me as from God, all that my reason has to do in this case is seriously, soberly, diligently, impartially and (I add) *humbly* to examine whether it comes with the true credentials of his authority, and has him for its real author or no. This is all that reason has to do in this matter, and when she has done this, she is to rise from the seat of judgment and resign it to faith, which either gives or refuses her assent, not as the thing proposed is comprehensible or not comprehensible, but as 'tis either revealed or not revealed.

REASON AND RELIGION, OR THE GROUNDS AND MEASURES OF DEVOTION
CONSIDERED FROM THE NATURE OF GOD AND THE NATURE OF MAN

The Introduction

There being nothing of greater consequence to the highest interest of man than the knowledge of God and himself, I thought I could not better employ my solitude, either for my own or for the world's advantage, than in exercising my severest contemplations upon these two great and important subjects, the nature of God and the nature of man.

It must indeed be confessed that there is nothing whereof we have or can have so little knowledge, as of these two things; and 'tis much to be lamented that there should lie our greatest ignorance, where we are most concerned to know. But thus it is: that of ourselves, which we are best acquainted with, is least of all ourselves; and the unknown part of this little world is much greater than the known. We know but little of our bodies, but infinitely less of our souls. God has not given us any idea of the latter, and whatever we can borrow from our senses will never be able to supply that defect. For there is a greater distance and disproportion between an immaterial substance and a sensible, than between one sensible and another. But now the understanding the nature of one sensible will not suffice to make us understand the nature of another. For a man born blind will never from his understanding of sounds come to understand colors. Much less therefore will our understanding of sensible things help us to understand the nature of immaterial substances.

And if not of immaterial substances in general, much less will it serve us to understand the essence of the great God, which infinitely transcends all other immaterial substances. The idea of God is least capable of all spiritual beings to be formed out of sensible phantasms. For I consider that by how much the more our mind is raised to the contemplation of spiritual things, by so much the more we always abstract from sensibles. But now the highest and last term of contemplation is the divine essence. Whence it follows necessarily that the mind which sees the divine essence must be totally and thoroughly absolved from all commerce with the corporeal senses, either by death, or some ecstatical and rapturous abstraction. So true is that which God said to Moses, "Thou canst not see my face, for there shall no man see me and live" (Ex. 33:20).

So far therefore are we from deriving any idea of God from our senses that they are our greatest impediment in divine contemplations. So great, that we cannot any other way clearly apprehend the essence of God while we are lodged in the prison of our senses. God cannot give us a distinct view of himself, while we hold any commerce with our senses. For he that knows exactly what proportion our present condition bears to his own divine glories has told us that no man shall see him and live. We must therefore forever despair of conceiving the divine essence clear and distinctly, not only from our senses, but even with them.

Not that there is any darkness or obscurity in God. No, God is the most knowable object in himself. For he is the First Being, and therefore the First Truth, and therefore the First Intelligible, and consequently the most Intelligible. One apostle says that he "dwells in light" [1 Tim. 6:16]; and another, that he "is light," and that there is no darkness at all in him [1 Jn. 1:5]. God therefore considered in his own nature is as well the most intelligible, as the most intelligent being in the world.

The difficulty therefore arises not from the obscurity of the object, but from the disproportion of the faculty. For our understandings stand affected to the most manifest objects, as the eye of a bat to the light of the sun, as the Philosopher observes in his *Metaphysics*.[1] God dwells in light, as the apostle says, but then 'tis such as no man can approach unto; he inhabits "unapproachable light," or a light which cannot be come at,

1. [ED.] Aristotle, *Metaphysics*, Bk. II, Ch. 1.

not for its distance (for he is not far from every one of us) but for its brightness [cf. 1 Tim. 6:16; Acts 17:27]. The very angels are forced to "veil their faces" when they see it; but for mortals, they cannot so much as come "nigh it." The short is, God is too intelligible to be here clearly understood by an embodied understanding; and too great a light hinders vision, as much as darkness.

But though we cannot here have a clear and distinct knowledge either of God or ourselves, yet we may know so much of both as may serve the ends of piety and devotion. We may by attending to that general idea of God which is by himself imprinted on our minds learn to unfold many of the perfections of his glorious and invisible essence; and though we cannot see his face and live, yet his "back-parts" (we know) were once seen by a mortal capacity [Ex. 33:23], and so may be again. And for ourselves, though God has not given us any idea of our own souls, yet the powers and operations, the condition, circumstances and accidents of our nature are things that may fall within the sphere of human consideration. And from both these we may derive measures for our due behavior towards the Great God. And this is the design of the present contemplations, viz., to consider so much of the nature of God and the nature of man, as may afford sufficient grounds and measures for true piety and devotion.

By "devotion" here I do not merely understand that special disposition or act of the soul whereby we warmly and passionately address ourselves to God in prayer (which is what is commonly meant by devotion) but I use the word in a greater latitude, so as to comprehend under it faith, hope, love, fear, trust, humility, submission, honor, reverence, adoration, thanksgiving—in a word all that duty which we owe to God. Nor by this acceptation do I stretch the word beyond what either for its rise it *may*, or by frequent use among the learned it *does* signify. Devotion is from *devoting* or giving up one's self wholly to the service of another. And accordingly those among the heathens who delivered and consigned themselves up to death for the safety of their country were called *devoti*. And so in like manner for a man to give up himself wholly and entirely to the service of God and actually to demean [2] himself towards him in the conduct of his life, as becomes a creature towards his creator, is devotion. And in this latitude the word is used by Aquinas, who defines devotion to be "a will readily to give up one's self to all those things which belong to the service of God." [3]

2. [ED.] I.e., to comport.
3. [ED.] Aquinas, *Summa Theologica*, Pt. II(II), Q.82, Art. 1.

This is what I here understand by devotion, and of which I intend in the following contemplations to assign the grounds and measures from the nature of God and the nature of man. But before I proceed to enforce and direct devotion from these two particular subjects of contemplation, I think it not improper to consider a little by way of preparation, how much contemplation or meditation in general contributes to the advantage of devotion.

They that make ignorance the mother of devotion cannot suppose contemplation any great friend to it. For the more a man contemplates, the more he will know; and the wiser he grows, the less apt upon their supposition he will be for devotion. But I would ask the men of this fancy this one question: is devotion a rational thing, or is it not? If not, why then do they recommend ignorance or anything else in order to it? For it may as well, nay, better, be let alone. But if it be a rational thing, then they must either say, that the more a man considers, the less he will discover the reasons of it, the less he will be persuaded to the practice of it. Both which propositions are absurd and ridiculous enough to be laughed at, but too ridiculous to be seriously refuted.

But to show how much contemplation serves to the advantage of devotion we need only consider, that devotion is an act of the will, that the object of the will is good apparent or good understood, and consequently that every act of the will is influenced and regulated by considerations. Devotion therefore is as much influenced by consideration as any other act of the will is. And therefore I cannot but admire at the disposers of the angelical hierarchies for making the seraphim excel in love and devotion, and the cherubim in knowledge. As if knowledge were not the best preparative for devotion.

I deny not but that knowledge and devotion often go asunder, and the wisest are not always the devoutest. But then this is not owing to the natural and direct influence of knowledge, but comes to pass only occasionally and accidentally, by reason of some other impediment—suppose pride, lust, covetousness, or some such indisposition of mind, which is of more force and prevalency to let [4] our devotion, than knowledge is to further it. And then no wonder that the heavier scale weighs down. But still knowledge is to further it. And then no wonder that the heavier scale weighs down. But still knowledge has a natural aptness to excite devotion, and will infallibly do it if not hindered by some other cause. So that we may take this for a never failing rule, that all other things being equal, the

4. [ED.] I.e., to hinder.

more knowing and considering, still the more devout. And in this sense also that of the Psalmist will be verified, "While I was musing the fire kindled" [cf. Ps. 39:3].

The great God so enlighten my mind and so govern my pen, that by these my meditations I may illustrate his ineffable excellence, and kindle holy flames of devotion, both in myself and in my reader. To him therefore I pray in the words of Moses, "I beseech thee, shew me thy glory" [Ex. 33:18]. Amen.

PART THREE

❖

*The Nature of Reality and Our
Knowledge of It*

❖   ❖   ❖   ❖   ❖   ❖   ❖   ❖

HENRY MORE

An Antidote Against Atheism

Editor's Introduction. The challenge of atheism was never absent for long
from the minds of the Cambridge Platonists. This may seem strange; the
seventeenth century was, one might think, a period which suffered from
too much faith, not from too little. But the turmoils of the Civil War had
lifted the restraints which had previously held speculation in check. New
sects had multiplied, thinkers had appeared who were sometimes hetero-
dox, occasionally frankly atheistic. These, however, were not the men who
alarmed the Cambridge Platonists. It was the hidden implications of current philosophy which seemed most to threaten the convictions which the
Cambridge men chiefly valued. Often the attack was indirect; it could be
met not so much by refutation as by the restatement of a sounder case.
More's *Antidote* (London, 1652) is much more than a critique of writers
like Hobbes; it is a brilliant and original interpretation of the position
which More shared with Cudworth, Smith and his other colleagues.
Book I (the section here reproduced) elaborates that position. As More
himself stated in his Epistle Dedicatory to the work, he believed that he
was providing a "careful draft of natural theology or metaphysics." Book
II is a painstaking but not uniformly convincing examination of order in
nature as supplying evidence of design and benevolent purpose. The final
section of the work is a consideration of phenomena which, according to
More, provided the most cogent confirmation of theism: werewolves,
poltergeists and spirit manifestations of all kinds. The *Antidote*, therefore,
illustrates a feature of More's work which is puzzling to a modern reader.
He could present an argument which was cogently reasoned and rigor-
ously intellectual, but at the same time he could believe (as did Joseph
Glanvill also) that witches and warlocks constituted important evidence
for the reality of the spirit world. It would be wrong to assume either that
More was intellectually erratic or that he was unduly inclined to superstition. He believed that matter and spirit were so inseparably related that
the former was the means by which the latter found expression. This was

why he criticized Descartes' dualism; this explains his interest in spirit manifestations. The materialism of Hobbes was therefore a challenge to convictions carefully pondered and firmly held. Mechanism, like materialism, was seen as certain to be a continuing and increasing threat to belief. The Cambridge Platonists could not anticipate exactly the problems that would be raised by a scientific and technological era, but they did foresee that some such problems would arise.

An inadequate religion, said More, is no defence against superstition, and superstition leads invariably to atheism. It might appear that religion could not be upheld so convincingly that all doubts would be dissipated, but this did not really benefit the atheists' case. The right approach to the problem of religious belief, he believed, had a distinctive character; it might differ from logical demonstration, but it was not necessarily any less cogent on that account. Those who wished to prove *that* God is must first discover *what* God is. As a working definition of God, More suggested "a Being absolutely perfect." This might be a proposition difficult to establish, but actually the idea of a spirit was as easy to accept as the notion of any other substance. The assurance of its reality might derive from a distinctive kind of knowledge, but it was perfectly reasonable that this should be so. The soul, said More, was furnished with innate truths. Among them was the idea of God, and the idea of God, by its very character, implied his necessary existence. As far as More was concerned, the argument was based on the innate idea of God. It is here that his theory of knowledge and his doctrine of reality meet. Descartes had insisted that the innate idea of God has a priority over all other ideas. More also regarded the idea as innate (though not inborn), and as necessary, inescapable and universal.

❖   ❖   ❖   ❖

BOOK I

Chapter I

The grand truth which we are now to be employed about and to prove is, that there is a God. And I made choice of this subject as very seasonable for the times we are in and are coming on, wherein divine Providence, more universally loosening the minds of men from the awe and tyranny of mere accustomary superstition and permitting a freer perusal of matters of religion than in former ages, the Tempter would take advantage where he may to carry men captive out of one dark prison into another, out of superstition into atheism itself. Which is a thing feasible enough for him to bring about in such men as have adhered to religion in a mere external way, either for fashion's sake or in a blind obedience to the authority of a Church. For when this external frame of godliness shall break about their ears, they being really at the bottom devoid of the true fear and love of God, and destitute of a more free and unprejudiced use of their faculties, by reason of the sinfulness and corruption of their nature, it will be an easy thing to allure them to an assent to that which seems so much for their present interest; and so being emboldened by the tottering and falling of what they took for the chief structure of religion before, they will gladly in their conceit cast down also the very object of that religious worship after it and conclude that there is as well no God as no religion. That is, they have a mind there should be none, that they may be free from all wringings of conscience, trouble of correcting their lives, and fear of being accountable before that great tribunal.

Wherefore for the reclaiming of these if it were possible, at least for the succoring and extricating of those in whom a greater measure of the love of God doth dwell (who may probably by some darkening cloud of melancholy, or some more than ordinary importunity of the Tempter be dissettled and entangled in their thoughts concerning this weighty matter), I held it fit to bestow mine endeavors upon this so useful and seasonable enterprise, as to demonstrate that there is a God.

Chapter II

But when I speak of demonstrating there is a God, I would not be suspected of so much vanity and ostentation as to be thought I mean to bring no arguments but such as are so convictive that a man's understanding shall be forced to confess that it is impossible to be otherwise than I have concluded. For, for mine own part I am prone to believe that there is nothing at all to be so demonstrated. For it is possible that mathematical evidence itself may be but a constant undiscoverable delusion, which our nature is necessarily and perpetually obnoxious unto, and that either fatally or fortuitously there has been in the world time out of mind such a being as we call *man*, whose essential property it is to be then most of all mistaken when he conceives a thing most evidently true. And why may not this be, as well as anything else, if you will have all things fatal or casual without a God? For there can be no curb to this wild conceit but by the supposing that we ourselves exist from some higher principle that is absolutely good and wise, which is all one as to acknowledge that there is a God.

Wherefore when I say that I will demonstrate that there is a God, I do not promise that I will always produce such arguments that the reader shall acknowledge so strong as he shall be forced to confess that it is utterly impossible that it should be otherwise. But they shall be such as shall deserve full assent and win full assent from any unprejudiced mind.

For I conceive that we may give full assent to that which notwithstanding may possibly be otherwise; which I shall illustrate by several examples. Suppose two men got to the top of Mount Athos, and there viewing a stone in the form of an altar with ashes on it and the footsteps of men on those ashes, or some words if you will, as "To the Greatest Good" or "To the Unknown God" [cf. Acts 17:23] or the like, written or scrawled out upon the ashes; and one of them should cry out, "Assumedly here have been some men here that have done this." But the other, more nice than wise, should reply, "Nay, it may possibly be otherwise. For this stone may have naturally grown into this very shape, and the seeming ashes may be no ashes, that is, no remainders of any fuel burnt there, but some inexplicable and imperceptible motions of the air, or other particles of this fluid matter that is active everywhere have wrought some parts of the matter into the form and nature of ashes, and have fridged [1] and played about so that they have also figured those intelligible characters into the same." But would not anybody deem it a piece of weakness no less than dotage for the other man one whit to recede from his former apprehension, but as fully as ever to agree with what he pronounced first, notwithstanding this bare possibility of being otherwise?

So of anchors that have been digged up, either in plain fields or mountain places, as also the Roman urns with ashes and inscriptions, . . . or Roman coins with the effigies and names of the Caesars on them; or that which is more ordinary, the skulls of men in every churchyard, with the right figure and all those necessary perforations for the passing of the vessels, besides those conspicuous hollows for the eyes and rows of teeth, the *Os Styloeides, Ethoeides,* and what not? If a man will say of them, that the motion of the particles of the matter, or some hidden spermatic power has gendered these both anchors, urns, coins and skulls in the ground, he doth but pronounce that which human reason must admit as possible. Nor can any man ever so demonstrate that those coins, anchors and urns were once the artifice of men, or that this or that skull was once a part of a

1. [ED.] I.e., fidgeted. Cf. O.E.D.

living man, that he shall force an acknowledgment that it is impossible that it should be otherwise. But yet I do not think that any man, without doing manifest violence to his faculties, can at all suspend his assent, but freely and fully agree that this or that skull was once part of a living man, and that those anchors, urns and coins were certainly once made by human artifice, notwithstanding the possibility of being otherwise.

And what I have said of assent is also true in dissent. For the mind of man not crazed nor prejudiced will fully and unreconcilably disagree, by its own natural sagacity, where notwithstanding the thing that it doth thus resolvedly and undoubtingly reject, no wit of man can prove impossible to be true. As if we should make such a fiction as this, that Archimedes with the same individual body that he had when the soldiers slew him, is now safely intent upon his geometrical figures under ground, at the center of the earth, far from the noise and din of this world that might disturb his meditations or distract him in his curious delineations he makes with his rod upon the dust; [2] which no man living can prove impossible. Yet if any man does not as unreconcilably dissent from such a fable as this, as from any falsehood imaginable, assuredly that man is next door to madness or dotage, or does enormous violence to the free use of his faculties.

Wherefore it is manifest that there may be a very firm and unwavering assent or dissent, when as yet the thing we thus assent to may be possibly otherwise; or that which we thus dissent from, cannot be proved impossible to be true.

Which point I have thus long and thus variously sported myself in, for making the better impression upon my reader, it being of no small use and consequence as well for the advertising [3] of him, that the arguments which I shall produce though I do not bestow that ostentative term of *demonstration* upon them, yet they may be as effectual for winning a firm and unshaken assent, as if they were in the strictest notion such; as also to remind him that if they be so strong and so patly fitted and suitable with the faculties of man's mind, that he has nothing to reply, but only that for all this it may possibly be otherwise, that he should give a free and full assent to the conclusion. And if he do not, that he is to suspect himself rather of some distemper, prejudice or weakness, than the arguments of want of strength.

But if the atheist shall contrary-wise pervert my candor and fair-dealing,

2. [ED.] Archimedes (c. 287-12 B.C.), Greek mathematician, was killed at the time of the fall of Syracuse; while he was drawing a mathematical diagram on the sand, a Roman soldier rushed upon him and ran him through the body.

3. [ED.] I.e., giving warning or information.

and fancy that he has got some advantage upon my free confession that the arguments that I shall use are not so convictive but that they leave a possibility of the thing being otherwise, let him but compute his supposed gains by adding the limitation of this possibility (viz., that it is no more possible than that the clearest mathematical evidence may be false—which is impossible if our faculties be true—or in the second place, than that the Roman urns and coins above mentioned may prove to be the works of nature, not the artifice of man, which our faculties admit to be so little probable, that it is impossible for them not fully to assent to the contrary) and when he has cast up his account, it will be evident that it can be nothing but his gross ignorance in this kind of arithmetic that shall embolden him to write himself down gainer and not me.

Chapter III

And now having premised thus much, I shall come on nearer to my present design. In prosecution whereof it will be requisite for me, first to define *what God is*, before I proceed to demonstration *that he is*. For it is obvious for man's reason to find arguments for the impossibility, possibility, probability or necessity of the existence of a thing, from the explication of the essence thereof.

And now I am come hither, I demand of any atheist that denies there is a God or of any that doubts whether there be one or no, what idea or notion they frame of that they deny or doubt of. If they will prove nice and squeamish, and profess they can frame no notion of any such thing, I would gladly ask them, why they will then deny or doubt of they know not what. For it is necessary that he that would rationally doubt or deny a thing should have some settled notion of the very thing he doubts of or denies. But if they profess that this is the very ground of their denying or doubting whether there be a God, because they can frame no notion of him, I shall forthwith take away that allegation by offering them such a notion as is as proper to God as any notion is proper to anything else in the world.

I define God therefore thus, *an essence or being fully and absolutely perfect*. I say *fully and absolutely perfect*, in counterdistinction to such perfection as is not full and absolute, but the perfection of this or that species or kind of finite beings, suppose of a lion, horse or tree. But to be fully and absolutely perfect is to be at least as perfect as the apprehension of a man can conceive, without a contradiction. For what is inconceivable or contradictious, is nothing at all to us, who are not now to wag one atom beyond our faculties, that I dare appeal to any atheist that hath yet any command of sense and reason left in him, if it be not very easy and intelligible at the first sight and that that if there be a God he is to be deemed of us such as this idea or notion sets forth.

But if he will sullenly deny that this is the proper notion of God, let him enjoy his own humor; this yet remains undeniable, that there is in man an *idea* of a *being absolutely and fully perfect,* which we frame out by attributing all conceivable perfection to it whatsoever, that implies no contradiction. And this notion is natural and essential to the soul of man, and cannot be washed out nor conveyed away by any force or trick of wit whatsoever, so long as the mind of man is not crazed but hath the ordinary use of her own faculties.

Nor will that prove anything to the purpose, when as it shall be alleged that this notion is not so connatural and essential to the soul, because she framed it from some occasions from without. For all those undeniable conclusions in geometry, which might be helped and occasioned from something without, are so natural notwithstanding and essential to the soul that you may as soon unsoul the soul as divide her from perpetual assent to those mathematical truths, supposing no distemper nor violence offered to her faculties. As, for example, she cannot but acknowledge in herself the several distinct ideas of the five regular bodies, as also, that it is impossible that there should be any more than five. And this idea of being absolutely perfect is as distinct and indelible an idea in the soul as the idea of the five regular bodies, or any other idea whatsoever.

It remains therefore undeniable, that there is an inseparable *idea* of a *being absolutely perfect* ever residing, though not always acting, in the soul of man.

Chapter IV

But now to lay out more particularly the perfections comprehended in this notion of a being absolutely and fully perfect, I think I may securely nominate these: self-subsistency, immateriality, infinity as well of duration as essence, immensity of goodness, omnisciency, omnipotency and necessity of existence. Let this therefore be the description of a being absolutely perfect, that it is a spirit, eternal, infinite in essence and goodness, omniscient, omnipotent and of itself necessarily existent. All which attributes being attributes of the highest perfection that falls under the apprehension of man and having no discoverable imperfection interwoven with them, must of necessity be attributed to that which we conceive absolutely and fully perfect. And if anyone will say that this is but to dress up a notion out of my own fancy, which I would afterwards slily insinuate to be the notion of a God, I answer, that no man can discourse and reason of anything without recourse to settled notions deciphered in his own mind. And that such an exception as this implies the most contradictious absurdities imaginable, to wit, as if a man should reason from something that never entered into his mind, or that is utterly out of the ken of his own faculties. But such groundless allegations as these discover nothing but an unwillingness to find themselves able to entertain any conception of God and a heavy propension to sink down into an utter oblivion of him, and to become as stupid and senseless in divine things as the very beasts.

But others it may be will not look on this notion as contemptible for the easy composure thereof out of familiar conceptions which the mind of man ordinarily figures itself into, but reject it rather out of some unintelligible hard terms in it, such as spirit, eternal and infinite, for they do profess they can frame no notion of spirit, and that anything should be eternal or infinite they do not know how to set their mind in a posture to apprehend and therefore some would have no such thing as a spirit in the world.

But if the difficulty of framing a conception of a thing must take away the existence of the thing itself, there will be no such thing as a body left in the world, and then will all be spirit or nothing. For who can frame so safe a notion of a body as to free himself from the entanglements that the extension thereof will bring along with it? For this extended matter consists of either indivisible points or of particles divisible *in infinitum*. Take which of these two you will (and you can find no third), you will be wound into the most notorious absurdities that may be. For if you say it consists of points, from this position I can necessarily demonstrate that every spear or spire-steeple or what long body you will is as thick as it is long; that the tallest cedar is not so high as the lowest mushroom; and that the moon and the earth are so near one another that the thickness of your hand will not go betwixt; that rounds and squares are all one figure; that even and odd numbers are equal one with another; and that the clearest day is as dark as the blackest night. And if you make choice of the other member of the disjunction, your fancy will be little better at ease. For nothing can be divisible into parts it has not. Therefore if a body be divisible into infinite parts, it has infinite extended parts; and if it has an infinite number of extended parts, it cannot be but a hard mystery to the imagination of man, that infinite extended parts should not amount to one whole infinite extension. And thus "a grain of mustard seed" [cf. Mk. 4:31] would be as well infinitely extended as the whole matter of the universe; and a thousandth part of that grain as well as the grain itself. Which things are more inconceivable than anything in the notion of a spirit. Therefore we are not scornfully and contemptuously to reject any notion, for seeming at first to be clouded and obscured with some difficulties and intricacies of conception; sith that, of whose being we seem most assured, is the most entangled and perplexed in the conceiving, of anything that can be propounded to the apprehension of a man. But here you will reply, that our senses are struck by so manifest impressions from the matter, that though the nature of it be difficult to conceive, yet the existence is palpable to us by what it acts upon us. Why, then, all that I desire is this, that when you shall be reminded of some actions and operations that arrive to the notice of your sense or understanding, which unless we do violence to our faculties we can never attribute to matter or body, that then you would not be so nice and averse from the admitting of such a substance as is called a spirit, though you fancy some difficulty in the convincing thereof.

But for mine own part I think the nature of a spirit is as conceivable and easy to be defined as the nature of anything else. For as for the very essence or bare substance of anything whatsoever, he is a very novice in speculation that does not acknowledge that utterly unknowable. But for "the essential and inseparable properties," they are as intelligible and explicable in a spirit as in any other subject whatever. As for example, I conceive the entire idea of a spirit in general, or at least of all finite created and subordinate spirits, to consist of these several powers or properties, viz., self-penetration, self-motion, self-contradiction and dilatation, and indivisibility; and these are those that I reckon more absolute. I will add also what has relation to another, and that is the power of penetrating, moving and altering the matter. These properties and powers put together make up the notion and idea of a spirit, whereby it is plainly distinguished from a body, whose parts cannot penetrate one another, is not self-movable, nor can contract nor dilate itself, is divisible and separable one part from another. But the parts of a spirit can be no more separated, though they be dilated, than you can cut off the rays of the sun by a pair of scissors made of pellucid crystal. And this will serve for the settling of the notion of a spirit; the proof of its existence belongs not unto this place.

And out of this description it is plain that a spirit is a notion of more perfection than a body, and therefore the more fit to be an attribute of what is absolutely perfect than a body is.

But now for the other two hard terms of *eternal* and *infinite*, if any one would excuse himself from assenting to the notion of a *God*, by reason of the incomprehensibleness of those attributes, let him consider that he shall (whether he will or no) be forced to acknowledge something *eternal*, either *God* or the *world*, and the intricacy is alike in either. And though he would shuffle off the trouble of apprehending an *infinite deity*, yet he will never extricate himself out of the entanglements of an *infinite space;* which notion will stick as closely to his soul as her power of imagination.

Now that goodness, knowledge and power, which are the three following attributes, are attributes of perfection, if a man consult his own faculties, it will be undoubtedly concluded and I know nothing else he can consult with. At least this will be returned as infallibly true, that a being absolutely perfect has these, or what supereminently contains these. And that knowledge, or something like it, is in God is manifest, because without animadversion [4] in some sense or other it is impossible to be happy. But that a being should be absolutely perfect and yet not happy is as impossible. But knowledge without goodness is but dry subtlety or mischievous craft; and goodness with knowledge devoid of power is but lame and ineffectual. Wherefore whatever is absolutely perfect is infinitely both good, wise and powerful.

And lastly it is more perfection that all this be stable, immutable and necessary, than contingent or but possible. Therefore the idea of a being absolutely perfect represents to our minds, that that of which it is the idea is necessarily to exist. And that which of its own nature doth necessarily exist must never fail to be. And whether the atheist will call this absolutely perfect being God or not, it is all one; I list not to contend about words. But I think any man else at the first sight will say that we have found out the true idea of God.

Chapter V

And now we have found out this idea of a being absolutely perfect, that the use which we shall hereafter make of it may take the better effect it will not be amiss by way of further preparation briefly to touch upon

4. [ED.] "Animadversion" as used here denotes the action or faculty of taking notice. Cf. O.E.D.

that notable point in philosophy, whether the soul of man be *abrasa tabula*, a table book in which nothing is writ; or whether she have some innate notions and ideas in herself. For so it is that she having taken first occasion of thinking from external objects, it hath so imposed upon some men's judgments, that they have conceited that the soul has no knowledge nor notion, but what is in a passive way impressed or delineated upon her from the objects of sense; they not warily enough distinguishing betwixt extrinsical occasions and the adequate or principal causes of things.

But the mind of man, more free and better exercised in the close observations of its own operations and nature, cannot but discover that there is an active and actual knowledge in a man, of which these outward objects are rather the reminders than the first begetters or implanters. And when I say actual knowledge, I do not mean that there is a certain number of ideas flaring and shining to the animadversive faculty like so many torches or stars in the firmament to our outward sight, or that there are any figures that take their distinct places and are legibly writ there like the red letters or astronomical characters in an almanack; but I understand thereby an active sagacity in the soul, or quick recollection as it were, whereby some small business being hinted unto her, she runs out presently into a more clear and larger conception.

And I cannot better describe her condition than thus: suppose a skillful musician fallen asleep in the field upon the grass, during which time he shall not so much as dream anything concerning his musical faculty, so that in one sense there is no actual skill or notion nor representation of anything musical in him; but his friend sitting by him that cannot sing at all himself jogs him and awakes him and desires him to sing this or the other song, telling him two or three words of the beginning of the song, whereupon he presently takes it out of his mouth and sings the whole song upon so slight and slender intimation. So the mind of man being jogged and awakened by the impulses of outward objects is stirred up into a more full and clear conception of what was but imperfectly hinted to her from external occasions. And this faculty I venture to call *actual knowledge* in such a sense as the sleeping musician's skill might be called actual skill when he thought nothing of it.

Chapter VI

And that this is the condition of the soul is discoverable by sundry observations. As for example, exhibit to the soul through the outward senses the figure of a circle, she acknowledgeth presently this to be one kind of figure, and can add forthwith that if it be perfected all the lines from some one point of it drawn to the perimeter must be exactly equal. In like manner show her a triangle, she will straightway pronounce that if that be the right figure it makes toward, the angles must be closed in indivisible points. But this accuracy either in the circle or the triangle cannot be set out in any material subject, therefore it remains that she hath a more full and exquisite knowledge of things in herself than the matter can lay before her.

Let us cast in a third instance, let somebody now demonstrate this triangle described in the matter to have its three angles equal to two right ones. "Why yes," saith the soul, "this is true, and not only in this particular triangle but in all plain triangles that can possibly be described in the matter." And thus you see the soul sings out the whole song upon the first hint, as knowing it very well before.

Besides this, there are a multitude of relative notions or ideas in the mind of man, as well mathematical as logical, which if we prove cannot be the impresses of any material object from without, it will necessarily follow that they are from the soul herself within, and are the natural furniture of human understanding. Such as are these, cause, effect, whole and part, like and unlike, and the rest. So equality and inequality, logos and analogia, proportion and analogy, symmetry and asymmetry and such like: all which relative ideas I shall easily prove to be no material impresses from without upon the soul, but her own active conception proceeding from herself whilst she takes notice of eternal objects. For that these ideas can make no impresses upon the outward senses is plain from hence, because they are no sensible nor physical affections of the matter. And how can that, that is no physical affection of the matter, affect our corporeal organs of sense?

But now that these relative ideas, whether logical or mathematical, be no physical affections of the matter, is manifest from these two arguments: First, they may be produced when there has been no physical motion nor alteration in the subject to which they belong, nay, indeed when there hath been nothing at all done to the subject to which they do accrue. As for example, suppose one side of a room whitened, the other not touched or meddled with, this other has thus become unlike; and hath the notion of *dissimile* necessarily belonging to it, although there has nothing at all been done thereunto. So suppose two pounds of lead, which therefore are two equal pieces of that metal; cut away half from one of them, the other pound, nothing at all being done unto it, has lost its notion of *equal* and hath acquired a new one of *double* unto the other. Nor is it to any purpose to answer that though there was nothing done to this pound of lead, yet there was to the other. For that does not at all enervate the reason but shows that the notion of *sub-double* which accrued to that lead which had half cut away is but our mode of conceiving, as well as the other, and not any physical affection that strikes the corporeal organs of the body, as hot and cold, hard and soft, white and black, and the like do. Wherefore the ideas of equal and unequal, double and sub-double, like and unlike, with the rest, are no external impresses upon the senses, but the soul's own active manner of conceiving those things which are discovered by the outward senses.

The second argument is that one and the same part of the matter is capable at one and the same time, wholly and entirely of two contrary ideas of this kind. As for example, any piece of matter that is a middle proportional betwixt two other pieces is double, suppose and sub-double, or triple and sub-triple at once. Which is a manifest sign that these ideas are no affections of the matter and therefore do not affect our senses, else they would affect the senses of beasts, and they might also grow good geometricians and arithmeticians. And they not affecting our senses, it is plain that we have some ideas that we are not beholding to our senses for, but are the mere exertions of the mind occasionally awakened by the appulses [5] of the outward objects; which the outward senses do not more teach us than he that awakened the musician to sing taught him his skill.

And now in the third and last place it is manifest, besides these single ideas I have proved to be in the mind, that there are also several complex notions in the same, such as are these: the whole is bigger than the parts; if you take equal from equal, the remainders are equal; every number is either even or odd; which are true to the soul at the very first proposal, as anyone that is in his wits does plainly perceive.

Chapter VII

And now we see so evidently the soul is not unfurnished for the dictating of truth unto us, I demand of any man, why under a pretence that she having nothing of her own but may be molded into an assent to anything, or that she does arbitrariously and fortuitously compose the several impresses she receives from without, he will be still so squeamish or

5. [ED.] I.e., drivings toward or against. Cf. O.E.D.

timorous as to be afraid to close with his own faculties, and receive the natural emanations of his own mind, as faithful guides.

But if this seem, though it be not, too subtile [6] which I contend for, viz., that the soul hath actual knowledge in herself, in that sense which I explained, yet surely this at least will be confessed to be true, that the nature of the soul is such, that she will certainly and fully assent to some conclusions, however she came to the knowledge of them, unless she do manifest violence to her own faculties. Which truths must therefore be concluded not fortuitous or arbitratious, but natural to the soul; such as I have already named, as that every finite number is either even or odd, if you add equal to equal the wholes are equal, and such as are not so simple as these, but yet stick as close to the soul once apprehended as that "the three angles in a triangle are equal to two right one," "that there are just five regular bodies, neither more nor less," and the like, which we will pronounce necessarily true according to the light of nature.

Wherefore now to reassume that we have for a while laid aside, *the idea of a being absolutely perfect* above proposed, it being in such set forth, that a man cannot rid his mind of it, but he must needs acknowledge it to be indeed the idea of such a being; it will follow that it is no arbitrarious nor fortuitous concept, but necessary, and therefore natural to the soul at least, if not ever actually there.

Wherefore it is manifest, that we consulting with our own natural light concerning the notion of a *being absolutely perfect*, that this oracle tells us that it is "a spiritual substance, eternal, infinite in essence and goodness, omnipotent, omniscient, of itself necessarily existent."

For this answer is such, that if we understand the sense thereof, we cannot tell how to deny it, and therefore it is true according to the light of nature. But it is manifest that that which is self-subsistent, infinitely good, omniscient and omnipotent is the root and original of all things. For omnipotency signifies a power that can effect anything that implies no contradiction to be effected; and creation implies no contradiction. Therefore this perfect being can create all things. But if it found the matter or other substances existing aforehand of themselves, this omnipotency and power of creation will be in vain, nay indeed a full omnipotency will not be in this absolute omnipotent; which the free and unprejudiced faculties of the mind of man do not admit of but look upon as a contradiction. Therefore the natural notion of a being absolutely perfect implies that the same being is lord and maker of all things. And according to natural light that

6. [ED.] I.e., rarefied, delicately formed.

which is thus, is to be adored and worshipped of all that has the knowledge of it, with all humility and thankfulness; and what is this but to be acknowledged to be God?

Wherefore I conceive I have sufficiently demonstrated that the notion or idea of God is as natural, necessary and essential to the soul of man as any other notion or idea whatsoever, and is no more arbitrarious or fictitious than the notion of a cube or tetraedrum, or any other of the regular bodies in geometry, which are not devised at our own pleasure (for such figments and chimaeras are infinite), but for these it is demonstrable that there can be no more than five of them. Which shows that their notion is necessary, not an arbitrarious compilement of what we please.

And thus having fully made good the notion of God, *what he is*, I proceed now to the next point, which is to prove, *that he is*.

Chapter VIII

And now verily casting my eyes upon the true idea of God which we have found out, I seem to myself to have struck further into this business than I was aware of. For if this idea or notion of God be true, as I have undeniably proved, it is also undeniably true that he doth exist. For this idea of God being no arbitrarious figment taken up at pleasure, but the necessary and natural emanation of the mind of man, if it signifies to us that the notion and nature of God implies in it necessary existence, as we have shown it does, unless we will wink against our own natural light, we are without any further scruple to acknowledge that God does exist.

Nor is it sufficient grounds to diffide [7] to the strength of this argument, because our fancy can shuffle in this abater, viz., that indeed this idea of God, supposing God did exist, shows us that his existence is necessary, but it does not show us that he doth necessarily exist. For he that answers thus, does not observe out of what prejudice he is enabled to make this answer, which is this: he being accustomed to fancy the nature or notion of everything else without existence, and so ever easily separating essence and existence in them, here unawares he takes the same liberty, and divides existence from that essence to which existence itself is essential. And that's the witty [8] fallacy his unwariness has entangled him in.

Again, whenas we contend that the true idea of God represents him as a

7. [ED.] I.e., to have or feel distrust.
8. [ED.] I.e., intelligent.

being necessarily existent, and therefore that he does exist; and you to avoid the edge of the argument reply, if he did at all exist; by this answer you involve yourself in a manifest contradiction. For first you say with us that the nature of God is such that in its very notion it implies its necessary existence, and then again you unsay it by intimating that notwithstanding this true idea and notion, God may not exist, and so acknowledge that what is absolutely necessary according to the free emanation of our faculties yet may be otherwise; which is a palpable contradiction as much as respects us and our faculties, and we have nothing more inward and immediate than these to steer ourselves by.

And to make this yet plainer at least if not stronger, when we say that the existence of God is necessary, we are to take notice that necessity is a logical term, and signifies so firm a connexion betwixt the subject and predicate (as they call them) that it is impossible that they should be dissevered, or should not hold together and therefore if they be affirmed one of the other, that they make *axioma necessarium,* an axiom that is necessary or eternally true. Wherefore there being a necessary connexion betwixt *God and existence,* this axiom, *God does exist,* is an axiom necessarily and eternally true. Which we shall yet more clearly understand if we compare necessity and contingency together. For as contingency signifies not only the manner of existence in that which is contingent according to its idea, but does intimate also a possibility of actual existence, so (to make up the true and easy analogy) *necessity* does not only signify the manner of existence in that which is necessary, but also that it does *actually exist* and could never possibly do otherwise. For necessity of being and impossibility of not being are all one with Aristotle and the rest of the logicians. But the atheist and the enthusiast are usually such professed enemies against logic; the one merely out of dotage upon outward gross sense, the other in a dear regard to his stiff and untamed fancy, that shop of mysteries and fine things.

Thirdly, we may further add, that whereas we must needs attribute to the idea of God either contingency, impossibility or necessity of actual existence (some one of these belonging to every idea imaginable) and that contingency is incompetible to an idea of a being absolutely perfect, much more impossibility, the idea of God being compiled of no notions but such as are possible according to the light of nature, to which we now appeal. It remains therefore that necessity of actual existence be unavoidably cast upon the idea of God, and that therefore God does actually exist.

But fourthly and lastly, if this seem more subtile, though it be no less true for it, I shall now propound that which is so palpable, that it is impossible for anyone that has the use of his wits for to deny it. I say, therefore, that either God or this corporeal and sensible world must of itself necessarily exist. Or thus, either God, or matter, or both do of themselves necessarily exist. If both, we have what we would drive at, the existency of God.

But yet to acknowledge the necessary existence of the *matter* of itself, is not so congruous and suitable to the light of nature. For if anything can exist independently of God, all things may; so that not only the omnipotency of God might be in vain, but beside there would be a letting in from hence of all confusion and disorder imaginable. Nay, of some grand devil of equal power and of as large command as God himself. Or, if you will, of six thousand millions of such monstrous gigantic spirits, fraught with various and mischievous passions, as well as armed with immense power, who in anger or humor appearing in huge shapes, might take the planets up in their prodigious clutches and pelt one another with them as boys are wont to do with snowballs. And that this has not yet happened will be resolved only into this, that the humor has not yet taken them. But the frame of nature and the generation of things would be still liable to this ruin and disorder. So dangerous a thing it is to slight the natural dependencies and correspondencies of our innate ideas and conceptions.

Nor is there any refuge in such a reply as this, that the full and perfect infinitude of the power of God is able easily to overmaster these six thousand millions of monsters and to stay their hands. For I say that six or fewer may equalize the infinite power of God. For if anything may be self-essentiated besides God, why may not a spirit of just six times less power than God exist of itself? And then six such will equalize him, a seventh will overpower him.

But such a rabble of self-essentiated and divided deities does not only hazard the pulling the world in pieces, but plainly takes away the existence of the true God. For if there be any power or perfection whatsoever which has its original from any other than God, it manifestly demonstrates that God is not God, that is, is not a being absolutely and fully perfect, because we see some power in the world that is not his, that is, that is not from him. But what is fully and wholly from him is very truly and properly his, as the thought of my mind is rather my mind's, than my thought's.

And this is the only way that I know to demonstrate that it is impossible that there should be any more than one true *God* in the world. For if we did admit another beside him, this other must be also self-originated; and so neither of them would be God. For the idea of God swallows up into itself all power and perfection conceivable, and therefore necessarily implies that whatever hath any being derives it from him.

But if you say the *matter* does only exist and not God, then this matter does necessarily exist of itself, and so we give that attribute unto the matter which our natural light taught us to be contained in the essential conception of no other thing besides God. Wherefore to deny that of God which is so necessarily comprehended in the true idea of him, and to acknowledge it in that in whose idea it is not at all contained (for necessary existence is not contained in the idea of anything but of a being absolutely perfect) is to pronounce contrary to our natural light and to do manifest violence to our faculties.

Nor can this be excused by saying that the corporeal matter is palpable and sensible unto us but God is not, and therefore we pronounce confidently that it is, though God be not, and also that it is necessary of itself, sith that which is without the help of another must necessarily be and eternally.

For I demand of you then, sith you profess yourselves to believe nothing but sense, how could sense ever help you to that truth you acknowledged last, viz., that that which exists without the help of another is necessary and eternal? For necessity and eternity are no sensible qualities and therefore are not the objects of any sense. And I have already very plentifully proved, that there is other knowledge and perception in the soul besides that of sense. Wherefore it is very unreasonable, whenas we have other faculties of knowledge besides the senses, that we should consult with the senses alone about matters of knowledge and exclude those faculties that penetrate beyond sense—a thing that the professed atheists themselves will not do when they are in the humor of philosophizing, for their principle of atoms is a business that does not fall under sense, as Lucretius at large confesses.[9]

But now seeing it is so manifest that the soul of man has other cognoscitive faculties besides that of sense (which I have clearly demonstrated), it is as incongruous to deny there is a God, because God is not an object fitted to the senses, as it were to deny there is matter or a body because that body or matter, in the imaginative notion thereof, lies so unevenly and troublesomely in our fancy and reason.

In the contemplation whereof our understanding discovereth such contradictious incoherencies that were it not that the notion is sustained by

9. [ED.] Lucretius, *De Rerum Natura*, Bk. II, lines 312–13; Bk. IV, lines 110–15.

the confident dictates of sense, reason appealing to those more crass representations of fancy, would by her shrewd dilemmas be able to argue it quite out of the world. But our reason being well aware that corporeal matter is the proper object of the sensitive faculty, she gives full belief to the information of sense in her own sphere, slighting the puzzling objections of perplexed fancy, and freely admits the existence of matter, the entanglements of imagination; as she does also the existence of God from the contemplation of his idea in our soul, notwithstanding the silence of the senses therein.

For indeed it were an inexcusable piece of folly and madness in a man, whenas he has cognoscitive faculties reaching to the knowledge of God and has a certain and unalterable idea of God in his soul, which he can by no device wipe out, as well as he has the knowledge of sense that reaches to the discovery of the matter; to give necessary self-existence to the matter, no faculty at all informing him so; and to take necessary existence from God, though the natural notion of God in the soul inform him to the contrary; and only upon this pretence, because God does not immediately fall under the knowledge of the senses; thus partially siding with one kind of faculty only of the soul and proscribing all the rest. Which is as humorsomely and foolishly done, as if a man should make a faction amongst the senses themselves and resolve to believe nothing to be but what he could see with his eyes and so confidently pronounce that there is no such thing as the element of air, nor winds, nor music, nor thunder. And the reason forsooth must be because he can see none of these things with his eyes, and that's the sole sense that he intends to believe.

Chapter IX

And hitherto I have argued from the natural notion or idea of God as it respects that of which it is the idea or notion. I shall now try what advantage may be made of it from the respect it bears unto our souls, the subject thereof, wherein it does reside.

I demand therefore who put this indelible character of God upon our souls? Why and to what purpose is it there?

Nor do not think to shuffle me off by saying, we must take things as we find them and not inquire of the final cause of anything; for things are necessarily as they are of themselves, whose guidance and contrivance is from no principle of wisdom or counsel, but every substance is now and ever was of what nature and capacity it is found; having its original from none other than itself; and all those changes and varieties we see in the world are but the result of an eternal scuffle of co-ordinate causes, bearing up as well as they can, to continue themselves in the present state they ever are, and acting and being acted upon by others, these varieties of things appear in the world, but every particular substance with the essential properties thereof is self-originated, and independent of any other.

For to this I answer that the very best that can be made of all this is but thus much, that it is merely and barely possible, nay if we consult our faculties and the idea of God, utterly impossible; but admit it possible; this bare possibility is so lax, so weak and so indeterminate a consideration, that it ought to have no power to move the mind this way or that way that has any tolerable use of her own reason, more than the faint breathings of the loose air have to shake a mountain of brass. For if bare possibility may at all entangle our assent or dissent in things, we cannot fully disbelieve the absurdest fable in Æsop or Ovid, or the most ridiculous figments that can be imagined: as suppose that ears of corn in the field hear the whistling of the wind and chirping of the birds; that the stones in the street are grinded with pain when the carts go over them; that the heliotrope eyes the sun and really sees him as well as turns about with him; that the pulp of the walnut, as bearing the signature of the brain, is endued with imagination and reason. I say no man can fully misbelieve any of these fooleries, if bare possibility may have the least power of turning the scales this way or that way. For none of these nor a thousand more such like as these imply a perfect and palpable contradiction and therefore will put in for their right of being deemed possible.

But we are not to attend to what is simply possible, but to what our natural faculties do direct and determine us to. As for example, suppose the question were, whether the stones in the street have sense or no, we are not to leave the point as indifferent, or that may be held either way, because it is possible and implies no palpable contradiction that they may have sense, and that a painful sense too. But we are to consult with our natural faculties and see whither they propend and they do plainly determinate the controversy by telling us, that what has sense and is capable of pain ought to have also progressive motion to be able to avoid what is hurtful and painful and we see it is so in all beings that have any considerable share of sense. And Aristotle, who was no doter on a deity, yet frequently does assume this principle, that nature does nothing in vain.[10] Which is either an acknowledgment of a God or an appeal to our own

10. [ED.] Aristotle, *De Coelo*, Bk. I, Ch. IV; Bk. II, Ch. V.

rational faculties; and I am indifferent which, for I have what I would out of either; for if we appeal to the natural suggestions of our own faculties they will assuredly tell us there is a God.

I therefore again demand (and I desire to be answered without prejudice or any restraint laid upon our natural faculties) to what purpose is this indelible image or idea of God in us, if there be no such thing as God existent in the world? or who sealed so deep an impression of that character upon our minds?

If we were travelling in a desolate wilderness, where we could discover neither man nor house, and should meet with herds of cattle or flocks of sheep upon whose bodies there were branded certain marks or letters, we should without any hesitancy conclude that these have all been under the hand of some man or other that has set his name upon them. And verily when we see writ in our souls in such legible characters the name or rather the nature and idea of God, why should we be so slow and backward from making the like reasonable inference? Assuredly he whose character is signed upon our souls has been here and has thus marked us that we and all may know to whom we belong, that "it is he that has made us, and not we ourselves, that we are his people and the sheep of his pasture" [Ps. 100:3]. And it is evidently plain from the idea of God, which includes omnipotency in it, that we can be made from none other than he, as I have before demonstrated. And therefore there was no better way than by sealing us with this image to make us acknowledge ourselves to be his and to do that worship and adoration to him that is due to our mighty Maker and Creator, that is to our God.

Wherefore things complying thus naturally and easily together, according to the free suggestions of our natural faculties, it is as perverse and forced a business to suspend assent as to doubt whether those Roman urns and coins I spoke of digged out of the earth be the works of nature or the artifice of men.

But if we cannot yet for all this give free assent to this position, that God does exist, let us at least have the patience a while to suppose it. I demand therefore, supposing God did exist, what can the mind of man imagine that this God should do better or more effectual for the making himself known to such a creature as man, endued with such and such faculties, than we find really already done? For God being a spirit and infinite, cannot ever make himself known necessarily and adequately by any appearance to our outward senses. For if he should manifest himself in any outward figures or shapes portending either love or wrath, terror or protection, our faculties could not assure us that this were God, but some particular genius good or bad; and besides, such dazzling and affrightful external forces are neither becoming the divine nature, nor suitable with the condition of the soul of man, whose better faculties and more free God meddles with, does not force nor amaze us by a more coarse and oppressing power upon our weak and brutish senses. What remains therefore but that he should manifest himself to our inward man? And what way imaginable is more fit than the indelible impression of the idea of himself, which is (not divine life and sense, for that's an higher prize laid up for them that can win it), but a natural representation of the Godhead and a notion of his essence, whereby the soul of man could no otherwise conceive of him than an "eternal spirit, infinite in goodness, omnipotent, omniscient and necessarily of himself existent." But this, as I have fully proved, we find *de facto* done in us, wherefore we being every way dealt with as if there were a God existing, and no faculty discovering anything to the contrary, what should hinder us from the concluding that he does really exist?

Chapter X

Hitherto we have argued for the existency of the Godhead from the natural idea of God, inseparably and immutably residing in the soul of man. There are also other arguments may be drawn from what we may observe to stick very close to man's nature; and such is natural remorse of conscience and a fear and disturbance from the committing of such things as notwithstanding are not punishable by men; as also a natural hope of being prosperous and successful in doing those things which are conceived by us to be good and righteous; and lastly religious veneration or divine worship—all which are fruits unforcedly and easily growing out of the nature of man, and if we rightly know the meaning of them, they all intimate that there is a God.

And first of natural conscience, it is plain that it is a fear and confusion of mind arising from the presage of some mischief that may befall a man beside the ordinary course of nature or the usual occurrences of affairs, because he has done thus or thus. Not that what is supernatural or absolutely extraordinary must needs fall unto him, but that at least the ordinary calamities and misfortunes which are in the world will be directed and levelled at him some time or other, because he hath done this or that evil against his conscience. And men do naturally in some heavy adversity, mighty tempest on the sea or dreadful thunder on the land (though these be but from natural causes) reflect upon themselves and their actions and so are invaded with fear or are unterrified, accordingly as they condemn or acquit themselves in their own consciences. And from this supposal is that magnificent expression of the poet concerning the just man,

Nec fulminantis magna Jovis manus,[11]

that he is not afraid of the darting down of thunder and lightning from heaven. But this fear, that one should be struck rather than the rest, or at this time rather than another time, because a man has done thus or thus, is a natural acknowledgment that these things are guided and directed from some discerning principle, which is all one as to confess that there is a God. Nor is it material that some allege that mariners curse and swear the loudest when the storm is the greatest, for it is because the usualness of such dangers have made them lose the sense of the danger, not the sense of a God.

It is also very natural for a man that follows honestly the dictates of his own conscience to be full of good hopes and much at ease and secure that all things at home and abroad will go successfully with him, though his actions and sincere motions of his mind act nothing upon nature or the course of the world to change them anyway. Wherefore it implies that there is a superintendent principle over nature and the material frame of the world, that looks to it so that nothing shall come to pass but what is consistent with the good and welfare of honest and conscientious men. And if it does not happen to them according to their expectations in this world, it does naturally bring in a belief of a world to come.

Nor does it at all enervate the strength of this argument that some men have lost the sense and difference betwixt good and evil, if there be any so fully degenerate; but let us suppose it, this is a monster, and I suspect of his own making. But this is no more prejudice to what I aim at who argue from the natural constitution of a man the existency of a God, than if because Democritus put out his eyes, some are born blind, others drink out their eyes and cannot see, that therefore you should conclude that there is neither light nor colors. For if there were, then every one would see them, but Democritus and some others do not see them. But the reason is plain: there hath been force done to their natural faculties and they have put out their sight.

11. [ED.] Horace, *Odes*, Bk III, Ode III: "Nec fulminantis magna manus Jovis: Not by the mighty hand of thundering Jove."

Wherefore I conclude from natural conscience in a man that puts him upon hope and fear of good and evil from what he does or omits, though those actions and omissions do nothing to the change of the course of nature or the affairs of the world, that there is an intelligent principle over universal nature that takes notice of the actions of men—that is, that there is a God; for else this natural faculty would be false and vain.

Now for adoration or religious worship, it is as universal as mankind, there being no nation under the cope of heaven that does not do divine worship to something or other and in it to God, as they conceive; wherefore according to the ordinary natural light that is in all men, there is a God.

Nor can the force of this argument be avoided by saying it is but an universal tradition that has been time out of mind spread among the nations of the world. For if it were so (which yet cannot at all be proved) in that it is universally received, it is manifest that it is according to the light of nature to acknowledge there is a God. For that which all men admit as true, though upon the proposal of another, is undoubtedly to be termed true according to the light of nature. As many hundreds of geometrical demonstrations that were first the inventions of some one man have passed undeniable through all ages and places for true according to the light of nature, with them that were but learners, not inventors of them. And it is sufficient to make a thing true according to the light of nature, that no man upon a perception of what is propounded and the reasons of it (if it be not clear at the first sight and need reasons to back it) will ever stick to acknowledge for a truth. And therefore if there were any nations that were destitute of the knowledge of a God, as they may be it is likely of the rudiments of geometry, so long as they admit of the knowledge of one as well as of the other, upon due and fit proposal, the acknowledgment of a God is as well to be said to be according to the light of nature as the knowledge of geometry which they thus receive.

But if it be here objected that a thing may be universally received of all nations and yet be so far from being true according to the light of nature, that is not true at all, as for example, that the sun moves about the earth, and that the earth stands still as the fixed center of the world, which the best of astronomers and the profoundest of philosophers pronounce to be false: I answer that in some sense it does stand still, if you understand by motion the translation of a body out of the vicinity of other bodies. But suppose it did not stand still, this comes not home to our case; for this is but the just victory of reason over the general prejudice of sense. And every one will acknowledge that reason may correct the impresses of sense;

otherwise we should, with Epicurus and Lucretius,[12] admit the sun and moon to be no wider than a sieve, and the bodies of the stars to be no bigger than the ordinary flame of a candle. Therefore you see here is a clashing of the faculties one against another, and the stronger carries it. But there is no faculty that can be pretended to clash with the judgment of reason and natural sagacity that so easily either concludes or presages that there is a God. Wherefore that may well go for a truth according to the light of nature that is universally received of men, be it by what faculty it will they receive it, no other faculty appearing that can evidence to the contrary. And such is the universal acknowledgment that there is a God.

Nor is it much more material to reply that though there be indeed a religious worship exercised in all nations upon the face of the earth, yet they worship many of them but stocks and stones or some particular piece of nature, as the sun, moon or stars. For I answer that first it is very hard to prove that they worship any image or statue without reference to some spirit at least, if not to the omnipotent God. So that we shall hence at least win thus much, that there are in the universe some more subtile and immaterial substances that take notice of the affairs of men, and this is as ill to a slow atheist as to believe that there is a God.

And for that adoration some of them do to the sun and moon, I cannot believe they do it to them under the notion of mere inanimate bodies, but they take them to be the habitation of some intellectual beings as the verse does plainly intimate to us,

The sun that hears and sees all things; [13]

and this is very near the true notion of a God.

But be this universal religious worship what it will, as absurd as you please to fancy it, yet it will not fail to reach very far for the proving of a deity. For there are no natural faculties in things that have not their object in the world; as there is meat as well as mouths, sounds as well as hearing, colors as well as sight, dangers as well as fear, and the like. So there ought in like manner to be a God as well as a natural propension in men to religious worship, God alone being the proper object thereof.

Nor does it abate the strength of the argument that this so deeply radicated property of religion in man, that cannot be lost, does so ineptly and ridiculously display itself in mankind.

---

12. [ED.] Lucretius, *De Rerum Natura*, Bk. IV, lines 478, 496; Bk. V, line 564; and Diogenes Laertius, *Life of Epicurus*.

13. [ED.] Homer, *The Iliad*, Bk. III, line 277.

For as the plying of a dog's feet in his sleep, as if here were some game before him, and the butting of a young lamb before he has yet either horns or enemies to encounter, would not be in nature were there not such a thing as a hare to be coursed or an horned enemy to be encountered with horns: so there would not be so universal an exercise of religious worship in the world, though it be done never so ineptly and foolishly, were there not really a due object of this worship and a capacity in man for the right performance thereof; which could not be unless there were a God.

But the truth is, man's soul in this drunken drowsy condition she is in has fallen asleep in the body and like one in a dream talks to the bed-posts, embraces her pillow instead of her friend, falls down before statues instead of adoring the eternal and invisible God, prays to stocks and stones instead of speaking to him that by his word created all things.

Aye, but you will reply that a young lamb has at length both his weapon and enemy to encounter, and the dreaming dog did once and may again pursue some real game. And so he that talks in his sleep did once confer with men awake and may do so once again. But whole nations for many successions of ages have been very stupid idolaters and do so continue to this day. But I answer that this rather informs us of another great mystery than at all enervates the present argument or obscures the grand truth we strive for. For this does plainly insinuate thus much, that mankind is in a lapsed condition, like one fallen down in a fit of an epilepsy, whose limbs by force of the convulsion are moved very incomposedly and ill-favoredly; but we know that he that does for the present move the members of his body so rudely and fortuitously, did before command the use of his muscles in a decent exercise of his progressive faculty, and that when the fit is over he will do so again.

This therefore rather implies that these poor barbarous souls had once the true knowledge of God and of his worship, and by some hidden providence may be recovered into it again, than that this propension to religious worship, that so conspicuously appears in them should be utterly in vain, as it would be both in them and in all men else if there were no God.

Chapter XI

We have done with all those more obvious faculties in the soul of man that naturally tend to the discovery of the existence of a God. Let us briefly, before we loose from ourselves and launch out into the vast ocean of the external phenomena of nature, consider the essence of the soul herself, what it is, whether a mere modification of the body or substance distinct therefrom; and then whether corporeal or incorporeal. For upon the clearing of this point we may happily be convinced that there is a spiritual substance, really distinct from the matter. Which whoso does acknowledge will be easilier induced to believe there is a God.

First, therefore, if we say that the soul is a mere modification of the body, the soul then is but one universal faculty of the body or a many faculties put together, and those operations which are usually attributed unto the soul must of necessity be attributed unto the body. I demand therefore to what in the body will you attribute spontaneous motion? I understand thereby a power in ourselves of moving or holding still most of the parts of our body, as our hand, suppose, or little finger. If you will say that it is nothing but the immission [14] of the spirits into such and such muscles, I would gladly know what does limit these spirits and direct them so curiously. Is it themselves, or the brain, or that particular piece of the brain they call the conarion or pine kernel? [15] Whatever it be, that which does thus immit them and direct them must have animadversion, and the same that has animadversion has memory also and reason. Now I would know whether the spirits themselves be capable of animadversion, memory and reason; for it indeed seems altogether impossible. For these animal spirits are nothing else but matter very thin and liquid, whose nature consists in this, that all the particles of it be in motion, and being loose from one another fridge [i.e., fidget] and play up and down according to the measure and manner of agitation in them.

I therefore now demand which of the particles in these so many loosely moving one from another has animadversion in it? If you say that they all

14. I.e., insertion, injection (from "immit," to inject).
15. [54.] The conarion (from the Greek diminutive of *conos*, a pine cone or kernel) is the pineal gland of the brain. The gland is the "vestigial remainder of an unpaired mesial eye." Its exact function is still not fully known. More refers to the conarion on other occasions (e.g., *Antidote Against Atheism*, Appendix; *The Immortality of the Soul*, Bk. II, Ch. iv–v). Descartes had aroused interest in the subject by his surmise that the conarion was the organ of common sense. More expressed more than one opinion of this surmise. In his Appendix to the *Antidote* he accepted it; in his *Immortality* he rejected it, but even then he took it seriously. Descartes' view had to be examined with care, he said, because "it bids the fairest of anything I have met withall, or ever hope to meet withall, for the resolution of the passions and properties of living creatures into mere corporeal motion" (*Immortality*, Bk. II, Ch. iv, §9).

put together have, I appeal to him that thus answers how unlikely it is that that should have animadversion that is so utterly incapable of memory and consequently of reason. For it is as impossible to conceive memory competible to such a subject, as it is, how to write characters in the water or in the wind.

If you say the brain emits and directs these spirits, how can that so freely and spontaneously move itself or another that has no muscles? Besides anatomists tell us that though the brain be the instrument of sense, yet it has no sense at all of itself; how then can that that has no sense, direct thus spontaneously and arbitrariously the animal spirits into any part of the body?—an act that plainly requires determinate sense and perception. But let the anatomists conclude what they will, I think I shall little less than demonstrate that the brains have no sense. For the same thing in us that has sense has likewise animadversion; and that which has animadversion in us has also a faculty of free and arbitrarious fancy and of reason.

Let us now consider the nature of the brain and see how competible those operations and powers are to such a subject. Verily if we take a right view of this lax pith or marrow in man's head, neither our sense nor understanding can discover anything more in this substance that can pretend to such noble operations as free imagination and the sagacious collections of reason, than we can discern in a cake of suet or a bowl of curds. For this loose pulp that is thus wrapped up within our cranium is but a spongy and porous body and pervious not only to the animal spirits but also to more gross juice and liquor, else it could not well be nourished, at least it could not be so soft and moistened by drunkenness and excess as to make the understanding inept and sottish in its operations. Wherefore I now demand in this soft substance which we call the brain (whose softness implies that it is in some measure liquid, and liquidity implies a several motion of loosened parts), in what part or parcel thereof does fancy, reason and animadversion lie? In this lax consistence that lies like a net all on heaps in the water, I demand in what knot, loop or interval thereof does this faculty of free fancy and active reason reside? I believe you will be ashamed to assign me any one in particular.

And if you will say in "all together," you must say that the whole brain is figured into this or that representation, which would cancel memory and take away all capacity of there being any distinct notes and places for the several species of things there represented.

But if you will say there is in every part of the brain this power of animadversion and fancy, you are to remember that the brain is in some measure a liquid body, and we must inquire how these loose parts understand one another's several animadversions and notions. And if they could (which is yet very inconceivable) yet if they could from hence do anything toward the immission and direction of the animal spirits into this or that part of the body, we must consider that they must do it (upon the knowing one another's minds) as it were by a joint contention of strength, as when many men at once, the word being given, lift or tug together for the moving of some so massy a body that the single strength of one could not deal with. But this is to make the several particles of the brain so many individual persons; a fitter object for laughter than the least measure of belief.

Besides, how come these many animadversions to seem but one to us, our mind being these, as is supposed? Or rather why, if the figuration of one part of the brain be communicated to all the rest, does not the same object seem situated both behind us and before us, above and beneath, on the right hand and on the left, and every way as the impress of the object is reflected against all the parts of the brains? But there appearing to us but one animadversion as but one site of things, it is a sufficient argument that there is but one; or if there be many, that they are not mutually communicated from the parts one to another, and that therefore can be no such joint endeavor toward one design; whence it is manifest that the brains cannot emit nor direct these animal spirits into what part of the body they please.

Moreover that the brain has no sense and therefore cannot impress spontaneously any motion on the animal spirits, it is no slight argument in that some being dissected have been found without brains and Fontanus [16] tells us of a boy at Amsterdam that had nothing but limpid water in his head instead of brains and the brains generally are easily dissolvable into a watery consistence, which agree with what I intimated before. Now I appeal to any free judge how likely these liquid particles are to approve themselves together for a moment of time to bear themselves so as with one joint contention of strength to cause an arbitrarious ablegation [sending abroad] of the spirits into this or that determinate part of the body. But the absurdity of this I have sufficiently insinuated already.

Lastly the nerves, I mean the marrow of them which is of the selfsame substance with the brain, have no sense, as is demonstrable from a catalep-

16. [ED.] Fontanus: Nicholas Fonteyn, a celebrated Dutch physician of the seventeenth century, professor of anatomy at Amsterdam, a prolific author of medical works: e.g., *Responsionum et curationum medicinalium*, Amsterdam, 1639.

sis or catochus: [17] but I will not accumulate arguments in a matter so palpable.

As for that little sprunt [sprung] piece of the brain which they call the conarion, that this should be the very substance whose natural faculty it is to move itself and by its motions and nods to determinate the course of the spirits into this or that part of the body, seems to me no less foolish and fabulous than the story of him that could change the wind as he pleased by setting his cap on this or that side of his head.

If you heard but the magnificent stories that are told of this little lurking mushroom, how it does not only hear and see, but imagines, reasons, commands the whole fabric of the body more dexterously than an Indian boy does an elephant, what an acute logician, subtle geometrician, prudent statesman, skillful physician and profound philosopher he is, and then afterwards by dissection you discover this worker of miracles to be nothing but a poor silly contemptible knob or protuberancy consisting of a thin membrane containing a little pulpous matter much of the same nature with the rest of the brain,

Spectatum admissi risum teneatis amici? [18]

Would you not sooner laugh at it than go about to confute it? And truly I may the better laugh at it now, having already confuted it in what I have afore argued concerning the rest of the brain.

I shall therefore make bold to conclude that the impress of spontaneous motion is neither from the animal spirits nor from the brain, and therefore that those operations that are usually attributed unto the soul are really incompetible to any part of the body; and therefore that the soul is not a mere modification of the body but a substance distinct therefrom.

Now we are to enquire whether this substance distinct from what ordinarily we call the body be also itself a corporeal substance, or whether it be incorporeal. If you say that it is a corporeal substance you can understand no other than matter more subtile and tenuous than the animal spirits themselves, mingled with them and dispersed through the vessels and porosities of the body, for there can be no penetration of dimensions. But I need no new arguments to confute this fond conceit, for what I said of the animal spirits before is applicable with all ease and fitness to this present

17. [ED.]"Catalepsis" (catalepsy), a disease characterized by seizure or trance, lasting for hours or days, with a suspension of sensation or consciousness; "catochus," a disease similar to catalepsy, but with rigidity of the limbs. Cf. O.E.D.

18. [ED.] Horace, *Ars Poetica*, 5: "My friends, if you were admitted to such a sight, could you refrain from laughter?"

case. And let it be sufficient that I advertise you so much, and so be excused from the repeating of the same things over again.

It remains therefore that we conclude that that which impresses spontaneous motion upon the body or more immediately upon the animal spirits, that which imagines, remembers and reasons, is an immaterial substance distinct from the body, which uses the animal spirits and the brains for instruments in such and such operations. And thus we have found a spirit in a proper notion and signification that has apparently these faculties in it: it can both understand and move corporeal matter.

And now the prize that we have won will prove for our design of very great consequence. For it is obvious here to observe that the soul of man is, as it were, "a compendious statue of the Deity." Her substance is a solid effigies [19] of God. And therefore as with ease we consider the substance and motion of the vast heavens on a little sphere or globe, so we may with like facility contemplate the nature of the Almighty in this little "medal of God," the soul of man, enlarging to infinity what we observe in ourselves when we transfer it unto God; as we do imagine those circles which we view on the globe to be vastly bigger while we fancy them as described in the heavens.

Wherefore we being assured of this, that there is a spiritual substance in ourselves in which both these properties do reside, viz., of understanding and of moving corporeal matter, let us both enlarge our minds so as to conceive as well as we can of a spiritual substance that is able to move and actuate all matter whatsoever never so far extended, and after what way and manner soever it please and that it has not the knowledge only of this or that particular thing, but a distinct and plenary cognoscence of all things; and we have indeed a very competent apprehension of the nature of the eternal and invisible God, who like the soul of man does not indeed fall under sense, but does everywhere operate so, that his presence is easily to be gathered from what is discovered by our outward senses.

19. [ED.] The archaic form of "effigy."

❖ ❖ ❖ ❖ ❖ ❖ ❖ ❖

RALPH CUDWORTH

The Existence of God and the Nature of Knowledge

Editor's Introduction. **One** of the interesting features of Cudworth's thought is his theory of knowledge. He criticizes the dualism of Descartes, not because it is dualistic but because it is falsely conceived. Similarly he repudiates the theory that the mind passively receives the impressions of sense. He is concerned to make clear the active, unifying, synthesizing function of the mind. Of this "action and comprehensive power" he offers illustrations chosen from a wide variety of fields, including political theory and aesthetics. His most telling example is taken from the nature of the universe. When we consider the cosmos, according to Cudworth, we become aware of wide diversity but also of a unifying principle which knits the whole together. In human experience the mind, he believes, is prior to the sensations it receives and from which it constructs concepts and judgments; similarly in the universe, the order and symmetry which we observe must be dependent on the ultimate source of rationality, i.e., "the mind of an omnipotent and infinitely perfect Being, comprehending itself and the extent of its own power." To Cudworth the conclusion is inescapable: "There must be a mind senior to the world and all sensible things, and such as comprehends in it the ideas of all intelligibles, their necessary scheses and relations to one another, and all their immutable truths."

Cudworth was using Platonic materials, and he was writing before the publication of Locke's *Essay*. The significance of the work reproduced here lies not merely in the freedom with which Cudworth handled his sources and by implication criticized his contemporaries, nor is it even in the remarkable extent to which he anticipates Kant; rather, it is in the way his epistemology is made to serve his primary theological concerns.

❖ ❖ ❖ ❖

The Demonstration of the Existence of a God ... from the Nature of Knowledge and Understanding

FROM *The True Intellectual System of the Universe*

CHAPTER V, SECTION I

Now we shall, for the present, only so far forth concern ourselves in confuting this atheistic doctrine, as to lay a foundation thereby for the demonstration of the contrary, namely, the existence of a God, or a Mind before the world, from the nature of knowledge and understanding. First, therefore, it is a sottish conceit of these atheists, proceeding from their not attending to their own cogitations, that not only sense but also knowledge and understanding in men is but a tumult, raised from corporeal things without, pressing upon the organs of their body; or else, as they declare themselves more distinctly, nothing but the activity of sensible objects upon them, and their passion from them. For if this were true, then would everything that suffered and reacted motion, especially polite [1] bodies, as looking-glasses, have something both of sense and of understanding in them. It is plain that there comes nothing to us from bodies without us but only local motion and pressure. Neither is sense itself the mere passion of those motions, but the perception of their passions in a way of fancy. But sensible things themselves (as for example light and colors) are not known or understood either by the passion or the fancy of sense, nor by any thing merely foreign and adventitious, but by intelligible ideas exerted from the mind itself, that is, by something native and domestic to it; nothing being more true than this of Boethius, that "whatsoever is known, is not known by its own force and power, but by the force and power, the vigor and activity of that thing itself, which knows or comprehends it." [2] Wherefore, besides the phantasms of singular bodies or of sensible things

---

1. [ED.] I.e., smoothed, polished, burnished. Cf. O.E.D.
2. [ED.] Boethius, *The Consolation of Philosophy*, Bk. V, Ch. IV. Cudworth quotes Boethius inexactly. A more faithful translation would be: "For all that is known is not grasped according to the force which it has in itself, but rather according to the faculty of those who know it."

existing without us (which are not mere passions neither), it is plain that our human mind hath other cogitations or conceptions in it; namely, the ideas of the intelligible natures and essences of things which are universal, and by and under which it understands singulars. It is a ridiculous conceit of a modern atheistic writer, that universals are nothing else but names, attributed to many singular bodies, because whatsoever *is*, is singular. For though whatsoever exists without the mind be singular, yet is it plain that there are conceptions in our minds objectively universal. Which universal objects of our mind, though they exist not as such anywhere without it, yet are they not therefore nothing, but have an intelligible entity for this very reason, because they are conceivable: for since nonentity is not conceivable, whatsoever is conceivable and an object of the mind, is therefore something. And as for axiomatical truths, in which something is affirmed or denied, as these are not all passions from bodies without us (for what local motions could impress this common notion upon our minds, that things which agree in one third agree amongst themselves, or any other?), so neither are these things only gathered by induction from repeated and reiterated sensations, we clearly apprehending at once that it is impossible they should be otherwise. Thus Aristotle ingeniously: "It is evident that there is no knowledge (of the universal theorems of geometry) by sense. For if we could perceive by sense that the three angles of a triangle were equal to two right, yet should we not rest satisfied in this, as having therefore a sufficient knowledge hereof; but would seek further after a demonstration of it; sense reaching only to singulars, but knowledge to universals." [3] When from the universal idea of a triangle, which is neither here nor there, nor anywhere without our mind, but yet hath an intelligible entity, we see a plain necessity, that its three angles must be equal to two right, then do we know the truth of this universal theorem, and not before; as also we understand, that every singular triangle (so far as it is true) hath this property in it. Wherefore the knowledge of this and the like truths is not derived from singulars, nor do we arrive to them in way of ascent from singulars to universals; but, on the contrary, having first found them in the universals, we afterwards descending, apply them to singulars; so that our knowledge here is not after singular bodies, and secondarily or derivatively from them, but in order of nature before them, and proleptical to them.

Now these universal conceptions, some of which are also abstract (as

3. [ED.] Aristotle, *Posterior Analytics*, Bk. I. Cudworth has conflated two passages; the order of the words is not that of Aristotle, but the sense is accurately reproduced.

life, sense, reason, knowledge and the like) many of them are of such things whose singulars do not at all fall under sense, which therefore could never possibly be impressed upon us from singular bodies by local motion, and again some such, as though they belong to corporeal and sensible things, yet, as their accuracy cannot be reached to by sense, so neither did they ever exist in that matter of this lower world which here encompasseth us, and therefore could not be stamped upon us from without: as for example, the ideas of a perfect straight line, and a plain superficies, or of an exact triangle, circle, sphere, or cube; no material thing here amongst us being terminated in so strait lines but that even by microscopes there may be discovered much irregularity and deformity in them; and very probable it is, that there are no perfectly straight lines, no such triangles, circles, spheres or cubes as answer to the exactness of our conceptions in any part of the whole material universe, nor never will be. Notwithstanding which, they are not absolute nonentities, since we can demonstrate things concerning them, and though they never were nor will be, yet are they possible to exist, since nothing can be conceived but it either is or else is possible to be. The human mind therefore hath a power of framing ideas and conceptions not only of what actually is, but also of things which never were, nor perhaps will be, they being only possible to be. But when from our conceptions, we conclude of some things, that though they are not, yet they are possible to be (since nothing that is not can be possible to be, unless there be something actually in being which hath sufficient power to produce it) we do implicitly suppose the existence of a God or omnipotent Being thereby, which can make whatsoever is conceivable, though it yet be not, to exist; and therefore material triangles, circles, spheres, cubes, mathematically exact.

The result of what we have hitherto said is this, that since singular bodies are not the only objects of our mind and cogitation, it having also universal and abstract ideas of the intelligible natures or essences of things (some of which are such, whose singulars do not at all fall under sense; others, though they belong to bodies, yet sense can never reach to them, nor were they ever in matter); moreover, since our mind can conceive of things which nowhere actually exist, but are only possible, and can have such a demonstrative science of universal truths, as sense can never ascend to: that therefore human knowledge and understanding itself is not the mere image and creature of singular bodies only; and so derivative, or ectypal from them, and in order of nature junior to them, but that, as it were hovering aloft over all the corporeal universe, it is a thing independent upon singular bodies, or proleptical to them, and in order of nature before them.

But what account can we then possibly give of knowledge and understanding, their nature and original, since there must be "that which is intelligible," in order of nature, before "intellection"? Certainly no other than this, that the first original knowledge is that of a perfect Being, infinitely good and powerful, comprehending itself and the utmost extent of its own fecundity and power, that is, the possibilities of all things; their ideas, with the several relations to one another; all necessary and immutable truths. Here therefore is there a knowledge before the world and all sensible things, that was archetypal and paradigmatical to the same. Of which one perfect mind and knowledge all other imperfect minds (being derived from it) have a certain participation; whereby they are enabled to frame intelligible ideas, not only of whatsoever doth actually exist, but also of such things as never were, nor will be, but are only possible, or objects of divine power.

Wherefore since it is certain that even human knowledge and understanding itself is not a mere passion from sensible things and singular bodies existing without (which is the only foundation of that forementioned atheistic argument, that "things made knowledge," and "not knowledge things"), and consequently it must needs have some other original: moreover, since knowledge and understanding apprehend things proleptically to their existence (mind being able to frame conceptions of all possible entities and modifications) and therefore in their nature do plainly suppose the actual existence of a perfect Being, which is infinitely fecund and powerful, and could produce all things possible or conceivable; the first original Knowledge, or Mind, from whence all other knowledges and minds are derived, being that of an absolutely perfect and omnipotent Being, comprehending itself, and the extent of its own power, or of its communicability, that is, the ideas of all possibilities of things, that may be produced by it, together with their relations to one another, and their necessary immutable truths; accordingly as wisdom and understanding are described to be "the breath (or vapor) of the power of God, and an efflux (or emanation) from the glory of the Almighty, . . . a clear mirror (or looking-glass) of his active energy or virtue, and the image of his goodness" [Wisd. 7:25,26]; I say, the result of all is this, that the nature of knowledge and understanding is so far from being a ground of disproving a Deity (as the atheists ignorantly pretend) that it affordeth a firm demonstration to us, on the contrary, of the existence of God, a perfect omnipotent Being, comprehending itself, and the extent of its own power, or all possibilities of things; a mind before the world, and senior to all things; no ectypal, but archetypal thing, which comprehended in it, as a kind of intellectual world, the paradigm or platform, according to which this sensible world was made.

And this may be further confirmed from what is generally acknowledged, and indeed cannot reasonably be denied by any, viz., that there are eternal verities, such as were never made, nor can ever be destroyed, or cease to be: as for example, such common notions as these, that equals added to equals make equals; that the cause is in the order of nature before the effect, &c., together with all geometrical theorems; as Aristotle himself declareth, he writing in his *Ethics* after this manner: "Concerning eternal (and immutable) things no man does consult; as for example, concerning the diameter or diagonal of a square, whether it should be incommensurable to the sides, or no." [4] Where he plainly affirmeth this geometrical theorem, that the diameter or diagonal of a square is incommensurable to the sides, to be an eternal truth. Neither are there such eternal truths as these only in mathematics, and concerning quantity, but also in ethics concerning morality; there being here "things eternally just," as Justin Martyr calls them,[5] which were not made such at certain times by law and arbitrary command, but, being such in their own nature immutably, were from everlasting to everlasting, and (as it is said of that eternal Word, which comprehends all truth) "the same yesterday, to-day, and for ever" [Heb. 13:8]. For of these is that famous passage of Sophocles in his *Antigone*: "These are not things of to-day, or yesterday, but they ever live, and no man knows their date, or from whence they came." [6] No man can declare the time when all common notions and geometrical truths were first made and generated out of nothing or brought out of antecedent non-existence into being. Certain it is, that such truths as these, that the "diameter and sides of a square are incommensurable, or that the power of the hypothenuse in a rectangular triangle is equal to the powers of both the sides," were not made by any man's thinking, or by those first geometricians who discovered or demonstrated the same; they discovering and demonstrating only that which was. Wherefore these truths were before there was any man to think of them, and they would continue still to be, though all the

---

4. [ED.] Aristotle, *Nicomachean Ethics*, Bk. III, Ch. v. Cudworth quotes only part of the passage.

5. [ED.] Justin Martyr, *Dialogue with Trypho*.

6. [ED.] Sophocles, *Antigone*, verses 467, 468.

men in the world should be annihilated; nay, though there were no material squares and triangles anywhere in the whole world neither, no nor
any matter at all; for they were ever without beginning before the world,
and would of necessity be ever after it, should it cease to be.

Now if there be eternal truths which were never made, and could not
but be, then must the *rationes rerum,* the "simple reasons" of things also,
or their intelligible natures and essences, out of which those truths are
compounded, be of necessity eternal likewise. For how can this be an
eternal truth, that the diameter of a square is incommensurable with the
sides, if the *rationes,* the "reasons" of a square, diameter, and sides, or their
intelligible essences, were not themselves eternal? These are therefore
called by Plato (a man of much meditation, and no contemptible philosopher) not only "things which are always the same, and unchangeable,"
but also, "things which were never made, but always are"; and sometimes,
"things that were neither made, nor can be destroyed"; sometimes, "things
ingenerable and incorruptible." [7] Of which Cicero thus: "These things
Plato affirmeth to have been never made, but always to be, and to be
contained in reason and understanding." [8] And though perhaps it may seem
strange, even Aristotle himself also, notwithstanding his so often clashing
with Plato's ideas, here really agreeth in the main that the forms and
species, or the universal intelligible essences of things, which are the proper
and immediate objects of science, were eternal and never made. Thus in
his *Metaphysics:* "No man makes the form, or species of a thing, nor was it
ever generated"; and again, "There is no generation of the essence of a
sphere"; and, "The forms or species of things are without any generation
or corruption." And he sometimes calleth these objects of science "an
immutable essence or nature." Lastly, where he writeth against the Hera-
clitics, and those other skeptics who denied all certainty of science, he first
discovers the ground of their error herein to have been this, that they
supposed the singular bodies, or sensibles existing without, to be the only
things or objects of the mind, or knowledge: "The original of these men's
mistake was this, because truth was to be looked for in things, and they
conceived the only things to be sensibles, in which it is certain there is
much of the indeterminate nature. Wherefore they, perceiving all the
nature of sensibles to be movable, or in perpetual flux and mutation, since
nothing can possibly be verified or constantly affirmed concerning that,
which is not the same but changeable, concluded that there could be no

7. [ED.] These are phrases which occur commonly in Plato.
8. [ED.] Cicero, *De Oratore ad Brutum,* Ch. III. 10.

truth at all, nor certainty of science; those things, which are the only objects of it, never continuing the same." And then he subjoins in way of
opposition to this skeptical doctrine of theirs, and the forementioned
ground thereof: "We would have these men therefore to know that there
is another kind of essence of things, besides that of sensibles, to which
belongeth neither motion, nor corruption, nor any generation at all." [9]
By which essences of things that have no generation nor corruption, he
could understand nothing else but those intelligible natures, species and
ideas, which are the standing and immutable objects of science. And
certain it is that there could be no constant and immutable science at all,
were there no other objects of the mind but singulars and sensibles, because these are all mutable. Wherefore the proper and immediate objects
of the geometrical science are no singular and material triangles, squares,
spheres and cubes, &c., not only because none of these are found mathematically exact, and because geometricians, in all the several distant ages
and places of the world, could not have the same singular bodies before
them, but also because they do none of them continue immutably the same;
all corporeal things being more or less in perpetual motion and mutation;
whereas, that of which any geometrical theorem is verified and demonstrated, must be immutably and unalterably the same. The triangles and
circles, spheres and cubes of Euclid, Archimedes, Pappus, Apollonius,
and all other ancient and modern geometricians, in all the distant places
and times of the world, were both indivisibly one and the same, and also
perfectly immutable and incorruptible, the science of geometry being such.
For which cause it is affirmed also of these mathematical things by the
forementioned Aristotle that they are nowhere as in a place, as all singular
bodies are: "It is absurd to make mathematical things to be in a place, as
solid bodies are; for place belongeth only to singulars, which are therefore
separable from one another by place; but mathematical things are not
anywhere." [10] Because they being universal and abstract, are only in minds;
nevertheless, for the same reason are they also everywhere, they being in
every mind that apprehends them. Lastly, these intelligible essences and
ideas of things are called also by Philo, "the most necessary essences," [11]
as being not only eternal, but having likewise necessary existence belong-

---

9. [ED.] Aristotle, *Metaphysics*. Cudworth refers to (and sometimes quotes from)
Bk. VII, Ch. VIII; Bk. XIV, Chs. II, III, VI; Bk. IV, Ch. V. But some of the passages
cannot easily be identified.

10. [ED.] Aristotle, *Metaphysics*, Bk. XII, Ch. v.

11. [ED.] Philo, *On the Allegories of the Sacred Laws*, Bk. I, Ch. XVIII.

ing to them; for though there be no absolute necessity that there should be matter or body, yet is there an absolute necessity that there should be truth.

If therefore there be eternal intelligibles or ideas and eternal truths, and necessary existence do belong to them, then must there be an eternal mind necessarily existing, since these truths and intelligible essences of things cannot possibly be anywhere but in a mind. For by the essences of things, when they are said to be eternal, must not be meant their very substances, as if everything were in itself eternal and uncreated; or that God in creation did only, as a modern writer abusively expresseth it, "clothe the antecedent essences of things with a new garment of existence"; but only their *esse cognitum*, their "possible and intelligible natures," as they were objects of infinite power and understanding, before they were made. There must be a mind senior to the world and all sensible things, and such as at once comprehends in it the ideas of all intelligibles, their necessary scheses [12] and relations to one another, and all their immutable truths; a mind, which doth not (as Aristotle writeth of it), sometimes understand, and sometimes not understand, as if it were sometimes awake and sometimes asleep, or like an eye, sometimes open and sometimes shut; but such a mind as is essentially act and energy, and hath no defect in it.[13] And this, as we have already declared, can be no other than the mind of an omnipotent and infinitely perfect Being, comprehending itself and the extent of its own power, or how far itself is communicable, that is, all the possibilities of things that may be made by it, and their respective truths; mind and knowledge, in the very nature of it, supposing the actual existence of an omnipotent or infinitely powerful Being, as its Νοητὸν, or "Intelligible"; it being nothing but the comprehension of the extent of infinite or divine power, and the measure of the same.

And hence it is evident also that there can be but one only original mind, or no more than one understanding Being self-existent; all other minds whatsoever partaking of one original mind, and being, as it were, stamped with the impression or signature of one and the same seal. From whence it cometh to pass, that all minds, in the several places and ages of the world, have ideas or notions of things exactly alike and truths indivisibly the same. Truths are not multiplied by the diversity of minds that apprehend them, because they are all but ectypal participations of one and the same original or archetypal mind and truth. As the same face may be reflected

12. [ED.] I.e., ways in which a thing is related to something else.
13. [ED.] Cf. Aristotle, *Metaphysics*, Bk. XIV, Ch. IX, though Cudworth is not quoting Aristotle exactly.

in several glasses, and the image of the same sun may be in a thousand eyes at once beholding it, and one and the same voice may be in a thousand ears listening to it, so when innumerable created minds have the same ideas of things and understand the same truths, it is but one and the same eternal light that is reflected in them all ("that light, which enlighteneth every man that cometh into the world" [Jn. 1:9]), or the same voice of that one everlasting Word, that is never silent, re-echoed by them. Thus was it concluded by Themistius, that one man, by teaching, could not possibly beget in the mind of another the very same notions, conceptions, and knowledges, which himself had in his own mind, "were not the minds both of the teacher and of the learner, as it were, printed and stamped alike." As also that men could not possibly so confer together as they do, presently apprehending one another's meaning and raising up the very same senses in their minds, and that merely by occasion of words and sounds, "were there not some one mind, which all men did partake of." [14] As for that antimonarchical opinion of many understanding beings, or minds, self-originated, and independent (none of which therefore could be omnipotent), is neither conceivable, how such should all agree in the same truths, there being no common measure of truth betwixt them, no more than any common rule of their wills; nor indeed how should they have any knowledge or understanding at all, properly so called, that being the comprehension of the possibilities of things, or of the extent of infinite power; whereas according to this hypothesis, there is no infinite power at all, the power of each of those many supposed principles or deities being limited and finite, and therefore indeed not creative of anything neither, since that which could create one thing could create all, and consequently would have all depending upon it. We conclude therefore that from the nature of mind and knowledge it is demonstrable that there can be but one original and self-existent Mind or understanding Being, from which all other minds were derived. And now have we, more copiously than we designed, confuted the first atheistic argument; we having not only asserted the idea of God, and fully answered and repelled all the atheistic pretences against the same; but also from this very idea of God, or a perfect Being, demonstrated his existence.

14. [ED.] Themistius, *Paraphrase of Aristotle's de Anima*. Themistius (317-?387) was a statesman, rhetorician and philosopher active at Constantinople. A new edition of his works, *Themistii Orationes quae supersunt* (Leipzig, 1965), has been prepared by Glanville Downey.

RALPH CUDWORTH

On Providence and God's Direction of Human Destiny

Editor's Introduction. In refuting the errors of the atheists, Cudworth indirectly developed certain positions of great importance in his own system of thought. What he called the "thirteenth atheistic argument" is the second phase of the attack on the idea of Providence. Cudworth had previously answered the contention that the disorder in nature made it impossible to believe in God's wise oversight of the world. He now turned to examine the kindred argument, that the disarray in human affairs was an equally serious obstacle to faith. A great truth, said Cudworth, was not really discredited simply because it had been distorted by trivial misconceptions. It was absurd to expect that the rewards of virtue and the punishments of vice would be either immediate or automatic. It was right that there should be "a doubtful and cloudy state of things, for the better exercise of virtue and faith": prompt and invariable rewards and punishments would debase religious conduct to the level of a calculating common sense. He conceded that completely to refute the atheists' arguments on this point would require a treatise far more extensive (even by his capacious standards!) than he could undertake, and therefore he merely advanced certain considerations which he believed would be helpful to those who believed in God.

In judging the works of God, we must not, Cudworth insists, concentrate our attention on the details. The parts must be seen in relation to the whole; and if there were uniformity of good fortune throughout the whole, the want of variety would produce monotony. Even a skillful dramatist avoided this mistake. Would God be likely to commit it? Furthermore, we must not confine God's activity to a context too limited to allow full scope to his purposes. The universe might not be infinite, but the astronomy of Cudworth's day had shown it to be vastly greater than had been commonly supposed, and it was thus reasonable to assume that within its bounds God could work out his purposes in ways men could not follow but which were nevertheless governed by the divine wisdom.

(Cudworth, it will be observed, was aware that the brilliant scientific developments of the seventeenth century could and should be related to theological thought.) Again, he argued, Providence must be set in a context which would be adequate in respect to time as well as space. Men must look both forward to the future and backward upon the past. Cudworth, it is clear, was not removing all the problems that arose; he was insisting that faith must examine human life in a setting suitable to the grandeur of the theme. When this was done, many of the difficulties would assume their proper proportions.

A third argument against Providence also demanded consideration; Cudworth noted that it had usually been advanced in one or other of two alternative forms. Some had argued that the size of the universe was so vast and its variety so infinite that it was inconceivable that any single being could exercise over it the kind of care that a doctrine of Providence presupposed. But this was to fall a prey to the cruder errors of anthropomorphism. Admittedly, the finite minds of men could not conceive such intelligence or power, but the discussion concerned not a human being or even human capacities magnified to the utmost degree. God was not man, and he could not be subjected to human standards. But opponents had also argued that even if God could control everything, he would not do so. A being infinitely powerful and happy would not concern himself about the welfare of others; his self-sufficiency would lift him above the trivialities of mundane existence. Once again, so to argue was to limit oneself to an arbitrary set of presuppositions concerning human life. It was to impose upon God a view of benevolence which many people would reject even when applied to their fellow men. If men were to think creatively about God, they must not let themselves be beguiled by such an indefensible use of what Bacon called "the idols of the cave."

❖   ❖   ❖   ❖

From *The True Intellectual System of the Universe,* Chapter V

The thirteenth atheistic argument, or second objection against Providence, is from the seeming confusion of human affairs; that all things fall alike to all; the innocent and the nocent, the pious and the impious, the religious and the profane; nay, that many times the worser causes and men prevail against the better, as is intimated in that passage of the poet, though in the person of a theist,

Victrix causa Deo placuit, sed victa Catoni; [1]

and that the unjust and ungodly often flow in all kind of prosperity, whilst the innocent and devout worshippers of the Deity, all their lives long, conflict with adversity. Whereas, were there a God and Providence, as they conceive, profane and irreligious persons would be presently thunder-struck from heaven, or otherwise made remarkable objects of divine vengeance, as also the pious miraculously protected and rescued from evil and harms.

Now we grant, indeed, that this consideration hath too much puzzled and staggered weak minds in all ages. Because "sentence against an evil work is not executed speedily, therefore the heart of the sons of men is fully set in them to do evil" [Eccles. 8:11]. And the Psalmist himself was sometimes much perplexed with this phenomenon, the prosperity of the ungodly, who "set their mouths against heaven, and whose tongue walketh through the earth" [Ps. 73:9]; so that he was tempted to think, "he had cleansed his heart in vain, and washed his hands in innocency" (till at length, entering into the sanctuary of God, his mind became illuminated, and his soul fixed in a firm trust and confidence upon divine providence: "Whom have I in heaven but thee," &c.; "My flesh and my heart faileth, but God is the strength of my heart, and my portion for ever" [Ps. 73:25–26]. For as some will from hence be apt to infer that there is no God at all, but that blind chance and fortune steer all ("The fool hath said in his heart there is no God" [Ps. 14:1]); so will others conclude, that though there be a God, yet he either does not know things done here below ("How does God know? and is there knowledge in the Most High?" [Ps. 73:11]), or else will not so far humble himself or disturb his own ease and quiet as to concern himself in our low human affairs.

First of all therefore, we here say that it is altogether unreasonable to require that divine Providence should miraculously interpose upon every turn in punishing the ungodly and preserving the pious, and thus perpetually interrupt the course of nature (which would look but like a botch or bungle, and a violent business), but rather carry things on in a still and silent path, and show his art and skill in making things of themselves fairly unwind, and clear up at last into a satisfactory close. Passion and self-interest is blind or short-sighted; but that which steers the whole

---

1. [ED.] Lucan, *The Civil War*, Bk. I, line 128: "If the victor had the gods on his side, the vanquished had Cato." Lucan is referring to the struggle between Julius Caesar and Pompey.

world is no fond, pettish, impatient and passionate thing, but an impartial, disinterested and uncaptivated nature. Nevertheless, it is certain, that sometimes we have not wanted instances, in cases extraordinary, of a θεὸς ἀπὸ μηχανῆς,[2] "God appearing, as it were, miraculously upon the stage," and manifesting himself in taking immediate vengeance upon notorious malefactors, or delivering his faithful servants from imminent dangers or evils threatened; as the same is often done also by a secret and undiscerned overruling of the things of nature. But it must be granted that it is not always thus, but the periods of divine Providence here in this world are commonly longer and the evolutions thereof slower; according to that of Euripides, which yet has a tang of profaneness in the expression, "The Deity is slow or dilatory, and this is the nature of it." [3] For it is not from slackness or remissness in the Deity, but either from his patience and long-suffering, he willing that men should repent, or else to teach us patience by his example (as Plutarch suggesteth) [4] or that all things may be carried on with more pomp and solemnity; or lastly, for other particular reasons, as Plutarch ventures to assign one, why it might not be expedient for Dionysius the tyrant, though so profane and irreligious a person, to have been cut off suddenly.[5] But wicked and ungodly persons oftentimes fail not to be met withal at last, and at the long-run, here in this life, and either in themselves or posterity, to be notoriously branded with the marks of divine displeasure; according to that of the poet: "It is seldom that wickedness altogether scapes punishment, though it come slowly after, limping with a lame foot"; [6] and those proverbial speeches amongst the pagans,

> Mills of the gods do slowly wind,
> But they at length to powder grind.

and, "Divine justice steals on softly with woollen feet, but strikes at last with iron hands." [7]

Nevertheless we cannot say that it is always thus neither, but that wicked persons may possibly sometimes have an uninterrupted prosperity here in this life and no visible marks of divine displeasure upon them; but as the generously virtuous will not envy them upon this account, nor

---

2. [ED.] "Deus ex machina."
3. [ED.] Euripides, *Orestes*, line 420.
4. [ED.] Plutarch, *De Sera Numinis Vindicta* (*Plutarchi Chaeronensis Quae Exstant Omnia* [Frankfort, 1599]), II, 550.
5. [ED.] Plutarch, *De Sera Numinis Vindicta*, II, 575.
6. [ED.] Horace, *Odes*, Bk. III, 2.
7. [ED.] Cf. Plutarch, *De Sera Numinis Vindicta*, II, 548.

repine at their own condition, they knowing, that "there is neither any thing truly evil to the good, nor good to the evil"; so are they so far from being staggered herewith in their belief of a God and Providence, that they are rather the more confirmed in their persuasions of a future immortality and judgment after death, when all things shall be set straight and right, and rewards and punishments impartially dispensed. That of Plutarch therefore is most true here: "That there is a necessary connexion betwixt those two things, divine Providence, and the permanence or immortality of human souls, one and the same reason confirming them both; neither can one of these be taken alone without the other." [8] But they who, because judgment is not presently executed upon the ungodly, blame the management of things as faulty and Providence as defective are like such spectators of a dramatic poem, as when wicked and injurious persons are brought upon the stage, for a while swaggering and triumphing, impatiently cry out against the dramatist and presently condemn the plot; whereas, if they would but expect the winding up of things and stay till the last close, they should then see them come off with shame and sufficient punishment. The evolution of the world, as Plotinus calls it, is ἀληθέστερον ποίημα, a "truer poem"; [9] and we men histrionical actors upon the stage, who, notwithstanding, insert something of our own into the poem too; but God Almighty is that skillful dramatist who always connecteth that of ours which went before with what of his follows after, into good coherent sense, and will at last make it appear that a thread of exact justice did run through all, and that rewards and punishments are measured out in geometrical proportion.

Lastly, it is in itself fit that there should be somewhere a doubtful and cloudy state of things, for the better exercise of virtue and faith. For as there could have been no Hercules had there not been monsters to subdue, so were there no such difficulties to encounter with, no puzzles and entanglements of things, no temptations and trials to assault us, virtue would grow languid and that excellent grace of faith want due occasions and objects to exercise itself upon. Here have we therefore such a state of things, and this world is, as it were, a stage erected for the more difficult part of virtue to act upon, and where we are to live by "faith" and not by "sight"—that faith which is "the substance of things to be hoped for and the evidence of things not seen" [Heb. 11:1], a belief in the goodness, power and wisdom of God, when all things are dark and cloudy round about us. "The just shall live by his faith" [Hab. 2:4; Rom. 1:17].

8. [ED.] Plutarch, *De Sera Numinis Vindicta*, II, 560.
9. [ED.] Plotinus, *The Enneads*, III.2.16.

We have now sufficiently confuted the second atheistic objection also against Providence, as to the conduct and economy of human affairs. Nevertheless this is a large field, and much more might be said in defence of Providence, both as to these and other instances, had we room here to expatiate in. Wherefore for a supplement of what remains we shall refer the reader to the writings of others, who have professedly undertaken apologies for Providence, both as to the fabric and economy of the world; but especially the learned and ingenious author of the *Divine Dialogues*.[10] Only we shall here add some few considerations, not so much for the confutation of atheists as for the better satisfaction of such religionists who, too easily concluding that all things might have been much better than they are, are thereupon apt to call in question the divine attribute of goodness in its full extent, which yet is the only foundation of our Christian faith.

First, therefore, we say that in judging of the works of God we ought not to consider the parts of the world alone by themselves; and then, because we could fancy much finer things, thereupon blame the Maker of the whole. As if one should attend only to this earth, which is but the lowest and most dreggy part of the universe; or blame plants, because they have not sense; brutes, because they have not reason; men, because they are not demons or angels; and angels, because they are not gods, or want divine perfection. Upon which account, God should either have made nothing at all, since there can be nothing besides himself absolutely perfect, or else nothing but the higher rank of angelic beings, free from mortality and all those other evils that attend mankind, or such fine things as Epicurus' gods were feigned to be, living in certain delicious regions, where there was neither blustering winds, nor any lowering clouds, nor nipping frosts, nor scorching heat, nor night, nor shadow, but the calm and unclouded ether, always smiling with gentle serenity, whereas were there but one kind of thing (the best) thus made, there could have been no music nor harmony at all in the world, for want of variety.[11] But we ought, in the first place, to consider the whole, whether that be not the best that could be made, having all that belongeth to it; and then the parts in reference to the whole, whether they be not, in their several degrees and ranks, congruous and agreeable thereunto. But this is a thing which hath been so well insisted upon by Plotinus, that we cannot speak better to it than in his words: "God made the whole most beautiful, entire, complete, and sufficient; all agreeing friendly with itself and its parts; both the

10. [ED.] Henry More, *Divine Dialogues* (1668).
11. [ED.] Cf. Lucretius, *De Rerum Natura*, Bk. III, lines 19–22.

nobler and the meaner of them being alike congruous thereunto. Whosoever therefore, from the parts thereof, will blame the whole is an absurd and unjust censurer. For we ought to consider the parts, not alone by themselves, but in reference to the whole, whether they be harmonious and agreeable to the same. Otherwise we shall not blame the universe, but some of its parts only taken by themselves; as if one should blame the hair or toes of a man, taking no notice at all of his divine visage and countenance; or omitting all other animals, one should attend only to the most contemptible of them; or, lastly, overlooking all other men, consider only the most deformed Thersites." [12] But that which God made was the whole as one thing, which he that attends to may hear it speaking to him after this manner: God Almighty hath made me, and from thence came I, perfect and complete and standing in need of nothing, because in me are contained all things—plants, and animals, and good souls, and men happy with virtue, and innumerable demons, and many gods. Nor is the earth alone in me adorned with all manner of plants and variety of animals; or does the power of soul extend at most no further than to the seas; as if the whole air and ether, and heaven, in the meantime, were quite devoid of soul and altogether unadorned with living inhabitants. Moreover, all things in me desire good and every thing reaches to it, according to its power and nature. For the whole depends upon that first and highest good, the gods themselves, who reign in my several parts, and all animals, and plants, and whatsoever seems to be inanimate in me. For some things in me partake only of being, some of life also, some of sense, some of reason, and some of intellect above reason. But no man ought to require equal things from unequal; nor that the finger should see, but the eye; it being enough for the finger to be a finger, and to perform its own office." And again, afterwards: "As an artificer would not make all things in an animal to be eyes, so neither has the divine λόγος or spermatic reason of the world, made all things gods; but some gods, and some demons, and some men, and some lower animals; not out of envy, but to display its own variety and fecundity. But we are like unskillful spectators of a picture, who condemn the limner, because he hath not put bright colors everywhere; whereas he had suited his colors to every part respectively, giving to each such as belonged to it. Or else are we like those who would blame a comedy or tragedy, because they were not all kings or heroes that acted in it, but some servants and rustic clowns introduced also, talking after their rude

---

12. [ED.] Plotinus, *The Enneads*, III.2.3. Thersites: the most ill-favored of the Greeks assembled before Troy and a man of evil tongue. He was severely chastised by Odysseus for defaming Agamemnon. Homer, *The Iliad*, Bk. II, lines 212–77.

fashion. Whereas the dramatic poem would neither be complete, nor elegant and delightful, were all those worser parts taken out of it." [13]

Again, we cannot certainly conclude that the works of God and his creation do not transcend those narrow limits which vulgar opinion and imagination sets them, that commonly terminates the universe, but a little above the clouds, or at most supposes the fixed stars, being all fastened in one solid sphere, to be the utmost wall, or arched roof, and rolling circumference thereof. Much less ought we, upon such groundless suppositions, to infer that the world might therefore have been made much better than it is, because it might have been much more roomy and capacious. We explode the atheistic infinity of distant worlds; nor can we admit that Cartesian, seemingly more modest, indefinite extension of one corporeal universe, which yet really, according to that philosopher's meaning, hath *nullos fines*, "no bounds nor limits at all." [14] For we persuade ourselves that the corporeal world is as incapable of a positive infinity of magnitude, as it is of time, there being no magnitude so great but that more still might be added to it. Nevertheless, as we cannot possibly imagine the sun to be a quarter or an hundredth part so big as we know it to be, so much more may the whole corporeal universe far transcend those narrow bounds which our imagination would circumscribe it in. The new celestial phenomena and the late improvements of astronomy and philosophy made thereupon, render it so probable that even this dull earth of ours is a planet and the sun a fixed star in the center of that vortex wherein it moves, that many have shrewdly suspected, that there are other habitable globes besides this earth of ours (which may be sailed round about in a year or two), as also more suns, with their respective planets, than one. However, the distance of all the fixed stars from us being so vast that the diameter of the great orb makes no discernible parallax in the site of them; from whence it is also probable that the other fixed stars are likewise vastly distant from one another: this, I say, widens the corporeal universe to us, and makes those *flammantia moenia mundi*, as Lucretius calls them, "those flaming walls of the world," [15] to fly away before us. Now, it is not reasonable to think that all this immense vastness should lie waste, desert or uninhabited, and have nothing in it that could praise the Creator thereof, save only this one small spot of earth. "In my Father's house" (saith our Savior) "are many mansions" [Jn. 14:2]. And Baruch, (Ch. 3, appointed by our church to be read publicly): "O Israel, how great is the

13. [ED.] Plotinus, *The Enneads*, III.2.3.
14. [ED.] Descartes, *Principles of Philosophy*, Pt. II, XXI.
15. [ED.] Lucretius, *De Rerum Natura*, Bk. I, line 74.

house of God, and how large is the place of his possession? Great and hath no end, high and immeasurable" [Baruch 3:24–25]. Which yet we understand not of an absolute infinity, but only such an immense vastness as far transcends vulgar opinion and imagination.

We shall add but one thing more, that to make a right judgment of the ways of Providence and the justice thereof as to the economy of mankind, we must look both forwards and backwards, or besides the present, not only upon the future but also the past time. Which rule is likewise thus set down by Plotinus: "Neither is that doctrine of the ancients to be neglected, that, to give an account of Providence, we ought to look back upon former periods as well as forward to what is future." [16] Indeed he and those other philosophers who were religious understood this so as to conclude a pre-existent state of all particular souls, wherein they were first created by God pure but by the abuse of their own liberty degenerated, to be a necessary hypothesis for the salving that phenomenon [17] of the depraved state of mankind in general here in this life. And not only so, but they endeavored in like manner to give an account also of those different conditions of particular persons as to morality, from their infancy, and their other different fates here, deriving them all "from their several demeanors heretofore in a pre-existent state." [18] And there have not wanted Christian doctors who have complied with these philosophers in both. But our common Christianity only agrees thus far, as to suppose a kind of imputative pre-existence in Adam, in whom all were created pure and so consequently involved in his after miscarriage, to salve the pravity of human nature; upon which account we are all said to be "by nature children of wrath" [Eph. 2:3]. But as for the different conditions of persons and their several fates, more disadvantageous to some than others, this indeed the generality of Christian doctors have been content to resolve only into an occult but just Providence. And thus does Origen himself sometimes modestly pass it over, as in his third book against Celsus: "It happeneth to many, so to have been brought up from their very childhood, as that, by one means or other, they could have no opportunity at all of thinking of the better things, &c. And it is very probable, that there are causes of these things in the reasons of Providence, though they do not easily fall under human notice." [19]

16. [ED.] Plotinus, *The Enneads*, III.2.13.
17. [ED.] "To salve the phenomenon": i.e., to account for it. Cf. O.E.D.
18. [ED.] This is a concept (and so an expression) often used by Origen.
19. [ED.] Origen, *Contra Celsum*, Bk. III, Ch. XXXVIII.

But there is yet a third atheistic objection against Providence behind, that "it is impossible any one Being should animadvert and order all things in the distant places of the world at once; and, were this possible, yet would such infinite negotiosity be very uneasy and distractious to it, and altogether inconsistent with happiness. Nor would a being irresistibly powerful, concern itself in the good or welfare of anything else, it standing in need of nothing, and all benevolence and good will arising from indigency and imbecility. Wherefore, such a being would wholly be taken up in the enjoyment of itself and its own happiness, utterly regardless of all other things."

To which the reply is, first, that though ourselves and all created beings have but a finite animadversion and narrow sphere of activity, yet does it not therefore follow that the case must be the same with the Deity, supposed to be a Being infinitely perfect, "that hath no manner of defect" either of knowledge or power in it. But this is a mere *idolum specus*, "an idol of the cave or den," men measuring the Deity by their own scantling and narrowness. And indeed, were there nothing at all but what we ourselves could fully comprehend there could be no God. Were the sun an animal and had life co-extended with its rays and light, it would see and perceive every atom of matter that its outstretched beams reached to and touched. Now all created beings are themselves, in some sense, but the rays of the Deity, which therefore cannot but feel and sensibly perceive all these its own effluxes and emanations. Men themselves can order and manage affairs in several distant places at once, without any disturbance; and we have innumerable notions of things in our own mind, that lie there easily together without crowding one another or causing any distraction to us.

Nevertheless the minds of weak mortals may here be somewhat eased and helped by considering what hath been before suggested, that there is no necessity God Almighty should "do all things himself immediately and drudgingly," but he may have his inferior ministers and executioners under him to discharge him of that supposed encumberment. As first of all, an artificial plastic nature, which, without knowledge and animal consciousness, disposes the matter of the universe according to the platform or idea of a perfect mind, and forms the bodies of all animals. And this was one reason why we did not before insist so much upon this artificial, regular and methodical nature, namely, that divine Providence might neither be excluded from having an influence upon all things in this lower world, as resulting only from the fortuitous motions of senseless matter, unguided by any mind; nor yet the Deity be supposed to do everything itself immediately and miraculously, without the subservient ministry of any natural causes, which would seem to us mortals to be not only a violent but also an operose, cumbersome and moliminous [20] business. And thus did Plato acknowledge that there were "certain causes of a prudent, that is artificial and orderly nature, which God makes use of as subservient to himself in the mundane economy." [21] Besides which, those instincts also impressed upon animals and which they are passive to, directing them to act for ends either not understood or not attended to by them, in order to their own good and the good of the universe, are another part of that divine fate which, inserted into things themselves, is the servant and executioner of Providence. Above all which, there are yet other knowing and understanding ministers of the Deity, as its eyes and hands, demoniac or angelic beings, appointed to preside over mankind, all mundane affairs, and the things of nature; they having their several distinct offices and provinces assigned them. Of which also Plato thus: "There are certain rulers or presidents appointed by the supreme God who governs the whole world, over all the several things and parts therein, even to the smallest distribution of them." [22] All which inferior causes are constantly overlooked and supervised by the watchful eye of God Almighty himself, who may also sometimes extraordinarily interpose.

We need not, therefore, restrain and confine divine Providence to a few greater things only, as some do, that we may thereby consult the ease of the Deity and its freedom from distraction, but may and ought to extend it to all things whatsoever, small as well as great. And indeed, the great things of the world cannot well be ordered neither, without some regard to the small and little: "as architects affirm that great stones cannot be well placed together in a building without little." [23] Neither can generals of armies, nor governors of families, nor masters of ships, nor mechanic artificers, discharge their several functions and do their works respectively as they ought, did they not mind small things also, as well the great. "Let us not therefore," saith the forementioned philosopher, "make God Almighty inferior to mortal opificers,[24] who, by one and the same art, can order small things as well as great; and so suppose him to be supine and

20. [54.] "Operose," involving much labor. "Moliminous," characterized by effort.
21. [ED.] Cf. Plato, *Timaeus*, 46.
22. [ED.] Plato, *Laws*, Bk. X, 903
23. [ED.] Plato, *Laws*, Bk. X, 903.
24. [ED.] Those who make or construct a work; makers, framers, fabricators.

negligent." [25] Nevertheless, the chief concernment and employment of divine Providence in the world is the economy of souls, or government of rational beings, which is by Plato contracted into this compendium: "There is no other work left for the supreme Governor of all than only to translate better souls into better places and conditions, and worser into worser"; or, as he after addeth, to dispose of every one in the world in such a manner as might best render "virtue victorious and triumphant over vice." [26] And thus may the slow and imperfect wits of mortals be satisfied, that providence to the Deity is no moliminous, laborious and distractious thing.

But that there is no higher spring of life in rational animals than contracted self-love, and that all good will and benevolence arises only from indigency and imbecility, and that no being whatsoever is concerned in the welfare of any other thing but only what itself stands in need of; and lastly therefore, that what is irresistibly powerful and needs nothing would have no manner of benevolence, nor concern itself in the good and welfare of anything whatsoever; this is but another idol of the atheists' den, and only argues their bad nature, low-sunk minds, and gross immorality. And the same is to be said also of that other maxim of theirs: that what is perfectly happy would have nothing at all to do, but only enjoy its own ease and quiet; whereas there is nothing more troublesome to ourselves than "this having nothing to do;" and the activity of the Deity, or a perfect Being, is altogether as easy to it as its essence.

The atheistic queries come next to be answered; which, being but three, are naturally to be disposed in this order: First, if there were a God, or perfect Being, who therefore was sufficiently happy in the enjoyment of himself, why would he go about to make a world? Secondly, if he must needs make a world, why did he not make it sooner?—this late production therefore looking as if he had but newly awaked out of a long sleep throughout infinite past ages, or else had in length of time contracted a satiety of his solitude. Thirdly and lastly, what tools or instruments? what machines or engines had he? Or how could he move the matter of the whole world, especially if incorporeal?—because then he would run through all things and could not lay hold, nor fasten upon anything.

To the first therefore we say, that the reason why God made the world was from his own overflowing and communicative goodness, that there might be other beings also happy besides him, and enjoy themselves. Nor

25. [ED.] Plato, *Laws*, Bk. X, 903.
26. [ED.] Plato, *Laws*, Bk. X, 904

does this at all clash with God's making of the world for his own glory and honor; though Plotinus were so shy of that: "It is ridiculous to say, that God made the world that he might be honored; this being to transfer the affections of human artificers and statuaries upon him." [27] But the chief reason of his saying so was, because that philosopher conceived the world to have proceeded, not so much from the will of the Deity, as the necessity of its nature. Though this be true also, that God did not make the world merely to ostentate his skill and power, but to communicate his goodness, which is chiefly and properly his glory, as the light and splendor of the sun is the glory of it. But the atheist demands, "What hurt had it been for us never to have been made?" And the answer is easy: we should then never have enjoyed any good, or been capable of happiness; and had there been no rational creatures at all made, it must have been either from impotent sterility in the Deity, or else from an invidious, narrow and contracted selfishness, or want of benignity and communicative goodness; both which are inconsistent with a perfect Being. But the argument may be thus retorted upon these atheists: What hurt would it be for us to cease to be, or become nothing? And why then are these atheists, as well as others, so unwilling to die?

But then in the next place they urge: Why was not the world made sooner, since this goodness of God was without date, and from everlasting? But this question may be taken in two different senses; either, "Why was not the world from eternity, as God and his goodness are eternal?" or else, secondly, "If the world could not be from eternity, yet, notwithstanding, why was it not sooner, but so lately made?" In both which queries the atomic atheists take it for granted that the system of the world was not from eternity but had a beginning. Now we say that the reason why the world was not made from eternity was not from any defect of goodness in the divine will, but because there is an absolute impossibility in the thing itself; or because the necessity and incapacity of such an imperfect being hindered. For we must confess that, for our parts, we are prone to believe that could the world have been from eternity it should certainly have been so. And just thus does Philoponus, in his confutation of Proclus' arguments for the world's eternity, declare himself, and no otherwise: "Ourselves also supposing the world not to have been eternal, do neither ascribe this to any defect either of goodness or of power in the Deity, but only to the impossibility of the thing itself." Where, in the following words, he gives a twofold account of this impossibility of the

27. [ED.] Plotinus, *The Enneads*, III.9.4.

world's eternity: "First, because there can be nothing actually infinite, and yet run through, as all the past duration of the world hath been; and secondly, because that which is made, or brought into being by another, as a distinct thing from it, cannot be co-eternal with its maker." [28] Where it is probable that Philoponus, being a Christian, designed not to oppose the eternal generation of the Son of God, but only to assert that nothing which was properly made or created by God, and nothing which was not itself God, could be from eternity, or without beginning. And now we see how those atheistic exceptions against the novity of the divine creation, as if God must therefore either have slept from eternity or else have at length contracted a satiety of his former solitude, and the like, do of themselves quite vanish into nothing. But then, as to the second sense of the question, "Why the world, though it could not possibly be from eternity, yet was no sooner, but so lately made?" We say, that this is an absurd question; both because time was made together with the world, and there was no "sooner" or "later" before time; and also because whatsoever had a beginning, must of necessity be once but a day old. Wherefore the world could not possibly have been so made by God in time, as not to be once but five or six thousand years old, and no more; as now it is. . . .

28. [ED.] Joannes Philoponus, *De Aeternitate Mundi Contra Proclum*, Bk. I, §4.

RALPH CUDWORTH

On the Indefensible Arguments of the Atheists

Editor's Introduction. The second chapter of *The True Intellectual System* was designed to state as accurately as possible the arguments which had, historically, been advanced in support of atheism. Cudworth followed this with an examination of the disagreements among atheists, as well as of those points concerning which they were united against theists. Cudworth was evidently aware that his "large account given of the pagan polytheism" had unduly postponed his essential purpose—"the full and copious confutation of them" (i.e., the atheists). So, with Chapter V he picks up the interrupted thread of his argument. He examines "the first atheistic argument, that there is no idea of God." Cudworth enunciates, and demolishes, five points that have been advanced in defence of this first position. He then proceeds to consider the second and third arguments advanced by the atheists; these are the sections here reproduced. The atheists have insisted, says Cudworth, that the idea of God must be false. Even believers, they say, concede that he is incomprehensible; what cannot be comprehended cannot be conceived; what cannot be conceived must be a non-entity. But this argument, retorts Cudworth, rests on a confusion of terms which runs back to a serious misunderstanding of intellectual processes. The third argument concerns infinity and its implications. Infinity, say the atheists, is really inconceivable and consequently impossible. This, replies Cudworth, is a modern objection. The ancient atheists had realized that infinity was a useful—even a necessary—concept, though they declined to associate with it the concept of deity. But the new generation of atheists have adopted a different (and, from Cudworth's point of view, much less defensible) attitude.

This section is closely related to one of Cudworth's central concerns. At last we see him systematically embarking on his announced intention: to confute the validity of the arguments which the atheists advance.

❖   ❖   ❖   ❖

God Is Incomprehensible and Eternal, Yet not Inconceivable

FROM *The True Intellectual System of the Universe*, CHAPTER V

The second pretence of atheists against the idea of God, and consequently his existence, is, because theists themselves acknowledging God to be incomprehensible, it may be from thence inferred that he is a nonentity. Which argumentation of the atheists supposes these two things: first, that what is incomprehensible is altogether inconceivable; and then, that what is inconceivable is nothing. The latter of which two, perhaps, may be granted to them, that what is so utterly inconceivable as that no man can frame any manner of idea or conception of it, is therefore either in itself, or at least to us, nothing. Because, though that of Protagoras be not true, in his sense: "That man is the measure of all things, either as existing or not existing"; he meaning indeed nothing else thereby, but that there was no absolute truth or falsehood of anything, but all was relative to particular persons, and fantastical or seeming only.[1] And though it must not be granted, that whatsoever any man's shallow understanding cannot easily and fully comprehend, is therefore presently to be expunged out of the catalogue of beings; which is the reason, or rather infidelity of the anti-trinitarians; yet is there notwithstanding some truth in that of Aristotle, that "the rational soul or mind is in a manner all things"; it being able to frame some idea and conception or other of whatsoever is in the nature of things, and hath either an actual or possible existence, from the very highest to the lowest. Mind and understanding is, as it were, a diaphanous and crystalline globe, or a kind of notional world, which hath some reflex image and correspondent ray or representation in it, to whatsoever is in the true and real world of being. And upon this account may it be said that whatsoever is in its own nature absolutely inconceivable is indeed a non-entity.

But the former is absolutely denied by us, that whatsoever is incomprehensible is inconceivable; and therefore when we affirm that God is incomprehensible, our meaning is only this, that our imperfect minds

1. [ED.] Plato, *Theaetetus.*

cannot have such a conception of his nature, as doth perfectly master, conquer and subdue that vast object under it; or at least is so fully adequate and commensurate to the same, as that it doth every way match and equalize it. Now it doth not at all follow from hence, because God is thus incomprehensible to our finite and narrow understandings, that he is utterly inconceivable by them, so that they cannot frame any idea at all of him, and he may therefore be concluded to be a non-entity. For it is certain, that we cannot fully comprehend ourselves, and that we have not such an adequate and comprehensive knowledge of the essence of any substantial thing as that we can perfectly master and conquer it. It was a truth, though abused by the skeptics, that there is "something incomprehensible" in the essence of the lowest substances. For even body itself, which the atheists think themselves so well acquainted with because they can feel it with their fingers and which is the only substance that they acknowledge either in themselves or the universe, hath such puzzling difficulties and entanglements in the speculation of it, that they can never be able to extricate themselves from. We might instance also in some accidental things, as time and motion. Truth is bigger than our minds, and we are not the same with it, but have a lower participation only of the intellectual nature, and are rather apprehenders than comprehenders thereof. This is indeed one badge of our creaturely state, that we have not a perfectly comprehensive knowledge, or such as is adequate and commensurate to the essences of things; from whence we ought to be led to this acknowledgment, that there is another perfect Mind or understanding Being above us in the universe, from which our imperfect minds were derived and upon which they do depend. Wherefore if we can have no idea or conception of anything whereof we have not a full and perfect comprehension, then can we not have an idea or conception of the nature of any substance. But though we do not comprehend all truth, as if our mind were above it or master of it, and cannot penetrate into and look quite through the nature of everything, yet may rational souls frame certain ideas and conceptions of whatsoever is in the orb of being proportionate to their own nature and sufficient for their purpose. And though we cannot fully comprehend the Deity nor exhaust the infiniteness of its perfection, yet may we have an idea or conception of a Being absolutely perfect; such a one as is *nostro modulo conformis*, "agreeable and proportionate to our measure and scantling"; as we may approach near to a mountain and touch it with our hands, though we cannot encompass it all round and enclasp it within our arms. Whatsoever is in its own nature absolutely inconceivable, is nothing; but not whatsoever is not fully comprehensible by our imperfect understandings.

It is true, indeed, that the Deity is more incomprehensible to us than anything else whatsoever, which proceeds from the fullness of its being and perfection and from the transcendency of its brightness; but, for the very same reason may it be said also, in some sense, that it is more knowable and conceivable than any thing. As the sun, though by reason of its excessive splendor it dazzle our weak sight, yet it is notwithstanding far more visible also, than any of "the small misty stars." Where there is more of light there is more of visibility; so where there is more of entity, reality and perfection, there is there more of conceptibility and cognoscibility; such an object filling up the mind more and acting more strongly upon it. Nevertheless, because our weak and imperfect minds are lost in the vast immensity and redundancy of the Deity, and overcome with its transcendent light and dazzling brightness, therefore hath it to us an appearance of darkness and incomprehensibility; as the unbounded expansion of light, in the clear transparent ether, hath to us the apparition of an azure obscurity; which yet is not an absolute thing in itself, but only relative to our sense and a mere fancy in us.

The incomprehensibility of the Deity is so far from being an argument against the reality of its existence, as that it is most certain on the contrary, that were there nothing incomprehensible to us, who are but contemptible pieces and small atoms of the universe; were there no other being in the world, but what our finite and imperfect understandings could span or fathom, and encompass round about, look through and through, have a commanding view of, and perfectly conquer and subdue under them; then there could be nothing absolutely and infinitely perfect, that is, no God. For though that of Empedocles be not true in a literal sense, as it seems to have been taken by Aristotle: [2] "That by earth we see earth, by water water, and by fire fire; and understand everything by something of the same within ourselves"; yet is it certain, that everything is apprehended by some internal congruity in that which apprehends, which perhaps was the sense intended by that noble philosophic poet. Wherefore it cannot possibly otherwise be, but that the finiteness, scantness, and imperfection of our narrow understandings must make them asymmetral or incommensurate to that which is absolutely and infinitely perfect.

And nature itself plainly intimates to us that there is some such absolutely perfect Being, which, though not inconceivable yet is incompre-

2. [ED.] Aristotle, *De Anima*, Bk. I, Ch. II.

hensible to our finite understandings, by certain passions which it hath implanted in us, that otherwise would want an object to display themselves upon; namely, those of devout veneration, adoration, and admiration, together with a kind of ecstasy and pleasing horror; which, in the silent language of nature, seem to speak thus much to us, that there is some object in the world, so much bigger and vaster than our mind and thoughts, that it is the very same to them that the ocean is to narrow vessels; so that when they have taken into themselves as much as they can thereof by contemplation and filled up all their capacity, there is still an immensity of it left without which cannot enter in for want of room to receive it, and therefore must be apprehended after some other strange and more mysterious manner, viz., by their being as it were plunged into it, and swallowed up or lost in it. To conclude, the Deity is indeed incomprehensible to our finite and imperfect understandings, but not inconceivable; and therefore there is no ground at all for this atheistic pretence, to make it a non-entity.

We come to the third atheistic argumentation: That because infinity (which according to theology is included in the idea of God and pervadeth all his attributes) is utterly inconceivable, the Deity itself is therefore an impossibility, and nonentity. To this sense sound sundry passages of a modern writer: as, "Whatsoever we know, we learn from our phantasms; but there is no phantasm of infinite, and therefore no knowledge or conception of it." [3] Again, "Whatsoever we imagine is finite, and therefore there is no conception or idea of that which we call infinite. No man can have in his mind an image of infinite time, or of infinite power. Wherefore the name of God is used not to make us conceive him, but only that we may honor him." [4] The true meaning whereof (as may be plainly gathered from other passages of the same writer) is thus to be interpreted; that there is nothing of philosophic truth and reality in the idea or attributes of God; nor any other sense in those words, but only to signify the veneration and astonishment of men's own confounded minds. And accordingly the word infinite is declared to signify nothing at all in that which is so called (there being no such thing really existing), but only the inability of men's own minds, together with their rustic astonishment and admiration. Wherefore when the same writer determines

3. [ED.] Hobbes, *Physics*, Pt. IV, Ch. xxvi. Cudworth omits certain phrases, but without modifying the sense.

4. [ED.] Hobbes, *Leviathan*, Pt. I, Ch. iii. This passage is also quoted with omissions.

that God must not be said to be finite, this being no good courtship nor compliment; [5] and yet the word infinite signifieth "nothing" in the thing itself, nor hath any conception at all answering to it; he either does plainly abuse his reader, or else he leaves him to make up this conclusion, that since God is neither finite nor infinite, he is an inconceivable nothing. In like manner, another learned well-willer to atheism declareth, that he who calleth any thing infinite, doth but "attribute an unintelligible name to a thing inconceivable; because all conception is finite, and it is impossible to conceive any thing that hath no bounds or limits. But that which is mistaken for infinite, is nothing but a confused chaos of the mind, or an unshapen embryo of thought; when men going on further and further, and making a continual progress, without seeing any end before them, being at length quite weary and tired out with this their endless journey, they sit down, and call the thing by this hard and unintelligible name, infinite." And from hence does he also infer, that because we can have no idea of infinite, as to signify any thing in that which is so called; we therefore cannot possibly have "any true and genuine idea or notion of God." Of which they who understand the language of atheists, know very well the meaning to be this: That there is indeed no such thing, or that he is a non-entity.

5. [ED.] Hobbes, *De Cive*, Ch. xv, §14.

❖ ❖ ❖ ❖ ❖ ❖ ❖ ❖

RALPH CUDWORTH

That God Is Not a Fiction Inspired by Fear

Editor's Introduction. Cudworth often developed his own position while refuting the negative arguments of his opponents. The "atheists" whom he attacked sometimes denied the existence of God, as did certain classical determinists; sometimes, like Hobbes, they professed belief in God while advocating views which Cudworth deemed incompatible with faith. The atheists insisted that religion was merely the product of man's fears, a psychological device for soothing the apprehensions created by living in an intimidating environment. Cudworth conceded that there was an element of fear in all religion, but argued that godly reverence was a very different thing from the servile dread which was the distinguishing mark of superstition. For him, the atheists misconceived fear because they misunderstood religion. Reason had its own place—and an important one—in the life of faith, but faith could not be reduced to a system of logical propositions. Man had within him an awareness of the infinite. This awakened a response of reverence and awe, and one who ignored it could neither appreciate nor explain the essential character of religious consciousness.

❖ ❖ ❖ ❖

FROM *The True Intellectual System of the Universe*, CHAPTER V

Thus have we fully declared the sense of the atheists, in their account of the phenomenon of religion and the belief of a God; namely, that they derive it principally from these three springs or originals: first, from men's own fear and solicitude concerning future events, or their good and evil fortune; secondly, from their ignorance of the causes both of those events and the phenomena of nature, together with their curiosity; and lastly, from the fiction of civil sovereigns, law-makers, and politicians. The weakness and foolery of all which we shall now briefly manifest. First, therefore, it is certain that such an excess of fear as makes any one constantly and obstinately to believe the existence of that which there is no manner of ground neither from sense nor reason for, tending also to the great disquiet of man's own lives and the terror of their minds, cannot be accounted other than a kind of crazedness or distraction. Wherefore, the atheists themselves acknowledging the generality of mankind to be possessed with such a belief of the Deity, when they resolve this into such an excess of fear as makes anyone constantly and obstinately to believe the existence of that which there is no manner of ground neither from sense nor reason for, tending also to the great disquiet of men's own lives and the terror of their minds, cannot be accounted other than a kind of crazedness or distraction. Wherefore, the atheists themselves acknowledging the generality of mankind to be possessed with such a belief of the Deity when they resolve this into such an excess of fear, it is all one as if they should affirm the generality of mankind to be frighted out of their wits, or crazed and distempered in their brains; none but a few atheists, who being undaunted and undismayed have escaped this panic terror, remaining sober and in their right senses. But whereas the atheists thus impute to the generality of mankind, not only light-minded fantastry but also such an excess of fear, as differs nothing at all from crazedness and distraction or madness, we affirm, on the contrary, that their supposed courage, stayedness and sobriety is really nothing else but the dull and sottish stupidity of their minds, dead and heavy incredulity, and earthly diffidence or distrust, by reason whereof they can believe nothing but what they can feel or see.

Theists indeed have a religious fear of God, which is consequent from him or their belief of him (of which more afterwards); but the Deity itself, or the belief thereof, was not created by any antecedent fear, that is, by fear concerning men's good and evil fortune; it being certain, that none are less solicitous concerning such events, than they who are most truly religious. The reason whereof is, because these place their chief good in nothing that is "alien" or "in another's power," and exposed to the strokes of fortune; but in that which is most truly their own, namely, the right use of their own will. As the atheists, on the contrary, must needs, for this very reason, be liable to great fears and solicitudes concerning outward events, because they place their good and evil in the "passion of pleasure and pain"; or at least, denying natural honesty, they acknowledge no other good but what belongs to the animal life only and so is under the empire of fortune. And that the atheists are indeed generally timorous and fearful, suspicious and distrustful things, seems to appear plainly from their building all their politics, civil societies and justice (improperly so called) upon that only foundation of fear and distrust.

But the grand error of the atheists here is this, that they suppose the Deity, according to the sense of the generality of mankind, to be nothing but a mormo, bugbear, or terriculum,[1] an "affrightful, hurtful," and "most undesirable thing": whereas men everywhere invoke the Deity in their straits and difficulties for aid and assistance, looking upon it as exorable and placable; and by their trust and confidence in it, acknowledge its goodness and benignity. Synesius affirms that though men were otherwise much divided in their own opinions, yet "They all everywhere, both wise and unwise, agree in this, that God is to be praised, as one who is good and benign." [2]

If among the pagans there were any who understood that proverbial speech, φθονερὸν τὸ δαιμόνιον, in the worst sense, as if God Almighty were of an "envious and spiteful nature"; these were certainly but a few ill-natured men, who therefore drew a picture of the Deity according to their own likeness. For the proverb, in that sense, was disclaimed and cried down by all the wiser pagans; as Aristotle, who affirmed the "poets to have lied in this, as well as they did in many other things"; [3] and Plutarch, who taxeth Herodotus for insinuating "the Deity universally (that is, all the gods) to be of an envious and vexatious or spiteful disposition"; [4] whereas himself appropriated this only to that evil demon or principle asserted by him, as appeareth from the life of P. Æmelius, written by him where he affirmeth, not that "the Deity universally was of an envious nature" but "that there is a certain deity or demon whose proper task it is to bring down all great and overswelling human prosperity, and so to temper every man's life that none may be happy in this world, sincerely and unmixedly, without a check of adversity"; [5] which is as if a Christian should ascribe it to the devil. And Plato plainly declares the reason of God's making the world at first, to have been no other than this: "Because he was good, and there is no manner of envy in that which is good." From whence he also concluded, "That God therefore willed all things should

---

1. [ED.] "Mormo," a hobgoblin or bugbear; "terriculum" (Latin), something that excites terror (the more usual form was "terricula," a source or object of terror).

2. [ED.] Synesius of Cyrene, *De Regno*, §9 (Migne, P. G. LXVI).

3. [ED.] Aristotle, *Metaphysics*, Bk. I, Ch. II.

4. [ED.] Plutarch, "*De Herodoti Malignitate*" (*Plutarchi Chaeronensis Quae Exstant Omnia*, Frankfort, 1599, II, 857).

5. [ED.] Plutarch, *Paulus Æmelius* (in *Works*, as above), I, 273.

be made the most like himself"; [6] that is, after the best manner. But the true meaning of that ill-languaged proverb seems at first to have been no other than what, besides Hesiod, the Scripture itself also attributes to God Almighty, that he affecteth to humble and abase the pride of men and to pull down all high, towering and lofty things, whether as noxious and hurtful to the men themselves or as in some sense invidious to him and derogatory from his honor, who alone ought to be exalted and no flesh to glory before him. And there hath been so much experience of such a thing as this in the world, that the Epicurean poet himself could not but confess that there was some hidden force or power which seemed to have a spite to all overswelling greatnesses, and affect to cast contempt and scorn upon the pride of men:

> Usque adeo res humanas vis abdita quaedam
> Opterit, et pulchros fascis saevasque secures
> Proculcare ac ludibrio sibi habere videtur.[7]

Where he plainly reeled and staggered in his atheism, or else was indeed a theist but knew it not; it being certain that there can be no such force as this "in the reign or empire of senseless atoms." And as for those among Christians who make such a horrid representation of God Almighty, as one who created far the greatest part of mankind for no other end or design but only this, that he might recreate and delight himself in their eternal torments; these also do but transcribe or copy out their own ill nature and then read it in the Deity; the Scriptures declaring on the contrary, that God is love. Nevertheless these very persons in the meantime dearly hug and embrace God Almighty in their own conceit, as one that is fondly good, kind and gracious to themselves; he having fastened his affections upon their very persons, without any consideration of their dispositions or qualifications.

It is true indeed, that religion is often expressed in the Scripture by the "fear of God," and fear hath been said to be "the first measure of the Divinity in us," or the first impression that religion makes upon men in this obnoxious and guilty state, before they have arrived to the true love of God and righteousness. But this religious fear is not a fear of God as a mere arbitrary omnipotent Being, much less as hurtful and mischievous (which could not be disjoined from hatred); but an awful regard of him,

6. [ED.] Plato, *Timaeus*, 29.

7. [ED.] Lucretius, *De Rerum Natura*, Bk. V, lines 1233–35: "All the while some unseen force crushes human affairs, and seems to trample the lictor's fasces [lit., the noble rods and the cruel axes] and regard them with ridicule."

as of one who is essentially just, and as well a punisher of vice and wickedness as a rewarder of virtue; Lucretius himself, when he describes this
religious fear of men, confessing it to be conjoined with a conscience of
their duty, or to include the same within itself:

Tunc [non] populi gentesque tremunt, . . .
Ne quod [ne quid] ob admissum foede dictumve superbe,
Poenarum grave sit solvendi tempus adactum.[8]

And this is the sense of the generality of mankind, that there being a
natural difference of good and evil moral, there is an impartial justice in
the Deity, which presideth over the same, and inclines it as well to punish
the wicked, as to reward the virtuous; Epicurus himself acknowledging
thus much: "Theists suppose that there are both great evils inflicted upon
the wicked from the gods; and also great rewards by them bestowed upon
the good." [9] And this fear of God is not only beneficial to mankind in
general, by repressing the growth of wickedness, but also wholesome and
salutary to those very persons themselves, that are thus religiously affected,
it being preservative of them both from moral evils and likewise from the
evils of punishment consequent thereupon. This is the true and genuine
fear of religion, which when it degenerates into a dark kind of jealous
and suspicious fear of God Almighty, either as a hurtful or as a mere
arbitrary and tyrannical being, then is it looked upon as the vice or extreme
of religion, and distinguished from it by the name of "superstition." Thus
is the character of a superstitious man given by Plutarch: "That he thinks
there are gods, but that they are noxious and hurtful;" and "A superstitious
man must needs hate God, as well as fear him." [10] "The true fear of God
(as the son of Sirach speaks) is the beginning of his love, and faith is the
beginning of cleaving to him" [Ecclus. 25:12]. As if he should have said,
the first entrance into religion is an awful regard to God as the punisher
of vice; the second step forwards therein is faith or confidence in God,
whereby men rely upon him for good and cleave to him; and the top and
perfection of all religion is the love of God above all, as the most amiable
being. Christianity, the best of religions, recommendeth faith to us as the
inlet or introduction into all true and ingenuous piety; for "he that
cometh to God, must not only believe that he is, but also that he is a

8. [ED.] Lucretius, *De Rerum Natura*, Bk. V, lines 1222, 1224–25: "Then [do not]
nations and peoples tremble . . . lest for some shameful act or some arrogant word
the solemn time of punishment approaches."

9. [ED.] Diogenes Laertius, *Life of Epicurus*, Bk. X, §124.

10. [ED.] Plutarch, *On Superstition*, §2. This is one of the short treatises usually
included among the *Moralia*.

rewarder of those that seek him" [Heb. 11:6]. Which faith is better defined in the Scripture, than by any scholastic, to be the substance of things
(that are to be) hoped for, and the evidence of things not seen; that is, a
confident persuasion of things that fall not under sight (because they are
either invisible or future) and which also are to be hoped for. So that
religious fear consisteth well with faith, and faith is near of kin to hope,
and the result of both faith and hope is love; which faith, hope and love,
do all suppose an essential goodness in the Deity. God is such a Being,
who, if he were not, were of all things whatsoever most to be wished for;
it being indeed no way desirable (as that noble emperor concluded) for a
man to live in a world void of a God and providence.[11] He that believes a
God, believes all that good and perfection in the universe which his heart
can possibly wish or desire. It is the interest of none that there should be
no God, but only of such wretched persons as have abandoned their first
and only true interest of being good and friends to God, and are
desperately resolved upon ways of wickedness.

The reason why the atheists do thus grossly mistake the notion of God
and conceive of him differently from the generality of mankind, as a thing
which is only to be feared and must consequently be hated, is from
nothing but their own vice and ill-nature. For first, their vice so far blind-
ing them as to make them think that the moral differences of good and evil
have no foundation in nature but only in law or arbitrary constitution,
which law is contrary to nature (nature being liberty, but law restraint),
as they cannot but really hate that which hinders them of their true liberty
and chief good, so must they needs interpret the severity of the Deity
so much spoken of against wickedness to be nothing else but cruelty and
arbitrary tyranny. Again, it is a wretched ill-natured maxim, which these
atheists have, that there is "no natural charity," but that "all benevolence
ariseth only from imbecility and fear";[12] that is, from being either obnoxious to another's power or standing in need of his help. So that all
that is now called love and friendship amongst men is, according to these,
really nothing but either a crouching under another's power, whom they
cannot resist, or else "a certain kind of merchandizing for utilities." And
thus does Cotta in Cicero declare their sense: "You conceive that no man
would be any way beneficent or benevolent to another, were it not for his
imbecility or indigence." But as for God Almighty, these atheists conclude that upon the supposition of his existence there could not be so
much as this spurious love or benevolence in him neither towards any

11. [ED.] Cf. *Meditations* of Marcus Aurelius Antoninus, Bk. II, §§3.11; Bk. XII, §14.
12. [ED.] Cicero, *On the Nature of the Gods*, Ch. XLIII.

thing; because by reason of his absolute and irresistible power, he would neither stand in need of anything, and be devoid of all fear. Thus the forementioned Cotta: "What is there more excellent than goodness and beneficence? which when you will needs have God to be utterly devoid of, you suppose that neither any god nor man is dear to the supreme God, or beloved of him. From whence it will follow, that not only men are neglected by the gods, but also the gods amongst themselves are neglected by one another." [13] Accordingly, a late pretender to politics,[14] who in this manner discards all natural justice and charity, determines concerning God, "That he has no other right of reigning over men, and of punishing those who transgress his laws, but only from his irresistible power." Which indeed is all one as to say, "That God has no right at all of ruling over mankind, and imposing commands upon them," but what he doth in this kind, he doth it only by force and power, right and might (or power) being very different things from one another, and there being no just or "right" without natural justice; so that the word "right" is here only abused. And consentaneously hereunto the same writer further adds: "That if God's right of commanding be derived only from his omnipotence, then it is manifest that men's obligation to obey him lies upon them only from their imbecility." Or, as it is further explained by him: "That men are therefore only subject to God, because they are not omnipotent, or have not sufficient power to resist him." [15] Thus do we see plainly how the atheists, by reason of their vice and ill-nature (which makes them deny all natural justice and honesty, all natural charity and benevolence), transform the Deity into a monstrous shape; such an omnipotent Being, as if he were, could have nothing neither of justice in him nor of benevolence towards his creatures, and whose only right and authority of commanding them would be his irresistible power; whom his creatures could not place any hope, trust and confidence in, nor have any other obligation to obey, than that of fear and necessity, proceeding from their imbecility or inability to resist him. And such a Deity as this is indeed a mormo or bugbear, a most formidable and affrightful thing.

But all this is nothing but the atheists' false imagination, true religion representing a most comfortable prospect of things from the Deity;

---

13. [ED.] All the above quotations are from the chapter of Cicero referred to in the previous note.

14. [ED.] Cudworth writes with Hobbes constantly in mind, but he almost never refers to him by name. "A late pretender to politics" is a characteristic periphrasis.

15. [ED.] Hobbes, *De Cive*, Ch. xv, §§4, 7.

whereas, on the contrary, the atheistic scene of things is dismal, hopeless and forlorn, that there should be no other good than what depends upon things wholly out of our own power, the momentary gratification of our insatiate appetites and the perpetual pouring into "a perforated and leaking vessel"; that ourselves should be but a congeries of atoms, upon the dissolution of whose compages, our life should vanish into nothing, and all our hope perish; that there should be no providence over us, nor any kind and good-natured being above to take care of us, there being nothing without us but dead and senseless matter. True indeed, there could be no spiteful designs in senseless atoms, or a dark unconscious nature. Upon which account, Plutarch would grant that even this atheistic hypothesis itself, as bad as it is, were notwithstanding to be preferred before that of an omnipotent, spiteful and malicious being [16] (if there can be any such hypothesis as this), a monarchy of the Manichean evil principle, reigning all alone over the whole world, without any corrival, and having an undisturbed empire. Nevertheless it is certain also that there could be no faith nor hope neither, in these senseless atoms, both necessarily and fortuitously moved, no more than there could be faith and hope in a whirlwind, or in a tempestuous sea whose merciless waves are inexorable and deaf to all cries and supplication. For which reason Epicurus himself confessed, that it was better to give credit to the fable of the gods (as he calls it) than to serve the atheistic fate, or that material necessity of all things, introduced by those atheistic philosophers, Leucippus and Democritus: "Because there is hope, that the gods may be prevailed with by worship and prayer; but the other [necessity] is altogether deaf and inexorable." [17] And though Epicurus thought to mend the matter and make the atheistic hypothesis more tolerable by introducing into it (contrary to the tenor of those principles) liberty of will in men, yet this being not a power over things without us, but ourselves only, could alter the case very little. Epicurus himself was in a panic fear lest the frame of heaven should sometime upon a sudden crack and tumble about his ears, and this fortuitous compilement of atoms be dissolved into a chaos:

> Tria talia texta
> Una dies dabit exitio; multosque per annos
> Sustentata ruet moles et machina mundi.[18]

16. [ED.] Plutarch, *On Superstition*, §4.

17. [ED.] Diogenes Laertius, *Life of Epicurus*, Bk. X, §134.

18. [ED.] Lucretius, *De Rerum Natura*, Bk. V, lines 94–96: " . . . these three textures so interwoven, one day shall consign to destruction; the mighty and complex system of the universe, sustained through many years, shall collapse."

And what comfort could his liberty of will then afford him, who placed all his happiness in security from external evils? "The atheistic design in shaking off the belief of a God was to be without fear," saith Plutarch; [19] but by means hereof, they framed such a system of things to themselves, as, under which, they could not have the least hope, faith or confidence. Thus running from fear, did they plunge themselves into fear; for they who are without hope can never be free from fear. Endless of necessity must the fears and anxieties of those men be who shake off that one fear of God, that would only preserve them from evil, and have no faith nor hope in him. Wherefore, we might conclude, upon better grounds than the atheists do of theism, that atheism (which hath no foundation at all in nature nor in reason) springs first from the imposture of fear. For the faith of religion being the substance or confidence of such things not seen as are to be hoped for, atheistic infidelity must needs, on the contrary, be a certain heavy diffidence, despondence and misgiving of mind, or a timorous distrust and disbelief of good to be hoped for, beyond the reach of sense; namely, of an invisible being omnipotent, that exerciseth a just, kind and gracious providence over all those who commit their ways to him, with an endeavor to please him both here in this life and after death. But vice, or the love of lawless liberty, prevailing over such disbelieving persons, makes them by degrees more and more desirous that there should be no God—that is, no such hinderer of their liberty—and to count it a happiness to be freed from the fear of him whose justice (if he were) they must needs be obnoxious to.

And now have we made it evident that the atheists, who make religion and the belief [in] a God to proceed from the imposture of fear, do first of all disguise the Deity, and put a monstrous, horrid and affrightful wizard upon it, transforming it into such a thing as can only be feared and hated; and then do they conclude concerning it (as well indeed they may) that there is no such thing as this really existing in nature, but that it is only a mormo, or bugbear, raised up by men's fear and fancy. Of the two, it might better be said, that the opinion of a God sprung from men's hope of good, than from their fear of evil; but really, it springs neither from hope nor fear (however in different circumstances it raises both those passions in our minds); nor is it the imposture of any passion, but that whose belief is supported and sustained by the strongest and clearest reason, as shall be declared in due place. But the sense of a Deity often

19. [ED.] Plutarch, *On Superstition*, §2.

preventing ratiocination in us, and urging itself more immediately upon us, it is certain that there is also, besides a rational belief thereof, a natural prolepsis or anticipation in the minds of men concerning it, which by Aristotle is called μαντεία, "a vaticination."

RALPH CUDWORTH

On Plastic Nature

Editor's Introduction. The Cambridge Platonists found that they were constantly obliged to wage war on two fronts. On the one hand, they attacked Hobbes and everything he represented; on the other, they struggled for a more liberal view than was permitted by the rigidities of Calvinistic orthodoxy.

The struggle became particularly explicit concerning the doctrine of nature. The Cambridge Platonists believed that Hobbes had propounded a pure materialism, a nature controlled at every point by mechanistic forces. The Calvinist doctrine of extreme Occasionalism, on the other hand, presupposed the continual intervention of God: the universe, even in its minutest details, had been created by God and was controlled by his constant care. But the Cambridge men insisted that there was a middle ground between these two extreme positions. Their answer was related to their understanding of mind (an absolute and independent spirit, "senior to the world and proleptical to it"). For them, God was the highest and most perfect example of spirit; he was the source of all spirit, and he had given to the world a spirit of its own. More termed it "the spirit of the world"; Cudworth called it "plastic nature." It was the instrument by means of which God accomplished his purposes in the world he had made. It was the force or principle diffused throughout the world, giving it unity, determining its form, preserving its life. Plastic nature must not be equated with God, though it derived its power from him. There were some tasks which it was unnecessary for God to perform in person. Actually it would be unworthy of him to do so. Consequently, "there is a plastic nature under God which as an inferior and subordinate instrument doth drudgingly execute that part of his providence which consists in the regular and orderly motion of matter." Plastic nature had its appropriate place on the grand staircase of life which led from God through angels and the rational soul to animals and unthinking things. Its powers worked unconsciously, but they were governed by purpose, not by chance. It was God's instrument in creation; its operation at the first had arranged all matter in the

234

proper order, and ever since it had worked immediately and within every parcel of matter to produce the forms of life which we know.

Plastic nature relieved God of the necessity of constantly interfering with the operation of the universe. It explained the dynamic element in a universe which clearly could not be dismissed as dead and lifeless. Because it derived from God, it was responsible for the order, the regularity and the beauty which men saw around them; because it was an unconscious force, it explained the slips and errors which constitute the minor blemishes in a glorious creation. Deformities were its mistakes. But normally it worked with an unobtrusive skill which contrasted strangely with the clumsy efforts of the highest human art. The difference was easily explained: plastic nature operated from within, creatively; man's artifice worked from without, artificially. The regular functioning of plastic nature did not eliminate the possibility of direct and purposive action on the part of God, but it did account for the regular operation of the world as we know it.

Cudworth insisted that it was impossible to resolve the universe into mechanical force. The universe, he believed, could be understood only in organic terms. In all organisms he detected an urge towards adventure and survival; the sub-human could not be treated as the domain of the machine. Hence he opposed Hobbes, and modified the position adopted by Descartes. He revived a view which had been popular with Renaissance thinkers, but he went behind them to his usual sources in Plotinus (whom he quoted repeatedly) and in Plato. He believed that he had found a means of preserving the essential message of the Bible and yet of reconciling it with the implications of the new science that was emerging in his day. But he also anticipated the philosophers who are intrigued by an *élan vital,* and the biologists who resist a crude materialism; he even has affinities with men like Teilhard, Toulmin, Margenau and Sinnott. To Cudworth the world was instinct with vitality and creativity. Within it lurked new and unsuspected possibilities. Its vitalism was related to universal truth, and was the reflection of absolute value.

❖   ❖   ❖   ❖

From *The True Intellectual System of the Universe* [1]

Unless there be such a thing admitted as a plastic nature, that acts ἕνεκα τοῦ, for the sake of something and in order to ends, regularly, arti-

1. [ED.] This passage occurs in Chapter III, and begins with Section xxxvii, 2.

ficially and methodically, it seems that one or other of these two things must be concluded: that either in the efformation and organization of the bodies of animals, as well as the other phenomena, everything comes to pass fortuitously and happens to be as it is, without the guidance and direction of any mind or understanding; or else, that God himself doth all immediately, and, as it were with his own hands, form the body of every gnat and fly, insect and mite, as of other animals in generations, all whose members have so much of contrivance in them, that Galen professed he could never enough admire that artifice, which was in the leg of a fly (and yet he would have admired the wisdom of nature more, had he been but acquainted with the use of microscopes). I say, upon supposition of no plastic nature, one or other of these two things must be concluded; because it is not conceived by any that the things of nature are all thus administered, with such exact regularity and constancy everywhere, merely by the wisdom, providence and efficiency of those inferior spirits, demons or angels. As also, though it be true that the works of nature are dispensed by a divine law and command, yet this is not to be understood in a vulgar sense, as if they were all effected by the mere force of a verbal law or outward command, because inanimate things are not commendable nor governable by such a law. And therefore besides the divine will and pleasure there must needs be some other immediate agent and executioner provided, for the producing of every effect, since not so much as a stone or other heavy body could at any time fall downward merely by force of a verbal law, without any other efficient cause; but either God himself must immediately impel it, or else there must be some other subordinate cause in nature for that motion. Wherefore the divine law and command, by which the things of nature are administered, must be conceived to be the real appointment of some energetic, effectual and operative cause for the production of every effect.

Now to assert the former of these two things—that all the effects of nature come to pass by material and mechanical necessity, or the mere fortuitous motion of matter, without any guidance or direction—is a thing no less irrational than it is impious and atheistical. Not only because it is utterly inconceivable and impossible, that such infinite regularity and artificialness,[2] as is everywhere throughout the whole world, should constantly result out of the fortuitous motion of matter; but also because there are many such particular phenomena in nature, as do plainly transcend the powers of mechanism, of which therefore no sufficient mechanical reasons can be devised—as the motion of respiration in animals; as

2. [ED.] I.e., that which reflects artifice or skill in workmanship.

there are also other phenomena that are perfectly cross to the laws of mechanism—as for example, that of the distant poles of the equator and ecliptic, which we shall insist upon afterward. Of both which kinds there have been other instances proposed by my learned friend Dr. More, in his *Enchiridion Metaphysicum,* and very ingeniously improved by him to this very purpose, namely, to evince that there is something in nature besides mechanism, and consequently substance incorporeal.

Moreover, those theists, who philosophize after this manner, by resolving all the corporeal phenomena into fortuitous mechanism, or the necessary and unguided motion of matter, make God to be nothing else in the world, but an idle spectator of the various results of the fortuitous and necessary motions of bodies; and render his wisdom altogether useless and insignificant, as being wholly inclosed and shut up within his own breast, and not at all acting abroad upon anything without him.

Furthermore, all such mechanists as these, whether theists or atheists, do, according to that judicious censure passed by Aristotle long since upon Democritus, but substitute as it were "a carpenter's or artificer's wooden hand, moved by strings and wires, instead of a living hand." [3] They made a kind of dead and wooden world, as it were a carved statue, that hath nothing neither vital nor magical at all in it. Whereas to those who are considerative, it will plainly appear that there is a mixture of life or plastic nature, together with mechanism, which runs through the whole corporeal universe.

And whereas it is pretended, not only that all corporeal phenomena may be sufficiently solved mechanically, without any final, intending and directive causality, but also that all other reasons of things in nature, besides the material and mechanical, are altogether unphilosophical,[4] the same Aristotle ingeniously exposes the ridiculousness of this pretence after this manner; telling us, that it is just as if a carpenter, joiner or carver should give this account, as the only satisfactory, of any artificial fabric or piece of carved imagery, "that because the instruments, axes and hatchets, planes and chisels happened to fall so and so upon the timber, cutting it here and there, that therefore it was hollow in one place, and plain in another, and the like; and by that means the whole came to be of such a form." [5] For is it not altogether as absurd and ridiculous, for men to undertake to give an account of the formation and organization of the

---

3. [ED.] Aristotle, *De Partibus Animalium,* Bk I, Ch. I.
4. [ED.] "Philosophical," in seventeenth-century usage, was often equivalent to "scientific."
5. [ED.] Aristotle, *De Partibus Animalium,* Bk. I, Ch. I.

bodies of animals, by mere fortuitous mechanism, without any final or in-tending causality, as why there was a heart here, and brains there; and why the heart had so many and such different valves in the entrance and outlet of its ventricles; and why all the other organic parts, veins and arteries, nerves and muscles, bones and cartilages, with the joints and members, were of such a form? Because, forsooth, the fluid matter of the seed happened to move so and so in several places, and thereby to cause all those differences, which are also diverse in different animals; all being the necessary result of a certain quantity of motion at first indifferently impressed upon the small particles of the matter of this universe turned round in a vortex. But as the same Aristotle adds, no carpenter or artificer is so simple as to give such an account as this, and think it satisfactory, but he will rather declare that himself directed the motion of the instruments, after such a manner, and in order to such ends: "A carpenter would give a better account than so, for he would not think it sufficient to say, that the fabric came to be of such a form, because the instruments happened to fall so and so, but he will tell you that it was because himself made such strokes, and that he directed the instruments and determined their motion after such a manner, to this end that he might make the whole a fabric fit and useful for such purposes." [6] And this is to assign the final cause. And certainly there is scarcely any man in his wits that will not acknowledge the reason of the different valves in the heart from the apparent usefulness of them, according to those particular structures of theirs, to be more satisfactory, than any which can be brought from mere fortuitous mechan-ism, or the unguided motion of the seminal matter.

And as for the latter part of the disjunction, that everything in nature should be done immediately by God himself; this, as according to vulgar apprehension, it would render divine Providence operose, solicitous and distractious, and thereby make the belief of it to be entertained with greater difficulty, and give advantage to atheists; so, in the judgment of the writer *De Mundo*, it is not so decorous in respect of God neither, that he should set his own hand, as it were, to every work, and immediately do all the meanest and triflingest things himself drudgingly, without making use of any inferior and subordinate instruments: "If it were not congruous in respect of the state and majesty of Xerxes the great king of Persia, that he should condescend to do all the meanest offices himself; much less can this be thought decorous in respect of God. But it seems far more august, and becoming of the divine majesty, that a certain power and virtue, de-

6. [ED.] Aristotle, *De Partibus Animalium*, Bk. I, Ch. I.

rived from him, and passing through the universe, should move the sun and moon, and be the immediate cause of those lower things done here upon earth." [7]

Moreover, it seems not so agreeable to reason neither, that nature, as a distinct thing from the Deity, should be quite superseded or made to signify nothing, God himself doing all things immediately and miraculously; from whence it would follow also, that they are all done either forcibly and violently, or else artificially only, and none of them by any inward principle of their own.

Lastly, this opinion is further confuted by that slow and gradual process, that is in the generations of things, which would seem to be but a vain and idle pomp, or a trifling formality, if the agent were omnipotent: as also by those ἁμαρτήματα (as Aristotle calls them), those errors and bungles, which are committed when the matter is inept and contumacious; which argue the agent not to be irresistible, and that nature is such a thing, as is not altogether uncapable (as well as human art) of being sometimes frustrated and disappointed, by the indisposition of matter. Whereas an omnipotent agent, as it could dispatch its work in a moment, so it would always do it infallibly and irresistibly; no ineptitude or stubbornness of matter being ever able to hinder such a one, or make him bungle or fumble in anything.

Wherefore since neither all things are produced fortuitously or by the unguided mechanism of matter, nor God himself may reasonably be thought to do all things immediately and miraculously, it may well be concluded, that there is a plastic nature under him, which, as an inferior and subordinate instrument, doth drudgingly execute that part of his providence which consists in the regular and orderly motion of matter; yet so as that there is also, besides this, a higher providence to be acknowledged, which, presiding over it, doth often supply the defects of it and sometimes overrule it; forasmuch as this plastic nature cannot act electively nor with discretion. And by this means the wisdom of God will not be shut up nor concluded wholly within his own breast, but will display itself abroad, and print its stamps and signatures everywhere throughout the world; so that God, as Plato (after Orpheus) speaks, will be not only the beginning and end, but also the middle of all things; they being as much to be ascribed to his causality, as if himself had done them all immediately, with-

7. [ED.] *De Mundo* ["Of the World"] was often attributed to Aristotle, but the attribution is now regarded as spurious. The work was probably written between 50 B.C. and A.D. 100. This quotation comes from Ch. VII.

out the concurrent instrumentality of any subordinate natural cause.[8] Notwithstanding which, in this way, it will appear also to human reason that all things are disposed and ordered by the Deity, without any solicitous care or distractious providence.

And indeed those mechanic theists who, rejecting a plastic nature, affect to concern the Deity as little as is possible in mundane affairs, either for fear to debasing and bringing him down to too mean offices or else of subjecting him to solicitous incumberment, and for that cause would have God to contribute nothing more to the mundane system and economy than only the first impressing of a certain quantity of motion upon the matter and the after-conserving of it, according to some general laws—these men (I say) seem not very well to understand themselves in this. Forasmuch as they must of necessity either suppose these their laws of motion to execute themselves, or else be forced perpetually to concern the Deity in the immediate motion of every atom of matter through the universe, in order to the execution and observation of them. The former of which, being a thing plainly absurd and ridiculous, and the latter that which these philosophers themselves are extremely abhorrent from, we cannot make any other conclusion than this, that they do but unskillfully and unawares establish that very thing which in words they oppose; and that their laws of nature concerning motion are really nothing else but a plastic nature, acting upon the matter of the whole corporeal universe, both maintaining the same quantity of motion always in it, and also dispensing it (by transferring it out of one body into another) according to such laws, there can be no reason given, why the same might not also extend farther to the regular disposal of that matter, in the formation of plants and animals and other things, in order to that apt coherent frame and harmony of the whole universe.

And as this plastic nature is a thing, which seems to be in itself most reasonable, so hath it also had the suffrage of the best philosophers in all ages. . . .[9]

But because some may pretend that the plastic nature is all one with an occult quality, we shall here show how great a difference there is betwixt these two. For he that asserts an occult quality for the cause of any phenomenon, does indeed assign no cause at all of it, but only declares his own

---

8. [ED.] Plato, *Laws*, Bk. IV, 716.

9. [ED.] At this point Cudworth launches into a detailed examination of Aristotle, Plato, Empedocles, Plotinus, Heraclitus and other ancient philosophers, to prove that his own teaching is not really a novelty.

ignorance of the cause. But he that asserts a plastic nature assigns a determinate and proper cause, nay the only intelligible cause, of that which is the greatest of all phenomena in the world, namely the "orderly, regular and artificial frame" of things in the universe, whereof the mechanic philosophers, however pretending to solve all phenomena by matter and motion, assign no cause at all. Mind and understanding is the only cause of orderly regularity, and he that asserts a plastic nature, asserts mental causality in the world. But the fortuitous mechanists, who, exploding final causes, will not allow mind and understanding to have any influence at all upon the frame of things, can never possibly assign any cause of this grand phenomenon, unless confusion may be said to be the cause of order, and fortune or chance of constant regularity, and therefore themselves must resolve into an occult quality. Nor indeed does there appear any great reason why such men should assert an infinite mind in the world, since they do not allow it to act anywhere at all, and therefore must needs make it to be in vain.

Now this plastic nature being a thing which is not without some difficulty in the conception of it, we shall here endeavor to do these two things concerning it: first, to set down a right representation thereof, and then afterwards to show how extremely the notion of it hath been mistaken, perverted and abused by those theists who would make it to be the only God Almighty or first principle of all things.

How the plastic nature is in general to be conceived, Aristotle instructs us in these words: "If the naupegical art, that is, the art of the shipwright, were in the timber itself operatively and effectually, it would there act just as nature doth." [10] And the case is the same for all other arts. If the oecodomical art, which is in the mind of the architect, were supposed to be transfused into the stones, bricks and mortar, there acting upon them in such a manner as to make them come together of themselves, and range themselves into the form of a complete edifice, as Amphion was said, by his harp, to have made the stones move, and place themselves orderly of their own accord, and so to have built the walls of Thebes; [11] or if the musical art were conceived to be immediately in the instruments and strings, animating them as a living soul and making them to move exactly,

10. [ED.] Aristotle, *Physics*, Bk. II, Ch. VIII.

11. [ED.] Amphion and Zethus, twin sons of Antiope by Zeus, seized the sovereignty of Thebes and fortified the city. Homer tells how Zethus brought up the stones with his strong arm, and that Amphion (a harper of more than mortal skill) fitted them together by the music of his lyre (*The Odyssey*, Bk. XI, lines 262–65).

according to the laws of harmony, without any external impulse: these, and such like instances, in Aristotle's judgment, would be fit iconisms or representations of the plastic nature, that being art itself acting immediately upon matter as an inward principle in it. To which purpose the same philosopher adds, that this thing might be further illustrated by another instance or resemblance. "Nature may be yet more clearly resembled to the medicinal art, when it is employed by the physician in curing himself." [12] So that the meaning of this philosopher is, that nature is to be conceived as art acting not from without and at a distance, but immediately upon the thing itself which is formed by it. And thus we have the first general conception of the plastic nature, that it is art itself, acting immediately on the matter as an inward principle.

In the next place, we are to observe that though the plastic nature be a kind of art, yet there are some considerable pre-eminences which it hath above human art. The first whereof is this, that whereas human art cannot act upon the matter otherwise than from without and at a distance, nor communicate itself to it but with a great deal of tumult and hurlyburly, noise and clatter (it using hands and axes, saws and hammers, and after this manner with much ado, by knocking and thrustings, slowly introducing its form or ideas—as for example of a ship or house—into the materials) nature in the meantime is another kind of art, which insinuating itself immediately into things themselves, and their acting more commandingly upon the matter as an inward principle, does its work easily, cleverly and silently. Nature is art as it were incorporated and embodied in matter, which doth not act upon it from without mechanically but from within vitally and magically; "Here are no hands, nor feet, nor any instrument, connate, or adventitious, there being only need of matter to work upon, and to be brought into a certain form, and nothing else. For it is manifest that the operation of nature is different from mechanism, it doing not its work by trusion or pulsion, by knockings or thrustings, as if it were without that which it wrought upon." [13] But as God is inward to everything, so nature acts immediately upon the matter, as an inward and living soul, or law in it.

Another pre-eminence of nature above human art is this, that whereas human artists are often to seek and at a loss, and therefore consult and deliberate, as also upon second thoughts mend their former work; nature, on the contrary, is never to seek what to do, nor at a stand; and for that

12. [ED.] Aristotle, *De Partibus Animalium*, Bk. I, Ch. 1.
13. [ED.] Plotinus, *The Enneads*, III.8.1.

reason also (besides another that will be suggested afterwards) it doth never consult nor deliberate. Indeed Aristotle intimates, as if this had been the grand objection of the old atheistic philosophers against the plastic nature, that because we do not see natural bodies to consult or deliberate, therefore there could be nothing of art, counsel or contrivance in them, but all came to pass fortuitously. But he confutes it after this manner: "It is absurd for men to think nothing to be done for ends, if they do not see that which moves to consult, although art itself doth not consult." [14] Whence he concludes that nature may act artificially, orderly and methodically, for the sake of ends, though it never consult or deliberate. Indeed human artists themselves do not consult properly as they are artists, but whenever they do it, it is for want of art, and because they are to seek, their art being imperfect and adventitious. But art itself or perfect art is never to seek, and therefore doth never consult or deliberate. And nature is this art, which never hesitates nor studies, as unresolved what to do, but is always readily prompted; nor does it ever repent afterwards of what it hath formerly done, or go about, as it were upon second thoughts, to alter and mend its former course; but it goes on in one constant unrepenting tenor, from generation to generation, because it is the stamp or impress of that infallibly omniscient art of the divine understanding, which is the very law and rule of what is simply the best in everything.

And thus we have seen the difference between nature and human art—that the latter is imperfect art, acting upon the matter from without and at a distance, but the former is art itself, or perfect art, acting as an inward principle in it. Wherefore when art is said to imitate nature, the meaning thereof is, that imperfect human art imitates that perfect art of nature, which is really no other than the divine art itself; as, before Aristotle, Plato had declared in his *Sophist,* in these words: "Those things, which are said to be done by nature, are indeed done by divine art." [15]

From what hath been hitherto declared concerning the plastic nature, it may appear that though it be a thing that acts for ends artificially, and which may be also called the divine art and the fate of the corporeal world, yet for all that it is neither god nor goddess, but a low and imperfect creature. Forasmuch as it is not master of that reason and wisdom according to which it acts, nor does it properly intend those ends which it acts for; nor indeed is it expressly conscious of what it doth, it not knowing, but only doing, according to commands and laws impressed

14. [ED.] Aristotle, *Physics*, Bk. II, Ch. VIII.
15. [ED.] Plato, *Sophist*, 265.

upon it. Neither of which things ought to seem strange or incredible, since nature may as well act regularly and artificially, without any knowledge and consciousness of its own, as forms of letters compounded together may print coherent philosophic sense, though they understand nothing at all. And it may also act for the sake of those ends that are not intended by itself but some higher being, as well as the saw or hatchet in the hand of the architect or mechanic doth—"the axe cuts for the sake of something, though itself does not ratiocinate, nor intend or design anything, but is only subservient to that which does so." [16] It is true that our human actions are not governed by such exact reason, art, and wisdom, nor carried on with such constancy, evenness and uniformity as the actions of nature are; notwithstanding which, since we act according to a knowledge of our own, and are masters of that wisdom by which our actions are directed, since we do not act fatally [17] only, but electively and intendingly, with consciousness and self-perception, the rational life that is in us ought to be accounted a much higher and more noble perfection than that plastic life of nature. Nay, this plastic nature is so far from being the first and highest life, that it is indeed the last and lowest of all lives, it being really the same thing with the vegetative, which is inferior to the sensitive. The difference betwixt nature and wisdom was before observed, that wisdom is the first and highest thing, but nature the last and lowest; this latter being but an umbratile [shadowy] imitation of the former. And to this purpose, this plastic nature is further described by the same philosopher, in these words: "The spermatic reason or plastic nature is no pure mind or perfect intellect, nor any kind of pure soul neither; but something which depends upon it, and being as it were an effulgency or eradiation from both together, mind and soul, or soul affected according to mind, generating the same as a lower kind of life." [18]

And though this plastic nature contain no small part of divine providence in it, yet, since it is a thing that cannot act electively nor with discretion, it must needs be granted, that there is a higher and diviner providence than this, which also presides over the corporeal world itself; which was a thing likewise insisted upon by that philosopher: "The things in the world are not administered merely by spermatic reasons, but by perileptic (that is, comprehensive intellectual reasons), which are in order of nature before the other, because in the spermatic reasons cannot be contained that which

---

16. [ED.] Simplicius, *On the Physics of Aristotle*, Bk. II.
17. [ED.] I.e., as directed or ordained by fate.
18. [ED.] Plotinus, *The Enneads*, III.2.16.

is contrary to them." [19] Where, though this philosopher may extend his spermatic reasons further than we do our plastic nature in this place (which is only confined to the motions of matter), yet he concludes that there is a higher principle presiding over the universe than this. So that it is not *ratio mersa et confusa*, a reason drowned in matter, and confounded with it, which is the supreme governor of the world, but a providence perfectly intellectual, abstract and released.

But though the plastic nature be the lowest of all lives, nevertheless since it is a life, it must needs be incorporeal, all life being such. For body being nothing but antitypous [material, solid] extension or resisting bulk, nothing but mere outside, *aliud extra aliud*, together with passive capability, hath no internal energy, self-activity or life belonging to it. It is not able so much as to move itself and therefore much less can it artificially direct its own motion. Moreover, in the efformation of the bodies of animals, it is one and the selfsame thing that directs the whole. That which contrives and frames the eye cannot be a distinct thing from that which frames the ear; nor that which makes the hand from that which makes the foot. The same thing which delineates the veins must also form the arteries, and that which fabricates the nerves must also project the muscles and joints. It must be the same thing that designs and organizes the heart and brain, with such communications betwixt them. One and the selfsame thing must needs have in it the entire idea and the complete model or platform of the whole organic body. For the several parts of matter distant from one another, acting alone by themselves, without any common directrix, being not able to confer together nor communicate with each other, could never possibly conspire to make up one such uniform and orderly system or compages [20] as the body of every animal is. The same is to be said likewise concerning the plastic nature of the whole corporeal universe, in which "all things are ordered together conspiringly into one." It must be one and the same thing which formeth the whole, or else it could never have fallen into such an uniform order and harmony. Now that which is one and the same, acting upon several distant parts of matter, cannot be corporeal.

Indeed, Aristotle is severely censured by some learned men for this, that though he talk everywhere of such a nature as acts regularly, artificially and methodically, in order to the best, yet he does nowhere positively declare whether this nature of his be corporeal or incorporeal, sub-

19. [ED.] Plotinus, *The Enneads*, IV.4.39.
20. [ED.] I.e., a whole formed by the compaction of parts, a complex structure.

stantial or accidental; which yet is the less to be wondered at in him, because he does not clearly determine these same points concerning the rational soul neither, but seems to stagger uncertainly about them. In the meantime it cannot be denied, but that Aristotle's followers do for the most part conclude this nature of his to be corporeal; whereas notwithstanding, according to the principles of this philosophy, it cannot possibly be such. For there is nothing else attributed to body in it besides these three, matter, form and accidents, neither of which can be the Aristotelic nature. First, it cannot be matter, because nature, according to Aristotle, is supposed to be the principle of motion and activity, which matter in itself is devoid of. Moreover, Aristotle concludes that they who assign only a material cause, assign no cause at all "of well and fit," [21] of that regular and artificial frame of things which is ascribed to nature; upon both which accounts, it is determined by that philosopher, that "nature is more a principle and cause than matter" [22] and therefore it cannot be one and the same thing with it. Again, it is as plain that Aristotle's nature cannot be the forms of particular bodies neither, as vulgar Peripatetics [23] seem to conceive, these being all generated and produced by nature, and as well corruptible as generable; whereas nature is such a thing as is neither generated nor corrupted, it being the principle and cause of all generation and corruption. To make nature and the material forms of bodies to be one and the selfsame thing is all one as if one should make the seal (with the stamper too) to be one and the same thing with the signature upon the wax. And lastly, Aristotle's nature can least of all be the accidents or qualities of bodies; because these act only in virtue of their substance, neither can they exercise any active power over the substance itself in which they are; whereas the plastic nature is a thing which domineers over the substance of the whole corporeal universe, and which, subordinately to the Deity, put both heaven and earth in this frame in which now it is. Wherefore since Aristotle's nature can be neither the matter nor the forms, nor the accidents of bodies, it is plain that, according to his own principles, it must be corporeal.

Now if the plastic nature be incorporeal, then it must of necessity be either an inferior power or faculty of some soul, which is also conscious, sensitive or rational; or else a lower substantial life by itself, devoid of

---

21. [ED.] Aristotle, *Metaphysics*, Bk. I, Ch. III.

22. [ED.] Aristotle, *De Partibus Animalium*, Bk. I, Ch. I.

23. [ED.] By "vulgar Peripatetics," Cudworth means the less significant members of the school of Aristotle.

animal consciousness. The Platonists seem to affirm both these together, namely, that there is a plastic nature lodged in all particular souls of animals, brutes and men, and also that there is a general plastic or spermatic principle of the whole universe, distinct from their higher mundane soul though subordinate to it and dependent upon it. "That which is called nature is the offspring of a higher soul, which hath a more powerful life in it." [24] And though Aristotle do not so clearly acknowledge the incorporeity and substantiality of souls, yet he concurs very much with this Platonic doctrine, that nature is either a lower power or faculty of some conscious soul, or else an inferior kind of life by itself, depending upon a superior soul.

And this we shall make to appear from his book, *De Partibus Animalium*,[25] after we have taken notice of some considerable preliminary passages in it in order thereunto. For having first declared that besides the material cause there are other causes also of natural generations, namely these two, "that for whose sake," or the final cause, "and that from which the principle of motion is," or the efficient cause, he determines that the former of these two is the principal: "The chiefest of these two causes seems to be the final or the intending cause; for this is reason, and reason is alike a principle in artificial and in natural things." Nay, the philosopher adds, excellently, that there is more reason and art in the things of nature, than there is in those things that are artificially made by men: "There is more of final or intending causality, and of the reason of good, in the works of nature, than in those of human art." After which he greatly complains of the first and most ancient physiologers, meaning thereby Anaximander and those other Ionics before Anaxagoras, that they considered only "the material principle and cause of things," without attending to those two other causes, the principle of motion, and that which aims at ends; they talking only of fire, water, air and earth, and generating the whole world from the fortuitous concourse of these senseless bodies. But at length Aristotle falls upon Democritus, who being junior to those others before mentioned, philosophized after the same atheistical manner but in a new way of his own, by atoms; acknowledging no other nature, neither in the universe nor in the bodies of animals, than that of fortuitous mechanism, and supposing all things to arise from the different compositions of magnitudes, figures, sites and motions. Of which Democritic

24. [ED.] Plotinus, *The Enneads*, III.8.3.
25. [ED.] The quotations in this paragraph and the next are all from this source, Bk. I, Ch. I.

philosophy he gives his censure in these following words: "If animals and their several parts did consist of nothing but figure and color, then indeed Democritus would be in the right: but a dead man hath the same form and figure of body that he had before, and yet for all that he is not a man; neither is a brazen or wooden hand a hand, but only equivocally, as a painted physician, or pipes made of stone are so called. No member of a dead man's body is that which it was before, when he was alive, neither eye, nor hand, nor foot. Wherefore this is but a rude way of philosophizing, and just as if a carpenter should talk of a wooden hand. For thus these physiologers declare the generations and causes of figures only, or matter out of which things are made, as air and earth. Whereas no artificer would think it sufficient to render such a cause of any artificial fabric, because the instrument happened to fall so upon the timber, that therefore it was hollow here, and plain there; but rather because himself made such strokes, and for such ends."

Now, in the close of all, this philosopher at length declares that there is another principle of corporeal things besides the material, and such as is not only the cause of motion but also acts artificially in order to ends: "There is such a thing as that which we call nature"—that is, not the fortuitous motion of senseless matter, but a plastic, regular and artificial nature, such as acts for ends and good; declaring in the same place what this nature is, namely that it is "soul, or part of soul, or not without soul"; and from thence inferring, that it properly belongs to a physiologer to treat concerning the soul also. But he concludes afterwards, "that the whole soul is not nature"; whence it remains that according to Aristotle's sense, nature is "either part of a soul, or not without soul"; that is, either a lower part or faculty of some conscious soul, or else an inferior kind of life by itself, which is not without soul, but subordinate to it and dependent on it. . . .[26]

But the grand objection against Aristotle's holding the world's animation is still behind; namely, from that in his *Metaphysics*, where he determines the highest starry heavens to be moved by an immovable mover, commonly supposed to be the Deity itself, and no soul of the world; and all the other spheres likewise to be moved by so many separate intelligences and not by souls.[27] To which we reply that indeed Aristotle's first immovable mover is no mundane soul, but an abstract intellect separate

26. [ED.] In the passage omitted at this point, Cudworth is concerned to show that Aristotle believed there was a plastic nature in animals, and similarly a plastic nature in the universe as a whole. This leads him to assert that Aristotle believed in a soul of the world.

27. [ED.] Aristotle, *Metaphysics*, Bk. XIV, Chs. VII–IX.

from matter, and the very Deity itself: whose manner of moving the heavens is thus described by him: "It moveth only as being loved." Wherefore, besides this supreme unmoved mover, that philosopher supposed another inferior moved mover also, that is a mundane soul, as the proper and immediate efficient cause of the heavenly motions; of which he speaks after this manner: "That which itself being moved," objectively, or by appetite and desire of the first good "moveth other things." [28] And thus that safe and sure-footed interpreter, Alex. Aphrodisius, expounds his master's meaning, that the heaven being animated, and therefore indeed moved by an internal principle of its own, is, notwithstanding, originally moved by a certain immovable and separate nature, which is above soul, "both by its contemplating of it, and having an appetite and desire of assimilating itself thereunto." [29] Aristotle seeming to have borrowed this notion from Plato, who makes the constant regular circumgyration of the heavens to be an imitation of the motion or energy of intellect.[30] So that Aristotle's first mover is not properly the efficient, but only the final and objective cause of the heavenly motions, and the immediate efficient cause thereof being "soul and nature."

Neither may this be confuted from those other Aristotelic intelligences of the lesser orbs; that philosopher conceiving in like manner concerning them, that they were also abstract minds or intellects of certain other inferior souls, which moved their several respective bodies or orbs circularly and uniformly, in a kind of imitation of them. For this plainly appears from hence, in that he affirms of these his inferior intelligences likewise, as well as of the supreme mover, that they do κινεῖν ὡς τέλος, "move only as the end."

Where it is evident that though Aristotle did plainly suppose a mundane intellectual soul, such as also contained, either in it or under it, a plastic nature, yet he did not make either of these to be the Supreme Deity; but resolved the first principle of things to be one absolutely perfect mind or intellect, separate from matter, which was "an immovable nature," [31] whose essence was his operation, and which moved only as being loved, or as the final cause; of which he pronounces in this manner: "That upon such a principle as this, heaven and nature depend"; [32] that is, the animated heaven, or mundane soul, together with the plastic nature of the

28. [ED.] Aristotle, *Metaphysics*, Bk. XIV, Ch. VIII.

29. [ED.] Alexander of Aphrodisias, *Quaestionum naturalium et moralium ad Aristotelis philosophiam*, Bk. I, Ch. I.

30. [ED.] Plato, *Laws*, Bk. X.

31. [ED.] Aristotle, *Metaphysics*, Bk. XIV, Ch. VI.

32. [ED.] Ibid., Ch. VII.

universe, must of necessity depend upon such an absolutely perfect and immovable mind or intellect.

Having now declared the Aristotelic doctrine concerning the plastic nature of the universe, with which the Platonic also agreed, that it is "either part of a mundane intellectual soul," that is, a lower power and faculty of it, "or else not without it, but some inferior thing depending on it"; we think fit to add in this place, that though there were no such mundane soul, as both Plato and Aristotle supposed, distinct from the Supreme Deity, yet there might notwithstanding be a plastic nature of the universe depending immediately upon the Deity itself. For the plastic nature essentially depends upon mind or intellect, and could not possibly be without it; according to those words before cited: "Nature depends upon such an intellectual principle"; and for this cause that philosopher does elsewhere join "mind and nature" both together.

Besides this general plastic nature of the universe, and those particular plastic powers in the souls of animals, it is not impossible but that there may be other plastic natures also (as certain lower lives, or vegetative souls) in some greater parts of the universe; all of them depending, if not upon some higher conscious soul, yet at least upon a perfect intellect presiding over the whole. As for example: though it be not reasonable to think that every plant, herb and pile of grass hath a particular plastic life or vegetative soul of its own, distinct from the mechanism of the body, nor that the whole earth is an animal endued with a conscious soul; yet there may possibly be, for aught we know, one plastic nature or life belonging to the whole terrestrial (or terraqueous) globe, by which all plants and vegetables, continuous with it, may be differently formed, according to their different seeds, as also minerals and other bodies framed, and whatsoever else is above the power of fortuitous mechanism effected, as by the immediate cause, though always subordinate to other causes; the chief whereof is the Deity. And this perhaps may ease the minds of those who cannot but think it too much to impose all upon one plastic nature of the universe.

And now we have finished our first task, which was to give account of the plastic nature, the sum whereof briefly amounts to this; that it is a certain lower life than the animal, which acts regularly and artificially, according to the direction of mind and understanding, reason and wisdom, for ends, or in order to good, though itself do not know the reason of what it does, nor is master of that wisdom according to which it acts, but only a servant to it, and drudging executioner of the same; it operating fatally and sympathetically, according to laws and commands prescribed to it by perfect intellect, and impressed upon it; and which is either a lower faculty of some conscious soul, or else an inferior kind of life or soul by itself; but essentially depending upon a higher intellect.

We proceed to our second undertaking; which was to show, how grossly those two sorts of atheists before mentioned, the Stoical or cosmoplastic, and the Stratonical or hylozoic,[33] both of them acknowledging this plastic life of nature, do mistake the notion of it, or pervert it and abuse it, to make a certain spurious and counterfeit God-Almighty of it (or a first principle of all things), thereby excluding the true Omnipotent Deity, which is a perfect mind or consciously understanding nature, presiding over the universe; they substituting this stupid plastic nature in the room of it.

Now the chief errors or mistakes of these atheists concerning the plastic nature, are these four following. First, that they make that to be the first principle of all, and the highest thing in the universe, which is the last and lowest of all lives; a thing essentially secondary, derivative and dependent. For the plastic life of nature is but a mere umbrage of intellectuality, a faint and shadowy imitation of mind and understanding; upon which it doth as essentially depend, as the shadow doth upon the body, the image in the glass upon the face, or the echo upon the original voice. So that if there had been no perfect mind or intellect in the world, there could no more have been any plastic nature in it, than there could be an image in the glass without a face, or an echo without an original voice. If there be φύσις, then there must be Νοῦς: [34] if there be a plastic nature, that acts regularly and artificially in order to ends and according to the best wisdom, though itself not comprehending the reason of it, nor being clearly conscious of what it doth; then there must of necessity be a perfect mind or intellect, that is, a Deity, upon which it depends. Wherefore Aristotle does like a philosopher in joining φύσις and Νοῦς, nature and mind both together; [35] but these atheists do very absurdly and unphilosophically,

33. [ED.] "Cosmoplastic," maintaining an inanimate plastic nature to be the highest principle of the universe. "Hylozoic," pertaining to the theory that matter has life, or that life is merely a property of matter. Cudworth mentions Strato as one of the chief proponents of "hylozoic atheism," but he probably also has Spinoza in mind. Cf. J. A. Passmore, *Ralph Cudworth*, 5.

34. [ED.] Φύσις, the natural form or constitution of a person or thing, may mean "dynamic operation" or "energy system"; Νοῦς, mind, thought, meaning, or (especially in Attic philosophy) intellect or reason, particularly as the center of rational direction of any "dynamic operation."

35. [ED.] Aristotle, *Metaphysics*, Bk. I, Ch. III.

that would make a senseless and unconscious plastic nature, and therefore without any mind or intellect, to be the first original of all things.

Secondly, these atheists augment the former error in supposing those higher lives of sense or animality, and of reason or understanding, to rise both of them from that lower senseless life of nature, as the only original fundamental light. Which is a thing altogether as irrational and absurd as if one should suppose the light that is in the air or ether to be the only original and fundamental light, and the light of the sun and stars but a secondary and derivative thing from it, and nothing but the light of the air modificated and improved by condensation; or as if one should maintain that the sun and moon and all the stars were really nothing else but the mere reflections of those images that we see in rivers and ponds of water. But this hath always been the sottish humor and guise of atheists, to invert the order of the universe and hang the picture of the world as of a man with his heels upwards. Conscious reason and understanding, being a far higher degree of life and perfection than that dull plastic nature which does only do but not know, can never possibly emerge out of it; neither can the duplication of corporeal organs be ever able to advance that simple and stupid life of nature into redoubled consciousness or self-perception; nor any triplication, or indeed millecuplation [36] of them, improve the same into reason and understanding.

Thirdly, for the better coloring of the former errors the hylozoists adulterate the notion of the plastic life of nature, confounding it with wisdom and understanding. And though themselves acknowledge that no animal sense, self-perception, and consciousness belongs to it, yet they will have it to be a thing perfectly wise, and consequently every atom of senseless matter that is in the whole world, to be infallibly omniscient, as to all its own capacities and congruities, or whatsoever itself can do or suffer; which is plainly contradictious. For though there may be such a thing as the plastic nature, that, according to the former description of it, can do without knowing and is devoid of express consciousness or self-perception, yet perfect knowledge and understanding without consciousness is nonsense and impossibility. Wherefore this must needs be condemned for a great piece of sottishness in the hylozoic atheists, that they attribute perfect wisdom and understanding to a stupid unconscious nature, which is nothing but the mere drudging instrument or manuary opificer [37] of a perfect mind.

36. [ED.] I.e., the action or process of increasing a thousandfold.

37. [ED.] "Drudging," performing servile labor; "manuary opificer," a manual fabricator.

Lastly, these atheists err in this, that they make this plastic life of nature to be a mere material or corporeal thing; whereas matter or body cannot move itself, much less therefore can it artificially order and dispose its own motion. And though the plastic nature be indeed the lowest of all lives, yet notwithstanding since it is a life, or internal energy and self-activity, distinct from local motion, it must needs be incorporeal, all life being essentially such. But the hylozoists conceive grossly both of life and understanding, spreading them all over upon matter, just as butter is spread upon bread or plaster upon a wall, and accordingly slicing them out in different quantities and bulks, together with it; they contending that they are but inadequate conceptions of body, as the only substance; and consequently concluding that the vulgarly received notion of God is nothing else but such an inadequate conception of the matter of the whole corporeal universe, mistaken for a complete and entire substance by itself, that is supposed to be the cause of all things; which fond dream or dotage of theirs will be further confuted in due place. But it is now time to put a period to this long though necessary digression concerning the plastic life of nature, or an artificial, orderly and methodical nature.

The Digression Concerning the Plastic Life of Nature, or an Artificial, Orderly, and Methodical Nature[38]

1. That neither the hylozoic nor cosmoplastic atheists are condemned for asserting an orderly and artificial plastic nature as a life distinct from the animal, however this be a thing exploded, not only by the atomic atheists, but also by some professed theists, who notwithstanding might have an undiscerned tang of the mechanically-atheistic humor hanging about them. 2. If there be no plastic artificial nature admitted, then it must be concluded that either all things come to pass by fortuitous mechanism and material necessity, (the motion of matter unguided) or else that God doth αὐτουργεῖν ἅπαντα, do all things himself immediately and miraculously, framing the body of every gnat and fly, as it were with his own hand; since divine laws and commands cannot execute themselves, nor be the proper efficient causes of things in nature. 3. To suppose all things to come to pass fortuitously or by the unguided motion of matter, a thing altogether as irrational as it is atheistical and impious; there being many phenomena, not only above the powers of mechanism, but also contrary to the laws of

38. [ED.] The "digression," an appendix to Chapter III of *The True Intellectual System*, summarizes in a series of propositions Cudworth's doctrine of plastic nature.

it. The mechanic theists make God but an idle spectator of the fortuitous
motions of matter and render his wisdom altogether useless and insignificant. Aristotle's judicious censure of the fortuitous mechanists, with the
ridiculousness of that pretence that material and mechanical reasons are
the only philosophical. 4. That it seems neither decorous in respect of God
nor congruous to reason that he should αὐτουργεῖν ἅπαντα, do all things himself immediately and miraculously, nature being quite superseded and
made to signify nothing. The same further confuted by the slow and gradual process of things in nature, as also by those errors and bungles that are
committed when the matter proves inept and contumacious, arguing the
agent not to be irresistible. 5. Reasonably inferred, that there is a plastic
nature in the universe, as a subordinate instrument of divine providence in
the orderly disposal of matter; but yet so as not without a higher providence presiding over it, forasmuch as this plastic nature cannot act electively or with discretion. Those laws of nature concerning motion which
the mechanic theists themselves suppose, really nothing else but a plastic
nature. 6. The agreeableness of this doctrine with the sentiments of the
best philosophers in all ages, Aristotle, Plato, Empedocles, Heraclitus,
Hippocrates, Zeno and the Paracelsians. Anaxagoras, though a professed
theist, severely censured, both by Aristotle and Plato, as an encourager of
atheism, merely because he used material and mechanical causes more than
mental and final. Physiologers and astronomers why vulgarly suspected of
atheism in Plato's time. 7. The plastic nature no occult quality, but the only
intelligible cause of that which is the grandest phenomena, the orderly
regularity and harmony of things, which the mechanic theists, however
pretending to solve all phenomena, can give no account at all of. A God
or infinite mind asserted by them in vain and to no purpose. 8. Two things
here to be performed by us; first, to give an account of the plastic nature,
and then to show how the notion of it hath been mistaken and abused by
atheists. The first general account of the plastic nature, according to
Aristotle, that it is to be conceived as art itself acting inwardly and immediately upon the matter; as if harmony living in the musical instruments
should move the strings of them without any external impulse. 9. Two
pre-eminences of the plastic nature above human art. First, that whereas
human art acts upon the nature from without, cumbersomely and molimi-
nously [laboriously], with tumult and hurlyburly, nature acting upon it
from within more commandingly doth its work easily, cleverly and
silently. Human art acts on the matter mechanically, but nature vitally
and magically. 10. The second pre-eminence of nature above human art,

that whereas human artists are often to seek and at a loss, anxiously consult and deliberate, and upon second thoughts mend their former works,
nature is never to seek, nor unresolved what to do, nor doth she ever
repent afterwards of what she hath done, changing her former course.
Human artists themselves consult not, as artists, but only for want of art;
and therefore nature, though never consulting, may act artificially. Concluded, that what is called nature is really the divine art. 11. Nevertheless,
that nature is not the divine art, pure and abstract, but concreted and embodied in matter, *ratio mersa et confusa* [reason immersed and disordered];
not the divine art archetypal, but ectypal. Nature differs from the divine
art, as the manuary opificer from the architect. 12. Two imperfections of
the plastic nature, in respect whereof it falls short even of human art; first,
that though it acts for ends artificially, yet itself neither intends those ends
nor understands the reason what it doth, and therefore cannot act electively. The difference between the spermatic reasons and knowledge.
Nature doth but ape or mimic the divine art or wisdom, being not master
of that reason according to which it acts, but only a servant to it, and
drudging executioner of it. 13. Proved that there may be such a thing as
acts artificially, though itself do not comprehend that art by which its
motions are governed; first, from musical habits; the dancer resembles the
artificial life of nature. 14. The same further evinced from the instincts of
brute animals, directing them to act rationally and artificially, in order to
their own good and the good of the universe, without any reason of their
own. The instincts in brutes but passive impresses of the divine wisdom,
and a kind of fate upon them. 15. The second imperfection of the plastic
nature, that it acts without animal fancy, συναίσθησις, express con-sense,[39]
and consciousness, and is devoid of self-perception and self-enjoyment.
16. Whether this energy of the plastic nature be to be called cogitation or
no, but a logomachy or contention about words. Granted, that what
moves matter vitally must needs do it by some energy of its own, distinct
from local motion; but that there may be a simple vital energy, without
that duplicity, which is in synaesthesis, or clear and express consciousness.
Nevertheless, that the energy of nature might be called a certain drowsy,
unawakened or astonished cogitation. 17. Instances which render it probable that there may be a vital consciousness. 18. The plastic nature, acting
neither knowingly nor fantastically, acts fatally, magically and sympathetically. The divine laws and fate, as to matter, not mere cogitation in

39. [ED.] Συναίσθησις, joint-sensation; "con-sense," joint-sense (equivalent to consciousness).

the mind of God, but an energetic and effectual principle; and the plastic nature, the true and proper fate of matter, or the corporeal world. What magic is, and that nature which acts fatally, acts also magically and sympathetically. 19. That the plastic nature, though it be the divine art and fate, yet for all that, it is neither god nor goddess, but a low and imperfect creature; it acting artificially and rationally no otherwise than compounded forms of letters, when printing coherent philosophic sense; nor for ends, than a saw or hatchet in the hands of a skillful mechanic. The plastic and vegetative life of nature the lowest of all lives, inferior to the sensitive. A higher providence than that of the plastic nature governing the corporeal world itself. 20. Notwithstanding which, forasmuch as the plastic nature is a life, it must needs be incorporeal. One and the same thing having in it an entire model and platform and acting upon several distant parts of matter at once coherently, cannot be corporeal; and though Aristotle nowhere declares whether his nature be corporeal or incorporeal (which he neither doth clearly concerning the rational soul), and his followers conclude it to be corporeal, yet, according to the very principles of that philosophy, it must needs be otherwise. 21. The plastic nature, being incorporeal, must either be a lower power lodged in souls that are also conscious, sensitive, or rational; or else a distinct substantial life by itself, and inferior kind of soul. How the Platonists complicate both these together; with Aristotle's agreeable determination, that nature is either part of a soul, or not without soul. 22. The plastic nature as to animals, according to Aristotle, a part or lower power of their respective souls. That the phenomena prove a plastic nature or *archaeus* [vital force] in animals, to make which a distinct thing from the soul is to multiply entities without necessity. The soul endued with a plastic power, the chief formatrix of its own body, the contribution of certain other causes not excluded. 23. That besides that plastic principle in particular animals, forming them as so many little worlds, there is a general plastic nature in the whole corporeal universe, which likewise, according to Aristotle, is either a part and lower power of a conscious mundane soul, or else something depending on it. 24. That no less according to Aristotle than Plato and Socrates, ourselves partake of life from the life of the universe, as well as we do of heat and cold, from the heat and cold of the universe; from whence it appears, that Aristotle also held the world's animation, with further undeniable proof thereof. An answer to two of the most considerable places of that philosopher, that seem to imply the contrary. That Aristotle's first immovable mover was no soul, but a perfect intellect abstract from matter; but that he supposed this to move only as a final cause, or as being loved, and besides it, a mundane soul and plastic nature, to move the heavens efficiently. Neither Aristotle's nature nor his mundane soul, the supreme Deity. However, though there be no such mundane soul as both Plato and Aristotle conceived, yet notwithstanding, there may be a plastic nature depending upon a higher intellectual principle. 25. No impossibility of some other particular plastic principles. And though it be not reasonable to think that every plant, herb, and pile of grass hath a plastic or vegetative soul of its own, nor that the earth is an animal; yet that there may possibly be one plastic inconscious nature in the whole terraqueous globe, by which vegetables may be severally organized and framed, and all things performed which transcend the power of fortuitous mechanism. 26. Our second undertaking, which was to show how grossly those atheists (who acknowledge this plastic nature) misunderstand it and abuse the notion, to make a counterfeit God Almighty or Numen of it, to the exclusion of the true Deity. First, in their supposing that to be the first and highest principle of the universe, which is the last and lowest of all lives, a thing as essentially derivative from and dependent upon a higher intellectual principle, as the echo on the original voice. 27. Secondly, in their making sense and reason in animals to emerge out of a senseless life of nature, by the mere modification and organization of matter. That no duplication of corporeal organs can ever make one single unconscious life to advance into redoubled consciousness and self-enjoyment. 28. Thirdly, in attributing perfect knowledge and understanding to this life of nature, which yet themselves suppose to be devoid of all animal sense and consciousness. 29. Lastly, in making the plastic life of nature to be merely corporeal; the hylozoists contending that it is but an inadequate conception of body, as the only substance; and fondly dreaming that the vulgar notion of God is nothing but such an inadequate conception of the matter of the whole universe, mistaken for a complete and entire substance by itself, the cause of all things.

PART FOUR

❖

Ethical Theory

HENRY MORE

On the Nature and Principles of Ethics

Editor's Introduction. Cudworth, as we have seen, expounded at length the general character of the ethical system to which the Cambridge Platonists adhered. At certain points, however, More's *Enchiridion Ethicum* (his chief contribution to this subject) is more explicit than anything that Cudworth wrote. For one thing, he defined with some care exactly what he meant by ethics. Furthermore, in a series of twenty-three "Noemata Moralia," he offered a systematic exposition of ethical principles. These principles, he declared, could be intuitively apprehended; their truth would strike the reader as immediately evident. It is interesting to note that though More saw his system as an alternative to that of Hobbes, he was quite prepared to admit into it a strong hedonistic element. Ethics, he assures us, is "the art of living both well and happily." Some of his principles presuppose an egotistic application, and apparently More accepted this as right and proper. He clearly differed from his contemporary opponents in his insistence that certain ethical principles required that the individual be prepared to sacrifice for the benefit of others. You must do "as you would be done by"; you must accept the principle of justice, that is, of "giving every man his own and letting him enjoy it without interference." This is particularly true in what More described as the abstract formula of benevolence, that "if it be good that one man should be supplied with the means of living well and happily, it is mathematically certain that it is doubly good that two should be so supplied, and so on."

It is usually easier to define what is right than to provide the impulse necessary to perform it. More is not very clear when he comes to explain the motivation that should induce us to prefer principles of social benefit to impulses of selfish desire. He seems to suggest that the principles he has defined reflect an absolute good, which is apprehended by the intellect. This would imply that man, as a rational being, ought to do what is absolutely good because his mind sees it as such and directs his will to act appropriately. But there was, More believed, another consideration which

261

affected the human understanding of the matter. A man might recognize absolute good, but "the sweetness and flavor" of it were apprehended by what More calls a "boniform faculty." What really induced men to submit to the constraint of the good was their awareness of the "sweetness and flavor" associated with true virtue. It is evident that on the one hand More recognized the power of goodness to awaken an awareness of the joys to which it leads, and on the other he so defined the happiness which constitutes his ethical motive that it would appeal with requisite intensity only to an exceptionally sensitive moral consciousness.

In More's moral theory we also detect a further instance of the constant mingling of Christian and Platonic elements in his thought. As the Gospel commands us, we are to seek our neighbor's benefit as earnestly as our own, and indeed the highest manifestation of the "boniform faculty" is in love to God and to our neighbor. Nevertheless, when More describes the various virtues, he assigns a place to the Christian duty of benevolence only under the guise of the Platonic ideal of liberality.[1]

❖ ❖ ❖ ❖

An Account of Virtue
Enchiridion Ethicum

Book I

Chapter I. *What Ethics or Morals Are*

Ethics are defined to be *the Art of Living Well and Happily*.

I. We understand in this place, by art, a methodical knowledge of such precepts as are consentaneous one to another. And therefore, since ethics are that art we design to treat of, our precepts must all partake thereof, and all conduce thereunto; for else they would not be consentaneous. So that you are not to expect precepts how to dispute, but how to live, and how to be happy.

The reason why in the definition above we call it *The Art of Living both Well and Happily*, is because a man may live well and yet not altogether so happily; which two differing kinds of life the Pythagoreans did rightly

---

1. [ED.] *Enchiridion Ethicum* was first published in 1667; by 1711 it had reached its fourth edition. An English translation of the Latin original was published in 1690 under the title, *An Account of Virtue: Or, Dr Henry More's Abridgment of Morals, Put into English*. The translator was Edward Southwell. This was reproduced in 1930 by The Facsimile Text Society, New York.

distinguish; for by their doctrine it is one thing to be perfect according to nature, another according to life.

II. Now such men are by nature perfect who are adorned with virtue. For, by the definition of those philosophers, "Virtue is the top and perfection of every nature." They term these men good only and not happy or blest. But such men are said to be perfect according to life who are not only good but also happy. For they define happiness to be the perfection of human life; and they define human life to be a collection or chronicle of human actions. Wherefore, seeing the event and success of such actions depend on fortune, no man can, without the benefits of fortune, enjoy a perfect state. . . .

CHAPTER II. *Of the Parts of Ethics, and of Happiness*

I. Ethics are divided into two parts, *the knowledge of happiness*, and *the acquisition of it*. The knowledge contains the doctrine of its nature, and of such things as the nature of happiness does, in some part, either comprehend or else refer unto. Whence in this first part we shall principally treat of the virtues and of the passions, and in the last part add somewhat about the external supports of life.

II. Happiness is that pleasure which the mind takes in from a sense of virtue, and a conscience of well-doing, and of conforming in all things to the rules of both. Wherefore we say that external comforts, or some moderate proportion of them, do much conduce to the making happiness complete. Here we call happiness a pleasure of the mind rather than an operation of it, since all men allow it to be the best and greatest of human fruitions. But as that cannot be the greatest which is subservient to another, so the operation of the mind cannot be said to be its greatest good, since it is but in order to pleasure. And it is upon this account, as Aristotle observes,[1] that we often heighten and raise our operations: not that we are pleased with the operation itself, but because we expect a pleasure from it, which we highly value, and which we look upon as an effect thereof.

III. Furthermore, to come closer to the mark, this pleasure by which we define happiness, is here considered as the flower and masterpiece of that very operation, in the ways of virtue, which makes up the excellency of life. For in every action we go about, it is pleasure that makes the operation complete; it is as the soul of the work which cannot be wanting. And so

---

1. [ED.] Aristotle, *Eudemian Ethics*, Bk. I., Ch. 7.

Aristotle says, "That it gives perfection to all our works, and even to life itself." [2]

It is plain that each creature hath its own particular pleasure, which is construed to be its supreme happiness. Whence we may infer that human happiness does also consist in human pleasure; but such, I mean, as ariseth from the sense of virtue. . . .

CHAPTER III. *Of Virtue in General: and of Right Reason*

I. *Virtue is an intellectual power of the soul, by which it overrules the animal impressions or bodily passions; so as in every action it easily pursues what is absolutely and simply the best.*

Here it seems fit, in the definition, to call virtue rather a power than a habit. First, because the word virtue implies as much, and signifies the same thing as fortitude. And next because an habit is not essential to virtue. For if a man had this intellectual power born in him, he would doubtless be virtuous, though it came not to him in the way of repeated actions, such as constitute a habit. For it is not the external causes, but the internal, which make the essence of a thing. Besides it is this idea of virtue which elevates and inclines the mind to love her and tread in her ways, and which argues virtue to be a quick and vigorous heat, by which the mind is easily and irresistibly moved to do things which are good and honorable. So that we esteem this very notion of virtue able to rouse up men from sloth and lethargy, and make those ashamed, who on a few moderate performances think to set up for men of virtue.

II. We term this a power intellectual, not only because of its situation, which is in the intellectual part of the soul (and not in the animal part of it, where that power resides which governs the members) but also because it is always excited by some principle which is intellectual or rational. By animal impressions we understand every motion of the body, which being obtruded with any sort of violence on the soul, brings danger of sin and error, if not carefully watched.

Therefore all such delusions and imaginations as strongly assault the mind may fittingly be referred to this head. By actions, I mean all motions made by the soul upon deliberation, which is to say, all such as may properly be termed human actions, whether they be such as the Schoolmen call *elicitae* or *imperatae:* that is, whether they do immediately proceed

2. [ED.] Aristotle, *Nicomachean Ethics,* Bk. X, Ch. 4.

from the soul itself, or whether they are occasioned from any outward impressions made upon the soul. Under which heads we may rightly comprehend the accepting or refusing any philosophical opinion, whether physical or metaphysical. And so of anything else.

III. As to the pursuit of the soul, we spake of: this was to set off and more openly express the intellectual power; for if it had not that force to pursue, it would not be virtue, but only a disposition towards it. So Theages the Pythagorean hath it: "The reason doth not beget in us a continency and forbearance, but by putting a forcible restraint upon lust and anger. And that when the passions do overcome, and put the same forcible restraint upon reason, she then gives place to incontinency and a softness of mind which receives all impressions; when as bare dispositions without such a forcible restraint, can only produce imperfect virtues and imperfect vices."

Wherefore the philosopher makes these interchangeable conflicts and dispositions of the soul to be but virtues half perfect, as also the vices but half inveterate.

And whereas we say, the soul pursues what was absolutely and simply the best, this was to manifest that famous distinction of a twofold good; one general, which was absolutely good or absolutely better. The other particular, and which in respect of some single inclination of any particular person, was good or better: that is to say, either grateful or more grateful. But what we hold to be the absolute good, or better thing, is that which proves grateful, or more grateful, to the boniform faculty [3] of the soul, which we have already pronounced to be a thing divine.

IV. Aristotle seems to me, in his Ethics to Nicomachus, to point at this very faculty, saying, "That what is best, in whatever subject it be, is not apparent but to a good man." [4] By which he means that men do discover that which is best in every subject (I mean really and simply best) not as they are knowing, but as they are good. So that methinks he had spoken more correctly had he styled this faculty "the very eye of the soul," than to call it that sort of natural industry, which seems too much bordering upon craft. But forasmuch as no man can feel the motives and dictates of this divine faculty but one who hath attained to it by diligent application, we must have recourse to some middle principle to serve as Mercury did of old, and be an interpreter between God and man. And for this we shall

3. [ED.] "Boniform faculty": distinctive phrase used by More to denote a faculty cognizant of moral goodness.
4. [ED.] Aristotle, *Nicomachean Ethics,* Bk. VI, Ch. 13.

constitute that which we call right reason, wherefore that certainly is absolutely and simply the best, which according to the circumstances of the case in question comes up closest to right reason or is rather consentaneous with it.

v. For right reason, which is in man, is a sort of copy or transcript of that reason or law eternal which is registered in the mind divine. However this law is not by nature made otherwise known unto us, than as 'tis communicated and reflected on our minds by the same right reason, and so shines forth. But by how much it shines forth, by so much doth it oblige the conscience, even as a law divine inscribed in our hearts. To this very sense the Pythagoreans pronounced of virtue: "That it was the habit of doing what ought to be done." They did not barely intend, the doing what was equal, and in a mean, or doing what needed neither addition nor subtraction, as being already what it ought to be: But the doing that which was obligatory, and of duty, and according to a law which was immutable. And so also did Epictetus famously pronounce, "Whatever appears to be best, let that be your inviolable law." [5]

vi. The height of virtue is this, constantly to pursue that which to right reason seems best. For indeed she herself is even absolutely and simply that best, not only as she is so consonant to divine reason, which does nothing partially for the sake of this or that particular; but as she generously dictates, like to a common parent, such laws as tend, in their own nature, to the happiness of all mankind. Hence Aristotle calls God, the law eternal, as regarding every way with equal benignity.[6] So also, as well among the Pythagoreans as the Stoics, it was held, That to follow God, or to follow Nature, was just the same thing as to follow Right Reason. For this alone is what constitutes our nature, and distinguishes a man from a beast.

CHAPTER IV. *Certain Axioms or Intellectual Principles: Into Which Almost All the Reasons of Morality May Be Reduced*

But since there is a race of men in the world, who are quite seared up [7] as to God, and all that is divine; who allow no such thing as superiority in the faculties, but assert obedience to that passion in particular, which shall

5. [ED.] Epictetus, *Enchiridion*, §51.

6. [ED.] *De Mundo*, Ch. VI. On the attribution of this work to Aristotle, see note 7, supra, 239.

7. [ED.] A metaphorical expression, derived from 1 Timothy 4:2, and commonly used in the sixteenth and seventeenth centuries to describe a conscience rendered incapable of feeling. Cf. O.E.D.

happen to usurp above the rest, and make it the top of human felicity to fulfill the desires thereof: to such as these, who would injuriously pass for men, which they are not, we must proceed by other steps than what are already set down. For we must not talk of our boniform faculty [8] as the measure of right reason and flowing from the divine part of the soul, but merely insist with them upon what refers to the intellect; since, as Aristotle notes, "Some things are intelligible, though men know not the reason why." [9]

From this magazine therefore let us draw forth a stock of such principles, as being immediately and irresistibly true, need no proof; such, I mean, as all moral reason may in a sort have reference unto; even as all mathematical demonstrations are found in some first undeniable axioms. And because these principles arise out of that faculty, which the Greeks call Νοῦς, that signifies the mind or intellect; and that the words *Noema* and *Noemata* derive therefrom, and properly signify rules intellectual, we do not therefore improperly style the rules that hereafter follow, Moral Noemas. But lest any should fancy them to be morose and unpracticable, I must here affirm they propose nothing for good, which at the same time is not grateful also and attended with delight.

Noema I. *Good is that which is grateful, pleasant and congruous to any being, which hath life and perception, or that contributes in any degree to the preservation of it.*

Noema II. *But, on the other side, whatever is ungrateful, unpleasant or any ways incongruous to any being which hath life and perception, is evil. And if it finally tend to the destruction of that being, it is the worst of evils.*

As for example sake, if anything should not only offend your eyes or ears but bring also blindness and deafness upon you, this were the worst that could happen. But if the sight and hearing were but only impaired thereby, this were but an inferior evil. And the reason holds the same in the other faculties.

Noema III. *Among the several kinds or degrees of sensible beings which are in the world, some are better and more excellent than others.*

Noema IV. *One good may excel another in quality, or duration, or in both.*

This is self-evident; yet it may be illustrated from this absurdity, that otherwise one life would not be better, nor one sort of happiness greater than another: so as gods, angels, men, horses and the vilest worm, would be happy alike; which none but a mad man can fancy. And as to duration there is no scruple thereof.

8. [ED.] Cf. note 3.
9. [ED.] Aristotle, *Eudemian Ethics*, Bk. V, Ch. 8.

Noema v. *What is good is to be chosen; what is evil to be avoided; but the more excellent good is preferable to the less excellent; and a less evil is to be borne, that we may avoid a greater.*

Noema vi. *In things of which we have no experience, we must believe those who profess themselves to have experience. Provided always that there be no suspicion of fraud or worldly contrivance, but that there be a conformity between their professions and their lives*

Noema vii. *'Tis more eligible to want a good, which for weight and duration is very great, than to bear an evil of the same proportion. And by how much any evil shall in weight and duration exceed the good, by so much the more willingly can we be without such good.*

Noema viii. *That which must certainly come to pass, ought to be reputed as present; inasmuch as the future will one day come upon us. And herein some proportion of reason holds in things future, which are very probable.*

Noema ix. *Good things which excel less are distinguished by weight and duration from those things which excel more.*

Noema x. *A present good is to be rejected or moderated, if there be a future good of infinite more value, as to weight and duration to be but probably expected; and much more therefore if such expectation be certain.*

Noema xi. *A present evil is to be borne, if there be a probable future evil infinitely more dangerous, as to weight and duration, to be avoided thereby: and this is much more strongly incumbent, if the future evil be certain.*

Noema xii. *A mind which is free from the prejudices that attend passion, judges more uprightly than a mind which by such passions, or any other corporeal impressions is solicited or disturbed. For even as a cloudy sky, and turbulent sea will neither transmit or reflect light, so a disturbed mind admits no reason, though it come never so plain and clear.*

Boethius sets this forth in very elegant verse, which thus begins,

> *Nubibus atris*   *Fundere possunt*
> *Condita nullum*   *Sidera Lumen*, &c.
> The stars, though of themselves so bright,
> When hid in clouds can give no light.[10]

And these are those rules or Noemata which almost suffice to engender in the soul that prudence, temperance and fortitude which regard the

---

10. [ED.] Boethius, *The Consolation of Philosophy*, Bk. I, Ch. VII.

duties we owe ourselves. Those which follow regard what we owe unto others; as to God, to man, and to virtue itself. And therefore they are the rules and principles of sincerity, justice, gratitude, mercy and piety. For I account piety among the moral virtues, inasmuch as God may by the light of nature be known.

Noema XIII. *We must pursue the greatest and most perfect good with the greatest zeal, and lesser goods with a zeal proportionably less. Nor must we subordinate greater goods to less, but less to greater.*

Noema XIV. *The good, which in any case in question, you would have another man do unto you, the same you are bound in the like case, to do unto him, so far forth as it may be done without prejudice to a third.*

Noema XV. *The evil you would not have done to yourself, you must abstain from doing the same to another, as far as may be done without prejudice to a third.*

Noema XVI. *Return good for good, and not evil for good.*

Noema XVII. *'Tis good for a man to have wherewithal to live well and happily.*

Noema XVIII. *If it be good for one man to have withal to be happy, it evidently follows, 'tis twice as good for two men to be happy, thrice for three, a thousand times for a thousand, and so of the rest.*

Noema XIX. *'Tis better that one man be disabled from living voluptuously, than that another should live in want and calamity.*

Noema XX. *'Tis good to obey the magistrate in things indifferent, even where there is no penalty to disobey.*

Noema XXI. *'Tis better to obey God than men, or even our own appetites.*

Noema XXII. *'Tis good and just to give every man what is his due, as also the use and possession thereof without any trouble.*

Noema XXIII. *However 'tis manifest, that a man may so behave himself, as that what was his own by acquisition or donation, may of right cease to be his own.*

These and such like sayings may justly be called moral axioms or noemas: for they are so clear and evident of themselves, that, if men consider impartially, they need no manner of deduction or argument, but are agreed to as soon as heard. And thus we are prepared, as with so many touchstones, to let the inquisitive know what *right reason* is. For in short, *it is that which by certain and necessary consequences is at length resolved into some intellectual principle which is immediately true.*

And if any ask after examples in this kind, that are suited to morality, they may have recourse to such as are above recited.

RALPH CUDWORTH

On the Essentials of Ethics

Editor's Introduction. It is typical of Cudworth that he consistently laid the foundations of enterprises which he failed to complete. His vast work on *The True Intellectual System of the Universe* moves majestically towards a conclusion which it was never to reach. Probably realizing that his *System* would remain unfinished, Cudworth wrote, during his later years, *A Treatise Concerning Eternal and Immutable Morality;* but here again he did not attain his objective. It provided a recapitulation of his earlier work (the *System*), obviously intended to serve as a basis for more complete ethical studies, but he neither completed his task nor published it. The *Eternal and Immutable Morality* (like his writings on free will) remained in manuscript and was published in 1731 by Bishop Chandler of Durham.

Though not a complete ethical system, Cudworth's work indicates clearly his fundamental presuppositions. He confronted two views of the nature of good and evil, both of which he was convinced were wrong. It was contended, on the one hand, that moral distinctions were determined by the will of God. This view was propounded by Duns Scotus and Ockham. It was held, in characteristic form and with characteristic force, by Calvin. In the seventeenth century, its principal representative was Descartes: God, he said, could make a cube a sphere if he so desired, and he could make the right to be the wrong, just as he had actually determined it to be the right. On the other hand, Hobbes declared that good and evil were fixed by the will of sovereigns, and that ethics accordingly became a branch of politics. Against both of these views Cudworth upheld the "essential and eternal distinctions of good and evil." According to his belief, the difference between right and wrong had an objective reality, and reason could grasp that difference as effectively as it did the relations of space or number. Man might be dependent on God for his knowledge of these distinctions, but it was divine reason, not the divine will, to which man owed his awareness of ethical truths. As Cudworth said in his sermon at Lincoln's Inn, "Virtue and holiness in creatures . . . are not therefore good because God loveth them and will have them to be accounted such; but rather God loveth them because they are in themselves good."

Ethical truths, therefore, could not be regarded as relative. They were inseparable from the universal essence of things. As a result, the presuppositions of ethics were as unalterably valid as the propositions of mathematics. This meant, of course, that God was no longer the sole guardian of ethics: "An eternal and immutable morality" did not require the kind of support traditionally demanded by systems of Christian ethics. But Cudworth had merely altered the function of God; he had not dispensed with it. From his point of view it was never required of the divine fiat to determine what was right or wrong. Supreme right and supreme power had always coinhered. What Cudworth realized was that the love of God must play a very important role in determining the pattern of ethics. God, he said, was "a fountain of goodness"; from him, as from its source, flowed the disinterestedness so necessary for the transformation of man's moral life.

❖   ❖   ❖   ❖

A Treatise Concerning Eternal and Immutable Morality

Book I

Chapter II

Wherefore in the first place, it is a thing which we shall very easily demonstrate, that moral good and evil, just and unjust, honest and dishonest (if they be not mere names without any signification, or names for nothing else but willed and commanded, but have a reality in respect of the persons obliged to do and avoid them), cannot possibly be arbitrary things, made by will without nature; because it is universally true, that things are what they are, not by will but by nature. As for example, things are white by whiteness, and black by blackness, triangular by triangularity, and round by rotundity, like by likeness, and equal by equality, that is, by such certain natures of their own. Neither can omnipotence itself (to speak with reverence) by mere will make a thing white or black without whiteness or blackness; that is, without such certain natures, whether we consider them as qualities in the objects without us according to the peripatetical philosophy, or as certain dispositions of parts in respect of magnitude, figure, site and motion, which beget those sensations or phantasms of white and black in us. Or, to instance in geometrical figures, omnipotence itself cannot by mere will make a body triangular, without having the nature and properties of a triangle in it—that is, without having three angles equal to right ones; nor circular without the nature of a circle —that is, without a circumference equidistant everywhere from the center or middle point. Or lastly, to instance in things relative only, omnipotent will cannot make things like or equal one to another, without the natures of likeness and equality. The reason whereof is plain, because all these things imply a manifest contradiction, that things should be what they are not. And this is a truth fundamentally necessary to all knowledge, that contradictories cannot be true, for otherwise nothing would be certainly true or false. Now things may as well be made white or black by mere will without whiteness or blackness, equal and unequal without equality and inequality, as morally good and evil, just and unjust, honest and dishonest, *debita* [obligatory] and *illicita* [unlawful], by mere will without any nature of goodness, justice, honesty. For though the will of God be the supreme efficient cause of all things, and can produce into being or existence, or reduce into nothing what it pleaseth, yet it is not the formal cause of anything besides itself, as the Schoolmen have determined in these words: "Deum ipsum non posse supplere locum causae formalis, That God himself cannot supply the place of a formal cause." And therefore it cannot supply the formal cause, or nature of justice or injustice, honesty or dishonesty. Now all that we have hitherto said amounts to no more than this, that it is impossible anything should be by will only, that is, without a nature or entity, or that the nature and essence of anything should be arbitrary.

And since a thing cannot be made anything by mere will without a being or nature, everything must be necessarily and immutably determined by its own nature, and the nature of things be that which it is and nothing else. For though the will and power of God have an absolute, infinite and unlimited command upon the existences of all created things to make them to be or not to be at pleasure, yet when things exist they are what they are, this or that, absolutely or relatively, not by will or arbitrary command but by the necessity of their own nature. There is no such thing as an arbitrarious essence, mode or relation, that may be made indifferently anything at pleasure; for an arbitrarious essence is a being without a nature, a contradiction, and therefore a non-entity. Wherefore the natures of justice and injustice cannot be arbitrarious things, that may be applicable by will indifferently to any actions or dispositions whatsoever. For the modes of all subsistent beings and the relations of things to one another are immutably and necessarily what they are, and not arbitrary, being not by will but by nature.

Now the necessary consequence of that which we have hitherto said is this, that it is so far from being true, that all moral good and evil, just and unjust are mere arbitrary and factitious things that are created wholly by will; that (if we would speak properly) we must needs say that nothing is morally good or evil, just or unjust, by mere will without nature, because everything is what it is by nature and not by will. For though it will be objected here that when God or civil powers command a thing to be done, that was not before *debitum* or *illicitum*, obligatory or unlawful, the thing willed or commanded doth forthwith become Δέον or *debitum*, obligatory, that which ought to be done by creatures and subjects respectively; in which the nature of moral good or evil is commonly conceived to consist. And therefore if all good and evil, just and unjust be not the creatures of mere will (as many assert) yet at least positive things must needs owe all their morality, their good and evil to mere will without nature. Yet notwithstanding, if we well consider it, we shall find that even in positive commands themselves, mere will doth not make the thing commanded just or *debitum*, obligatory, or beget and create any obligation to obedience. Therefore it is observable that laws and commands do not run thus, to will that this or that thing shall become *justum* or *injustum, debitum* or *illicitum*, just or unjust, obligatory or unlawful, or that men shall be obliged and bound to obey, but only to require that something be done or not done or otherwise to menace punishment to the transgressors thereof. For it was never heard of, that anyone founded all his authority of commanding others, and others' obligation or duty to obey his commands, in a law of his own making that men should be required, obliged or bound to obey him. Wherefore since the thing willed in all laws is not that men should be bound or obliged to obey, this thing cannot be the product of the mere will of the commander but it must proceed from something else; namely, the right or authority of the commander which is founded in natural justice and equity and an antecedent obligation to obedience in the subjects; which things are not made by laws, but presupposed before all laws to make them valid. And if it should be imagined that anyone should make a positive law to require that others should be obliged or bound to obey him, everyone would think such a law ridiculous and ab-

surd; for if they were obliged before, then this law would be in vain and
to no purpose; and if they were not before obliged, then they could not
be obliged by any positive law, because they were not previously bound
to obey such a person's commands. So that obligation to obey all positive
laws is older than all laws and previous or antecedent to them. Neither is it
a thing that is arbitrarily made by will, or can be the object of command,
but that which either is or is not by nature. And if this were not morally
good and just in its own nature before any positive command of God,
that God should be obeyed by his creatures, the bare will of God himself
could not beget an obligation upon any to do what he willed and commanded, because the natures of things do not depend upon will, being not
Γιγνόμενα but ὄντα, "things that are arbitrarily made," but "things that are."
To conclude, therefore, even in positive laws and commands it is not
mere will that obligeth, but the natures of good and evil, just and unjust,
really existing in the world.

Wherefore that common distinction betwixt things φύσει καὶ θέσει, things
naturally and positively good and evil, or (as others express it) betwixt
things that are therefore commanded because they are good and just, and
things that are therefore good and just because they are commanded,
stands in need of a right explication that we be not led into a mistake
thereby as if the obligation to do thetical [1] and positive things did arise
wholly from will without nature; whereas it is not the mere will and
pleasure of him that commandeth that obligeth to do positive things commanded, but the intellectual nature of him that is commanded. Wherefore
the difference of these things lies wholly in this, that there are some things
which the intellectual nature obligeth to *per se*, of itself, and directly, absolutely and perpetually, and these things are called φύσει, naturally good
and evil. Other things there are which the same intellectual nature obligeth
to by accident only and hypothetically, upon condition of some voluntary
action either of our own or some other persons, by means whereof those
things which were in their own nature indifferent, falling under something
that is absolutely good or evil and thereby acquiring a new relation to the
intellectual nature, do for the time become *debita* or *illicita*, such things as
ought to be done or omitted being made such not by will but by nature.
As for example, to keep faith and perform covenants is that which natural
justice obligeth to absolutely; therefore *ex hypothesi* upon the supposition
that anyone maketh a promise, which is a voluntary act of his own, to do
something which he was not before obliged to by natural justice, upon

1. [ED.] I.e., of the nature of or involving direct or positive statement.

the intervention of this voluntary act of his own, that indifferent thing promised falling now under something absolutely good, and becoming the matter of promise and covenant, standeth for the present in a new relation to the rational nature of the promiser, and becometh for the time a thing which ought to be done by him, or which he is obliged to do. Not as if the mere will or words and breath of him that covenanteth had any power to change the moral natures of things, or any ethical virtue of obliging; but because natural justice and equity obligeth to keep faith and perform covenants. In like manner natural justice, that is, the rational or intellectual nature, obligeth not only to obey God but also civil powers, that have lawful authority of commanding, and to observe political order amongst men, and therefore if God or civil powers command anything to be done that is not unlawful in itself, upon the intervention of this voluntary act of theirs, those things that were before indifferent become by accident for the time *debita*, obligatory, such things as ought to be done by us, not for their own sakes but for the sake of that which natural justice absolutely obligeth to.

And these are the things that are commonly called θέσει, positively good and evil, just or unjust, such as though they are adiaphorous or indifferent in themselves, yet natural justice obligeth to accidentally *ex hypothesi*, on supposition of the voluntary action of some other person rightly qualified in commanding, whereby they fall into something absolutely good. Which things are not made good or *debita*, due, by the mere will or pleasure of the commander, but by that natural justice which gives him right and authority of commanding and obligeth others to obey him; without which natural justice, neither covenants nor commands could possibly oblige anyone. For the will of another doth no more oblige in command than our own will in promises and covenants. To conclude therefore, things called naturally good and *debita*, due, are such things as the intellectual nature obliges to immediately, absolutely and perpetually and upon no condition of any voluntary action that may be done or omitted intervening, but those things that are called positively good and due are such as natural justice or the intellectual nature obligeth to accidentally and hypothetically, upon condition of some voluntary act of another person invested with lawful authority in commanding.

And that it is not the mere will of the commander that makes these positive things to oblige or become *debita*, due, but the nature of things appears evidently from hence, because it is not the volition of everyone that obligeth but of a person rightly qualified and invested with lawful authority and because the liberty of commanding is circumscribed within certain bounds and limits, so that if any commander go beyond the sphere and bounds that nature sets him, which are indifferent things, his commands will not at all oblige.

But if we would speak yet more accurately and precisely, we might rather say, that no positive commands whatsoever do make anything morally good and evil, just and unjust, which nature had not made such before. For indifferent things commanded, considered materially in themselves, remain still what they were before in their own nature, that is, indifferent, because (τὸ φύσει ἀκίνητον, as Aristotle speaks) will cannot change nature. And those things that are φύσει ἀδιάφορα, by nature indifferent, must needs be as immutably so as those things that are φύσει δίκαια or ἄδικα, καλὰ or αἰσχρὰ, by nature just or unjust, honest or shameful. But all the moral goodness, justice and virtue that is exercised in obeying positive commands and doing such things as are θέσει, positive only and to be done for no other cause but because they are commanded, or in respect to political order, consisteth not in the materiality of the actions themselves, but in that formality of yielding obedience to the commands of lawful authority in them. Just as when a man covenanteth or promiseth to do an indifferent thing which by natural justice he was not bound to do, the virtue of doing it consisteth not in the materiality of the action promised, but in the formality of keeping faith and performing covenants. Wherefore in positive commands, the will of the commander doth not create any new moral entity, but only diversely modifies and determines that general duty or obligation of natural justice to obey lawful authority and keep oaths and covenants, as our own will in promising doth but produce several modifications of keeping faith. And therefore there are no new δίκαια, *justa* or *debita*, things just or due made by either of them, besides what was alway φύσει, by nature such, to keep our own promises, and obey the lawful commands of others.

We see then that it is so far from being true, that all moral good and evil, just and unjust (if they be anything) are made by mere will and arbitrary commands (as many conceive) that it is not possible that any command of God or man should oblige otherwise than by virtue of that which is φύσει δίκαιον, naturally just. And though particular promises and commands be made by will, yet it is not will but nature that obligeth to the doing of things promised and commanded, or makes them *debita*, such things as ought to be done. For mere will cannot change the moral nature of actions nor the nature of intellectual beings. And therefore if there were no natural justice, that is, if the rational or intellectual nature in itself were indetermined and unobliged to anything, and so destitute of all morality, it were not possible that anything should be made morally good or evil, *debitum* or *illicitum*, obligatory or unlawful, or that any moral obligation should be begotten by any will or command whatsoever.

Chapter III

But some there are that will still contend that, though it should be granted that moral good and evil, just and unjust do not depend upon any created will, yet notwithstanding they must needs depend upon the arbitrary will of God, because the natures and essences of all things and consequently all verities and falsities, depend upon the same. For if the natures and essences of things should not depend upon the will of God, it would follow from hence, that something that was not God was independent upon God.

And this is plainly asserted by that ingenious philosopher Renatus Des Cartes [i.e., René Descartes] who, in his answer to the Sixth Objector against his *Metaphysical Meditations*,[2] writes thus:

It is a contradiction to say, that the will of God was not from eternity indifferent to all things which are or ever shall be done; because no good or evil, nothing to be believed or done or omitted, can be fixed upon, the idea whereof was in the divine intellect before that his will determined itself to effect that such a thing should be. Neither do I speak this concerning priority of time, but even there was nothing prior in order or by nature, or reason as they call it, so as that that idea of good inclined God to choose one thing rather than another. As for example sake, he would therefore create the world in time because that he saw that it would be better so than if he had created it from eternity; neither willed he that the three angles of a triangle should be equal to two right angles, because he knew it could not be otherwise. But on the contrary, because he would create the world in time, therefore it is better than if he had created it from eternity; and because he would that the three angles of a triangle should necessarily be equal to two right angles, therefore this is true and can be no otherwise; and so of other things. And thus the greatest indifference in God is the greatest argument of his omnipotence.

2. [ED.] Descartes published six *Metaphysical Meditations*. Subsequently he issued a set of six *Objections* to his *Meditations*, together with his replies. The objections were sometimes forwarded by celebrated individuals—the third set came from Thomas Hobbes, the fifth from P. Gassendi—sometimes by groups of enquirers or critics. The sixth set, to which Descartes here gives his answers, was "urged by divers theologians and philosophers."

And again afterward, "To him that considers the immensity of God it is manifest that there can be nothing at all which doth not depend upon him, not only nothing subsisting, but also no order, no law, no reason of truth and goodness."

And when he was again urged by the Sixth Objector, "Could not God cause that the nature of a triangle should not be such? And how, I pray thee, could he from eternity cause that it should not be true, that twice four are eight?",[3] he confesseth ingenuously that those things were not intelligible to us; but yet notwithstanding they must be so, because nothing in any sort of being can be which doth not depend upon God. Which doctrine of Cartesius is greedily swallowed down by some servile followers of his that have lately written of the old philosophy.

Perhaps some may make a question for all this, whether Cartesius were any more in earnest in this than when he elsewhere goes about to defend the doctrine of Transubstantiation by the principles of his new philosophy, because in his Meditations upon the old philosophy (where it is probable he would set down the genuine sense of his own mind more undisguisedly, before he was assaulted by these objectors, and thereby forced to turn himself into several shapes) he affirmeth that the essences of things were eternal and immutable; but being afterward urged by Gassendus with this inconvenience, that then something would be eternal and immutable be- sides God, and so independent upon God, he doth in a manner unsay it again and betakes himself to this pitiful evasion. "As the poets feign that the Fates were indeed fixed by Jupiter, but that when they were fixed, he had obliged himself to the preserving of them; so I do not think that the essences of things and those mathematical truths which can be known of them, are independent on God; but I think nevertheless that because God so willed, and so ordered, therefore they are immutable and eternal"— which is plainly to make them in their own nature mutable. But whether Cartesius were in jest or earnest in this business it matters not, for his bare authority ought to be no more valued by us than the authority of Aristotle and other ancient philosophers was by him whom he so freely dissents from.

For though the names of things may be changed by anyone at pleasure, as that a square may be called a circle, or a cube a sphere, yet that the nature of a square should not be necessarily what it is, but be arbitrarily convertible into the nature of a circle and so the essence of a circle into the

3. [ED.] In each of these extracts from Descartes, Cudworth quotes the Latin version in full before providing an English translation.

essence of a sphere, or that the selfsame body, which is perfectly cubical, without any physical alteration made in it should, by this metaphysical way of transformation of essences, by mere will and command, be made spherical or cylindrical; this doth most plainly imply a contradiction and the compossibility of contradictions destroys all knowledge and the definite natures or notions of things. Nay, that which implies a contradiction is a non-entity and therefore cannot be the object of divine power. And the reason is the same for all other things, as just and unjust; for everything is what it is immutably by the necessity of its own nature; neither is it any derogation at all from the power of God to say that he cannot make a thing to be that which it is not. Then there might be no such thing as knowledge of God himself. God might will that there should be no such thing as knowledge.

And as to the being or not being of particular essences, as that God might, if he pleased, have willed that there should be no such thing as a triangle or circle, and therefore nothing demonstrable or knowable of either of them, which is likewise asserted by Cartesius, and those that make the essences of things dependent upon the arbitrary will in God: this is all one as if one should say that God could have willed, if he had pleased, that neither his own power nor knowledge should be infinite.

Now it is certain that if the natures and essences of all things, as to their being such or such, do depend upon a will of God that is essentially arbitrary, there can be no such thing as science or demonstration, nor the truth of any mathematical or metaphysical proposition be known any otherwise, than by some revelation of the will of God concerning it, and by a certain enthusiastic or fanatic faith and persuasion thereupon that God would have such a thing to be true or false at such a time, or for so long. And so nothing would be true or false φύσει but θέσει, naturally but positively only, all truth and science being mere arbitrarious things. Truth and falsehood would be only names. Neither would there be any more certainty in the knowledge of God himself, since it must wholly depend upon the mutability of a will in him essentially indifferent and undetermined; and if we would speak properly according to this hypothesis, God himself would not know or be wise by knowledge or by wisdom, but by will.

Wherefore as for that argument, that unless the essences of things and all verities and falsities depend upon the arbitrary will of God there would be something that was not God, independent upon God; if it be well considered, it will prove a mere bugbear and nothing so terrible and formidable as Cartesius seemed to think it. For there is no other genuine consequence deducible from this assertion, that the essences and verities of things are independent upon the will of God but that there is an eternal and immutable wisdom in the mind of God, and thence participated by created beings independent upon the will of God. Now the wisdom of God is as much God as the will of God and whether of these two things in God, that is, will or wisdom, should depend upon the other will be best determined from the several natures of them. For wisdom in itself hath the nature of a rule and measure, it being a most determinate and inflexible thing; but will being only a blind and dark thing, as considered in itself, but also indefinite and indeterminate, hath therefore the nature of a thing regulable and measurable. Wherefore it is the perfection of will as such to be guided and determined by wisdom and truth; but to make wisdom, knowledge and truth to be arbitrarily determined by will, and to be regulated by such a κανὼν μολύβδινος, "plumbean [4] and flexible rule" as that is, is quite to destroy the nature of it; for science or knowledge is κατάληψις τοῦ ὄντος, the comprehension of that which necessarily is and there can be nothing more contradictious than truth or falsehood arbitrary. Now all the knowledge and wisdom that is in creatures, whether angels or men, is nothing else but a participation of that one eternal, immutable and uncreated wisdom of God, or several signatures of that one archetypal seal, or like so many multiplied reflections of one and the same face, made in several glasses, whereof some are clearer, some obscurer, some standing nearer, some further off.

Moreover, it was the opinion of the wisest of the philosophers (as we shall show afterward) that there is also in the scale of being a nature of goodness superior to wisdom, which therefore measures and determines the wisdom of God, as his wisdom measures and determines his will, and which the ancient cabbalists were wont to call כתר, a crown, as being the top or crown of the Deity, of which more afterward. Wherefore although some novelists make a contracted idea of God, consisting of nothing else but will and power, yet his nature is better expressed by some in this mystical or enigmatical representation of an infinite circle, whose inmost center is simple goodness, the radii, the rays and expanded area, plat [5] thereof, all-comprehending and immutable wisdom, the exterior periphery or interminate circumference, omnipotent will or activity, by which everything without God is brought forth into existence. Wherefore the will and power of God have no *imperium ad intra*, command inwardly either upon

---

4. [ED.] I.e., leaden.
5. [ED.] I.e., a plane surface, a flat extension.

the wisdom and knowledge of God, or upon the ethical and moral disposition of his nature which is his essential goodness; but the sphere of its activity is *extra Deum*, without God, where it hath an absolute command upon the existences of things; and is always free, though not always indifferent, since it is its greatest perfection to be determined by infinite wisdom and infinite goodness. But this is to anticipate what according to the laws of method should follow afterward in another place.

Book II

Chapter I

Now the demonstrative strength of our cause lying plainly in this, that it is not possible that anything should be without a nature, and the natures or essences of all things being immutable, therefore upon supposition that there is anything really just or unjust, *debitum* or *illicitum*, due or unlawful, there must of necessity be something so, both naturally and immutably, which no law, decree, will nor custom can alter. There have not wanted some among the old philosophers that rather than they would acknowledge anything immutably just or unjust, would not stick to shake the very foundations of all things and to deny that there was any immutable nature or essence of anything, and by consequence any absolute certainty of truth or knowledge; maintaining this strange paradox that both all being and knowledge was fantastical and relative only, and therefore that nothing was good or evil, just or unjust, true or false, white or black, absolutely and immutably, but relatively to every private person's humor or opinion. . . .

Book IV

Chapter VI

We have now abundantly confuted the Protagorean philosophy,[6] which, that it might be sure to destroy the immutable natures of just and unjust,

6. In Bk. II, Ch. 1, Cudworth gives, as the best summary of Protagoras' philosophy, the words in Plato's *Theaetetus:* "That nothing was anything in itself absolutely, but was always made so to something else, and essence or being was to be removed from everything."

would destroy all science or knowledge and make it relative and fantastical. Having showed that this tenet is not only most absurd and contradictious in itself but also manifestly repugnant to that very atomical physiology on which Protagoras endeavored to found it and than which nothing can more effectually confute and destroy it; and also largely demonstrated that, though sense be indeed a mere relative and fantastical perception, as Protagoras thus far rightly supposed; yet notwithstanding there is a superior power of intellection and knowledge of a different nature from sense, which is not terminated ἐν τῷ φαινομένῳ, in mere seeming and appearance only but ἐν τῷ ὄντι, in the truth and reality of things, and reaches to the comprehension of that which really and absolutely is, whose objects are the eternal and immutable essences and natures of things, and their unchangeable relations to one another.

To prevent all mistake I shall again remember, what I have before intimated, that where it is affirmed that the essences of all things are eternal and immutable, which doctrine the theological schools have constantly avouched, this is only to be understood of the intelligible essences and *rationes* of things as they are the objects of the mind. And that there neither is nor can be any other meaning of it than this, that there is an eternal knowledge and wisdom, or an eternal mind or intellect, which comprehends within itself the steady and immutable *rationes* of all things and their verities, from which all particular intellects are derived and on which they do depend. But not that the constitutive essences of all individual created things were eternal and uncreated, as if God in creating of the world, did nothing else but, as some sarcastically express it, *sartoris instar rerum essentias vestire existentia*, "only clothed the eternal, increated, and antecedent essences of things with a new outside garment of existence, and not created the whole of them": and as if the constitutive essences of things could exist apart separately from the things themselves, which absurd conceit Aristotle frequently and no less deservedly chastises.

Wherefore the result of all that we have hitherto said is this, that the intelligible natures and essences of things are neither arbitrary nor fantastical, that is neither alterable by any will whatsoever, nor changeable by opinion; and therefore everything is necessarily and immutably to science and knowledge what it is, whether absolutely or relatively, to all minds and intellects in the world. So that if moral good and evil, just and unjust, signify any reality, either absolute or relative, in the things so denominated, as they must have some certain natures, which are the actions or souls of men, they are neither alterable by mere will nor opinion.

Upon which ground that wise philosopher Plato, in his *Minos*, determines that Νόμος, a law, is not δόγμα πόλεως, any arbitrary decree of a city or supreme governors, because there may be unjust decrees which therefore are no laws, but τοῦ ὄντος ἐξεύρεσις, but the invention of that which is, or what is absolutely or immutably just, in its own nature. Though it be very true also, that the arbitrary constitutions of those that have lawful authority of commanding, when they are not materially unjust, are laws also in a secondary sense, by virtue of that natural and immutable justice of law that requires political order to be observed.

But I have not taken all this pains only to confute skepticism or fantasticism, or merely to defend and corroborate our argument for the immutable natures of just and unjust, but also for some other weighty purposes that are very much conducing to the business that we have in hand. And first of all, that the soul is not a mere *rasa tabula*, a naked and passive thing, which has no innate furniture or activity of its own, nor anything at all in it, but what was impressed upon it without; for if it were so, then there could not possibly be any such thing as moral good and evil, just and unjust; forasmuch as these differences do not arise merely from the outward objects, or from the impresses which they make upon us by sense, there being no such thing in them, in which sense it is truly affirmed by the author of the *Leviathan*, that there is no common rule of good and evil to be taken from the nature of the objects themselves, that is, either considered absolutely in themselves or relatively to external sense only,[7] but according to some other interior analogy which things have to a certain inward determination in the soul itself, from whence the foundation of all this difference must needs arise, as I shall shew afterwards; not that the anticipations of morality spring merely from intellectual forms and notional ideas of the mind, or from certain rules or propositions, arbitrarily printed upon the soul as upon a book, but from some other more inward and vital principle in intellectual beings as such whereby they have a natural determination in them to do some things and to avoid others, which could not be if they were mere naked passive things. Wherefore since the nature of morality cannot be understood without some knowledge of the nature of the soul, I thought it seasonable and requisite here to take this occasion offered and to prepare the way to our following discourse, by showing in general that the soul is not a mere passive and receptive thing, which hath no innate active principle of its own, because upon this hypothesis there could be no such thing as morality.

7. [ED.] T. Hobbes, *Leviathan*, Pt. I, Ch. VI.

Again, I have the rather insisted upon this argument also because that which makes men so inclinable to think that justice, honesty and morality are but thin, airy and fantastical things, that have little or no entity or reality in them besides sensuality, is a certain opinion in philosophy which doth usually accompany it, that matter and body are the first original and source of all things; that there is no incorporeal substance superior to matter and independent upon it: and therefore that sensible things are the only real and substantial things in nature, but souls and minds springing secondarily out of body, that intellectuality and morality which belong unto them are but thin and evanid shadows of sensible and corporeal things, and not natural but artificial and factitious things that do as it were border upon the confines of nonentity.

This is a thing excellently well observed by Plato and therefore I shall set down his words at large concerning it. "These men making this distribution of things, that all things that are, are either by nature or art or chance, they imagine that the greatest and most excellent things that are in the world are to be attributed to nature and chance; which working upon those greater things which are made by nature does form and fabricate certain smaller things afterwards, which we commonly call artificial things. To speak more plainly, fire, water, air and earth, they attribute wholly to nature and chance but not to any art or wisdom; in like manner those bodies of the earth, the sun, moon and stars, they will have to be made out of them fortuitously agitated; and so by chance causing both divers systems and compages of things. Thus they would have the whole heavens made, and all the earth and animals, and all the seasons of the year, not by any mind intellect, or God, not by art or wisdom, but all by blind nature and chance. But art and mind afterwards springing up out of these, to have begotten certain ludicrous things which have little truth and reality in them, but are like images in a glass, such as picture and music produces. Wherefore these men attribute all ethics, politics, morality and laws, not to nature, but to art whose productions are not real and substantial." [8]

Now this philosopher, that he may evince that ethics, politics and morality are as real and substantial things and as truly natural as those things which belong to matter, he endeavors to show that souls and minds do not spring secondarily out of matter and body, but that they are real things in nature, superior and antecedent to body and matter. His words are these: "These men are all ignorant concerning the nature of mind and

8. [ED.] Plato, *Laws*, Bk. X, 889. Cudworth quotes the Greek in full.

soul, as in other regards, so especially in respect of its original, as it is in order of nature before matter and body and does not result out of it; but does command it, govern it, and rule it." [9]

And I have in like manner in this antecedent discourse endeavored to show that wisdom, knowledge, mind and intellect are no thin shadows or images of corporeal and sensible things, nor do result secondarily out of matter and body and from the activity and impressions thereof, but have an independent and self-subsistent being, which in order of nature is before body, all particular created minds being but derivative participations of one infinite eternal mind, which is antecedent to all corporeal things.

Now from hence it naturally follows, that those things which belong to mind and intellect, such as morality, ethics, politics and laws, which Plato calls "the offspring and productions of mind," are no less to be accounted natural things, or real and substantial, than those things which belong to stupid and senseless matter. For since mind and intellect are first in order of nature before matter and body, those things which belong to the mind must needs be in order of nature before those things which belong to the body. "Wherefore mind and intellect, art and law, ethics and morality are first in order of nature, before hard and soft, light and heavy, long and broad, which belong to body"; and therefore more real and substantial things. For since mind and intellect are a higher, more real and substantial thing than senseless body and matter, and what hath far the more vigor, activity and entity in it, modifications of mind and intellect, such as justice and morality, must of necessity be more real and substantial things than the modifications of mere senseless matter, such as hard and soft, thick and thin, hot and cold, and the like are. And therefore that grave philosopher excellently well concludes that "the greatest and first works and actions are of art or of mind, which were before body; but those things which are said to be by nature (in which they abuse the word nature, appropriating it only to senseless and inanimate matter) are afterwards being governed by mind and art." [10]

Wherefore I thought our former discourse seasonable to confute the dullness and grossness of those philosophasters that make corporeal things existing without the soul, to be the only solid and substantial things, and make their grossest external senses the only judges of reality of things,

9. [ED.] Plato, *Laws*, Bk. X, 892. Plato is less emphatic than Cudworth: "Nearly all men appear to be ignorant. . . ."
10. [ED.] Plato, *Laws*, Bk. X, 892.

"and so conclude nothing is or has any reality but what they can grasp in their hands, or have some gross or palpable sense of."

Whereas notwithstanding it is most true that those corporeal qualities which they think to be such real things existing in bodies without them are for the most part fantastic and imaginary things and have no more reality than the colors of the rainbow; and, as Plotinus expresseth it, "have no reality at all in the objects without us, but only a seeming kind of entity in our own fancies"; [11] and therefore are not absolutely anything in themselves but only relative to animals. So that they do in a manner mock us when we conceive of them as things really existing without us, being nothing but our own shadows and the vital passive energies of our own souls.

Though it was not the intention of God or nature to abuse us herein, but a most wise contrivance thus to beautify and adorn the visible and material world, to add luster or embellishment to it, that it might have charms, relishes and allurements in it, to gratify our appetites; whereas otherwise really in itself the whole corporeal world in its naked hue is nothing else but a heap of dust or atoms, of several figures and magnitudes, variously agitated up and down; so that these things, which we look upon as such real things without us, are not properly the modifications of bodies themselves but several modifications, passions and affections of our own souls.

Neither are these passive and sympathetical energies of the soul, when it acts confusedly with the body and the pleasures resulting from them, such real and substantial things as those that arise from the pure noetical energies of the soul itself intellectually and morally; for since the mind and intellect is in itself a more real and substantial thing, and fuller of entity than matter and body, those things which are the pure offspring of the mind and sprout from the soul itself must needs to be more real and substantial than those things which blossom from the body, and from the soul enfeebled by it and slumbering in it.

Wherefore that philosopher professing and understanding to confute atheists and to show that all atheists, "though they pretend to wit never so much, are but bunglers at reason, and sorry philosophers," he, not without cause, fetches his discourse from hence, that "they that thus infect men's minds with impiety and atheism, make that which is the first cause of all generation and corruption to be the last thing in the universe, and that which is the last to be the first. From hence proceeds their error con-

11. [ED.] Plotinus, *The Enneads*, IV.3.10.

cerning the being of God"; that is, they make mind and soul to be the last thing, and body and matter to be the first.

This therefore is the only course and method which this philosopher proceeds in to confute the atheists, to show "that mind and soul in the order of the universe, are before body and not posterior to it; mind and soul being that which rules in the universe, and body that which is ruled and ordered by it." And there is no phenomenon in the world but may be salved from this hypothesis.

Now this he demonstrates, even from local motion, because body and matter has no self-moving power, and therefore it is moved and determined in its motion by a higher principle, a soul or mind; which argument is further improved by the author of that excellent philosophical Treatise, Book II, Chapter 11.

Now for the selfsame cause I have endeavored to demonstrate in the foregoing discourse that knowledge and intellection cannot possibly spring from sense, nor the radiation or impresses of matter and body upon that which knows, but from an active power of the mind, as a thing antecedent to matter and independent upon it, whereby it is enabled from within itself to exert intelligible ideas of all things.

Lastly, I have insisted the rather so largely upon this argument for this further reason also because it is not possible that there should be any such thing as morality unless there be a God, that is, an infinite eternal mind that is the first original and source of all things, whose nature is the first rule and exemplar of morality; for otherwise it is not conceivable whence any such thing should be derived to particular intellectual beings. Now there can be no such thing as God if stupid and senseless matter be the first original of all things; and if all being and perfection that is found in the world, may spring up and arise out of the dark womb of unthinking matter. But if knowledge and understanding, if soul, mind and wisdom may result and emerge out of it, then doubtless everything that appears in the world may; and so night, matter and chaos must needs be the first and only original of all things.

Wherefore Plato, as I have already intimated, taking notice of the opinion of divers pretenders to philosophy, "that fire, water, air and earth are the first beings of all, to which senseless and inanimate things they appropriate the title of nature: but that soul did spring up afterward out of these as a secondary thing," and as a mere shadow of them, he immediately adds concerning it, "We have here found and discovered the true fountain of all that atheistical madness that possesses most of those that deal in physiology or questions of natural philosophy," [12] viz., that they are all possessed with this sottishness, that matter and body is the original of all things; and therefore it is observed by the same author that the same persons that held all things were derived from body, blind nature and chance did both deny the existence of God and, which is consentaneous thereunto, asserted that justice and morality have no nature or entity at all, saying they were nothing but passion from corporeal things, without the sentient or the renitence [13] or the reaction made upon local motion in a body duly mixed and tempered; that is, if soul and mind, knowledge and wisdom may thus arise from the contemplation of mere senseless matter and radiation or impression that is the mere local motion of corporeal objects without, then, as we said before, there cannot possibly be the least shadow of argument left to prove a deity by, since not only the souls of men but also all that wisdom, counsel and contrivance that appears in the frame of the whole visible world might first arise in like manner from the mere casual concourse and contemperation [14] of the whole matter; either in these particular bodies of the sun and stars, or else in the whole system and compages [15] of the material world itself.

Wherefore we have not only showed that all intellection and knowledge does not emerge or emane [16] out of sense, but also that sense itself is not a mere passion or reception of corporeal impresses without, but that it is an active energy and vigor though sympathetical in the sentient. And it is no more possible that this should arise out of senseless matter and atoms, by reason of any peculiar contemperation or contexture of them in respect of figure, site and motion, than that which all atheists stoutly deny, that something should arise out of nothing.

And here we can never sufficiently applaud that ancient atomical philosophy, so successfully revived of late by Cartesius, in that it shows distinctly what matter is and what it can amount unto, namely, nothing else but what may be produced from mere magnitude, figure, site, local motion and rest; from whence it is demonstrably evident and mathematically certain that no cogitation can possibly arise out of the power of matter; whereas that other philosophy which brings in a dark unintelligible matter that is nothing and everything, out of whose potentiality not only in-

12. [ED.] Plato, *Laws*, Bk. X, 891.
13. [ED.] I.e., the resistance of a body to pressure.
14. [ED.] I.e., a blending together.
15. [ED.] I.e., a complex structure.
16. [ED.] I.e., emanate.

numerable qualities, but also substantial forms and sensitive souls (and therefore why not rational also, since all reason emerges out of sense), may be educed, must of necessity perpetually brood and hatch atheism. Whereas we cannot but extremely admire that monstrous dotage and sottishness of Epicurus and some other spurious pretenders to this atomical philosophy, that notwithstanding they acknowledge nothing else in matter besides magnitude, figure, site and motion, yet would make not only the power of sensation, but also of intellection and ratiocination, and therefore all human souls, to arise from the mere contexture of corporeal atoms, and utterly explode all incorporeal substances; than which two assertions nothing can be more contradictious. And this is far more absurd to make reason and intellection to arise from magnitude, figure and motion, than to attribute those unintelligible qualities to matter which they explode.

PART FIVE

❖

The Freedom of the Will

❖ ❖ ❖ ❖ ❖ ❖ ❖ ❖

The Freedom of the Will

Editor's Introduction. The problem of free will was one which the Cambridge Platonists could not evade. It had been raised in an acute form by Thomas Hobbes. In his work, *Of Liberty and Necessity* (1654), a man who had begun as a materialist revealed himself as a determinist, thus precipitating one of the major controversies of the seventeenth century. The most celebrated exchange on the subject took place between Hobbes and Bishop Bramhall, but other writers were inevitably drawn into the debate. Cudworth, as usual, wrote on so unmanageable a scale that his work (*A Discourse of Liberty and Necessity*) was never published. Perhaps it was never even finished, though in the eighteenth century Thomas Birch reported that he had seen the complete work. The manuscript survives at the British Museum only in fragments, from among which John Allen selected the one he published in 1838 under the title *A Treatise of Freewill.*

Cudworth, it is clear, believed that the challenge posed by all forms of determinism could best be met by giving immediate attention to the work of Hobbes. In so doing, Cudworth's first step was to demonstrate the reality of spirit. The logical arguments in support of free will could then be accorded their proper weight, and the appeal to experience could be properly assessed. It was one thing to prove that such a thing as free will existed; it was quite another to define the nature of the phenomenon. Cudworth was convinced that it was a distinctively human attribute: man alone, he believed, had the power of free choice. The will was obviously involved, and not merely as the servant of reason; the soul had the power "to return upon itself." ("It can command or turn itself this way and that way.") [1] But the power it possessed was not unrestricted, since the will had an inherent bias towards the good.

Cudworth developed his argument on a scale equalled by none of his colleagues; but they were unanimous in emphasizing the importance of the concept of free will. John Smith considered the problem in his *Discourse Concerning the Existence and Nature of God*, notably in a brief

1. B.M. Add. MSS. 4979, f.5; quoted by S. Mintz, *The Hunting of Leviathan*, 131.

passage of Chapter II. Smith, it will be noticed, equated freedom with the possession of reason. Cudworth had recognized that only reasonable creatures are free, but he had also been conscious that there is a subtle and elusive relationship between the reason and the will. Smith, since he wrote before Hobbes had thrust the subject into the forefront of ethical debate, could afford to be less precise than Cudworth.

Henry More also repeatedly returned to the problem. References to it are scattered throughout his works; the chapter he devoted to it in his *Enchiridion Ethicum* is the most satisfactory summary of his position. His views are further illuminated by an exchange of letters with John Norris that took place shortly before More's death. Norris had sent More a copy of one of his published sermons, on which he invited More's comments. In the course of the correspondence, More clarified his own opinions and criticized certain of Norris's. One point, in particular, is worth noting, since it was also a matter with which Cudworth would be deeply concerned. "You fall," he writes in his third letter,

> upon a very subtle subject, viz., what it is in which our pretence to free agency may be safely grounded, whether in the will or understanding. And in order to decide the point in hand, you do with great judgment declare against talking of the will and understanding as faculties really distinct either from one another or the soul herself. But though you begin thus hopefully, yet methinks you run yourself into an unnecessary noose of fatality by granting the soul necessarily wills as she understands. You know that of the poet: "Video meliora proboque, deteriora sequor [2] [I see and approve the better; I pursue the worse]." And for my part, I suspect there are very few men if they will speak out, but they have experience of that truth.

As an appendix to the correspondence, Norris fortunately summarized in seventeen propositions the points he considered essential to the debate— an epitome that may fittingly conclude this section.[3]

2. [ED.] Ovid, *Metamorphoses*, VII, 18.

3. [ED.] Among the works which could not be included in this collection, but which will abundantly repay study, is Peter Sterry's *Discourse of the Freedom of the Will* (1675).

❖ ❖ ❖ ❖ ❖ ❖ ❖ ❖

RALPH CUDWORTH

Of Free Will

We seem clearly to be led by the instincts of nature to think that there is something ἐφ' ἡμῖν, *in nostra potestate,* in our own power (though dependently upon God Almighty), and that we are not altogether passive in our actings, nor determined by inevitable necessity in whatsoever we do. Because we praise and dispraise, commend and blame men for their actings much otherwise than we do inanimate beings or brute animals. When we blame or commend a clock or automaton, we do it so as not imputing to that automaton its being the cause of its own moving well or ill, agreeably or disagreeably to the end it was designed for, this being ascribed by us only to the artificer; but when we blame a man for any wicked actions, as for taking away another man's life either by perjury or by willful murder, we blame him not only as doing otherwise than ought to have been done, but also than he might have done, and that it was possible for him to have avoided it, so that he was himself the cause of the evil thereof. We do not impute the evil of all men's wicked actions to God the creator and maker of them after the same manner as we do the faults of a clock or watch wholly to the watchman. All men's words at least free God from the blame of wicked actions, pronouncing ὁ θεὸς ἀναίτιος, God is causeless and guiltless of them, and we cast the blame of them wholly on the men themselves, as principles of action and the true causes of the moral defects of them. So also do we blame men's acting viciously and immorally in another sense than we blame a halting or a stumbling horse, or than we blame the natural and necessary infirmities of men themselves when uncontracted by vice. For in this case we so blame the infirmities as to pity the men themselves, looking upon them as unfortunate but not as faulty. But we blame men's vices with a displeasure against the persons themselves.

The same sense of nature's instincts appears yet more plainly from men's blaming, accusing and condemning themselves for their own actions, when done either rashly, inconsiderately and imprudently, to their own private disadvantage, or else immorally and viciously and against the dictate of honesty. In which latter case men have an inward sense of guilt (besides shame), remorse of conscience, with horror, confusion and astonishment, and they repent of those their actions afterward with a kind of self-detestation and sometimes not without exercising revenge upon themselves as being a piece of justice due. No man accuses or condemns himself nor looks upon himself as guilty for having had a fever, the stone, or the gout, when uncontracted by vice; and if all human actions were necessary, men would be said no more to repent of them than of diseases, or that they were not born princes or heirs to a thousand pounds a year.

Lastly, we have also a sense of retributive, punitive, vindictive justice, as not mere fancy but a thing really existing in nature, when punishments are inflicted upon malefactors for their unjust and illegal actions past by civil magistrates in particular commonwealths. For though it be true that these civil magistrates do in part look forward to prevent the like for the future by terrifying others from doing the same, or to hinder these male-factors themselves from doing the like mischief again by cutting them off by death, as we kill noxious animals, wolves and vipers and serpents and mad dogs, yet it is not true that this is all the meaning of them and that they have no retrospect to the actions past; as being satisfaction to the equitable nature of rational beings, when they see wicked men who have both abused and debased themselves and also acted injuriously to others, to have disgrace and pain for their reward.

But men's natural instincts do more strongly suggest to them a notion of vindictive justice in the Supreme Governor of this great mundane repub-lic, God Almighty; in inflicting punishments upon notorious wicked persons, even here in this life, though sometimes but slowly, as Plutarch has observed.[1] But besides this the generality of mankind have always had a strong presage of punishments to be inflicted by the Deity after death; and the Scripture assures us that there is a solemn day of judgment ap-pointed, in which God will conspicuously, palpably and notoriously render to every one according to his works or actions past. And that these punishments in Hell, after death, will respect only the future and are no otherwise designed than as iatrical and medicinal, in order to the curing or recovering of the deceased souls punished, as some have imagined (from whence they infer that there can be no eternal punishments), is neither agreeable to Scripture nor sound reason. But if all actions be necessary, there seems to be no more reason why there should be a day of judgment

1. [ED.] Plutarch, "De his qui sero a numine puniuntur" (*Plutarchi Chaeronensis Quae Exstant Omnia* [Frankfort, 1599], II, 549).

appointed to punish men for murders and adultery, injustice and intemperance, than for agues and fevers, palsies and lethargies.

Hence it is that moralists, looking upon men's free and voluntary actions as blameworthy in a peculiar sense, have called the evil of them *malum culpae*, an evil of fault, in way of distinction from those other necessary evils which are without fault, that is of which the doer himself was not properly the cause. Concerning which Cicero thus—"Hoc tibi persuade nihil homini pertimescendum praeter culpam"; i.e., that no other evil is to be feared by a man comparatively to the evil of fault, according to that Stoical doctrine that the truest and greatest goods and evils of rational beings, consists ἐν τοῖς προαιρεπκοῖς or ἐν τοῖς ἐφ' ἡμῖν, in their own free willed actions or things in their own power.

Wherefore according both to the genuine instincts of nature, rightly interpreted, and the tenor of the Christian religion, we are to conclude that there is something ἐφ' ἡμῖν, in our own power, and that absolute necessity does not reign over all human actions, but that there is something of contingent liberty in them. This being an article of Christ's faith, that God hath appointed a day in which he will judge the world, and render rewards and punishments to men for their actions past in this life, good and evil. Glory, honor, power to every man that hath done well, but tribulation and anguish to every soul of man that hath done evil. We cannot possibly maintain the justice of God in this, if all men's actions are necessary either in their own nature or by divine decrees and influx. That is, we cannot possibly maintain the truth of Christianity without a liberty from necessity.

❖ ❖ ❖ ❖ ❖ ❖ ❖ ❖

JOHN SMITH

Of Free Will

FROM *A Discourse Concerning the Existence and Nature of God*

CHAPTER II

We may, in the next place, consider that freedom and liberty which we find in our own souls, which is founded in our reason and understanding; and this is therefore infinite in God, because there is nothing that can bound the first mind, or disobey an almighty power. We must not conceive God to be the freest agent because he can do and prescribe what he pleaseth and so set up an absolute will which shall make both law and reason as some imagine. For as God cannot know himself to be any other than what indeed he is, so neither can he will himself to be anything else than what he is, or that anything else should swerve from those laws which his own eternal nature and understanding prescribe to it. For this were to make God free to dethrone himself and set up a liberty within him, that should contend with the royal prerogative of his own boundless wisdom.

To be short: When we converse with our own souls, we find the spring of all liberty to be nothing else but reason. And therefore no unreasonable creature can partake of it and that it is not so much any indifferency in our wills of determining without reason, much less against it, as the liberal election of and complacency in that which our understandings propound to us as most expedient. And our liberty most appears when our will most of all congratulates the result of our own judgments; and then shows itself most vigorous when either the particularity of that good with which the understanding converseth or the weak knowledge that it hath of it restrains it not. Then is it most pregnant and flows forth in the fullest stream when its object is most full and the acquaintance with it most ample; all liberty in the soul being a kind of liberality in the bestowing of our affections, and the want or scarce measure of it, parsimoniousness. And, therefore, the more the results of our judgments tend to an indifference,

the more we find our wills dubious and in suspense what to choose; contrary inclinations arising and falling within interchangeably, as the scales
of a balance equally laden with weights; and all this while the soul's
liberty is nothing else but a fluctuation between uncertainties, and lan-
guisheth away in the impotency of our understandings. Whereas the
divine understanding, beholding all things most clearly, must needs beget
the greatest freedom that may be; which freedom as it is bred in it, so it
never moves without the compass of it. And though the divine will be not
determined always to this or that particular, yet it is never bereft of eternal
light and truth to act by; and, therefore, though we cannot see a reason for
all God's actions, yet we may know they were neither done against it nor
without it.

✤ ✤ ✤ ✤ ✤ ✤ ✤ ✤

HENRY MORE

Of Free Will

Enchiridion Ethicum, BOOK III

CHAPTER I

We have hitherto treated about the way to know happiness, or rather virtue; which is the principal part of happiness, if not its full perfection. The next thing is about the way to attain it. And in this part we shall be the rather brief, since what is hitherto delivered goes far to that end. And we are not willing to have that swelled which we call an epitome. So then we shall here expose what may look like "Heads of Meditation in the Search of Virtue," rather than any extended treatise of it.

But before we can well enter into this province, there is a thing called free will of which it is needful previously to speak, since till this be cleared and asserted all exhortation to virtue seems but in vain.

Aristotle has sometimes proposed a famous question (but Plato in his *Menon* handles it more largely), and it hath affinity with this our subject of free will; as namely, "Whether virtue gets into men by custom or by nature or by some divine fate" [1] (which is the same as good fortune)? There are some men extremely scandalized at the affirmative part of this question, as thinking it a derogation from human nature to make men at this rate necessarily good, and to deprive them of all free will. For they judge a thing voluntarily done to be of far different merit from what happens by compulsion; which yet (I confess) sounds to me as if God, who is good, should be the less adorable because he cannot be naught. For I will presume that whoever is good, either by nature or the divine fate, is also endowed with so true and efficacious a sense of honesty that he can no more go against this sense than that a sober man should stab himself with a dagger.

Were there but a race of such men, they were of all others the most

---

1. [ED.] Aristotle, *Nicomachean Ethics*, Bk. X, Ch. 10; *Eudemian Ethics*, Bk. VI, Ch. 14.

fitted for heroes, and as deriving virtue from the gods. 'Tis of such that
Homer speaks,

Nec eum esse putares
Mortali Genitore satum, at Genus esse Deorum.
(You'd think a man of such heroic frame
Not made below but that from heaven he came.)[2]

Aristotle quotes this very verse in his description of heroical virtue, and
thinks such virtue more given from above than the product of human
industry.[3] My opinion is that if all such force or power from above were
united and either by impression or inspiration fixed in the mind at once,
yet it might properly be called virtue. For according to our definition
virtue is a power or energy, not a habit. And though habit be a sort of
power arising from exercise and custom, yet this very way and circumstance of acquiring virtue is nothing material as to the true nature of it.
For if this power or energy be got within us and operates in our souls as
by a native spring or elasticity, what matter is it whether it came by
repeated actions or by inspiration?

But forasmuch as the blessings of this kind come rarely (if at all) to the
lot of any, we need not overlabor the difficulty of this point. We need not
study admonitions for such sorts of men, who by nature or some divine
fate are already so well and so necessarily inclined, but rather press and
convince the necessity of virtue unto other mortals, who, while they may
exercise the liberty of their wills to either side, should be urged and
excited by all that can be said to incline their wills to that side where right
reason and a sense of their duty calls them.

They must, above all things, be told of that excellent and almost divine
pre-eminence which they enjoy. For while all other creatures have their
senses tied down to the service of the body, or some particular delights,
they can mount aloft, and are enabled by a liberty in their wills to shake
off or gradually destroy those ill desires with which they are beset, and by
the help of Heaven to assert that liberty which is most suitable to a
creature made by God's image and a partaker of divine sense.

And as this is a most true persuasion and hath wonderful power among
men to draw them to virtue, and also to corroborate their minds against
the allurements or assaults of vice, let those men be ashamed who have so
tampered with mankind to persuade the contrary. This (in truth) has been
vigorously and studiously attempted by Mr. Hobbes in his book, *Of*

2. [ED.] Homer, *The Iliad*, XXIV, lines 258–59.
3. [ED.] Aristotle, *Nicomachean Ethics*, Bk. VII, Ch. 1.

Liberty and Necessity. But we think his principal arguments are all laid low in our treatise *Of the Soul's Immortality* unto which we therefore refer.[4]

In the meantime I cannot here forget that where among other motives he contends to have man's will necessarily determined to any profligate action, he owns that this his opinion of necessity takes place among the rest. But certainly, if that false opinion have such force as to what is vicious and bad, it follows that the true opinion, touching liberty to fly from evil, deserves equal force at least as to virtue and good life. And therefore, that a persuasion so efficaciously contributing to our advantage should be adhered unto and strongly contended for by us.

But to make the truth of this opinion more manifest, let us take notice what this *liberum arbitrium* or free will is, and then demonstrate that there is really such a principle within us. First, liberty of the will, which the Greeks call *autexousion*, seems almost to imply the having a power to act or not act within ourselves. Now in that free will is a principle of acting within one's self, it so far agrees with what the Greeks call *hecousion* (which is the same as spontaneous), and which (as Andronicus defines it) is that "whose principle of acting is wholly in the agent." Yet what he straight subjoins in the same chapter, saying, "That in what a man acts, as moved thereunto by himself, he is lord and master of doing it, or letting it alone," [5] this I think is not altogether so exact.

For a man may act out of his own mere motion; that is to say from such inbred principles of virtue and so strong and efficacious a sense of honesty, as not to be able to act otherwise or to draw his will to any different thing. For instance, an honest man has power indeed, by his wit and bodily force, treacherously to destroy an innocent man and even one that has well deserved of him. But can that honest man do this thing? No, God forbid! He dare not let himself do it. For that vigorous and lively sense of what is honest, and with which his mind is tinctured and possessed, can by no means permit him to execute so horrid a villainy. Now as such a person, though never so much solicited by promises and rewards, starts back, and (in the sense of Antonine) stops all his faculties of motion, and does not

4. [ED.] H. More, *Of the Immortality of the Soul*, Bk. II, Ch. 3.

5. [ED.] Andronicus Rhodius, *Ethicorum Nicom., Paraphrasis*, Bk. III, Ch. 1. Andronicus was the eleventh head of the Peripatetic School. He arranged the writings of Aristotle and of Theophrastus, and wrote paraphrases and commentaries on them. All his works have disappeared; what was known as his commentary on Aristotle's *Nicomachean Ethics* was probably written either by Constantine Palaeocappa or by John Callistus.

resign himself to so base a fact; this doubtless is entirely from himself, and none else is the cause why that advantage is not taken. However, I say he is not, in this case, so much master of his forbearance as that it is in his power not to forbear. I grant (indeed) that if he would he were able to commit so wicked a thing; but that he is able to will it, or bring his will unto it, is what I utterly deny.

We say therefore there is some difference between having free will and being a voluntary or spontaneous agent. The former is more restrained and particular and obtains in fewer cases, the latter is more large and general. When we say that a man has *liberum arbitrium* or free will, we add a particular difference to the general notion of voluntariness, that is to say, we suppose he is such a voluntary agent as can act and not act as he pleases; whereas to the being a voluntary agent, simply or generally speaking, there is no such difference required. It is sufficient to denominate any agent to be such, whose principle of action is in himself,[6] and who understands and takes cognizance of his own actions and the circumstances that relate to them; though in the meantime, it may not be in his power, every time he acts, to act otherwise than he does.

This now being the notion of spontaneous or voluntary, we see plainly what is the opposite to it, namely, everything that proceeds either from ignorance or outward force. Whatever action is done from either of these principles must needs be inspontaneous and involuntary. For in the one case (that of force) the agent does not act from his own principles but is compelled from without. In the other case (that of ignorance) though he act from his own principle, yet he has no notice of the moral circumstances of the action, which if he had known, he would not have done that action.

But now as to *liberum arbitrium*, or freedom of the will: what we call by that name is only that sort of spontaneity or voluntariness in us which is so free and undetermined that it is in our power to will or act this way or the other way, as we please. This (I say) is properly free will, and it supposeth a free election or choice in ourselves. And accordingly Andronicus (from Aristotle) defines it to be, "A deliberate wishing or appetition of those things which are within our power."[7] For those things (says he) are the subjects of deliberation, whereof everyone is master to do them or to leave them undone. And these are those very things which he declares to be within our power.

6. [ED.] Andronicus Rhodius, Bk. III, Ch. 2
7. [ED.] Andronicus Rhodius, Bk. III, Ch. 4.

Now this power of not acting, when it regards those things which are base and dishonest, is a great perfection; but when it has respect to things that are noble and honest, 'tis a great imperfection. For 'tis in the very next degree to acting dishonestly to be able to incline the will towards an action that is vile.

However, to know we are able and possessed with a power to abstain from a vile thing (though possibly we do not abstain), this is a sort of perfective state and of high consequence for a man to discover in himself whether he have it or no.

Now that such a real power is planted in man of being able to abstain from doing ill, though he fails at some times to exert that power, is very plain from the instances that follow

We need not bring hereunto any other help than what was noted before in the chapter about the interpretation of the passions. For as we feel the checks of conscience after doing some things which were doubtingly acted, and without mature deliberation, even from hence it is manifest that we sometimes act so, as that to have willed and acted otherwise was in our power. And this power of abstaining from ill is that very thing which is truly called free will.

The reason also of repentance is close of relation hereunto. For when we are captivated by some appetite and commit what we know and are very sensible is against the dictates of honesty, 'tis of these things we are afterwards said to repent. 'Tis not said we lament such things as misfortunes, which they ought in reason to pass for, if either by fate or a necessary chain of causes we were always destined or irresistibly determined to them, and that it had never been within our power or capacity to have avoided them. For no man repents himself of his misfortunes, but of his sins; because these are committed by his own crime, when he might have abstained and done otherwise. But to repent of sins which were never in our power to withstand is as if a man should greatly lament his improbity and malice, or undertake some sharp penance for not having been created an angel or else born a prince. As to the like effect we have hinted before.

But in the last place, to what purpose do we reprehend some men for what they act, pardon others, and have pity on the rest, if mankind be destitute of free will, if it be not given him to turn away from what is vile, and to embrace what is laudable and just. For we might, in point of justice, insist upon it, that if men are tied to sin and do it by necessity and cannot otherwise act, there is both pardon and commiseration due unto them.

Also by how much a man's sins were crying and flagitious, by so much would they become the more worthy of such pardon and moral pity. But since these things are repugnant to common sense and the inbred characters of our mind it follows of necessity that we must acknowledge some actions at least of man to be free; that is to say, that they spring from such a principle as we have out of Aristotle described and which we call free will. And we hope no man will doubt hereof, when we shall have satisfied the two principal objections wherewith the champions of the other side do so loudly and with such clamors contend.

❖ ❖ ❖ ❖ ❖ ❖ ❖ ❖

JOHN NORRIS

Summary of His Correspondence
with Henry More on Free Will[1]

I shall now sum up the whole matter in this order of reasoning.

1. That a creature void of liberty cannot be capable of law or obligation, virtue or vice, reward or punishment, is certain.

2. That man is capable of all these is certain.

3. That man therefore is endowed with liberty is certain.

4. That liberty is a rational perfection, or a perfection belonging to an intellectual nature is certain.

5. That therefore this liberty must be subjected either in the understanding or will or (to speak more properly) in the soul as intelligent or in the soul as volent, is certain.

6. That it cannot be subjected in that part which acts necessarily, is certain.

7. That the will necessarily follows the dictate of the understanding, or that the soul necessarily wills according as she understands, is certain.

8. That therefore this liberty cannot be immediately subjected in the will or in the soul as volent, is certain.

9. That therefore it must be subjected in the soul as intelligent, is certain.

10. That even the soul as intelligent so far as it acts necessarily cannot be the immediate subject of liberty, is also certain.

11. That the soul as intelligent necessarily judges according as the object appears to her, is certain.

12. That therefore the soul as judging or forming a judgment, can no more be the immediate subject of liberty, than the soul as volent, is certain.

13. That, since the soul necessarily wills as she judges and necessarily judges as things appear, we have thus far no glimpse of liberty, is certain.

1. [ED.] In his *The Theory and Regulation of Love* (Oxford, 1688), Norris included "Letters Philosophical and Moral to Dr. Henry More, with the Doctor's Answers." This series of propositions is Norris's appendix to that correspondence.

14. That therefore our liberty must be founded upon the "No Necessity" of some certain things appearing determinately thus or thus, or that we have no liberty at all, is certain.

15. That things appearing thus or thus (unless in self-evident propositions) depends upon the various degrees of advertency or attention, and nothing else, is certain.

16. That therefore we have an immediate power of attending or not attending, or of attending more or less, is certain.

17. That therefore this indifferency of the soul as to attending or not attending or attending more or less is the prime root and immediate subject of human liberty, is no less certain, which was the point to be demonstrated.

PART SIX

❖

Liberty of Conscience

$$\text{❖ ❖ ❖ ❖ ❖ ❖ ❖ ❖}$$

The Plea for Toleration

Editor's Introduction. The plea for toleration is one of the most consistent strains in the writings of the Cambridge Platonists (see General Introduction). In his demands for liberty of thought, Henry More repeated what others had also said, but the wider scope of his writings enabled him to deal with the subject at greater length than his associates. The plea for toleration occupies an important place in his *Divine Dialogues*. It inspired his protests against the hideous anomaly of religious persecution (see the preface to "A Platonic Song of the Soul," in *Complete Poems*). Imbedded in his vast work on *The Mystery of Godliness* is a relatively brief but carefully wrought statement of his position on the subject.

More's approach was governed by certain presuppositions which he shared with the other Cambridge Platonists. He believed that the dignity of man was violated by any attempt to coerce his mind. More's whole concept of the role of reason in religion meant that he could never acquiesce in any attempt to substitute compulsion for persuasion. Only when there was freedom to pursue the truth would Christianity recover its authentic character as a spiritual religion.

According to More, the privilege of toleration should be extended to all men—but only so long as they satisfied certain essential conditions. More was not content with general commendations of an abstract virtue. Toleration presupposed certain convictions: a belief in God, since atheism struck at all social stability; a belief in the immortality of the soul, which alone could give man's life the dimensions necessary for an appreciation of its true issues; and a belief in a moral universe, where good is ultimately rewarded and evil punished. Moreover, those who claimed the benefits of toleration must show that they were worthy to enjoy them. A plea for freedom of conscience must not be used as a cloak for anarchism. The correlative of liberty was responsibility, and More insisted that those who threatened the security of society could not at the same time invoke the protection of society. More, in other words, realized that toleration was one aspect of the complicated problem of church and state. Though he emphasized strongly that toleration must not be denied those who deserved it, he was equally firm in withholding it from those who had for-

311

feited the right to it. This distinction accounts for his attacks on those who, in his day, seemed to agree with him most fully in condemning persecution—for example, the Quakers, whose plea for freedom of conscience More refused to honor precisely because they also claimed the right to attack the beliefs and to disrupt the religious practices of others. In the stormy and turbulent early days of Quakerism, many observers regarded as the distinctive mark of the new sect its apparent assertion of a divine right to interfere with the religion of others, and to denounce those responsible for maintaining the social order. The passage on religious toleration reproduced here comes from Chapters x and xi of the tenth book of *The Mystery of Godliness*. In the twelfth chapter, which examined in greater detail those whom the magistrate should or should not protect in the maintenance of their peculiar convictions, More passed directly to a strong denunciation of Quaker practices. It is one of the ironies of seventeenth-century history that this stout defender of toleration should have seen its greatest enemies in those who are now counted among its most courageous champions.

HENRY MORE

On Liberty of Conscience

FROM *The Mystery of Godliness,* BOOK X

CHAPTER X

Before we can well understand the power of the magistrate in matters of religion, we must first consider the common right of mankind in this point, provided they be not degenerated into atheism and profaneness. For he that believes there is no God, nor reward nor punishment after this life, what pretence can he have of claiming a right to liberty of conscience? Or how improper is it to talk of his right in matters of religion who professedly has no religion at all, nor any tie of conscience upon him to make that wicked profession? For atheism, as it is very coarsely [1] and palpably false in itself to any man that has the clear exercise of his reason, so is it intolerably mischievous and destructive even to the present happiness of states and kingdoms, and therefore to be shunned and repressed as the very plague and pest of human polities.

But for those that seriously make profession of the existence of God the Creator of all things and of his Providence, and acknowledging that there is a life to come wherein the wicked shall be punished and the good and virtuous rewarded; who are altogether upright and sincere, maintaining no religious opinion or practice that is contrary to or inconsistent with sound and genuine morality; who are so thoroughly possessed with an awful regard and reverential fear of the divine majesty that they cannot but preserve a good conscience in all things, acting always as in the sight of God; who are of an unshaken loyalty towards their prince, and ready and desirous to obey their spiritual rulers in anything their conscience will permit, the integrity and soundness whereof is such that it finds itself obliged to obey them in all things indifferent and not contrary to the commands of God; who have so great a regard of decency and order and

1. [ED.] As used here, the word means ordinarily or usually.

of the public good of religion that they are willing to submit themselves to any reasonable punishment, rather than their right of freedom should minister occasion to others of abusing this liberty of conscience to the neglect and contempt of all religion; those, I say, who are thus disposed seem verily to me to have naturally obtained such a right of liberty in matters of religion as is altogether inviolable, and which the power of the magistrate cannot lawfully invade, unless something so untoward should chance to be mingled therewith as might cause them justly to forfeit this their otherwise undoubted right.

In the meantime, supposing there to be nothing but simple mistake, which they of the contrary religion will call superstition, yet the conscience of the other party being bound up to this, it is his natural right to have his freedom therein, because his conscience is naturally subjected thereby to a greater power than any is on earth; and therefore not to give him the liberty of his religion is both a piece of inhumanity and injustice towards him and a kind of rebellion against God whose liege subject he is.

And certainly if this is true of a sincere professor of religion in general it is manifest that 'tis no less true of a sincere Christian—a Christian man, I mean, of an upright heart, a true Nathaniel in whom there is no guile, whose character it will not be difficult to draw, partly from that general description of a sincere professor of religion and partly from his particular nature. He is then a man of a conversation unblameable, steadfastly believing what is essential to the Christian religion, of a conscience unstained, being one who manages all his affairs in the sight and presence of God, of an invincible loyalty toward his prince, and obeying the Church to the utmost of what his conscience will allow him, that is, in all things that are indifferent or truly dubious and disputable, and whose conscience is so well ordered that he judges it his duty thus to do; and lastly, who is affected with so great and so profound a regard for the order and unity of the Church and hath upon him such a care and fear lest the common good of "Christianity truly apostolical" should in any manner be impaired or injured by unprofitable and pernicious divisions, that though it should fall to his own share to suffer (as being himself unable to comply with every institution of the Church because of some scruples he cannot get over) yet he would most willingly undergo any tolerable punishments rather than his immunity should afford an occasion to insolent or malicious men of abusing this privilege of liberty to subvert and destroy the peace and security of the truly Christian and Catholic Church. This is he who, beyond all others, ought freely to enjoy this natural right of liberty of conscience.

Which, were it indeed reserved entire for him, would not surely endamage the interest almost of any Church but that of Rome, which is so exceedingly corrupted and yet with so much assurance lays claim to infallibility that I freely acknowledge that nothing is more to be dreaded by her than this right of liberty of conscience how much soever guarded and limited by these harmless circumstances. But as for the Reformed Churches, whose religion is the truly infallible oracles of God contained in the Holy Scriptures, there is no reason why they should at all entertain any apprehensions of such a liberty, nor would it verily be hurtful or indecent for them to use an indulgence so skillfully cautioned towards their genuine children and sincere members, who are Christians so perfectly formed that they heartily believe all the essential parts of our religion, being only at a loss as to some opinions and difficulties preteressential. But in the meantime they are under the true and substantial dispensation of the Life and Spirit, of which their skillful guides being sufficiently convinced, 'tis verily no more unbecoming for them to allow unto such some peculiar privilege than for a tender mother to make much of her infant that is about teeth or otherwise weak or indisposed, or for the master of a family to permit, at least, if not to provide some proper accommodations apart to those of the household whose infirmities or bodily sicknesses render them unfit to dine or sup at the common table. For this is no lessening of his authority, but a more prudent and commendable exercise thereof. Where all things are as lifeless statues and pictures, each may be ordered according to the will or pleasure of the painter or statuary; and virgins who are idle and barren may with less danger lace up their bodies to that measure of slenderness as best agrees with the curiosity of their foolish fancy. But every Church of Christ wherein is found the "dispensation of life" (and that this ought indeed to be her condition is surely never to be forgotten) is like a woman big with child, who should therefore take a special care that she be not girded or laced too tight for fear of miserably miscarrying. These things are indeed so just and almost necessary that none can be ignorant thereof to whom the "life of God" hath been manifested.

And verily the ancient Fathers of the Church have spoken of this matter more freely and without such cautions and limitations. Hereof Grotius in his book *De Jure Belli et Pacis* [*Concerning the Law of War and Peace*] produceth many examples.[2] He quotes a canon of the Council of Toledo which runs thus: "It is ordained by the Holy Synod that henceforth no violence be used to any man; for God hath mercy on whom he will, and whom he will he hardeneth." To this purpose he cites the Clementine

2. [ED.] H. Grotius, *De Jure Belli et Pacis*, Bk. II, Ch. 20.

Constitutions, as likewise Athanasius and Chrysostom, who expressly exclude violence and compulsion in bringing over men to Christianity. That
also is worthy to be remarked which is cited by Jewel [3] out of Chrysostom
in his nineteenth homily upon St. Matthew: "Was it ever seen that a sheep
did persecute the wolf? No, but contrariwise. So also Cain persecuted Abel
but not Abel Cain. So Ishmael persecuted Isaac, not Isaac Ishmael. So the
Jews did Christ, not Christ the Jews. The heretics Christians, not the
Christians heretics. Wherefore by their fruits you shall know them."
Whereby he plainly intimates that persecution upon the account of conscience is a manifest evidence of Antichristianism. And again precisely in
the same homily: "He whom thou perceivest to take delight in persecution
and bloodshed is a ravening wolf." And lastly that intimation of the
apostle is very apposite: "He that was born after the flesh persecuted him
that was born after the spirit" [Gal. 4:29]. So great an antipathy is there
found to be between the carnal and the truly regenerate Christian. Which
thing ought to strike terror into a man as often as he perceives any motions
to persecution arising in his mind, such being manifest indications of the
Cainitish, Ismaelitish and wolfish nature, and a certain sign that he belongs
not to the sheepfold of Christ.

And so much, by the bye, for the opinion of the ancient Fathers in this
matter. But there yet remain arguments deduced from the nature of the
thing itself, whereby it may be demonstrated how great an injustice it is
towards men and rebellion against God himself not to allow to such a
serious professor of religion as I have above described this his right of
liberty of conscience. For first, that he speaks and acts according to the
unavoidable persuasions of his mind is not a sin, it arising according to our
hypothesis out of invincible ignorance, nor is he supposed to act anything
against the known laws of nature, and therefore no just right of any one is
impaired or endamaged. But in the meantime the sovereignty of the Godhead is fully acknowledged, and the loyalty and integrity of the sincere
professor of religion is exerted as well as exercised therein.

Wherefore what reason can there be that any one for so good an action,
that is not exceptionable for anything that is properly sinful, should be
rudely treated, punished or in any violent way disturbed or hindered? For
whosoever endeavors his forcible hindrance does not only suppress an innocent and laudable action, but he does himself necessarily perpetrate a foul
and sinful one. For such is the solicitation of others to the omission of that
duty of loyalty which in their own conscience they are persuaded they

3. [ED.] *The Works of John Jewel* (Parker Society ed.), III, 182.

owe to God. Wherefore he that hinders the sincere religionist from the profession of his religion constrains and necessitates him to sin against God; which no powers in the world have a right to do, but are *ipso facto* guilty of rebellion against their Maker, by thus corrupting his liege subjects and urging them to faithlessness and neglect of their duty. How exceeding culpable then are they in forcing them and haling them to such actions as they are persuaded God has severely forbid them? Verily if this be not unjust to command him who is under the power of another, I cannot imagine what is, nor what can be deemed a sin against God if urging others to sin against him be not. So that it is plain the sovereign power of God sets the sincere religionist free in matters of religion from any external force or power whatsoever.

Now as this position recommends itself sufficiently from its own native concinnity and solidity, so will it also appear still more solid and more consonous [4] to reason if we consider the absurdity of the contrary position, namely, that liberty of conscience is by no means to be granted in religion. For from hence it follows that every religion may, nay ought to prohibit and suppress all other religions with all care and diligence possible. For every man's conscience tells him his own religion is the best, or else he would not be of it; nay, that there is none true and saving but his own. For if they will say they may be saved in others, then is our former argument a perfect demonstration against them, that they are not only injurious to men but absolute rebels against God indeed, in treating those so ill that are his liege people, and whom he loves so well that he intends to save them, and in persecuting them even for those very actions wherein they do most seriously express their obedience to him and seek their salvation.

But if there be but one true and saving religion at once in the world, this is the greatest disinterest to it that can be imagined. For upon this position it will be as carefully kept out and as forcibly as any of the rest; which in my apprehension is very foul play and therefore this is another evidence of the truth of our thesis, viz., that the contrary is the greatest injury and disinterest to the true religion that can be supposed, which nothing but external force hinders from spreading over all. For "magna est veritas et praevalebit [great is truth and it will prevail"; cf. I Esdras 4:41], I mean in the minds and consciences of those men where she may have free audience, not in the noise and terror of tyrannical impositions

4. [ED.] "Concinnity," skillful fitting together of parts, harmony; "consonous," harmonious.

and obtrusions. Besides the frequent misery and calamity this position brings upon nations and kingdoms, viz., wars, bloodshed, subversion of families, deposing, stabbing or poisoning of princes, perpetual enmity and hatred and all the works and actions of the kingdom of darkness. Of so mischievous consequence is this opinion we do oppose. Whenas if it were acknowledged universally that liberty of religion is the natural right of mankind, all these mischiefs would be prevented. The prince could not pretend any quarrel against the people, nor the people against the prince or against one another, but in civil rights that are more plain and intelligible.

Chapter XI

It is manifest therefore that liberty of religion is the common and natural right of all nations and persons, that is to say, that they have a power, as they are men and indued with reason and believe there is a God and a life to come and sincerely lead their life according to this faith, to examine what is the best way to serve God, for their own advantage in another life; and not to be tied up so to that religion as first proposed to them, but that they have a right to suspect, especially if they do not like it, that there is some better, and therefore that they may confer with those of other religions, send for them out of one nation into another and entertain them when they are arrived, hear them diligently and, if they be convinced, openly profess their religion. Or if they come of their own accord, they are to be entertained with the same security that an agent of state is, and may freely converse with them of the nation that have a mind to hear them. For this is a piece of their right of liberty, to *speak* as well as the other to *hear*. Which transactions would breed no disturbance at all, if this right of liberty of religion was universally understood and acknowledged by all the nations of the world—as certainly it is their right.

And it being so, it seems plainly to follow that any nation or people that do heartily acknowledge the reasonableness of this right and their practice is accordingly, that there accrues to them this part of the right also, that they may send of those of the religion themselves are into their neighboring nations to communicate their religion to them and to try if they can convince them of that which they are persuaded is true, and to show them the errors of their own; but at seasonable times, and without reproach or tumult or any way confronting them in the exercise of their religion—a thing very barbarous and insufferable at home, much more abroad in countries where they are strangers.

For the avoiding of which wild enormities, it seems reasonable in itself and a thing fit to be agreed upon that there shall be no security to any stranger that takes upon him to gather the people together under pretence of instructing them in a more perfect religion unless he be an agent from his own nation for that purpose. Nor is he to begin with the rude people privately and by underhand ways, but to act above-board and to make his applications to the governors of the places where he arrives, and not to pretend to the jugglings of inspirations and the irresistible blusters and impetuosities of an unacountable conscience; but first with a discreet candor to allow and commend what is good and praiseworthy in the religion of the place; and then, after an unaffected profession of the love and kindness of them that sent him towards the nation, with all prudent insinuations possible to lay before them the groundlessness or gross falsities which are in their religion; and after that to show the most demonstrative reasons he has for the recommending of his own, namely, such as are agreed upon by the mature deliberation and counsel of them that sent him upon this errand, to which it should be criminal to add, upon their authority, any foolish inventions of his own.

And if these agents for religion, neither injuring nor defrauding any one of their civil rights, shall be evilly entreated by those they offer to instruct, if they abuse them by imprisonment or any other hard dealing or finally put them to death, that state or kingdom to which they belong may lawfully revenge their death and require their blood at the hands of that people, as having grossly and barbarously transgressed against the law of nations and the common right of all mankind that have not forfeited it some way or other. As these have not, they allowing this liberty among themselves and to all others that have a sense and conscience of the same right and being firmly resolved, if it should come to a war and they be conquerors of their ill neighbors, to use no other means to turn their new subjects from their old religion but by peaceably and patiently showing them the vanity thereof and the excellency and solidity of their own. Which therefore cannot by any means be called the propagation of religion by the sword, when there shall not be so much force put upon them to change their former religion, if they be found conscientious, as to compel them to be present at the solemnities of the new, though but as hearers and spectators. Only they shall swear fealty to their conquerors and be well indoctrinated in that common right of mankind, "that no man is to be persecuted for religion, if he have not forfeited that right by taking upon him the liberty of persecuting others or committing something else of a like nature." And therefore they may enjoy their religion if they can still like it, upon equal terms with the conquerors, as to their private capacities. If the Spaniard had made himself master of the Indies upon these conditions and had abstained from his execrable cruelties, he might have justified himself to all the world. For this had not been to propagate religion by the sword, but to maintain a man's natural right.

This theory I think is very sound at the bottom, and that it is very clear what ought to be, but hugely impracticable by reason of that general perverseness and corruption of men. Yet I thought it worth the while to expose it to view, the acknowledgment thereof being the greatest advantage to Christian religion that can possibly be conceived, there being nothing so effectual for the easy fall of Turkism and paganism into the profession of Christ as this principle we have explained; our religion being not only solid in itself, but incomparably more demonstrable to all rational spirits than any religion ever extant in the world. Besides, though its use will not extend so far at first, yet it may be something serviceable to these parts of the world whose eyes are more open to the truth than others are. And verily in my judgment this principle I do thus recommend, as it seems to me to deserve the reception of all men as true, so of all Christians especially, not only upon point of policy but as more suitable to that spirit they are of, abhorring from force and cruelty; who are therefore to permit full liberty of conscience to all those that do not forfeit it by mixing with their religion such principles as are contrary to good manners and civil right or repugnant to this very principle of liberty we speak of.

Wherefore those that under pretence of religion would corrupt the people with such doctrines as plainly countenance vice and tend to the rooting out of the sense of true honor and virtue out of a nation, have lost this common right we contend for, as being notorious infectors and poisoners of the people amongst whom they live; and therefore the public magistrate of what nation or religion soever has a power to restrain them, their doctrine being so dangerous and destructive to the welfare of a state and contrary to the light of nature and suffrage of the wisest men in all places of the world and in all ages. No religion fraught with such rotten ware as this is to be received in any coast where they would put in, but to be kept out by strangers and suppressed at home.

Again, those also would forfeit this right of liberty whose religion should contain anything in it that would destroy or impair the strength and safety of the state which received it. As if there were some such absurd superstition therein, as upon pretence of an high esteem of virginity and extreme abhorrence from war should urge the emasculation of every third male child or the luxation or cutting off of their forefinger or thumb, whereby the country would be deprived of many of its people and such as remained be made unserviceable for the defence thereof. There is no question but the magistrate might inhibit such a religion as this.

As he might also in the last place all such religions as have intermixed with them that wolfish and ferine humor of persecuting others for their religion, that would live quietly by them and would not force any one to their own faith nor disturb the public exercise of religion in others. For these have no right to be suffered further than at the discretion of the magistrate, nor can more reasonably plead for liberty than the wolf or fox crave leave to have their kennels or holes in the midst of a sheepfold, or the owl or night raven to put in their note amidst a choir of nightingales.

But, you'll say, all religions and sects are such foxes and wolves and therefore there is no liberty of religion at all to be given. Those that are so, I confess, are at the mercy of the magistrate, as having justly lost or forfeited their right of liberty. Which forfeiture he may exact more or less severely accordingly as he has more or less security that these crafty and wild creatures may do no mischief. But I do not believe that all men that do profess religion are of this partial nature; nay, on the contrary, I do verily believe that they that are the most truly religious are the most abhorrent from persecution for conscience sake. Wherefore as many as are ready to profess, and that upon oath if it be required, that it is their judgment (and their practice does not contradict it) that no man is to be incommodated in his civil rights, in his liberty, estate or life, for the cause of such a religion as whose principles reach not to incommodate others, and do avow that theirs is such, and that they will be as faithful to the prince or state in which they live as those of his own religion; these having in no wise forfeited their right of liberty, neither this way nor any other, by intermingling practices or principles against the light of nature and laudable morality; it were the highest piece of injustice that can be committed to abridge them of the safe profession thereof.

PART SEVEN

❖

The Immortality of the Soul

The Immortality of the Soul

Editor's Introduction. It was natural—indeed, it was inevitable—that the Cambridge Platonists should be concerned about the immortality of the soul. They were consciously indebted to Plato, and it was he who first made personal immortality an essential part of philosophical teaching. The Neo-Platonists further developed the concept: Plotinus devoted his fourth *Ennead* to a full consideration of the soul, and in the seventh tractate he provided a careful discussion of immortality. It had become abundantly clear that immortality must be the crown of all Platonic interpretations of human existence and destiny. In due course Christian teaching coalesced with Platonic philosophy; divine revelation and classical wisdom thus united to afford a confident answer to man's perennial surmise about his future. But ever since the Renaissance there had been sporadic attacks on the concept of immortality. In the seventeenth century that concept became one of the most urgent subjects of debate. Almost every significant writer on theology and philosophy had something to say on the topic, and many dealt with it at considerable length.

John Smith was convinced that immortality is one of the cardinal themes in any religious system; "for the chief natural way," he said, "whereby we climb up to the understanding of the Deity is by a contemplation of our own souls." Smith believed that the principal threat to this necessary foundation of faith came from the persistence of ancient forms of atheism, and he devoted a great deal of care to the refutation of writers like Lucretius.

For Cudworth, though the attack on immortality clearly was being made by his own contemporaries, it became necessary to show how deeply the belief in the soul's immortality was rooted in the thought of the most ancient Greek philosophers. Plato, he believed, only made explicit what had long before been present in principle; accordingly, Cudworth dealt with the problem as a perennial issue in human thought. For this reason he considered it important to expose the errors committed by certain ancient thinkers, whose mistakes had been revived century after century. Henry More regarded immortality as one of the essential elements in his philosophic system. Norris also gave the subject a good deal of careful attention.[1]

The most sustained and effective contributions by the Cambridge Platonists to this subject are those of Smith and More. The writings of both men are too extensive to be be reproduced in full; excerpts only can be given.

1. [ED.] Cudworth's treatment of immortality begins early in Book I, Chapter 1 of *The True Intellectual System,* and continues intermittently throughout the work. Norris's chief contribution to the subject is *A Philosophical Discourse Concerning the Natural Immortality of the Soul* (1708). More's *Immortality of the Soul* was published in 1659; he also annotated Glanvill's *Lux Orientalis* (1682).

JOHN SMITH

A Discourse Demonstrating the Immortality of the Soul

Editor's Introduction. It will be observed that Smith first sets down certain general considerations and then proceeds to develop a number of arguments specifically intended to prove the immortality of the soul. There is, he points out, an almost universal belief that the soul is immortal. A man's spiritual experience had an important bearing on the degree of his conviction concerning this truth. It must also be accepted as a principle that "no substantive and indivisible thing ever perisheth." But was there any convincing evidence, he asked, for the belief that the soul is immortal? He adduced four considerations: the first was derived from the soul's incorporeality, the second from its spontaneity, the third from its power of framing necessary and immutable truths, the fourth from the indestructibility of its moral attributes.

Because of the length of the discourse, extracts from certain chapters have been limited to the summaries prefixed to them, and extensive excisions have been made even from chapters that are more fully represented.

❖ ❖ ❖ ❖

CHAPTER I

Having finished our two short discourses concerning those two *anti-deities*, viz., *superstition and atheism*,[1] we shall now proceed to discourse more largely concerning the main heads and principles of religion.

And here we are to take notice of those two cardinal points which the author of the Epistle to the Hebrews makes the necessary foundations of all religion, viz., "That God is, and that he is a rewarder of them that seek him" [Heb. 11:6]. To which we should add, *the immortality of the reasonable soul*, but that *that* may seem included in the former. And, indeed,

1. [ED.] Of Smith's *Discourses*, the first four clearly form a sequence. "On the True Way or Method of Attaining Divine Knowledge" was the first; this is the fourth. The second and third, on Superstition and Atheism, are relatively brief.

we can neither believe any invisible reward of which he there speaks, without an anterior belief of the soul's immortality, neither can we entertain a serious belief of that, but the notions of *poena* and *praemium* will naturally follow from it. We never met with any who were persuaded of the former, that ever doubted of the latter. And therefore the former two have been usually taken alone for the first principles of religion, and have not been most insisted upon by the Platonists. . . .

But if we will have the fundamental articles of Christian religion, we must add to the former, *the communication of God to mankind through Christ;* which last the Scripture treats of at large, so far as concerns our practice, with that plainness and simplicity, that I cannot but think that whosoever shall, ingenuously and with humility of spirit addressing himself to God, converse therewith, will see the bright beams of divinity shining forth in it, and, it may be, find the text itself much plainer than all those glosses that have been put upon it; though perhaps it is not so clear in matters of speculation as some magisterial men are apt to think it is.

Now for these three articles of faith and practice, I think if we duly consider the Scriptures, or the reason of the thing itself, we shall easily find all practical religion to be referred to them and built upon them. *The nature of God and of our own immortal souls* both show us what our religion should be, and also the necessity of it; and the doctrine of *free grace in Christ*, the sweet and comfortable means of attaining to that perfection and blessedness which the other belief teaches us to aim at.

In pursuing these, we shall first begin with *the immortality of the soul*, which, if it be once cleared, we can neither leave any room for atheism (which those, I doubt, are not ordinarily very free from, that have gross material notions of their own souls) nor be wholly ignorant what God is; for indeed the chief natural way whereby we can climb up to the understanding of the Deity is by a contemplation of our own souls. We cannot think of him but according to the measure and model of our own intellect, or frame any other idea of him than what the impressions of our own souls will permit us. And therefore the best philosophers have always taught us to inquire for God within ourselves. "Reason in us," as Cicero tells us, being "made a partaker of the likeness of eternal reason"; [2] and accordingly some good expositors have interpreted that place in St. John's Gospel, "He is that true light which enlightens every man that cometh into the

2. [ED.] The sense of this passage is common enough in Cicero, but the quotation is actually taken from Thomas Aquinas, *Summa Theologica*, Pt. I, Q. LXXXIV, 5.

world" [Jn. 1:9]; which if I were to gloss upon in the language of the Platonists, I should do it thus: "The Eternal Word is the light of souls"; which the vulgar [Vulgate] Latin referred to in Psalm 4:7, "Signatum est supra nos lumen vultus tui, Domine," as Aquinas observes.[3] But we shall not search into the full nature of the soul, but rather make our inquiry into the immortality of it, and endeavor to demonstrate that.

CHAPTER II

Some considerations preparatory to the proof of the soul's immortality.

But before we fall more closely upon this, viz., the demonstrating the soul's immortality, we shall premise three things.

1. *That the immortality of the soul doth not absolutely need any demonstration to clear it, but might be assumed rather as a principle or postulatum, seeing the notion of it is apt naturally to insinuate itself into the belief of the most vulgar sort of men.* Men's understandings commonly lead them as readily to believe that their souls are immortal as that they have any existence at all. And though they be not all so wise and logical as to distinguish aright between their souls and their bodies, or tell what kind of thing that is which they commonly call their soul, yet they are strongly inclined to believe that some part of them shall survive another, and that that soul, which, it may be, they conceive by a gross phantasm, shall live when the other more visible part of them shall molder into dust. . . .

2. The *second* thing I should premise should be in place of a *postulatum* to our following demonstrations, or rather a caution about them, which is: *that to a right conceiving of the force of any such arguments as may prove the soul's immortality, there must be an antecedent converse with our own souls.* It is no hard matter to convince any one, by clear and evident principles, fetched from his own sense of himself, who hath ever well meditated on the powers and operations of his own soul, that it is immaterial and immortal. . . .

3. There is one thing more to be considered, which may serve as a common basis or principle to our following arguments, and it is this hypothesis: *that no substantial and indivisible thing ever perisheth.* . . .

3. [ED.] In the passage cited above, Aquinas quotes the Vulgate passage to which Smith refers: "Lift up the light of thy countenance upon us, O Lord!" (Ps. 4:6b in versions other than the Vulgate).

CHAPTER III

The first argument for the immortality of the soul. That the soul of man is not corporeal. The gross absurdities upon the supposition that the soul is a complex of fluid atoms, or that it is made up by a fortuitous concourse of atoms; which is the notion of Epicurus concerning body. The principles and dogmas of the Epicurean philosophy in opposition to the immaterial and incorporated nature of the soul, asserted by Lucretius; but discovered to be false and insufficient. That motion cannot arise from body or matter. Nor can the power of sensation arise from matter; much less can reason. That all human knowledge hath not its rise from sense. The proper function of sense, and that it is never deceived. An addition of three considerations for the enforcing of this first argument, and further clearing the immateriality of the soul. That there is in man a faculty which, 1st, controls sense, and 2ndly, collects and unites all the perceptions of our several senses. 3rdly, that memory and prevision are not explicable upon the supposition of matter and motion.

We shall therefore now endeavor to prove that the soul of man is something really distinct from his body, of an indivisible nature, and so cannot be divided into such parts as should flit one from another; and, consequently that it is apt of its own nature to remain to eternity, and so will do, except the decrees of Heaven should abandon it from being.

And first we shall prove it *ab absurdo*, and here do as the mathematicians use to do in such kind of demonstrations: we will suppose that, if the reasonable soul be not of such an immaterial nature, then it must be a body, and so suppose it to be made up as all bodies are; where, because the opinions of philosophers differ, we shall take only one, viz., that of Epicurus, which supposeth it to be made up by a fortuitous concourse of atoms; and in that demonstrate against all the rest. . . .[4]

Thus I hope, by this time, we have found out "some more noble power in the soul than that is,"[5] by which it accommodates itself to the body, and, according to the measure and proportion thereof, converseth with external matter. And this is the true reason why we are so apt to be mistaken in sensible objects, because our souls, sucking in the knowledge of external things thereby, and not minding the proportion that is between

4. [ED.] This leads to a long and searching examination of Epicurean teaching, especially as it is reflected in Lucretius' *De Rerum Natura*. Cf. the Cambridge ed. (1859), 70–80.

5. [ED.] Proclus, *On the Timaeus of Plato*, 76E.

the body and them, mindless of its own notions, collates their corporeal impressions with external objects themselves, and judgeth of them one by another. But whensoever our souls act in their own power and strength, untwisting themselves from all corporeal complications, they then can find confidence enough to judge of things in a seeming contradiction to all those other *visa corporea* [corporeal appearances].

And so I suppose this argument will amount to no less than a demonstration of the soul's immateriality, seeing to all sincere understanding it is necessary that it should thus abstract itself from all corporeal correspondence, and return from thence nearer into itself.

Now what we have to this purpose more generally intimated, we shall further branch out in these two or three particulars.

First, That that mental faculty and power whereby we judge and discern things is so far from being a body, that it must retract and withdraw itself from all bodily operation whensoever it will nakedly discern truth. For should our souls always mold their judgment of things according to those παθήματα and impressions which seem to be framed thereof in the body, they must then do nothing else but chain up errors and delusions one with another instead of truth. As, should the judgments of our understandings wholly depend upon the sight of our eyes, we should then conclude that our mere accesses and recesses from any visible object have such a magical power to change the magnitudes of visible objects and to transform them into all varieties of figures and fashions; and so attribute all that variety to them which we find in our corporeal perceptions. . . . Which is an unquestionable argument that that power whereby we discern things and make judgments of them different and sometimes contrary to those perceptions that are the necessary results of all organical functions is something distinct from the body; and therefore, though the soul, as Plato hath well observed, be various and divisible accidentally in these sensations and motions wherein it extends and spreads itself, as it were, upon the body, and so according to the nature and measure thereof perceived its impressions, yet it is indivisible, returning into itself.[6] Whensoever it will speculate on truth itself, it will not then listen to the several clamors and votes of these rude senses which always speak with divided tongues, but it consults some clearer oracle within itself. . . .

Secondly, we also find such a faculty within our own souls as collects and unites all the perceptions of our several senses, and is able to compare them together; something in which they all meet as in one center; which

6. [ED.] Plato, *Timaeus*, 35A.

Plotinus hath well expressed: "That in which all those several sensations meet, as so many lines drawn from several points in the circumference and which comprehends them all, must needs be one." [7] For should that be various and consisting of several parts, which thus receives all these various impressions, then must the sentence and judgment passed upon them be various too. Aristotle says, "That must be one that judgeth things to be diverse"; and that must judge too, setting all before it at once.[8] Besides we could not conceive how such an immense variety of impressions could be made upon any piece of matter, which should not obliterate and deface one another. And therefore Plotinus hath well disputed against them who make all sensation τυπώσεις καὶ ἐνσφραγίσεις ἐν ψυχῇ [9]—which brings me to the third.

Thirdly, that knowledge which the soul retains in itself of things past, and in some sort prevision of things to come, whereby many grow so sagacious in foreseeing future events that they know how to deliberate and dispose of present affairs, so as to be ready furnished and prepared for such emergencies as they see in a train and series of causes which sometimes work contingently—I cannot think Epicurus himself could, in his cool thoughts, be so unreasonable as to persuade himself that all the shuffling and cutting of atoms could produce such a divine piece of wisdom as this is. What matter can thus bind up past, present and future time together? which while the soul of man doth, it seems to imitate God's eternity, as far as its own finite nature will permit it to strive after an imitation of it; and grasping and gathering together a long series of duration into itself, makes an essay to free itself from the rigid laws of it, and to purchase to itself the freedom of a true eternity. And as, by its χρονικαὶ πρόοδοι (as the Platonists are wont to speak) "chronical and successive operations," it unravels and unfolds the contexture of its own indefinite intellectual powers by degrees; so, by this memory and prevision, it recollects and twists them all up together again into itself. And though it seems to be continually sliding from itself in those several vicissitudes and changes which it runs through, in the constant variety of its own effluxes and emanations, yet is it always returning back again to its first original, by a swift remembrance of all those motions and multiplicity of operations which have begot in it the first sense of this constant efflux. As if we

7. [ED.] Plotinus, *The Enneads*, IV.7.6.
8. [ED.] Aristotle, *De Anima*, Bk. III, Ch. 2.
9. [ED.] Plotinus, *The Enneads*, IV.6.1.: "Imprints and impressions on the soul." The quotation is not exact, but the meaning of the passage is not affected.

should see a sunbeam perpetually flowing forth from the bright body of the sun and yet ever returning back to it again; it never loseth any part of its being, because it never forgets what itself was. And though it may number out never so vast a length of its duration, yet it never comes nearer to its old age but carrieth a lively sense of its youth and infancy along with it, which it can at pleasure lay a fast hold on.

But if our souls were nothing else but a complex of fluid atoms, how should we be continually roving and sliding from ourselves and how soon forget what we once were! The new matter that would come in to fill up that vacuity which the old had made by its departure would never know what the old was nor what that should be that would succeed: "That new pilgrim and strangerlike soul would always be ignorant of what the other before it knew, and we should be wholly some other bulk of being than we were before," as Plotinus hath excellently observed.[10] It was a famous speech of wise Heraclitus, "A man cannot enter twice into the same river";[11] by which he was wont symbolically to express the constant flux of matter, which is the most unstable thing that may be. And if the philosophy of Epicurus could free this heap of refined atoms, which it makes the soul to be, from this inconstant and flitting nature and teach us how it could be some stable and immutable thing, always resting entire while it is in the body; though we would thank him for such a goodly conceit as this is, yet we would make no doubt but it might as well be able to preserve itself from dissolution and dissipation *out* of this gross body as *in* it; seeing it is no more secured from the constant impulses of that more gross matter, which is restlessly moving up and down in the body, than it is out of it; and yet, for all that, we should take the leave to ask Cicero's question with his sober disdain: "Quid enim? obsecro te, terrane tibi aut hoc nebuloso et caliginoso caelo aut sata aut concreta videtur tant vis memoriae?"[12] Such a jewel as this is too precious to be found in a dunghill: mere matter could never thus stretch itself over all its own former pre-existences. We may as well suppose this dull and heavy earth we tread upon to know how long it hath dwelt in this part of the universe it now dwells in, and what variety of creatures have in all ages sprung forth from it, and all these occurrences and events which have, during all this time, happened upon it.

10. [ED.] Plotinus, *The Enneads*, IV.7.5.
11. [ED.] Plutarch, *De El Delphico*, 392B.
12. [ED.] Cicero, *Tusculan Disputations*, Bk. I, xxv: "For consider, I pray, can you really think that it is from earth, where our atmosphere is so watery and foggy, that the prodigious power of memory has originated or been formed?"

CHAPTER IV

The second argument for the immortality of the soul. Actions either automatical or spontaneous. That spontaneous and elicit actions evidence the distinction of the soul from the body. The evasion of Lucretius very slight and weak. That the liberty of the will is inconsistent with the Epicurean principles. That the conflict of reason against the sensitive appetite argues a being in us superior to matter.

We have done with that which we intended for the first part of our discourse of the soul's immortality. We have hitherto looked at it rather *in concreto* than *in abstracto*—rather as a thing complicated with, and united to the body; and therefore considered it in those operations which, as they are not proper to the body, so neither are they altogether independent of it, but are rather of a mixed nature.

We shall now take notice of it in those properties in the exercise whereof it hath less commerce with the body and more plainly declares its own high descent to us; that it is able to subsist and act without the aid and assistance of this matter which it informs. . . .

CHAPTER V

The third argument for the immortality of the soul. That mathematical notions argue the soul to be of a truly spiritual and immaterial nature. . . .

CHAPTER VI

The fourth argument for the immortality of the soul. That those clear and stable ideas of truth which are in man's mind evince an immortal and immaterial substance residing in us, distinct from the body. The soul more knowable than the body. Some passages out of Plotinus and Proclus for the further confirming of this argument. . . .

CHAPTER VII

What it is that, beyond the highest and most subtle speculations whatsoever does clear and evidence to a good man the immortality of his soul. That true goodness and virtue beget the most raised sense of this immortality. The excellent discourse of Plotinus to this purpose.

And now, that we may conclude the argument in hand, we shall add but this one thing further to clear the soul's immortality, and it is, indeed, that which breeds a true sense of it, viz., *true and real goodness*. Our highest speculations of the soul may beget a sufficient conviction thereof within us, but yet it is only true goodness and virtue in the souls of men that can make them both know and love, believe and delight themselves in their own immortality. Though every good man is not so logically subtile as to be able, by fit mediums, to demonstrate his own immortality, yet he sees it in a higher light. His soul, being purged and enlightened by true sanctity, is more capable of those divine irradiations whereby it feels itself in conjunction with God, and by a συναύγεια (as the Greeks speak), the light of divine goodness mixing itself with the light of its own reason, sees more clearly not only that it may, if it please the supreme Deity, of its own nature exist eternally, but also that it shall do so. It knows it shall never be deserted of that free goodness that always embraceth it; it knows that almighty love which it lives by to be stronger than death and more powerful than the grave; it will not suffer those holy ones that are partakers of it to lie in Hell, or their souls to see corruption; and, though worms may devour their flesh and putrefaction enter into those bones that fence it, yet it knows that its Redeemer lives and that it shall at last see him with a pure intellectual eye,[13] which will then be clear and bright, when all that earthly dust, which converse with this mortal body filled it with shall be removed; it knows that God will never forsake his own life which he hath quickened in it; he will never deny those ardent desires of a blissful fruition of himself, which the lively sense of his own goodness hath excited within it. Those breathings and gaspings after an eternal participation of him are but the energy of his own breath within us. If he had had any mind to destroy it, he would never have shewn it such things as he hath done. He would not raise it up to such mounts of vision, to shew it all the glory of that heavenly Canaan, flowing with eternal and unbounded pleasures, and then precipitate it again into that deep and darkest abyss of death and non-entity. Divine goodness cannot—it will not—be so cruel to holy souls that are such ambitious suitors for his love. The more they contemplate the blissful effluxes of his divine love upon themselves, the more they find themselves strengthened with an undaunted confidence in him; and look not upon themselves in these poor bodily relations and dependencies, but in their eternal alliances, ὡς κόσμιοι, ὡς υἱοὶ τοῦ θεοῦ (as Arrian sometimes speaks) [14]—as the sons of God, who is the Father of souls, souls

---

13. [ED.] Cf. Song 8:6; Ps. 16:10; Acts 2:27; Job 19:25,26.
14. [ED.] Arrian, *On Epictetus*, Bk. I, Ch. IX.

that are able to live anywhere in this spacious universe, and better out of this dark and lonesome cell of bodily matter which is always checking and clogging them in their noble motions, than in it: as knowing that, when they leave this body, they shall then be "received into everlasting habitations" [Lk. 16:9] and converse freely and familiarly with that Source of life and spirit which they conversed with in this life in a poor, disturbed and straitened manner. It is, indeed, nothing else that makes men question the immortality of their souls so much as their own base and earthly loves, which first makes them *wish* their souls were not immortal, and then to *think* they are not; which Plotinus hath well observed, and accordingly hath soberly pursued this argument.

I cannot omit a large recital of his discourse, which tends so much to disparage that flat and dull philosophy which these latter ages have brought forth; as also those heavy-spirited Christians that find so little divine life and activity in their own souls as to imagine them to fall into such a dead sleep as soon as they leave this earthly tabernacle that they cannot be awakened again, till that last trumpet and the voice of an archangel shall rouse them up. [At this point, Smith introduces a very long quotation, extending for a couple of pages, from Plotinus, *The Enneads*, IV.7.10.]

I might, after all this, add many more reasons for a further confirmation of this present thesis, which are as numerous as the soul's relations and production themselves are; but to every one who is willing to do justice to his own soul, this evidence we have already brought in is more than sufficient.

HENRY MORE

The Immortality of the Soul

Editor's Introduction. More and his contemporaries alike considered *The Immortality of the Soul* one of his most important works. That he included it among his philosophical rather than his theological writings is a clear indication that for him immortality was a subject demanding careful and rigorous examination. To understand his approach we must remember the intense interest during the seventeenth century in the soul's nature, status and destiny. On the eagerly debated question of pre-existence, not even the Cambridge Platonists were agreed. Culverwel did not believe in the pre-existence of the soul; More, Glanvill and Rust did. More repeated a popular argument: existence is good for the soul, God is infinitely merciful, therefore he will not delay the conferring of this blessing on the soul. To the general discussion of immortality, almost every major writer of the period contributed in some degree. The work from which the following passage is taken is a long and closely reasoned attempt to fit More's concept of the soul into his understanding of reality. The extract here given includes a large proportion of the two opening chapters, followed by the axioms (occurring mainly in Book I, but also scattered throughout the work) which More saw as undergirding the belief in the soul's immortality.

The Immortality of the Soul (1659) belongs to More's early vigorous period.

❖ ❖ ❖ ❖

Of all the speculations the soul of man can entertain herself withal, there is none of greater moment or of closer concernment to her than this of her own immortality and independence on this terrestrial body. For hereby not only the intricacies and perplexities of Providence are made more easy and smooth to her and she becomes able, by unravelling this clue from end to end, to pass and repass safe through this labyrinth wherein many both anxious and careless spirits have lost themselves, but also (which touches her own interest more particularly) being once raised into the knowledge and belief of so weighty a conclusion, she may view from this prospect the most certain and most compendious way to her own happiness; which is, the bearing a very moderate affection to whatever tempts her, during the time of this her pilgrimage, and a careful preparation of herself for her future condition, by such noble actions and heroical qualifications of mind as shall render her most welcome to her own country.

Which belief and purpose of hers will put her in an utter incapacity of either envying the life or successes of her most embittered enemies or of over-lamenting the death or misfortunes of her dearest friends; she having no friends but such as are friends to God and virtue, and whose afflictions will prove advantages for their future felicity, and their departure hence a passage to present possession thereof.

Wherefore being fully grounded and rooted in this so concerning a persuasion, she is freed from all poor and abject thoughts and designs, and as little admires him that gets the most of this world, be it by industry, fortune or policy, as a discreet and serious man does the spoils of school boys, it being very inconsiderable to him who got the victory at cocks or cob-nut or whose bag returned home the fullest stuffed with counters or cherry-stones.

She has therefore no emulation, unless it be of doing good and of out-stripping, if it were possible, the noblest examples of either the present or past ages; nor any contest, unless it be with herself, that she has made no greater proficiency towards the scope she aims at. And aiming at nothing but what is not in the power of men to confer upon her, with courage she sets upon the main work; and being still more faithful to herself and to that light that assists her, at last tastes the first fruits of her future harvest and does more than presage that great happiness that is accruing to her. And so quit from the troubles and anxieties of this present world, stays in it with tranquility and content, and at last leaves it with joy.

The knowledge, therefore, and belief of the immortality of the soul being of so grand importance, we are engaged more carefully and punctually to handle this so weighty a theory; which will not be performed by multiplying of words, but by a more frugal use of them, letting nothing fall from our pen but what makes closely to the matter, nor omitting anything material for the evincing the truth thereof.

And to stop all creep-holes and leave no place for the subterfuges and evasions of confused and cavilling spirits, I shall prefix some few axioms of that plainness and evidence that no man in his wits but will be ashamed to deny them, if he will admit anything at all to be true. But as for perfect skepticism, it is a disease incurable and a thing rather to be pitied or laughed at than seriously opposed. For when a man is so fugitive and unsettled that he will not stand to the verdict of his own faculties, one can no more fasten anything upon him than he can write in the water or tie knots of the wind. But for those that are not in such a strange despondency, but that they think they know something already and may learn more, I do not doubt but by a seasonable recourse to these few rules, with others I shall set down in their due place, that they will be persuaded, if not forced, to reckon this truth of the immortality of the soul amongst such as must needs appear undeniable to those that have parts and leisure enough accurately to examine and throughly to understand what I have here written for the demonstration thereof.

Axiom I

Whatever things are in themselves, they are nothing to us but so far forth as they become known to our faculties or cognitive powers. . . .

Axiom II

Whatsoever is unknown to us or is known but as merely possible is not to move us or determine us any way or make us undetermined; but we are to rest in the present light and plain determination of our own faculties.

Axiom III

All our faculties have not a right of suffrage for determining of truth, but only common notions, external sense and evident and undeniable deductions of reason. . . .

Axiom IV

What is not consonant to all or some of these is mere fancy, and is of no moment for the evincing of truth or falsehood, by either its vigor or perplexiveness. . . .

Axiom V

Whatever is clear to any one of these three faculties is to be held undoubtedly true, the other having nothing to evidence to the contrary. . . .

Axiom VI

What is rejected by one, none of the other faculties giving evidence for it, ought to go for a falsehood. . . .

Axiom VII

What is plainly and manifestly concluded, ought to be held undeniable, when no difficulties are alleged against it, but such as are acknowledged to be found in other conclusions held by all men undeniably true. . . .

Axiom VIII

The subject, or naked essence or substance of a thing, is utterly inconceivable to any of our faculties. . . .

Axiom IX

There are some properties, powers and operations immediately appertaining to a thing of which no reasons can be given nor ought to be demanded, nor the way or manner of the cohesion of the attribute with the subject can by any means be fancied or imagined. . . .

So the immediate properties of spirit or immaterial substance are *penetrability* and *indiscerpibility*.[1] The necessary cohesion of which attributes with the subject is as little demonstrable as the former. For supposing that, which I cannot but assert, to be evidently true, That there is no substance but it has in some sort or other the three dimensions; this substance which we call *matter*, might as well have been penetrable as impenetrable, and yet have been substance. But now that it does so certainly and irresistibly keep one part of itself from penetrating another, it is so, we know not why.

1. [ED.] I.e., incapable of being divided into parts. After about the middle of the eighteenth century, the word was more usually spelled "indiscerptible."

For there is no necessary connexion discernible betwixt substance with three dimensions and impenetrability. For what some allege, that it implies a contradiction that extended substance should run one part into another (for so part of the extension, and consequently of the substance, would be lost), this, I say (if nearly looked into) is of no force. For the substance is no more lost in this case than when a string is doubled and redoubled or a piece of wax reduced from a long figure to a round.... And as what was lost in longitude was gotten in latitude or profundity before, so what is lost here in all or any two of the dimensions is kept safe in *essential spissitude*.[2] For so I will call this mode or property of a substance, that is able to receive one part of itself into another. Which fourth mode is as easy and familiar to my understanding as that of the three dimensions to my sense or fancy. For I mean nothing else by spissitude but the redoubling or contracting of substance into less space than it does sometimes occupy. And analogous to this is the lying of two substances of several kinds in the same place at once. To both these may be applied the terms of reduplication and saturation; the former when essence or substance is but once redoubled into itself, the latter when so oft that it will not easily admit anything more. And that more extensions than one may be commensurate, at the same time, to the same place, is plain, in that motion is co-extended with the subject where it is, and both with space. And motion is not nothing; wherefore two things may be commensurate to one space at once.

Now then extended substance (and all substances are extended) being of itself indifferent to penetrability or impenetrability, and we finding one kind of substance so impenetrable that one part will not enter at all into another (which with as much reason we might expect to find so irresistibly united one part with another that nothing in the world could dissever them. For this *indiscerpibility* has as good a connexion with substance as impenetrability has, they neither falling under the cognoscence of reason or demonstration but being immediate attributes of such a subject. For a man can no more argue from the extension of substance, that is discerpible, than that is penetrable; there being as good a capacity in extension for penetration as discerption) I conceive, I say, from hence we may as easily admit that some substance may be of itself indiscerpible, as well as others impenetrable; and that as there is one kind of substance, which of its own nature is impenetrable and discerpible, so there may be another indiscerpible and penetrable. Neither of which a man can give any other account of, than that they have the immediate properties of such a subject.

2. [ED.] I.e., density, thickness, compactness. Cf. O.E.D.

Axiom X

The discovery of some power, property or operation, incompetible to one subject, is an infallible argument of the existence of some other, to which it must be competible.[3]

[More now adds certain axioms "that tend to the demonstrating how the center or first point of the primary substance of a spirit may be indiscerpible; several others that demonstrate how the secondary substance of a spirit may be indiscerpible."]

Axiom XI

A globe touches a plane in something, though in the least that is conceivable to be real.

Axiom XII

The least that is conceivable is so little that it cannot be conceived to be discerpible into less.

Axiom XIII

As little as this is, the repetition of it will amount to considerable magnitudes.

Axiom XIV

Magnitude cannot arise out of mere non-magnitudes.

Axiom XV

The same thing by reason of its extreme littleness may be utterly indiscerpible, though intellectually divisible.

3. [ED.] I.e., appropriate, suitable; competent.

Axiom XVI

An emanative cause is the notion of a thing possible. By emanative cause is understood such a cause as merely by being, no other activity or causality interposed, produces an effect. That this is possible is manifest, it being demonstrable that there is *de facto* some such cause in the world; because something must move itself. Now if there be no spirit, matter must of necessity move itself, where you cannot imagine any activity or causality, but the bare essence of the matter from whence this motion comes. . . .

Axiom XVII

An emanative effect is co-existent with the very substance of that which is said to be the cause thereof.

Axiom XVIII

No emanative effect that exceeds not the virtues and powers of a cause can be said to be impossible to be produced by it.

Axiom XIX

There may be a substance of that high virtue and excellency, that it may produce another substance by emanative causality, provided that substance produced be in due gradual proportions inferior to that which causes it.

[Having discussed at considerable length the nature of spirit, and having also examined the implications of the teachings of both Hobbes and Descartes, More adds "more axioms for the demonstrating that there is a spirit or immaterial substance in man."]

Axiom XX

Motion or reaction of one part of the matter against another, or at least a due continuance thereof, is really one and the same with sense and perception, if there be any sense or perception in matter.

Axiom XXI

So far as this continued reaction reaches, so far reaches sense or perception and no farther.

Axiom XXII

That diversity there is of sense or perception does necessarily arise from the diversity of the magnitude, figure, position, vigor and direction of motion in parts of the matter.

Axiom XXIII

Matter in all the variety of those perceptions it is sensible of, has none but such as are impressed by corporeal motions, that is to say, that there are perceptions of some actions or modificated impressions of parts of matter bearing one against another.

Axiom XXIV

The distinct impression of any considerable extent of variegated matter cannot be received by a mere point of matter.

Axiom XXV

Whatever impression or parts of any impression are not received by this perfect parvitude or real point of matter, are not at all perceived by it.

Axiom XXVI

Whatever sense or motion there is now in matter, it is a necessary impression from some other part of matter and does necessarily continue till some part or other of matter has justled it out.

Axiom XXVII

The soul separate from this terrestrial body is not released from all vital union with matter.

Axiom XXVIII

There is a triple vital congruity in the soul, namely aethereal, aerial and terrestrial.

Axiom XXIX

According to the usual custom of nature, the soul awakes orderly into these vital congruities, not passing from one extreme to another without any stay in the middle.

Axiom XXX

The soul in her aerial vehicle in capable of sense properly so called, and consequently of pleasure and pain.

Axiom XXXI

The soul can neither impart to nor take away from the matter of her vehicle of air any considerable degree of motion, but yet can direct the particles moved which way she pleases by the imperium of her will.

Axiom XXXII

Though the soul can neither confer nor take away any considerable degree of motion from the matter of her airy vehicle, yet nothing hinders but that she may do both in her aethereal.

Axiom XXXIII

The purer the vehicle is, the more quick and perfect are the perceptive faculties of the soul.

Axiom XXXIV

The soul has a marvellous power of not only changing the temper of her airy vehicle but also of the external shape thereof.

Axiom XXXV

It is rational to think that as some faculties are laid asleep in death or after death, so others may awake that are more suitable for that state.

Axiom XXXVI

Whether the vital congruity of the soul expire, as whose period being quite unwound, or that of the matter be defaced by any essential disharmony, vital union immediately ceases.

PART EIGHT

✤

On Political Sovereignty

RALPH CUDWORTH

Civil Authority and Religious Belief

Editor's Introduction. During the seventeenth century, theory and experience were combined in a widespread concern with politics. Early in the century, King James I had advanced an extreme view of the nature of sovereignty and its religious foundations. When in due course this interpretation was challenged by the leaders of the parliamentary opposition and by their Puritan allies, the Cambridge Platonists were not immediately involved in the struggle, either as participants in political life or as theorists about it. It is probable that during the Civil War they favored the parliamentary cause, but they had neither the temper nor the outlook of partisans. As university teachers, they were intellectually preoccupied with man and how he attained to truth rather than with the corporate structures erected by him. But for the very reason that they were so vitally interested in the nature of man, they could not ignore the challenge of Thomas Hobbes—who, for both Cudworth and More, stood forth as the great contemporary exponent of the ancient errors which they incessantly attacked, namely the atheistic interpretation of the universe and the materialistic view of man. And because Hobbes was primarily concerned with the nature of political sovereignty, it was inevitable that a work so comprehensive as Cudworth's *The True Intellectual System of the Universe* should concern itself with political theory.

Cudworth was bound to oppose Hobbes's position on many grounds. He would have been unmoved by the plea that Hobbes was attempting to erect a theory of human conduct on the basis of natural science; it seemed clear to him that Hobbes was merely repeating errors that could be traced back to the determinists of classical times. At various points, Bodin in France had anticipated the views of Hobbes on the absolute nature of political authority; and in England the supporters of divine right were advancing somewhat similar claims. But Hobbes was unique in his radically secular approach to the origin of political power. In his *De Cive* (1642), he argued that in every state there must be a supreme power to whom obedience is due in all things, spiritual no less than temporal. This frank and uncompromising Erastianism was perhaps natural; after all, Hobbes was expounding a system of political absolutism which would replace the political supremacy of the medieval Church. He did not discard religious institutions, but he took a strictly utilitarian view of them and of everything they represented.

Cudworth opposed Hobbes's doctrine of sovereignty not merely because he disliked its implications; his fundamental objection was to the principles on which it rested. From the first four books of the *Leviathan* (1651), which dealt with man, it was obvious to Cudworth that Hobbes's absolutism cut at the very root of morality. The distinction between good and evil became unreal. Conscience was dismissed because it was inconsistent with public authority. To this "villainizing of human nature" Cudworth opposed all the resources at his command. It is interesting to note that whereas Hobbes's argument was based on psychological and sociological considerations, Cudworth attacked it with the weapons of logic and metaphysics.

I

Now, we deny not but that politicians may sometimes abuse religion, and make it serve for the promoting of their own private interests and designs; which they could not do so well neither, were the thing itself a mere cheat and figment of their own, and had no reality at all in nature, nor anything solid at the bottom of it. But since religion obtains so universally everywhere, it is not conceivable how civil sovereigns throughout the whole world, some of which are so distant, and have so little correspondence with one another, should notwithstanding all so well agree in this one cheating mystery of government, or piece of state-cozenage; nor, if they could, how they should be able so effectually to possess the generality of mankind (as well wise as unwise) with such a constant fear, awe and dread of a mere counterfeit thing and an invisible nothing, and which hath not only no manner of foundation neither in sense nor reason, but also (as the atheists suppose) tends to their own great terror and disquietment and so brings them at once under a miserable vassalage both of mind and body. Especially since men are not generally so apt to think that how much the more any have of power and dignity, they have therefore so much the more of knowledge and skill in philosophy and the things of nature, above others. And it is not strange that the world should not all this while have suspected or discovered this cheat and juggle of politicians, and have smelt out a plot upon themselves in the fiction of religion, to take away their liberty, and enthrall them under bondage; and that so many of these politicians and civil sovereigns themselves also, should have been unacquainted herewith, and as simply awed with fear of this invisible nothing, as any others? All other cheats and juggles, when they are once never so little detected, are presently thereupon dashed quite out of countenance, and have never any more the confidence to obtrude themselves upon the world. . . .

But that religion is no figment of politicians, will further unquestionably appear from that which now shall follow. As the religion of an oath is a necessary vinculum of civil society, so obligation in conscience, respecting the Deity as its original and as the punisher of the violation thereof, is the very foundation of all civil sovereignty. For pacts and covenants (into which some would resolve all civil power) without this obligation in conscience, are nothing but mere words and breath; and the laws presuppose it, as a thing in order of nature before them, and without which they would be invalid. Which is a truth so evident that the writer *De Cive* could not dissemble it (though he did not rightly understand this natural obligation) but acknowledgeth it in the words: "The obligation to civil obedience, by the force of which all the civil laws become valid, is before those civil laws. And if any prince should make a law to this purpose, that no man should rebel against him, this would signify nothing, because unless they to whom it is made were before obliged to obey, or not to rebel, the law is invalid; and if they were, then it is superfluous." [1] Now this previous obligation to civil obedience cannot be derived (as the forementioned writer [of] *De Cive* and of the *Leviathan* supposes) from men's private utility only; because every man being judge of this for himself, it would then be lawful for any subject to rebel against his sovereign prince, and to poison or stab him, whensoever he could reasonably persuade himself that it would tend to his own advantage or that he should thereby procure the sovereignty. Were the obligation to civil obedience made only by men's private utility, it would as easily be dissolved by the same. It remaineth, therefore, that conscience and religious obligation to duty is the only basis and essential foundation of a polity or commonwealth, without which there could be no right or authority of commanding in any sovereign, nor validity in any

1. [ED.] Hobbes, *De Cive*, Ch. 14, §21.

laws. Wherefore religious obligation cannot be thought to be the fiction or imposture of civil sovereigns, unless civil sovereignty itself be accounted a fiction and imposture, or a thing which hath no foundation in nature, but is either wholly artificial or violent.

Moreover, had a religious regard to the Deity been a mere figment or invention of politicians to promote their own ends and keep men in obedience and subjection under them, then would they doubtless have so framed and contrived it as that it should have been every way flexible and compliant; namely, by persuading the world, that whatsoever was commanded by themselves was agreeable to the divine will, and whatever was forbidden by their laws was displeasing to God Almighty, and would be punished by him; God ruling over the world no otherwise than by and in these civil sovereigns as his viceregents and as the only prophets and interpreters of his will to men. So that the civil law of every country and the arbitrary will of sovereigns should be acknowledged to be the only measure of just and unjust (there being nothing naturally such), the only rule of conscience and religion; for, from religion thus modelled, civil sovereigns might think to have an absolute power or an infinite right of doing or commanding whatsoever they pleased, without exception, nothing being unlawful to them and their subjects being always obliged, in conscience, without the least scruple, to obey.

But this is but a mere larva of religion and would be but a mocking of God Almighty, and indeed this is the only religion that can be called a political figment. Neither could the generality of mankind be ever yet thus persuaded that the arbitrary will of civil sovereigns was the only rule of justice and conscience, and that God Almighty could command nothing, nor reveal his will concerning religion to mankind otherwise than by these as his prophets and interpreters. True religion and conscience are no such waxen things, servilely addicted to the arbitrary wills of men, but immorigerous,[2] stiff and inflexible; they respecting the Deity only, his eternal or everlasting laws, and his revealed will; with which whensoever human laws clash (a thing not impossible), they conclude that then God ought to be obeyed, and not men. For this cause the profane politicians declare open war against this religion, as a thing utterly inconsistent with civil sovereignty; because it introduces a fear greater than the fear of the Leviathan, namely, that of him who can inflict eternal punishments after death; as also because it clashes with that monstrous, infinite and unlimited power of theirs, which is such a thing as is not attributed by genuine theists to God

2. [ED.] I.e., unyielding, rebellious.

Almighty himself; a power of making their mere arbitrary will the rule of justice, and not justice the rule of their will. Thus does a modern writer of politics condemn it for seditious doctrine, tending to the dissolution of a commonwealth: "That subjects may make a judgment of good and evil, just and unjust, or have any other conscience besides the law of the land." [3] As also this: "That subjects may sin obeying the command of their sovereign." [4] He likewise adds: "That it is impossible a commonwealth should stand, where any other than the sovereign hath a power of giving greater rewards than life, and of inflicting greater punishments than death. Now, eternal life is a greater reward than the life present, and eternal torment than the death of nature." [5] Wherefore God Almighty being the dispenser of eternal rewards and punishments, this is all one as if he should have said it is impossible a commonwealth should stand where the belief of a God, who can punish with eternal torments after this life, is entertained. Thus does the same writer declare, that if the "superstitious fear of spirits" (whereof God is the chief) "and things depending thereupon, were taken away, men would be much more fitted than they are, for civil obedience": [6] and that they who assert the immortality of souls, or their capability of receiving punishments after death, "fright men from obeying the laws of their country, with empty names, as men fright birds from the corn, with an empty doublet, a hat and a crooked stick." [7] And accordingly he concludes, that civil sovereigns do not only make justice but religion also; and that no scripture or divine revelation can oblige, unless it be first made law, or stamped with their authority. Now, since that which can make religion and gods must itself needs be greater than all gods, it follows, according to the tenor of this doctrine, that the civil sovereign is in reality the supreme Numen; or else at least, that the Leviathan (the king over all the children of pride) is the highest Deity, next to senseless omnipotent matter; the one of these being the atheists' natural, the other their artificial god. Nevertheless we shall here observe by the way that whilst these atheistic politicians thus endeavor to swell up the civil sovereign and to bestow upon him an infinite right, by removing to that end out of his way natural justice, conscience, religion and God himself, they do indeed thereby absolutely divest him of all right and authority, since the subject is now no

3. [ED.] Hobbes, *Leviathan*, Ch. 29.
4. [ED.] Hobbes, *De Cive*, Ch. 12, §2.
5. [ED.] Hobbes, *Leviathan*, Ch. 38.
6. [ED.] Ibid., Ch. 2. Cudworth omits certain clauses without seriously altering the sense.
7. [ED.] Ibid., Ch. 46.

longer obliged in conscience to obey him; and so instead of true right and authority, they leave him nothing but mere brutish force. Wherefore, since theism and true religion are thus plainly disowned and disclaimed by these politicians as altogether inconsistent with their designs, they cannot be supposed to have been the figments of civil sovereigns or the mere creatures of political art. And thus have we abundantly confuted those three atheistic pretences to solve the phenomenon of religion; from fear, and the ignorance of causes, and the fiction of politicians.

II

And now come we to the last atheistic argumentation, wherein they endeavor to recommend their doctrine to civil sovereigns, and to persuade them that theism or religion is absolutely inconsistent with their interest; their reasons for which are these three following. First, because the civil sovereign reigns only in fear; and therefore, if there be any power and fear greater than the power and fear of the Leviathan, civil authority can signify little. Secondly, because sovereignty is in its own nature absolutely indivisible, and must be either infinite, or none at all; so that divine laws (natural and revealed) superior to it, circumscribing it, would consequently destroy it. Wherefore religion and theism must of necessity be displaced and removed out of the way, to make room for the Leviathan to roll and tumble in. Thirdly and lastly, private judgment of good and evil, just and unjust, is also contradictious to the very being of a body politic, which is one artificial man, made up of many natural men united under one head, having one common reason, judgment and will ruling over the whole. But conscience, which religion introduceth, is private judgment of good and evil, just and unjust, and therefore altogether inconsistent with true politics, that can admit of no private consciences, but only one public conscience of the law.

In way of answer to the first of which, we must here briefly unravel the atheistic ethics and politics. The foundation whereof is first laid in the villainizing of human nature; as that, which has not so much as any the least seeds, either of politicalness or ethicalness at all in it; nothing of equity and philanthropy (there being no other charity or benevolence anywhere, according to them, save what resulteth from fear, imbecility, and indigency); nothing of public or common concern, but all private and selfish; appetite and utility, or the desires of sensual pleasure, and honor, dominion, and precellency [1] before others, being the only measures of good in nature. So that there can be nothing naturally just or unjust, nothing in itself sinful or unlawful, but every man by nature hath *jus ad omnia*, "a right to everything," whatsoever his appetite inclineth him unto, or himself judgeth profitable, even to other men's bodies and lives. "Si occidere cupis, jus habes, if thou desirest to kill, thou hast then naturally a right thereunto"; that is, a liberty to kill without any sin or injustice. For *jus* and *lex*, or *justicia*, "right" and "law," or "justice," in the language of these atheistic politicians are directly contrary to one another; their right being a belluine [2] liberty, not made or left by justice but such as is founded in a supposition of its absolute non-existence. Should therefore a son not only murder his own parents who had tenderly brought him up, but also exquisitely torture them, taking pleasure in beholding their rueful looks and hearing their lamentable shrieks and outcries, there would be nothing of sin or injustice at all in this, nor in anything else; because justice is no nature, but a mere factitious and artificial thing, made only by men and civil laws. And, according to these men's apprehensions, nature has been very kind and indulgent to mankind herein, that it hath thus brought us into the world, without any fetters or shackles upon us, free from all duty and obligation, justice and morality, these being to them nothing but restraints and hindrances of true liberty. From all which it follows that nature absolutely dissociates and segregates men from one another, by reason of the inconsistency of those appetites of theirs that are all carried out only to private good, and consequently that every man is, by nature, in a state of war and hostility against every man.

In the next place, therefore, these atheistic politicians further add that though this their state of nature, which is a liberty from all justice and obligation, and a lawless, loose or belluine right to every thing, be in itself absolutely the best; yet nevertheless by reason of men's imbecility and the equality of their strengths and inconsistency of their appetites, it proves by accident the worst; this war with every one making men's right or liberty to everything indeed a right or liberty to nothing; they having no security of their lives, much less of the comfortable enjoyment of them. For as it is not possible that all men should have dominion (which were indeed the most desirable thing, according to these principles), so the generality must needs be sensible of more evil in such a state of liberty with an universal war against all than of good. Wherefore, when men had

1. [ED.] I.e., pre-eminence.
2. [ED.] I.e., characteristic of beasts, brutal.

been a good while hewing and slashing and justling against one another, they became at length all weary thereof, and conceived it necessary by art to help the defect of their own power here, and to choose a lesser evil, for the avoiding of a greater; that is, to make a voluntary abatement of this their infinite right, and to submit to terms of equality with one another, in order to a sociable and peaceable cohabitation: and not only so, but also for the security of all, that others should observe such rules as well as themselves, to put their necks under the yoke of a common coercive power, whose will being the will of them all, should be the very rule and law and measure of justice to them.

Here therefore these atheistic politicians, as they first of all slander human nature, and make a villain of it, so do they in the next place, reproach justice and civil sovereignty also, making it to be nothing but an ignoble and bastardly brat of fear; or else a lesser evil, submitted to merely out of necessity, for the avoiding of a greater evil, that of war with every one, by reason of men's natural imbecility. So that according to this hypothesis, justice and civil government are plainly things not good in themselves, nor desirable (they being a hindrance of liberty, and nothing but shackles and fetters), but by accident only, as necessary evils. And thus do these politicians themselves sometimes distinguish betwixt good and just, that "Bonum amatur per se, justum per accidens—Good is that which is loved for itself, but just by accident." From whence it follows unavoidably, that all men must of necessity be "unwillingly just," or not with a full and perfect but mixed will only; just being a thing that is not sincerely good but such as hath a great dash or dose of evil blended with it. And this was the old atheistic generation of justice, and of a body politic, civil society, and sovereignty. For though a modern writer affirm this hypothesis (which he looks upon as the only true scheme of politics) to be a new invention, as the circulation of the blood, and no older than the book *De Cive*,[3] yet is it certain, that it was the commonly received doctrine of the atheistic politicians and philosophers before Plato's time; who represents their sense concerning the original of justice and civil society in this manner: [4] "I am to declare first what justice is, according to the sense of these philosophers, and from whence it was generated. They say therefore, that by nature, lawless liberty, and to do that which is now called injustice, and injury to other men, is good; but to suffer it from others, is evil. But of the two, there is more of evil in suffering it, than of

3. [ED.] In this work Hobbes first seriously expounded his political theories.
4. [ED.] Plato, *The Republic*, Bk. II.

good in doing it: whereupon when men had clashed a good while, doing and suffering injury, the greater part, who by of their imbecility were not able to take the former without the latter, at length compounded the business amongst themselves, and agreed together by pacts and covenants, neither to do nor suffer injury, but to submit to rules of equality, and make laws by compact, in order to their peaceable cohabitation, they calling that which was required in those laws by the name of just." And then it is added:

> And this is, according to these philosophers, the generation and essence of justice, as a certain middle thing betwixt the best and the worst. The best, to exercise a lawless liberty of doing whatsoever one please to other men without suffering any inconvenience from it; and the worst, to suffer evil from others without being able to revenge it. Justice, therefore, being a middle thing betwixt both these is loved, not as that which is good in itself, but only by reason of men's imbecility, and their inability to do injustice. Forasmuch as he, that had sufficient power, would never enter into such compacts, and submit to equality and subjection. As for example, if a man had Gyges' his magical ring,[5] that he could do whatsoever he listed, and not be seen or taken notice of by any, such a one would certainly never enter into covenants, nor submit to laws of equality and subjection.

Agreeably whereunto, it hath been concluded also by some of the old atheistic philosophers, that justice was, "not properly and directly one's own good, the good of him that is just, but another man's good, partly of the fellow-citizens, but chiefly of the ruler, whose vassal he is." And it is well known that after Plato's time, this hypothesis concerning justice, that it was a mere factitious thing, and sprung only from men's fear and imbecility, as a lesser evil, was much insisted on by Epicurus also.

But let us in the next place see how our modern atheistic philosophers and politicians will manage and carry on this hypothesis, so as to consociate men by art into a body politic, that are naturally dissociated from one another, as also make justice and obligation artificial, when there is none in nature. First of all, therefore, these artificial justice-makers, city-makers and authority-makers tell us that though men have an infinite right by nature, yet may they alienate this right, or part thereof, from them-

5. [ED.] Plato's *Republic*, Book II (359D) tells how Gyges, a Lydian shepherd, found in a cavern a bronze horse, inside which was a corpse from which he took a ring. Having discovered that by turning the seal of the ring inward he could become invisible, he was able to kill the king, take the queen as his wife, and become "tyrant" of Lydia.

selves, and either simply renounce it or transfer the same upon some other person; by means whereof it will become unlawful for themselves afterwards to make use thereof. Thus a late writer, men "may by signs declare that it is their will it shall no longer be lawful for them to do something, which before they had a right to do"; and this is called by him a simple renunciation of right. And further, saith he, they "may declare again that it is their will, it shall be no longer lawful for them to resist this or that particular person, whom before they might lawfully have resisted"; [6] and this is called a translation of right. But if there be nothing in its own nature unlawful, then cannot this be unlawful for a man afterwards to make use of such liberty as he had before in words renounced or abandoned. Nor can any man, by his mere will, make anything unlawful to him which is not so in itself, but only suspend the exercise of so much of his liberty as he thought good. But however, could a man by his will oblige himself, or make anything unlawful to him, there would be nothing got by this, because then might he by his will disoblige himself again, and make the same lawful as before. For what is made merely by will may be destroyed by will. Wherefore these politicians will yet urge the business further and tell us that no man can be obliged but by his own act, and that the essence of injustice is nothing else but *dati repetitio*, the "taking away of that which one had before given." [7] To which we again reply that were a man naturally unobliged to anything then could he no way be obliged to stand to his own act, so that it should be really unjust and unlawful for him at any time upon second thoughts, voluntarily to undo what he had before voluntarily done. But the atheists here plainly render injustice a mere ludicrous thing when they tell us that it is nothing but such an absurdity in life, as it is in disputation, when a man denies a proposition that he had before granted; which is no real evil in him as a man, but only a thing called an absurdity, as a disputant. That is, injustice is no absolute evil of the man, but only a relative incongruity in him as a citizen. As when a man speaking Latin observes not the laws of grammar, this is a kind of injustice in him as a Latinist or grammarian, so, when one who lives in civil society observes not the laws and conditions thereof, this is, as it were, the false Latin of a citizen, and nothing else. According to which notion of injustice, there is no such real evil or hurt in it, as can any way withstand the force of appetite and private utility and oblige men to civil obedience, when it is contrary to the same. But these political jugglers and

6. [ED.] Hobbes, *De Cive*, Ch. 2, §4.
7. [ED.] Hobbes, *De Cive*, Ch. 3, §3.

enchanters will here cast yet a further mist before men's eyes with their pacts and covenants. For men by their covenants, say they, may unquestionably oblige themselves, and make things unjust and unlawful to them that were not so before. Wherefore injustice is again defined by them, and that with more speciousness, to be the breach of covenants.[8] But though it be true that if there be natural justice, covenants will oblige, yet, upon the contrary supposition that there is nothing naturally unjust, this cannot be unjust neither, to break covenants. Covenants, without natural justice, are nothing but mere words and breath (as indeed these atheistic politicians themselves, agreeably to their own hypothesis, call them); and therefore can they have no force to oblige. Wherefore, these justice-makers are themselves at last necessitated to fly to laws of nature, and to pretend this to be a law of nature, that men should stand to their pacts and covenants.[9] Which is plainly to contradict their main fundamental principle, that by nature nothing is unjust or unlawful; for if it be so, then can there be no laws of nature; and if there be laws of nature, then must there be something naturally unjust and unlawful. So that this is not to make justice, but clearly to unmake their own hypothesis, and to suppose justice to have been already made by nature or to be in nature; which is a gross absurdity in disputation, to affirm what one had before denied. But these their laws of nature are indeed nothing but juggling equivocation, and a mere mockery; themselves again acknowledging them to be no laws, because law is nothing but the word of him who hath command over others; but only conclusions or theorems concerning what conduces to the conservation and defence of themselves, upon the principle of fear; that is, indeed, the laws of their own timorous and cowardly complexion; for they, who have courage and generosity in them, according to this hypothesis, would never submit to such sneaking terms of equality and subjection, but venture for dominion; and resolve either to win the saddle or lose the horse. Here, therefore, do our atheistic politicians plainly dance round in a circle, they first deriving the obligation of civil laws from that of covenants, and then that of covenants from the laws of nature; and lastly, the obligation both of these laws of nature and of covenants themselves, again, from the law, command and sanction of the civil sovereign, without which neither of them would at all oblige. And thus it is manifest how vain the attempts of these politicians are to make justice artificially, when there is no such thing naturally (which is indeed no less than to make something out of

8. [ED.] Hobbes, *De Cive*, Ch. 3, §3.
9. [ED.] Hobbes, *De Cive*, Ch. 3, §1.

nothing); and by art to consociate into bodies politic those, whom nature had dissociated from one another; a thing as impossible as to tie knots in the wind or water, or to build up a stately palace or castle out of sand. Indeed, the ligaments by which these politicians would tie the members of their huge Leviathan or artificial man together, are not so good as cobwebs, they being really nothing but mere will and words. For if authority and sovereignty be made only by will and words, then is it plain that by will and words they may be unmade again at pleasure.

Neither indeed are these atheistic politicians themselves altogether unaware hereof, that this their artificial justice and obligation can be no firm vinculum of a body politic, to consociate those together and unite them into one who are naturally dissociated and divided from one another; they acknowledging that "covenants without the sword, being but words and breath, are of no strength to hold the members of their Leviathan, or body politic together." Wherefore, they plainly betake themselves at length from art to force and power, and make their civil sovereign really to reign only in fear.[10] And this must needs be their meaning, when they so constantly declare all obligation, just and unjust, to be derived only from law; they by law there understanding "a command directed to such as by reason of their imbecility are not able to resist.": [11] so that the will and command of the more powerful obliges by the fear of punishment threatened. Now, if the only real obligation to obey civil laws be from the fear of punishment, then could no man be obliged to hazard his life for the safety of his prince and country; and they, who could reasonably promise themselves impunity, would be altogether disobliged, and consequently might justly break any laws, for their own advantage. An assertion so extravagant that these confounded politicians themselves are ashamed plainly to own it, and therefore disguise it, what they can, by equivocation; themselves sometimes also confessing so much of truth, that "punishment does not oblige, but only hold those to their duty who were before obliged." [12] Furthermore, what is made by power and force only may be unmade by power and force again. If civil sovereigns reign only in the fear of their own sword, then is that right of theirs, so much talked of, indeed nothing else but might, and their authority, force; and consequently successful and prosperous rebellion, and whatsoever can be done by power, will be *ipso facto* thereby justified. Lastly, were civil sovereigns

10. [ED.] Hobbes, *Leviathan*, Ch. 17.
11. [ED.] This is not an exact quotation from Hobbes; cf. *De Cive*, Ch. 14, §1.
12. [ED.] Hobbes, *De Cive*, Ch. 14, §2.

and bodies politic mere violent and contra-natural things, then would they all quickly vanish into nothing, because nature will prevail against force and violence; whereas men constantly everywhere fall into political order, and the corruption of one form of government is but the generation of another.

Wherefore, since it is plain that sovereignty and bodies politic can neither be merely artificial nor yet violent things, there must of necessity be some natural bond or vinculum to hold them together, such as may both really oblige subjects to obey the lawful commands of sovereigns, and sovereigns in commanding to seek the good and welfare of their subjects; whom these atheistic politicians (by their infinite and belluine right) quite discharge from any such thing. Which bond or vinculum can be no other than natural justice, and something of a common and public, of a cementing and conglutinating, nature in all rational beings; the original of both which is from the Deity. The right and authority of God himself is founded in justice; and of this is the civil sovereignty also a certain participation. It is not the mere creature of the people and of men's wills, and therefore annihilable again by their wills at pleasure; but hath a stamp of divinity upon it, as may partly appear from hence, because that "power of life and death" which civil sovereigns have was never lodged in singulars, before civil society; and therefore could not be conferred by them. Had not God and nature made a city, were there not a natural conciliation of all rational creatures and subjection of them to the Deity as their head (which is Cicero's "one city of gods and men" [13]), had not God made "ruling and being ruled," superiority and subjection, with their respective duty and obligation, men could neither by art or political enchantment, nor yet by force, have made any firm cities or polities. The civil sovereign is no Leviathan, no beast, but a god ("I have said ye are gods" [Ps. 82:6]); he reigns not in mere brutish force and fear, but in natural justice and conscience and in the right and authority of God himself. Nevertheless we deny not but that there is need of force and fear too, to constrain those to obedience to whom the conscience of duty proveth ineffectual. Nor is the fear of the civil sovereign's own sword alone sufficient for this neither, unassisted by religion, and the fear of an invisible Being omnipotent, who seeth all things, and can punish secret as well as open transgressors, both in this life and after death; which is a thing so confessedly true, that atheists have therefore pretended religion to have been at first a mere political figment. We conclude therefore that

13. [ED.] Cicero, *Concerning the Nature of the Gods*, Bk. II, Ch. 62.

the civil sovereign reigneth not merely in the fear of his own power and sword, but first in the justice and authority, and then in the power and fear also of God Almighty. And thus much for the first atheistic pretence, from the interests of civil sovereigns.

To their second, that sovereignty is essentially infinite, and therefore altogether inconsistent with religion, that would limit and confine it, we reply, that the right and authority of civil sovereigns is not, as these our atheistic politicians ignorantly suppose, a mere belluine liberty, but it is a right essentially founded in the being of natural justice, as hath been declared. For authority of commanding is such a right as supposes obligation in others to obey, without which it could be nothing but mere will and force. But none can be obliged in duty to obey but by natural justice; commands, as such, not creating obligation, but presupposing it. For if persons were not before obliged to obey, no commands would signify anything to them. Wherefore the first original obligation is not from will but nature. Did obligation to the things of natural justice, as many suppose, arise from the will and positive command of God only by reason of punishments threatened and rewards promised, the consequence of this would be that no man was good and just, but only by accident and for the sake of something else; whereas the goodness of justice or righteousness is intrinsical to the thing itself, and this is that which obligeth (and not anything foreign to it), it being a different species of good from that of appetite and private utility, which every man may dispense withal. Now, there can be no more infinite justice than there can be an infinite rule or an infinite measure. Justice is essentially a determinate thing and therefore can there not be an infinite *jus*, "right or authority." If there be anything in its own nature just and obliging, or such as ought to be done, then must there of necessity be something unjust or unlawful, which therefore cannot be obligingly commanded by any authority whatsoever. Neither ought this to be thought any impeachment of civil authority, it extending universally to all, even to that of the Deity itself. The right and authority of God himself, who is the supreme sovereign of the universe, is also in like manner bounded and circumscribed by justice. God's will is ruled by his justice, and not his justice ruled by his will; and therefore, God himself cannot command what is in its own nature unjust. And thus have we made it evident that infinite right and authority of doing and commanding anything without exception, so that the arbitrary will of the commander should be the very rule of justice itself to others and consequently might oblige to any thing, is an absolute contradiction and a non-entity; it supposing nothing to be in its own nature just or unjust; which, if there were not, there could be no obligation nor authority at all. Wherefore the atheists, who would flatter civil sovereigns with this infinite right, as if their will ought to be the very rule of justice and conscience, and upon that pretence prejudice them against religion, do as ill deserve of them as of religion hereby; they indeed, absolutely divesting them of all right and authority and leaving them nothing but mere brutish force and belluine liberty. And could civil sovereigns utterly demolish and destroy conscience and religion in the minds of men (which yet is an absolute impossibility), they thinking thereby to make elbow-room for themselves, they would certainly bury themselves also in the ruins of them. Nevertheless, thus much is true, that they in whom the sovereign legislative power of every polity is lodged (whether single persons or assemblies), they who make civil laws, and can reverse them at pleasure, though they may unquestionably sin against God, in making unjust laws, yet can they not sin politically or civilly, as violators or transgressors of those laws cancelled and reversed by them, they being superior to them. Nor is this all; but these sovereign legislative powers may be said to be absolute also in another sense, as being, "unjudicable," or uncensurable by any human court; because, if they were so obnoxious, then would that court or power which had a right to judge and censure them be superior to them; which is contrary to the hypothesis. And then, if this power were again judicable by some other, there must either be an infinite progress, or endless circulation (a thing not only absurd, but also utterly inconsistent with government and property; because, there being no ultimate judgment unappealable from, there could never be any final determination of controversies); or else at last, all must be devolved to the multitude of singulars, which would be a dissolution of the body politic and a state of anarchy. And thus have we fully confuted the second atheistic pretence also, for the "inconsistency of religion with civil sovereignty."

Their third and last follows: "That private judgment of good and evil is contradictious to civil sovereignty and a body politic, this being one artificial man that must be all governed by one reason and will." But conscience is private judgment of good and evil, such as is absolutely inconsistent with civil sovereignty, there being, according to them, nothing in nature of a public or common good, nothing of duty or obligation, but all private appetite and utility, of which also every man is judge for himself. For if this were so, then, whenever any man judged it most for his private utility to disobey laws, rebel against sovereigns, nay, to poison or stab them, he would be unquestionably bound by nature and the reason of his own good, as the highest law, to do the same. Neither can these atheistic politicians be ever able to bring men out of this state of private good, judgment and will, which is natural to them, by any artificial tricks and devices or mere enchantments of words, as "artificial justice," and an "artificial man," and a "common person" and "will," and a "public conscience," and the like. Nay, it is observable that themselves are necessitated by the tenor of these their principles casuistically to allow such private judgment and will as is altogether inconsistent with civil sovereignty; as, that any man may lawfully resist in defence of his own life; and that they, who have once rebelled, may afterwards justly defend themselves by force. Nor indeed can this private judgment of men, according to their appetite and utility, be possibly otherwise taken away than by natural justice, which is a thing not of a private but of a public and common nature; and by conscience, that obligeth to obey all the lawful commands of civil sovereigns, though contrary to men's appetites and private interest. Wherefore conscience also is, in itself, not of a private and partial but of a public and common nature; it respecting divine laws, impartial justice and equity, and the good of the whole, when clashing with our own selfish, good and private utility. This is the only thing that can naturally consociate mankind together, lay a foundation for bodies politic, and take away that private will and judgment, according to men's appetite and utility, which is inconsistent with the same; agreeably to that of Plato's: that "which is of a common and public nature, unites; but that, which is of a private, segregates and dissociates." [14] It is true, indeed, that particular persons must make a judgment, in conscience for themselves (a public conscience being nonsense and ridiculous), and that they may also err therein; yet is not the rule neither by which conscience judgeth, private; nor itself unaccountable, unless in such mistaken fanatics as professedly follow private impulses; but either the natural and eternal laws of God, or else his revealed will, things more public than the civil laws of any country, and of which others also may judge. Nevertheless, we deny not but that evil persons may and do sometimes make a pretence of conscience and religion, in order to sedition and rebellion, as the best things may be abused. But this is not the fault of religion, but only of the men; conscience obliging, though first to obey God, yet, in subordination to him, the laws of civil sovereigns also. To conclude, conscience and religion oblige subjects actively to obey all the lawful commands of civil sovereigns or legis-

14. [ED.] Plato, *Laws*, Bk. IX.

lative powers, though contrary to their own private appetite, interest and utility; but, when these same sovereign legislative powers command unlawful things, conscience, though it here obliges to "obey God, rather than man" [Acts 5:29], yet does it, notwithstanding, oblige not to resist. Romans 13:2: "Whosoever resisteth the power, resisteth the ordinance of God, and they that resist shall receive to themselves damnation." And Matthew 26:52: "All they that take the sword, shall perish with the sword."—"Here is the patience and the faith of the saints" [Rev. 13:10]. And thus does religion "give unto Caesar, the things that are Caesar's, as well as unto God the things that are God's" [Mk. 12:17].

And now, having fully confuted all the atheistic grounds, we confidently conclude that the first original of all things was neither stupid and senseless matter fortuitously moved, nor a blind and nescient, but orderly and methodical plastic nature; nor a living matter, having perception or understanding natural, without animal sense or consciousness; nor yet did everything exist of itself necessarily from eternity, without a cause. But there is one only necessary existent, the cause of all other things; and this an absolutely perfect Being, infinitely good, wise and powerful; who hath made all that was fit to be made, and according to the best wisdom, and exerciseth an exact providence over all; whose name ought to be hallowed and separated from all other things: "To whom be all honor, and glory, and worship, for ever and ever. Amen."

PART NINE

❖

Homiletical

❖ ❖ ❖ ❖ ❖ ❖ ❖ ❖

RALPH CUDWORTH

Sermon Preached Before the Honorable House of Commons

Editor's Introduction. In the religious and political life of the turbulent decades between 1640 and 1660, the sermons preached before the House of Commons often played a significant role. Among the eminent preachers invited to discharge this service, Ralph Cudworth occupied a distinctive place. Although he evidently sympathized with the parliamentary cause, he was in no sense a party man, and he was gravely concerned about the situation that was developing. By 1647 the tensions within the victorious parliamentary party were reaching an acute stage. All its members agreed that the defeated king must never again exercise arbitrary power in either church or state. But concerning how this desired end could be achieved, the differences were many and pronounced. On whom would devolve the powers stripped from the king? At every point civil and religious problems were intertwined, to the infinite complication of both. On the parliamentary side, parties were beginning to proliferate. The Presbyterians still controlled the House of Commons; the Independents increasingly dominated the army. A small group of Erastians wanted to see religious problems settled by political means. The radical bodies, scarcely represented in parliament, were increasing rapidly in the army and in the capital. But the "City of London" was conservative in outlook and Presbyterian in sympathy. The king—who, though robbed by defeat of any effective party, was still an important factor in the intricate maneuvers for some kind of settlement—was proving increasingly mendacious and untrustworthy. The Westminster Assembly of Divines was in session, and the Independents, though outnumbered, were showing an exasperating skill in Fabian tactics. In a few months, the rising unrest in the army would lead to the celebrated Putney debates (autumn 1647).[1] Before long the king's machinations were to result in the Second Civil War. At every point of tension, theological issues were involved.

1. Cf. *The Clarke Papers*, ed. C. H. Firth, 4 vols. (London, 1891–1901); also *Puritanism and Liberty*, ed. A.S.P. Woodhouse (London, 1938).

In this highly explosive atmosphere Cudworth preached to the House of Commons. He was well aware of what he calls "those many opinions about religion that are everywhere so eagerly contended for on all sides." He knew at first hand the people who "were so apt to spend all their zeal upon a violent obtruding of their own opinions and apprehensions upon others." He realized that this was "like to be the bellows that will blow a fire of discord and contention in Christian commonwealths." Cudworth therefore came "not to contend for this or that opinion, but only to persuade men to the life of Christ as the pith and kernel of all religion." The sermon, in fact, was a courageous as well as an eloquent protest against the very tendencies so conspicuously present among his congregation.

❖ ❖ ❖ ❖ ❖ ❖ ❖ ❖

[Dedication]

To The Honorable House of Commons

The scope of this sermon, which not long since exercised your patience, worthy senators, was not to contend for this or that opinion, but only to persuade men to the life of Christ, as the pith and kernel of all religion; without which, I may boldly say, all the several forms of religion in the world, though we please ourselves never so much in them, are but so many several dreams. And those many opinions about religion, that are everywhere so eagerly contended for on all sides, where this doth not lie at the bottom, are but so many shadows fighting with one another: so that I may well say of the true Christian, that is indeed possessed of the life of Christianity, in opposition to all those that are but lightly tinctured with the opinions of it, in the language of the poet: Οἶος πέπνυται τοὶ δ᾽ ὡς ϲκιαὶ ἀΐσσουϲι.[1] Wherefore I could not think anything else either more necessary for Christians in general or more seasonable at this time than to stir them up to the real establishment of the righteousness of God in their hearts, and that participation of the divine nature which the apostle speaketh of. That so they might not content themselves with mere fancies and conceits of Christ, without the Spirit of Christ really dwelling in them and Christ himself inwardly formed in their hearts; nor satisfy themselves with the mere holding of right and orthodox opinions, as they

1. [ED.] "He who is wise is like shadows which flit in every direction."

conceive, whilst they are utterly devoid within of that divine life, which Christ came to kindle in men's souls; and therefore are so apt to spend all their zeal upon a violent obtruding of their own opinions and apprehensions upon others, which cannot give entertainment to them; which, besides its repugnancy to the doctrine and example of Christ himself, is like to be the bellows that will blow a fire of discord and contention in Christian commonwealths; whilst in the meantime these hungry and starved opinions devour all the life and substance of religion, as the lean kine in Pharaoh's dream did eat up the fat [Gen. 41:2-4], Nor, lastly, please themselves only in the violent opposing of other men's superstitions, according to the genius of the present times, without substituting in the room of them an inward principle of spirit and life in their own souls. For I fear many of us that pull down idols in churches may set them up in our hearts; and whilst we quarrel with painted glass, make no scruple at all of entertaining many foul lusts in our souls, and committing continual idolatry with them.

This, in general, was the design of this following discourse, which you were pleased, noble senators, not only to express your good acceptance of, but also to give a real signification of your great undeserved favor to the author of it. Who therefore cannot but, as the least expression of his thankfulness, humbly devote it to you presenting it here again to your eye in the same form in which it was delivered to your ear; desirous of nothing more, than that it might be some way useful to you, to kindle in you the life and heat of that which is endeavored here to be described upon paper; that you may express it both in your private conversations and likewise in all your public employments for the commonwealth. That you may, by your kindly influence, effectually encourage all goodness; and by virtue of your power and authority (to use the phrase of Solomon) "scatter away all evil with your eye" [cf. Prov. 20:8] as the sun by his beams scattereth the mists and vapors. That from you "judgment may run down like waters, and righteousness like a mighty stream" [Amos 5:24] to refresh this whole land that thirsteth after them: which, whilst you distribute them plentifully to others, will bestow both strength and honor to yourselves. For justice and righteousness are the establishment of every throne, of all civil power and authority; and if these should once forsake it, though there be lions to support it, it could not stand long. These, together with a good peace, well settled in a commonwealth, are all the outward felicity we can expect, till that happy time come, which the prophet foretelleth, and is therefore more than a Platonical idea; when "the wolf shall dwell with the lamb, and the leopard shall lie down with the kid, and the calf, and the young lion, and the fatling together, and a little child lead them": when "the sucking child shall play on the hole of the asp, and the weaned child shall put his hand on the cockatrice den": when "they shall not hurt nor destroy in all God's holy mountain; for the earth shall be full of the knowledge of the Lord, as the waters cover the sea" [Is. 11:6–9].

I have but one word more, if you please to give me leave; that after your care for the advancement of religion, and the public good of the commonwealth, you would think it worthy of you to promote ingenuous learning and cast a favorable influence upon it. I mean not that only which furnisheth the pulpit, which you seem to be very regardful of; but that which is more remote from such popular use, in the several kinds of it, which yet are all of them both very subservient to religion, and useful to the commonwealth. There is indeed a ψευδοπαιδεία, as the philosopher tells us, a bastardly kind of literature, and a ψευδώνυμος γνῶσις, as the apostle instructeth us, a knowledge falsely so called; [2] which deserve not to be pleaded for. But the noble and generous improvement of our understanding faculty, in the true contemplation of the wisdom, goodness, and other attributes of God, in this great fabric of the universe, cannot easily be disparaged, without a blemish cast upon the Maker of it. Doubtless we may as well enjoy that which God hath communicated of himself to the creatures, by this larger faculty of our understandings, as by those narrow and low faculties of our senses; and yet nobody counts it to be unlawful to hear a lesson played upon the lute or to smell at a rose. And these raised improvements of our natural understandings may be as well subservient and subordinate to a Divine light in our minds, as the natural use of these outward creatures here below to the life of God in our hearts. Nay, all true knowledge doth of itself naturally tend to God, who is the fountain of it; and would ever be raising of our souls up upon its wings thither, did not we κατέχειν ἐν ἀδικίᾳ, detain it, and hold it down, in unrighteousness, as the apostle speaketh [Rom. 1:18]. All philosophy to a wise man, to a truly sanctified mind, as he in Plutarch speaketh, is but ὕλη τῆς θεολογίας, matter for Divinity to work upon. Religion is the queen of all those inward endowments of the soul; and all pure natural knowledge, all virgin and undeflowered arts and sciences, are her handmaids, that rise up and call her blessed. I need not tell you how much skill of tongues and languages, besides the excellent use of all philology in general, conduceth to the right understanding of the letter of sacred writings, on which the spiritual

2. [ED.] Cebes, *Philosophus*, II; 1 Tim. 6:20.

notions must be built; for none can possibly be ignorant of that, which have but once heard of a translation of the Bible. The apostle exhorteth private Christians to "whatsoever things are lovely, whatsoever things are of good report, if there be any virtue, if there be any praise, to think on those things" [Phil. 4:8]; and therefore it may well become you, noble gentlemen, in your public sphere to encourage so noble a thing as knowledge is, which will reflect so much lustre and honor back again upon yourselves. That God would direct you in all your counsels, and still bless you and prosper you in all your sincere endeavors for the public good is the hearty prayer of,

Your most humble servant,
RALPH CUDWORTH

SERMON

And hereby we do know that we know him, if we keep his commandments. He that saith, I know him, and keepeth not his commandments, is a liar, and the truth is not in him.—I John 2:3,4.

We have much inquiry concerning knowledge in these latter times. The sons of Adam are now as busy as ever himself was about the tree of knowledge of good and evil, shaking the boughs of it, and scrambling for the fruit; whilst, I fear, many are too unmindful of the tree of life. And though there be now no cherubims with their flaming swords to fright men off from it, yet the way that leads to it seems to be so solitary and untrodden as if there were but few that had any mind to taste the fruit of it [Gen. 2:9,17; 3:6,24]. There be many that speak of new glimpses and discoveries of truth, of dawnings of Gospel light, and no question but God hath reserved much of this for the very evening and sunset of the world, for in the latter days knowledge shall be increased. But yet I wish we could in the meantime see that day to dawn, which the apostle speaks of, and that "day-star to arise in men's hearts" [cf. 2 Pet. 1:19]. I wish, whilst we talk of light and dispute about truth, we could walk more as "children of the light" [Eph. 5:8]. Whereas, if St. John's rule be good here in the text, that no man truly knows Christ, but he that keepeth his commandments. It is much to be suspected that many of us who pretend to light have a thick and gloomy darkness within, overspreading our souls.

There be now many large volumes and discourses written concerning Christ, thousands of controversies discussed, infinite problems determined concerning his divinity, humanity, union of both together, and what not;

so that our bookish Christians, that have all their religion in writings and papers, think they are now completely furnished with all kinds of knowledge concerning Christ; and when they see all their leaves lying about them, they think they have a goodly stock of knowledge and truth and cannot possibly miss of the way to Heaven; as if religion were nothing but a little book-craft, a mere paper skill.

But if St. John's rule here be good, we must not judge of our knowing of Christ by our skill in books and papers, but by our keeping of his commandments. And that, I fear, will discover many of us (notwithstanding all this light which we boast of round about us) to have nothing but Egyptian darkness within our hearts.

The vulgar sort think that they know Christ enough out of their creeds and catechisms and confessions of faith;[3] and if they have but a little acquainted themselves with these, and like parrots conned the words of them, they doubt not but that they are sufficiently instructed in all the mysteries of the Kingdom of Heaven. Many of the more learned, if they can but wrangle and dispute about Christ, imagine themselves to be grown great proficients in the school of Christ.

The greatest part of the world, whether learned or unlearned, think that there is no need of purging and purifying of their hearts for the right knowledge of Christ and his Gospel; but though their lives be never so wicked, their hearts never so foul within, yet they may know Christ sufficiently out of their treatises and discourses, out of their mere systems and bodies of divinity; which I deny not to be useful in a subordinate way, although our Savior prescribeth his disciples another method to come to the right knowledge of divine truths, by doing of God's will. "He that will do my Father's will (saith he) shall know of the doctrine, whether it be of God" [Jn. 7:17]. He is a true Christian indeed, not he that is only book-taught, but he that is God-taught; he that hath an unction from the Holy One (as our apostle calleth it) that teacheth him all things; he that hath the Spirit of Christ within him, that searcheth out the deep things of God: "For as no man knoweth the things of a man, save the spirit of man, which is in him; even so the things of God knoweth no man, but the Spirit of God" [1 Cor. 2:11].

Ink and paper can never make us Christians, can never beget a new

3. [ED.] This was a particularly topical comment, and possibly a provocative one. The Westminster Assembly of Divines (actively in session from July 1643 to February 1649) had completed the Westminster Confession of Faith in December 1646—four months before Cudworth preached this sermon. The Westminster Catechisms (finished in the autumn of 1647) were already taking form.

nature, a living principle in us; can never form Christ, or any true notions of spiritual things, in our hearts. The Gospel, that new law which Christ delivered to the world, it is not merely a dead letter without us, but a quickening spirit within us. Cold theorems and maxims, dry and jejune disputes, lean syllogistical reasonings could never yet of themselves beget the least glimpse of true heavenly light, the least sap of saving knowledge in any heart. All this is but the groping of the poor dark spirit of man after truth, to find it out with his own endeavors, and feel it with his own cold and benumbed hands. Words and syllables, which are but dead things, cannot possibly convey the living notions of heavenly truths to us. The secret mysteries of a divine life, of a new nature, of Christ formed in our hearts, they cannot be written or spoken, language and expressions cannot reach them; neither can they be ever truly understood, except the soul itself be kindled from within and awakened into the life of them. A painter that would draw a rose, though he may flourish some likeness of it in figure and color, yet he can never paint the scent and fragrancy; or if he would draw a flame, he cannot put a constant heat into his colors; he cannot make his pencil drop a sound, as the echo in the epigram mocks at him;

Si vis similem pingere, pinge sonum.[4]

All the skill of cunning artisans and mechanics cannot put a principle of life into a statue of their own making. Neither are we able to enclose in words and letters the life, soul, and essence, of any spiritual truths, and, as it were, to incorporate it in them.

Some philosophers have determined that ἀρετὴ is not διδακτὸν, virtue cannot be taught by any certain rules or precepts. Men and books may propound some directions to us, that may set us in such a way of life and practice, as in which we shall at last find it within ourselves, and be experimentally acquainted with it; but they cannot teach it us like a mechanic art or trade. No, surely, "there is a spirit in man; and the inspiration of the Almighty giveth them understanding" [Job 32:8]. But we shall not meet with this spirit any where but in the way of obedience: the knowledge of Christ, and the keeping of his commandments, must always go together and be mutual causes of one another.

"Hereby we know that we know him, if we keep his commandments."

"He that saith, I know him, and keepeth not his commandments, is a liar, and the truth is not in him."

I come now unto these words themselves, which are so pregnant that I

4. [ED.] "If you wish to paint a likeness, paint a sound."

shall not need to force out anything at all from them. I shall therefore only take notice of some few observations which drop from them of their own accord, and then conclude with some application of them to ourselves.

1. First, then, if this be the right way and method of discovering our knowledge of Christ, by our keeping his commandments, then we may safely draw conclusions concerning our state and condition from the conformity of our lives to the will of Christ.

Would we know, whether we know Christ aright, let us consider whether the life of Christ be in us. "Qui non habet vitam Christi, Christum non habet: He that hath not the life of Christ in him, he hath nothing but the name, nothing but a fancy of Christ, he hath not the substance of him." He that builds his house upon this foundation, not an airy notion of Christ swimming in his brain, but Christ really dwelling and living in his heart, as our Savior himself witnesseth, he "buildeth his house upon a rock"; and when the floods come, and the winds blow, and the rain descends, and beats upon it, it shall stand impregnably. But he that builds all his comfort upon an ungrounded persuasion, that God from all eternity hath loved him, and absolutely decreed him to life and happiness, and seeketh not for God really dwelling in his soul; he builds his house upon a quicksand, and it shall suddenly sink and be swallowed up [Mt. 7:24-27]: "His hope shall be cut off, and his trust shall be a spider's web; he shall lean upon his house, but it shall not stand; he shall hold it fast, but it shall not endure" [Job 8:14-15].

We are nowhere commanded to pry into these secrets, but the wholesome counsel and advice given us is this, "to make our calling and election sure" [2 Pet. 1:10]. We have no warrant in Scripture to peep into these hidden rolls and volumes of eternity, and to make it our first thing that we do, when we come to Christ, to spell out our names in the stars, and to persuade ourselves that we are certainly elected to everlasting happiness, before we see the image of God, in righteousness and true holiness, shaped in our hearts. God's everlasting decree is too dazzling and bright an object for us at first to set our eye upon. It is far easier and safer for us to look upon the rays of his goodness and holiness as they are reflected in our own hearts, and there to read the mild and gentle characters of God's love to us, in our love to him and our hearty compliance with his heavenly will; as it is safer for us, if we would see the sun, to look upon it here below in a pail of water, than to cast up our daring eyes upon the body of the sun itself, which is too radiant and scorching for us. The best assurance that any one can have of his interest in God is doubtless the conformity of his soul to him. Those divine purposes, whatsoever they be, are altogether unsearchable and unknowable by us. They lie wrapped up in everlasting darkness, and covered in a deep abyss. Who is able to fathom the bottom of them?

Let us not therefore make this our first attempt towards God and religion, to persuade ourselves strongly of these everlasting decrees: for if at our first flight we aim so high, we shall haply but scorch our wings, and be struck back with lightning, as those giants of old were, that would needs attempt to invade and assault heaven. And it is indeed a most gigantical essay to thrust ourselves so boldly into the lap of heaven; it is the prank of a Nimrod, of a mighty hunter [Gen. 10:9], thus rudely to deal before God, and to force Heaven and happiness before his face, whether he will or no. The way to obtain a good assurance indeed of our title to Heaven, is not to clamber up to it by a ladder of our own ungrounded persuasions, but to dig as low as Hell by humility and self-denial in our own hearts. And though this may seem to be the farthest way about, yet it is indeed the nearest and safest way to it. We must ἀναβαίνειν κάτω and καταβαίνειν ἄνω, as the Greek epigram speaks, ascend downward and descend upward, if we would indeed come to Heaven, or get any true persuasion of our title to it.

The most gallant and triumphant confidence of a Christian riseth safely and surely upon this low foundation, that lies deep underground, and there stands firmly and steadfastly. When our heart is once tuned into a conformity with the word of God, when we feel our will perfectly to concur with his will, we shall then presently perceive a spirit of adoption within ourselves, teaching us to cry, Abba, Father [Rom. 8:15]. We shall not then care for peeping into those hidden records of eternity, to see whether our names be written there in golden characters; no, we shall find a copy of God's thoughts concerning us written in our own breasts. There we may read the characters of his favor to us; there we may feel an inward sense of his love to us, flowing out of our hearty and unfeigned love to him. And we shall be more undoubtedly persuaded of it than if any of those winged watchmen above, that are privy to Heaven's secrets, should come and tell us that they saw our names enrolled in those volumes of eternity. Whereas, on the contrary, though we strive to persuade ourselves never so confidently, that God from all eternity hath loved us and elected us to life and happiness, if we do yet, in the meantime, entertain any iniquity within our hearts and willingly close with any lust; do what we can, we shall find many a cold qualm every now and then seizing upon us at approaching dangers. And when death itself shall grimly look us in the face, we shall feel our hearts even to die within us and our spirits quite faint away, though we strive to raise them and recover them never so much with the strong waters and *aquavitae*[5] of our ungrounded presumptions. The least inward lust willingly continued will be like a worm, fretting the gourd of our jolly confidence and presumptuous persuasion of God's love, and always gnawing at the root of it; and though we strive to keep it alive, and continually besprinkle it with some dews of our own, yet it will be always dying and withering in our bosoms. But a good conscience within will be always better to a Christian, than "health to his navel, and marrow to his bones" [Prov. 3:8]; it will be an everlasting cordial to his heart; it will be softer to him than a bed of down, and he may sleep securely upon it in the midst of raging and tempestuous seas, when the winds bluster, and the waves beat round about him. A good conscience is the best looking-glass of Heaven, in which the soul may see God's thoughts and purposes concerning it, as so many shining stars reflected to it. "Hereby we know that we know Christ, hereby we know that Christ loves us, if we keep his commandments."

II. Secondly, if hereby only we know that we know Christ, by our keeping his commandments, then the knowledge of Christ doth not consist merely in a few barren notions, in a form of certain dry and sapless opinions.

Christ came not into the world to fill our heads with mere speculations, to kindle a fire of wrangling and contentious dispute amongst us and to warm our spirits against one another with nothing but angry and peevish debates, whilst in the meantime our hearts remain all ice within towards God and have not the least spark of true heavenly fire to melt and thaw them. Christ came not to possess our brains only with some cold opinions that send down nothing but a freezing and benumbing influence upon our hearts. Christ was *vitae magister*, not *scholae* [master of life, not of the schools]; and he is the best Christian whose heart beats with the truest pulse towards heaven, not he whose head spinneth out the finest cobwebs.

He that endeavors really to mortify his lusts and to comply with that truth in his life which his conscience is convinced of, is nearer a Christian, though he never heard of Christ, than he that believes all the vulgar articles of the Christian faith and plainly denieth Christ in his life.

Surely the way to Heaven that Christ hath taught us is plain and easy, if

5. [ED.] This was a technical term in alchemy, but the word was popularly used to denote any form of ardent spirits taken as a drink.

we have but honest hearts. We need not many criticisms, many school distinctions, to come to a right understanding of it. Surely Christ came not to ensnare us and entangle us with captious niceties, or to puzzle our heads with deep speculations and lead us through hard and craggy notions into the Kingdom of Heaven. I persuade myself that no man shall ever be kept out of Heaven for not comprehending mysteries that were beyond the reach of his shallow understanding, if he had but an honest and good heart, that was ready to comply with Christ's commandments. "Say not in thy heart, Who shall ascend into Heaven?"—that is, with high speculations, to bring down Christ from thence; or "Who shall descend into the abyss beneath?"—that is, with deep searching thoughts to fetch up Christ from thence: but lo, "The word is nigh thee, even in thy mouth, and in thy heart" [Rom. 10:6–8].

But I wish it were not the distemper of our times, to scare and fright men only with opinions and make them only solicitous about the entertaining of this and that speculation, which will not render them anything the better in their lives, or the liker unto God; whilst in the meantime there is no such care taken about keeping of Christ's commandments and being renewed in our minds according to the image of God in righteousness and true holiness. We say, "Lo, here is Christ," and, "Lo, there is Christ" [Mt. 24:23], in these and these opinions, whereas in truth Christ is neither here nor there nor anywhere, but where the Spirit of Christ, where the life of Christ is.

Do we not now-a-days open and lock up Heaven with the private key of this and that opinion of our own, according to our several fancies, as we please? And if any one observe Christ's commandments never so sincerely, and serve God with faith and a pure conscience, that yet haply skills not of some contended-for opinions, some darling notions, he hath not the right *shibboleth* [Judg. 12:6], he hath not the true watch-word, he must not pass the guards into Heaven. Do we not make this and that opinion, this and that outward form, to be the wedding-garment, and boldly sentence those to outer darkness that are not invested therewith? Whereas, every true Christian finds the least dram of hearty affection towards God to be more cordial and sovereign to his soul than all the speculative notions and opinions in the world; and though he study also to inform his understanding aright, and free his mind from all error and misapprehensions, yet it is nothing but the life of Christ deeply rooted in his heart which is the chemical elixir that he feeds upon. Had he "all faith, that he could remove mountains" (as St. Paul speaks), had he "all knowledge, all tongues and languages" [cf. 1 Cor. 13:2], yet he prizeth one dram of love beyond them all. He accounteth him that feeds upon mere notions in religion to be but an airy and chameleon-like Christian. He findeth himself now otherwise rooted and centered in God than when he did before merely contemplate and gaze upon him; he tasteth and relisheth God within himself; he hath *quendam saporem Dei,* a certain savor of him, whereas before he did but rove and guess at random at him. He feeleth himself safely anchored in God and will not be dissuaded from it, though perhaps he skill not many of those subtilties, which others make the *alpha* and *omega* of their religion. Neither is he scared with those childish affrightments with which some would force their private conceits upon him; he is above the superstitious dreading of mere speculative opinions as well as the superstitious reverence of outward ceremonies; he cares not so much for subtlety as for soundness and health of mind. And, indeed, as it was well spoken by a noble philosopher, ἄνευ ἀρετῆς θεὸς ὄνομα μόνον, that "without purity and virtue, God is nothing but an empty name"; so it is as true here that without obedience to Christ's commandments, without the life of Christ dwelling in us, whatsoever opinions we entertain of him, Christ is but only named by us, he is not known.

I speak not here against a free and ingenuous inquiry into all truth, according to our several abilities and opportunities; I plead not for the captivating and enthralling of our judgments to the dictates of men; I do not disparage the natural improvement of our understanding faculties by true knowledge, which is so noble and gallant a perfection of the mind. But the thing which I aim against is the dispiriting of the life and vigor of our religion by dry speculations, and making it nothing but a mere dead skeleton of opinions, a few dry bones, without any flesh and sinews, tied up together, and the misplacing of all our zeal upon an eager prosecution of these, which should be spent to better purpose upon other objects.

Knowledge indeed is a thing far more excellent than riches, outward pleasures, worldly dignities, or anything else in the world besides holiness and the conformity of our wills to the will of God; but yet our happiness consisteth not in it, but in a certain divine temper and constitution of soul, which is far above it.

But it is a piece of that corruption that runneth through human nature, that we naturally prize truth more than goodness, knowledge more than holiness. We think it a gallant thing to be fluttering up to Heaven with our wings of knowledge and speculation, whereas the highest mystery of a divine life here, and of perfect happiness hereafter, consisteth in nothing but mere obedience to the divine will. Happiness is nothing but that inward sweet delight that will arise from the harmonious agreement between our wills and God's will.

There is nothing contrary to God in the whole world, nothing that fights against him, but self-will. This is the strong castle that we all keep garrisoned against Heaven in every one of our hearts, which God continually layeth siege unto; and it must be conquered and demolished, before we can conquer Heaven. It was by reason of this self-will, that Adam fell in paradise; that those glorious angels, those morning-stars, kept not their first station, but dropped down from heaven like falling stars, and sunk into this condition of bitterness, anxiety, and wretchedness in which now they are. They all entangled themselves with the length of their own wings, they would needs will more and otherwise than God would will in them; and, going about to make their wills wider and to enlarge them into greater amplitude, the more they struggled, they found themselves the faster pinioned, and crowded up into narrowness and servility; insomuch that now they are not able to use any wings at all, but, inheriting the serpent's curse, can only creep with their bellies upon the earth. Now, our only way to recover God and happiness again is, not to soar up with our understandings, but to destroy this self-will of ours; and then we shall find our wings to grow again, our plumes fairly spread, and ourselves raised aloft into the free air of perfect liberty, which is perfect happiness.

There is nothing in the whole world able to do us good or hurt, but God and our own will: neither riches nor poverty, nor disgrace nor honor, nor life nor death, nor angels nor devils; but willing or not willing, as we ought to do. Should Hell itself cast all its fiery darts against us, if our will be right, if it be informed by the divine will, they can do us no hurt; we have then (if I may so speak), an enchanted shield, that is impenetrable, and will bear off all. God will not hurt us and Hell cannot hurt us if we will nothing but what God wills. Nay, then we are acted by God himself, and the whole Divinity floweth in upon us; and when we have cashiered this self-will of ours, which did but shackle and confine our souls, our wills shall then become truly free, being widened and enlarged to the extent of God's own will. Hereby we know that we know Christ indeed, not by our speculative opinions concerning him, but by our keeping of his commandments.

III. Thirdly, if hereby we are to judge whether we truly know Christ, by our keeping of his commandments, so that he that saith he knoweth him and keepeth not his commandments, is a liar; then this was not the plot and design of the Gospel, to give the world an indulgence to sin, upon what pretence soever.

Though we are too prone to make such misconstructions of it, as if God had intended nothing else in it but to dandle our corrupt nature and contrive a smooth and easy way for us to come to happiness, without the toilsome labor of subduing our lusts and sinful affections: or, as if the Gospel were nothing else but a declaration to the world, of God's engaging his affections from all eternity on some particular persons in such a manner as that he would resolve to love them and dearly embrace them, though he never made them partakers of his image in righteousness and true holiness; and though they should remain under the power of all their lusts, yet they should still continue his beloved ones, and he would, notwithstanding, at last bring them undoubtedly into heaven. Which is nothing else but to make the God that we worship, the God of the New Testament, an accepter of persons, and one that should encourage that in the world which is diametrically opposite to God's own life and being.

And, indeed, nothing is more ordinary than for us to shape out such monstrous and deformed notions of God unto ourselves, by looking upon him through the colored medium of our own corrupt hearts, and having the eye of our soul tinctured by the suffusions of our own lusts. And therefore because we mortals can fondly love and hate, and sometimes hug the very vices of those to whom our affections are engaged and kiss their very deformities, we are so ready to shape out a Deity like unto ourselves, and to fashion out such a God as will, in Christ at least, hug the very wickedness of the world, and in those that be once his own, by I know not what fond affection, appropriated to himself, connive at their very sins, so that they shall not make the least breach betwixt himself and them. Truly I know not whether of the two be the worse idolatry and of a deeper stain, for a man to make a god out of a piece of wood, and fall down unto it and worship it, and say, "Deliver me, for thou art my God," as it is expressed in the prophet Isaiah [Is. 44:17]; or to set up such an idol-god of our own imagination as this is, fashioned out according to the similitude of our own fondness and wickedness: and when we should paint out God with the liveliest colors that we can possibly borrow from any created being, with the purest perfections that we can abstract from them; to draw him out thus with the blackest coal of our own corrupt hearts, and to make the very blots and blurs of our own souls to be the letters which we spell out his name by. Thus do we, that are children of the night, make black and ugly representations of

God unto ourselves, as the Ethiopians were wont to do, copying him out according to our own likeness and setting up that unto ourselves for a god which we love most dearly in ourselves, that is, our lusts. But there is no such god as this anywhere in the world, but only in some men's false imaginations, who know not, all this while, that they look upon themselves instead of God, and make an idol of themselves, which they worship and adore for him; being so full of themselves, that whatsoever they see round about them, even God himself, they color with their own tincture; like him that Aristotle speaks of, that wheresoever he went and whatsoever he looked upon, he saw still his own face, as in a glass, represented to him. And therefore it is no wonder, if men seem naturally more devoutly affected toward such an imaginary god as we have now described than to the true real God, clothed with his own proper attributes; since it is nothing but an image of themselves, which, Narcissus-like, they fall in love with. No wonder if they kiss and dandle such a baby-god as this, which, like little children, they have dressed up out of the clouts of their own fond fancies, according to their own likeness, of purpose that they might play and sport with it.

But God will ever dwell in spotless light, howsoever we paint him and disfigure him here below; he will still be circled about with his own rays of unstained and immaculate glory. And though the Gospel be not God as he is in his own brightness, but God veiled and masked to us, God in a state of humiliation and condescent, as the sun in a rainbow, yet it is nothing else but a clear and unspotted mirror of divine holiness, goodness, purity; in which attributes lie the very life and essence of God himself. The Gospel is nothing else but God descending into the world in our form, and conversing with us in our likeness; that he might allure and draw us up to God, and make us partakers of his Divine form, θεὸς γέγονεν ἄνθρωπος (as Athanasius speaks), ἵνα ἡμᾶς ἐν ἑαυτῷ θεοποίησῃ, "God was therefore incarnated and made man, that he might deify us" [6]—that is (as St. Peter expresseth it), make us partakers of the divine nature [2 Pet. 1:4]. Now, I say, the very proper character and essential tincture of God himself is nothing else but goodness. Nay, I may be bold to add that God is therefore God, because he is the highest and most perfect good; and good is not therefore good, because God out of an arbitrary will of his would have it so. Whatsoever God doth in the world, he doth it as it is suitable to the highest goodness; the first idea and fairest copy of which is his own essence.

6. [ED.] Athanasius, *De Incarnatione*, 54.

Virtue and holiness in creatures, as Plato well discourseth in his *Euthyphro*, are not therefore good because God loveth them and will have them be accounted such, but rather God therefore loveth them because they are in themselves simply good. Some of our own authors go a little further yet, and tell us that God doth not fondly love himself because he is himself, but therefore he loveth himself because he is the highest and most absolute goodness; so that if there could be anything in the world better than God, God would love that better than himself. But because he is essentially the most perfect good, therefore he cannot but love his own goodness infinitely above all other things. And it is another mistake, which sometimes we have of God, by shaping him out according to the model of ourselves, when we make him nothing but a blind, dark, impetuous self-will running through the world; such as we ourselves are furiously acted with, that have not the ballast of absolute goodness to poise and settle us.

That I may therefore come nearer to the thing in hand: God, who is absolute goodness, cannot love any of his creatures and take pleasure in them, without bestowing a communication of his goodness and likeness upon them. God cannot make a Gospel to promise men life and happiness hereafter, without being regenerated and made partakers of his holiness. As soon may Heaven and Hell be reconciled together and lovingly shake hands with one another, as God can be fondly indulgent to any sin, in whomsoever it be. As soon may light and darkness be espoused together, and midnight be married to the noonday, as God can be joined in a league of friendship to any wicked soul.

The great design of God in the Gospel is to clear up this mist of sin and corruption, which we are here surrounded with, and to bring up his creatures out of the shadow of death to the region of light above the land of truth and holiness. The great mystery of the Gospel is to establish a god-like frame and disposition of spirit, which consists in righteousness and true holiness in the hearts of men. And Christ, who is the great and mighty Savior, came on purpose into the world, not only to save us from fire and brimstone but also to save us from our sins. Christ hath therefore made an expiation of our sins by his death upon the cross, that we, being thus delivered out of the hands of these our greatest enemies, might serve God without fear, in holiness and righteousness before him all the days of our life [Lk. 1:74–75]. This "grace of God, that bringeth salvation," hath therefore "appeared unto all men, in the Gospel, that it might teach us to deny ungodliness and worldly lusts, and that we should live soberly, righteously and godlily in this present world; looking for that blessed hope, and glorious appearing of the great God and our Savior Jesus Christ, who gave himself for us, that he might redeem us from all iniquity, and purify unto himself a peculiar people, zealous of good works" [Tit. 2:11–14]. "These things I write unto you" (saith our apostle a little before my text) "that you sin not"; therein expressing the end of the whole Gospel, which is, not only to cover sin by spreading the purple robe of Christ's death and sufferings over it, whilst it still remaineth in us with all its filth and noisomeness unremoved; but also to convey a powerful and mighty spirit of holiness, to cleanse us and free us from it. And this is a greater grace of God to us, than the former, which still go both together in the Gospel; besides the free remission and pardon of sin in the blood of Christ, the delivering of us from the power of sin by the Spirit of Christ dwelling in our hearts.

Christ came not into the world only to cast a mantle over us, and hide all our filthy sores from God's avenging eye, with his merits and righteousness; but he came likewise to be a surgeon and physician of souls, to free us from the filth and corruption of them; which is more grievous and burdensome, more noisome to a true Christian, than the guilt of sin itself.

Should a poor wretched and diseased creature, that is full of sores and ulcers, be covered all over with purple or clothed with scarlet, he would take but little contentment in it, whilst his sores and wounds remain upon him; and he had much rather be arrayed in rags, so he might obtain but soundness and health within. The Gospel is a true Bethesda, a pool of grace, where such poor, lame and infirm creatures as we are, upon the moving of God's Spirit in it, may descend down, not only to wash our skin and outside, but also to be cured of our diseases within [cf. Jn. 5:2–4]. And whatever the world thinks, there is a powerful Spirit that moves upon these waters, the waters of the Gospel, for this new creation, the regeneration of souls; the very same Spirit that once moved upon the waters of the universe at the first creation, and spreading its mighty wings over them did hatch the newborn world into this perfection: I say, the same almighty spirit of Christ still worketh in the Gospel, spreading its gentle, healing, quickening wings over our souls. The Gospel is not like Abana and Pharpar, those common rivers of Damascus, that could only cleanse the outside, but it is a true Jordan, in which such leprous Naamans as we all are, "may wash and be clean" [2 Kings 5:13]. "Blessed indeed are they, whose iniquities are forgiven, and whose sins are covered: Blessed is the man to whom the Lord will not impute sin" [Ps. 32:1–2]; but yet rather blessed are they, whose sins are removed like a morning cloud, and quite taken away from them [Hos. 13:3]. Blessed, thrice "blessed are they, that hunger and thirst after righteousness, for they shall be satisfied; blessed are the pure in heart, for they shall see God" [Mt. 5:6,8].

Our Savior Christ came (as John the Baptist tells us) "with a fan in his hand, that he might thoroughly purge his floor, and gather his wheat into his garner; but the chaff he will burn up with unquenchable fire" [Lk. 3:17]. He came (as the prophet Malachi speaks) "like a refiner's fire, and like fullers' soap; to sit as a refiner and purifier of silver, and to purify all the sons of Levi, and purge them as gold and silver, that they may offer unto the Lord an offering in righteousness" [Mal. 3:2,3].

Christ came not only to write "Holiness to the Lord" upon Aaron's forehead, and to put his Urim and Thummim upon his breast-plate [Ex. 28:30, 36,38]; but, "This is the covenant, saith the Lord, that I will make with them in those days; I will put my law in their inward parts, and write it in their hearts; and then I will be their God, and they shall be my people" [Jer. 31:33]. They shall be all kings and priests unto me. "God sent his own Son" (saith St. Paul) "in the likeness of sinful flesh, and by a sacrifice for sin condemned sin in the flesh; that the righteousness of the law might be fulfilled in us, who walk not after the flesh, but after the spirit" [Rom. 8:3,4].

The first Adam, as the Scripture tells us, brought in a real defilement, which, like a noisome leprosy, hath overspread all mankind; and therefore the second Adam must not only fill the world with a conceit of holiness and mere imaginary righteousness; but he must really convey such an immortal seed of grace into the hearts of true believers as may prevail still more and more in them, till it have at last quite wrought out that poison of the serpent.

Christ, that was nothing but Divinity dwelling in a tabernacle of flesh, and God himself immediately acting a human nature, came into the world to kindle here that divine life amongst men, which is certainly dearer unto God than anything else whatsoever in the world, and to propagate this celestial fire from one heart still unto another until the end of the world. Neither is he, nor was he, ever absent from this spark of his Divinity kindled amongst men, wheresoever it be, though he seem bodily to be withdrawn from us. He is the standing, constant, inexhausted fountain of this divine light and heat, that still toucheth every soul that is enlivened by it, with an outstretched ray, and freely lends his beams and disperseth his influence to all, from the beginning of the world to the end of it. "We all received of his fullness grace for grace" [Jn. 1:16]; as all the stars in heaven are said to light their candles at the sun's flame. For though his body be withdrawn from us, yet by the lively and virtual contact of his Spirit he is always kindling, cheering, quickening, warming and enlivening hearts. Nay, this divine life, begun and kindled in any heart, wheresoever it be, is something of God in flesh, and, in a sober and qualified sense, Divinity incarnate; and all particular Christians, that are really possessed of it, so many mystical Christs.

And God forbid that God's own life and nature, here in the world, should be forlorn, forsaken, and abandoned of God himself. Certainly, wherever it is, though never so little, like a sweet, young, tender babe, once born in any heart, when it crieth unto God the father of it, with pitiful and bemoaning looks imploring his compassion, it cannot choose but move his fatherly bowels, and make them yearn and turn towards it, and by strong sympathy draw his compassionate arm to help and relieve it. Never was any tender infant so dear to those bowels that begat it, as an infant new-born Christ, formed in the heart of any true believer, to God the father of it. Shall the children of this world, the sons of darkness, be moved with such tender affection and compassion towards the fruit of their bodies, their own natural offspring?—and shall God, who is the father of lights, the fountain of all goodness, be moved with no compassion towards his true spiritual offspring, and have no regard to those sweet babes of light, engendered by his own beams in men's hearts, that, in their lovely countenances, bear the resemblance of his own face, and call him their father? Shall he see them lie fainting and gasping and dying here in the world, for want of nothing to preserve and keep them, but an influence from him who first gave them life and breath? No, hear the language of God's heart, hear the sounding of his bowels towards them: "Is it Ephraim, my dear son? is it that pleasant child? Since I spake of him, I do earnestly remember him; my bowels," my bowels "are troubled for him; I will surely have mercy upon him, saith the Lord" [cf. Jer. 31:20]. If those expressions of goodness and tender affection here among the creatures be but drops of that full ocean that is in God, how can we then imagine, that this father of our spirits should have so little regard to his own dear offspring, I do not say our souls, but that, which is the very life and soul of our souls, the life of God in us (which is nothing else but God's own self communicated to us, his own Son born in our hearts), as that he should suffer it to be cruelly murdered in its infancy by our sins, and like young Hercules, in its very cradle to be strangled by those filthy vipers that he should see him to be crucified by wicked lusts, nailed fast to the cross by invincible corruptions, pierced and gored on every side with the poisonous spears of the devil's temptations, and at last to give up the ghost; and yet his tender heart not at all relent nor be at all this while impassionated with so sad a spectacle? Surely we cannot think he hath such an adamantine breast, such a flinty nature, as this is.

What then? Must we say that though indeed he be willing, yet he is not able to rescue his crucified and tormented Son now bleeding upon the cross; to take him down from thence, and save him; then must sin be more powerful than God; that weak, crazy and sickly thing more strong than the Rock of ages; and the devil, the prince of darkness, more mighty than the God of light. No, surely, there is a weakness and impotency in all evil, a masculine strength and vigor in all goodness; and therefore, doubtless, the highest good, the πρῶτον ἀγαθὸν as the philosopher calls it, is the strongest thing in the world. "Nil potentius summo Bono." [7] God's power, displayed in the world, is nothing but his goodness strongly reaching all things from height to depth, from the highest Heaven to the lowest Hell; and irresistibly imparting itself to everything, according to those several degrees in which it is capable of it.

Have the fiends of darkness then, those poor forlorn spirits, that are fettered and locked up in the chains of their own wickedness, any strength to withstand the force of infinite goodness, which is infinite power? or do they not rather skulk in holes of darkness, and fly, like bats and owls, before the approaching beams of this Sun of Righteousness? Is God powerful to kill and to destroy, to damn and to torment? and is he not powerful to save? Nay, it is the sweetest flower in all the garland of his attributes, it is the richest diamond in his crown of glory, that he is "mighty to save" [Is. 63: 1]—and this is far more magnificent for him, than to be styled "mighty to destroy." For that, except it be in the way of justice, speaks no power at all, but mere impotency; for the root of all power is goodness.

Or must we say, lastly, that God indeed is able to rescue us out of the power of sin and Satan, when we sigh and groan towards him; but yet sometimes, to exercise his absolute authority, his uncontrollable dominion, he delights rather in plunging wretched souls down into infernal night and everlasting darkness? What shall we then make the God of the whole world? Nothing but a cruel and dreadful *Erinnys* [8] with curled fiery

7. [ED.] "Nothing is more powerful than the Supreme Good."
8. [ED.] The Erinyes were Greek goddesses of vengeance. Homer speaks sometimes of one, sometimes of several. Euripides put their number at three. The grim details given by Cudworth are from the *Eumenides* of Aeschylus. The Erinyes were the avengers of offences against the natural order, especially those which might endanger society. The Roman Furies are to be identified with them.

snakes about his head and firebrands in his hands, thus governing the world? Surely this will make us either secretly to think that there is no God at all in the world, if he must needs be such; or else to wish heartily there were none. But, doubtless, God will at last confute all these our mis-apprehensions of him; he will unmask our hypocritical pretences, and clearly cast the shame of all our sinful deficiencies upon ourselves, and vindicate his own glory from receiving the least stain or blemish by them. In the meantime let us know, that the Gospel now requireth far more of us than ever the law did; for it requireth a new creature, a divine nature, Christ formed in us. But yet withal it bestoweth a quickening spirit, an enlivening power, to enable us to express that which is required of us. Whosoever therefore truly knows Christ, the same also keepeth Christ's commandments. But "he that saith, I know him, and keepeth not his commandments, is a liar, and the truth is not in him."

I have now done with the first part of my discourse, concerning those observations which arise naturally from the words and offer themselves to us. I shall, in the next place, proceed to make some general application of them all together.

Now therefore, I beseech you, let us consider whether or no we know Christ indeed, not by our acquaintance with systems and models of divinity, not by our skill in books and papers, but by our keeping of Christ's commandments. All the books and writings which we converse with, they can but represent spiritual objects to our understandings, which yet we can never see in their own true figure, color and proportion, until we have a Divine light within to irradiate and shine upon them. Though there be never such excellent truths concerning Christ and his Gospel set down in words and letters, yet they will be but unknown characters to us until we have a living Spirit within us, that can decipher them; until the same Spirit, by secret whispers in our hearts, do comment upon them, which did at first indite them. There be many that understand the Greek and Hebrew of the Scripture, the original languages in which the text was written, that never understood the language of the Spirit.

There is a *caro* and a *spiritus*, a flesh and a spirit, a body and a soul in all the writings of the Scriptures. It is but the flesh and body of divine truths that is printed upon paper; which many moths of books and libraries do only feed upon; many walking skeletons of knowledge, that bury and entomb truths in the living sepulchers of their souls, do only converse with; such as never did anything else but pick at the mere bark and rind of truths, and crack the shells of them. But there is a soul and spirit of divine truths that could never yet be congealed into ink, that could never be blotted upon paper; which, by a secret traduction and conveyance, passeth from one soul unto another, being able to dwell or lodge nowhere but in a spiritual being, in a living thing, because itself is nothing but life and spirit. Neither can it, where indeed it is, express itself sufficiently in words and sounds, but it will best declare and speak itself in actions, as the old manner of writing among the Egyptians was not by words but things. The life of divine truths is better expressed in actions than in words, because actions are more living things than words. Words are nothing but the dead resemblances and pictures of those truths which live and breathe in actions; and "the kingdom of God (as the apostle speaketh) consisteth not in word" [1 Cor. 4:20], but in life and power. Τὰ πρόβατα οὐ χόρτον φέροντα τοῖς ποιμέσιν ἐπιδεικύει πόσον ἔφαγεν (saith the moral philosopher), ἀλλὰ τὴν νομὴν ἔσω πέψαντα ἔριον ἔξω φέρει καὶ γάλα: "Sheep do not come and bring their fodder to their shepherd, and show him how much they eat; but inwardly concocting and digesting it, they make it appear by the fleece which they wear upon their backs, and by the milk which they give." [9] And let not us Christians affect only to talk and dispute Christ, and so measure our knowledge of him by our words; but let us shew ἀπὸ τῶν θεωρημάτων πεφθέντων τὰ ἔργα, "our knowledge concocted into our lives and actions"; and then let us really manifest that we are Christ's sheep indeed, that we are his disciples, by that fleece of holiness which we wear, and by the fruits that we daily yield in our lives and conversations: for "herein" (saith Christ) "is my Father glorified, that ye bear much fruit; so shall ye be my disciples" [Jn. 15:8].

Let us not, I beseech you, judge of our knowing Christ by our ungrounded persuasions that Christ from all eternity hath loved us and given himself particularly for us, without the conformity of our lives to Christ's commandments, without the real partaking of the image of Christ in our hearts. The great mystery of the Gospel doth not lie only in Christ without us (though we must know also what he hath done for us), but the very pith and kernel of it consists in Christ inwardly formed in our hearts.

Nothing is truly ours but what lives in our spirits. Salvation itself cannot save us as long as it is only without us, no more than health can cure us and make us sound, when it is not within us but somewhere at a distance from us; no more than arts and sciences, whilst they lie only in books and papers without us, can make us learned. The Gospel, though it be a sovereign and medicinal thing in itself, yet the mere knowing and believing

9. [ED.] Epictetus, *The Enchiridion*, 46.

of the history of it will do us no good; we can receive no virtue from it, till it be inwardly digested and concocted into our souls, till it be made ours and become a living thing in our hearts. The Gospel if it be only without us, cannot save us, no more than that physician's bill could cure the ignorant patient of his disease, who, when it was commended to him, took the paper only, and put it up in his pocket, but never drank the potion that was described in it.

All that Christ did for us in the flesh, when he was here upon earth, from his lying in a manger when he was born in Bethlehem to his bleeding upon the cross on Golgotha, it will not save us from our sins unless Christ by his Spirit dwell in us. It will not avail us to believe that he was born of a virgin, unless the power of the Most High overshadow our hearts, and beget him there likewise. It will not profit us to believe that he died upon the cross for us unless we be baptized into his death by the mortification of all our lusts, unless the old man of sin be crucified in our hearts. Christ indeed hath made an expiation for our sins upon his cross, and the blood of Christ is the only sovereign balsam to free us from the guilt of them; but yet, besides the sprinkling of the blood of Christ upon us, we must be made partakers also of his spirit. Christ came into the world, as well to redeem us from the power and bondage of our sins, as to free us from the guilt of them. "You know" (saith St. John) "that he was manifested to take away our sins; whosoever therefore abideth in him, sinneth not; whosoever sinneth, hath not seen nor known him" [cf. 1 Jn. 3:5,6]. Lo the end of Christ's coming into the world! Lo, a design worthy of God manifested in the flesh!

Christ did not take all those pains to lay aside his robes of glory, and come down hither into the world, to enter into a virgin's womb, to be born in our human shape, and to be laid a poor crying infant in a manger, and having no form or comeliness at all upon him, to take upon him the form of a servant, to undergo a reproachful and ignominious life, and at last to be abandoned to a shameful death, a death upon the cross; I say, he did not do all this merely to bring a notion into the world, without producing any real and substantial effect at all; without the changing, mending and reforming of the world, so that men should still be as wicked as they were before, and as much under the power of the prince of darkness, only they should not be thought so; they should still remain as full of all the filthy sores of sin and corruption as before, only they should be accounted whole. Shall God come down from heaven, and pitch a tabernacle amongst men? Shall he undertake such a huge design, and make so great a noise of doing something, which, when it is all summed up, shall not at last amount to a reality? Surely Christ did not undergo all this to so little purpose; he would not take all this pains for us, that he might be able at last to put into our hands nothing but a blank. He "was with child," he "was in pain and travail"; and hath "he brought forth nothing but wind? Hath he been delivered of the east wind?" [loosely quoted from Is. 26:18]. Is that great design, that was so long carried in the womb of eternity, now proved abortive, or else nothing but a mere windy birth? No surely: the end of the Gospel is life and perfection; it is a divine nature; it is a god-like frame and disposition of spirit; it is to make us partakers of the image of God in righteousness and true holiness, without which salvation itself were but a notion.

Christ came indeed into the world to make an expiation and atonement for our sins; but the end of this was, that we might eschew sin; that we might forsake all ungodliness and worldly lusts. The Gospel declares pardon of sin to those that are heavy laden with it and willing to be disburdened, to this end, that it might quicken and enliven us to new obedience. Whereas otherwise the guilt of sin might have detained us in horror and despair, and so have kept us still more strongly under the power of it, in sad and dismal apprehensions of God's wrath provoked against us and inevitably falling on us. But Christ hath now appeared like a day-star, with most cheerful beams; nay, he is the Sun of Righteousness himself, which hath risen upon the world with his healing wings, with his exhilarating light, that he might chase away all those black despairing thoughts from us [cf. 2 Pet. 1:19; Mal. 4:2]. But Christ did not rise that we should play and sport and wantonize with his light; but that we should do "the works of the day" in it [cf. Jn. 9:4]; that we should walk εὐσχημόνως [decently] (as the apostle speaketh) not in our night-clothes of sinful deformity, but clad all over with the comely garments of light [cf. 1 Thess. 4:12; Eph. 5:8]. The Gospel is not big with child of a fancy, of a mere conceit of righteousness without us, hanging at a distance over us, whilst our hearts within are nothing but cages of unclean birds, and like houses continually haunted with devils, nay, the very rendezvous of those fiends of darkness.

Holiness is the best thing that God himself can bestow upon us, either in this world or the world to come. True evangelical holiness, that is, Christ formed in the hearts of believers, is the very cream and quintessence of the Gospel. And were our hearts sound within, were there not many thick and dark fumes that did arise from thence and cloud our understandings, we could not easily conceive the substance of Heaven itself to be anything else but holiness, freed from those encumbrances that did ever clog it and accloy it here; neither should we wish for any other Heaven besides this. But many of us are like those children, whose stomachs are so vitiated by some disease, that they think ashes, coal, mud wall, or any such trash, to be more pleasant than the most wholesome food; such sickly and distempered appetites have we about these spiritual things, that hanker after I know not what vain shows of happiness, whilst in the mean time we neglect that which is the only true food of our souls, that is able solidly to nourish them up to everlasting life.

Grace is holiness militant, holiness encumbered with many enemies and difficulties, which it still fights against, and manfully quits itself of; and glory is nothing else but holiness triumphant, holiness with a palm of victory in her hand, and a crown upon her head: "Deus ipse cum omni sua bonitate, quatenus extra me est, non facit me beatum, sed quatenus in me est: God himself cannot make me happy, if he be only without me, and unless he give in a participation of himself and his own likeness into my soul." Happiness is nothing but the releasing and unfettering of our souls from all these narrow, scant and particular good things; and the espousing of them to the highest and most universal good, which is not this or that particular good, but goodness itself; and this is the same thing that we call holiness. Which, because we ourselves are so little acquainted with (being for the most part ever courting a mere shadow of it), therefore we have such low, abject and beggarly conceits thereof; whereas it is in itself the most noble, heroical and generous thing in the world. For I mean by holiness nothing else but God stamped and printed upon the soul. And we may please ourselves with what conceits we will; but so long as we are void of this, we do but dream of Heaven, and I know not what fond paradise; we do but blow up and down an airy bubble of our own fancies, which riseth out of the froth of our vain hearts; we do but court a painted Heaven, and woo happiness in a picture, whilst in the meantime a true and real Hell will suck in our souls into it, and soon make us sensible of a solid woe and substantial misery.

Divine wisdom hath so ordered the frame of the whole universe, as that everything should have a certain proper place, that should be a receptacle for it. Hell is the sink of all sin and wickedness. The strong magic of nature pulls and draws everything continually to that place, which is suitable to it, and to which it doth belong; so all these heavy bodies press downwards towards the center of our earth, being drawn in by it; in like manner Hell, wheresoever it is, will by strong sympathy pull in all sin, and magnetically draw it to itself; as true holiness is always breathing upwards, and fluttering towards Heaven, striving to embosom itself with God; and it will at last undoubtedly be conjoined with him. No dismal shades of darkness can possibly stop it in its course or beat it back.

'Ὡς αἰεὶ τὸ ὅμοιον ἄγει θεὸς εἰς τὸ ὅμοιον.[10]

Nay, we do but deceive ourselves with names. Hell is nothing but the orb of sin and wickedness, or else that hemisphere of darkness in which all evil moves; and Heaven is the opposite hemisphere of light, or else, if you please, the bright orb of truth, holiness and goodness; and we do actually in this life instate ourselves in the possession of one or other of them. Take sin and disobedience out of Hell, and it will presently clear up into light, tranquility, serenity, and shine out into a Heaven. Every true saint carrieth his Heaven about with him in his own heart; and Hell, that is without him, can have no power over him. He might safely wade through Hell itself, and, like the three children, pass through the midst of that fiery furnace, and yet not at all be scorched with the flames of it; he might walk through the valley of the shadow of death, and yet fear no evil [cf. Dan. 3:25; Ps. 23:4].

Sin is the only thing in the world that is contrary to God. God is light, and that is darkness. God is beauty, and that is ugliness and deformity. All sin is direct rebellion against God; and with what notions soever we may sugar it and sweeten it, yet God can never smile upon it. He will never make a truce with it. God declares open war against sin and bids defiance to it, for it is a professed enemy to God's own life and being. God, which is infinite Goodness, cannot but hate sin, which is purely evil. And though sin be in itself but a poor, impotent and crazy thing, nothing but straitness, poverty, and nonentity, so that of itself it is the most wretched and miserable thing in the world, and needeth no farther punishment besides itself; yet divine vengeance beats it off still farther and farther from God, and, wheresoever it is, will be sure to scourge it and lash it continually. God and sin can never agree together.

That I may therefore yet come nearer to ourselves: this is the message that I have now to declare unto you, that "God is light, and in him is no darkness at all. If we say, that we have fellowship with him, and walk in darkness, we lie, and do not the truth" [1 Jn. 1:5–6]. Christ and the Gospel are light, and there is no darkness at all in them; if you say, that you know

10. [ED.] Homer, *The Odyssey*, Bk. XVII, line 218: "As ever the god is bringing the like and the like together."

Christ and his Gospel, and yet keep not Christ's commandments but dearly hug your private darling corruptions, you are liars and the truth is not in you; you have no acquaintance with the God of light, nor with the Gospel of light. If any of you say that you know Christ and have an interest in him, and yet (as I fear too many do) still nourish ambition, pride, vain-glory within your breasts, harbor malice, revengefulness and cruel hatred to your neighbors in your hearts, eagerly scramble after this worldly pelf, and make the strength of your parts and endeavors serve that blind mammon, the god of this world; if you wallow and tumble in the filthy puddle of fleshly pleasures, or if you aim only at yourselves in your lives and make yourself the compass by which you sail and the star by which you steer your course, looking at nothing higher and more noble than yourselves; deceive not yourselves, you have neither seen Christ nor known him. You are deeply incorporated (if I may so speak) with the spirit of this world, and have no true sympathy with God and Christ, no fellowship at all with them.

And, I beseech you, let us consider: be there not many of us, that pretend much to Christ, that are plainly in our lives as proud, ambitious, vain-glorious as any others? Be there not many of us, that are as much under the power of unruly passions, as cruel, revengeful, malicious, censorious as others? that have our minds as deeply engaged in the world, and as much envassalled to riches, gain, profit, those great admired deities of the sons of men, and their souls as much overwhelmed and sunk with the cares of this life? Do not many of us as much give ourselves to the pleasures of the flesh, and though not without regrets of conscience, yet ever now and then secretly soak ourselves in them? Be there not many of us that have as deep a share likewise in injustice and oppression, in vexing the fatherless and the widows? I wish it may not prove some of our cases at that last day, to use such pleas as these unto Christ in our behalf: "Lord I have prophesied in thy name; I have preached many a zealous sermon for thee; I have kept many a long fast; I have been very active for thy cause in church, in state; nay, I never made any question, but that my name was written in thy book of life": when yet, alas! we shall receive no other return from Christ but this: "I know you not; depart from me, ye workers of iniquity" [cf. Mt. 25:41]. I am sure there be too many of us, that have long pretended to Christ, which make little or no progress in true Christianity, that is, holiness of life; that ever hang hovering in a twilight of grace, and never seriously put ourselves forward into clear daylight, but esteem that glimmering *crepusculum* which we are in, and like that faint twilight better than broad open day; whereas "the path of the just (as the wise man speaks) is as the shining light, that shineth more and more unto the perfect day" [Prov. 4:18]. I am sure there be many of us that are perpetual dwarfs in our spiritual stature, like those silly women (that St. Paul speaks of) laden with sins, and led away with divers lusts, that are "ever learning and never able to come to the knowledge of the truth" [2 Tim. 3:6–7]; that we are not now one jot taller in Christianity than we were many years ago, but have still as sickly, crazy and unsound a temper of soul as we had long before.

Indeed, we seem to do something; we are always moving and lifting at the stone of corruption that lies upon our hearts, but yet we never stir it notwithstanding, or at least never roll it off from us. We are sometimes a little troubled with the guilt of our sins, and then we think we must thrust our lusts out of our hearts; but afterwards we sprinkle ourselves over with I know not what holy water, and so are contented to let them still abide quietly within us. We do every day truly confess the same sins, and pray against them; and yet still commit them as much as ever, and lie as deeply under the power of them. We have the same water to pump out in every prayer, and still we let the same leak in again upon us. We make a great deal of noise, and raise a great deal of dust with our feet; but we do not move from off the ground on which we stood, we do not go forward at all; or if we do sometimes make a little progress, we quickly lose again the ground which we had gained; like those upper planets in the heaven, which (as the astronomers tell us) sometimes move forwards, sometimes quite backwards, and sometimes perfectly stand still; have their stations and retrogradations as well as their direct motions. As if religion were nothing else but a dancing up and down upon the same piece of ground, and making several motions and friskings on it; and not a sober journeying and travelling onwards toward some certain place. We do and undo; we do "*Penelopes telam texere* [weave Penelope's web]"; we weave sometimes a web of holiness, but then we let our lusts come, and undo and unravel all again. Like Sisyphus in the fable, we roll up a mighty stone with much ado, sweating and tugging up the hill; and then we let it go, and tumble down again unto the bottom; and this is our constant work. Like those Danaides which the poets speak of, we are always filling water into a sieve, by our prayers, duties and performances, which still runs out as fast as we pour it in.[11]

11. In *The Odyssey*, Penelope, wife of Odysseus, deferred giving an answer to her suitors by telling them that she must first finish her weaving; each night she unravelled

What is it that thus cheats us and gulls us of our religion?—that makes us thus constantly to tread the same ring and circle of duties, where we make no progress at all forwards, and the farther we go are still never the nearer to our journey's end? What is it that thus starves our religion, and makes it look like those kine in Pharaoh's dream, ill-favored and lean-fleshed [Gen. 41:3], that it hath no color in its face, no blood in its veins, no life nor heat at all in its members? What is it that doth thus bedwarf us in our Christianity? What low, sordid, and unworthy principles do we act by, that thus hinder our growth, and make us stand at a stay, and keep us always in the very porch and entrance where we first began? Is it a sleepy, sluggish conceit that it is enough for us if we be but once in a state of grace; if we have but once stepped over the threshold, we need not take so great pains to travel any farther? Or is it another damping, choking, stifling opinion, that Christ hath done all for us already without us, and nothing need more to be done within us? no matter how wicked we be in ourselves, for we have holiness without us; no matter how sickly and diseased our souls be within, for they have health without them. Why may we not as well be satisfied and contented to have happiness without us too to all eternity, and so ourselves for ever continue miserable? "Little children, let no man deceive you; he that doeth righteousness is righteous, even as he is righteous; but he that committeth sin is of the devil" [1 Jn. 3:7–8]. I shall therefore exhort you in the wholesome words of St. Peter: "Give all diligence to add to your faith, virtue; and to virtue, knowledge; and the knowledge, temperance; and to temperance, patience; to patience, godliness; and to godliness, brotherly kindness; and to brotherly kindness, charity. For if these things be in you and abound, they make you, that ye shall neither be barren nor unfruitful in the knowledge of our Lord Jesus Christ" [2 Pet. 1:5–8]. The apostle still goes on, and I cannot leave him yet: "But he that lacketh these things is blind, and cannot see far off, and hath forgotten that he was once purged from his old sins. Wherefore the rather, brethren, give diligence to make your calling and election sure; for if ye do these things, ye shall never fall" [2 Pet. 1:9–10]. Let us not only talk and dispute of Christ, but let us indeed put on the Lord Jesus Christ [cf. Rom. 13:14]. Having those great and precious promises which he

---

what she had woven during the day. Sisyphus, king of Corinth (also in *The Odyssey*), was condemned in Hades to roll a huge stone up a hill; and when he reached the top it always rolled down again. The daughters of Danaus, king of Argos, murdered their husbands on their wedding night and were condemned eternally to fill sieves with water. The Danaides are mentioned by Apollodorus, but this myth comes from the *Axiochus*, a work falsely attributed to Plato.

hath given us, let us strive to be made partakers of the divine nature, escaping corruption that is in the world through lust [cf. 2 Pet. 1:4]; and being begotten again to a lively hope of enjoying Christ hereafter, let us purify ourselves, as he is pure [cf. 1 Pet. 1:3; 1 Jn. 3:3].

Let us really declare that we know Christ, that we are his disciples, by our keeping of his commandments; and, amongst the rest, that commandment especially, which our Savior Christ himself commendeth to his disciples in a peculiar manner: "This is my commandment, that ye love one another, as I have loved you"; and again, "These things I command you that you love one another. Let us follow peace with all men, and holiness, without which no man shall see God. Let us put on, as the elect of God, holy and beloved, bowels of mercies, kindness, humbleness of mind, meekness, long-suffering; forbearing one another, and forgiving one another, if any man have a quarrel against any, even as Christ forgave us: and above all these things let us put on charity, which is the bond of perfectness. Let us in meekness instruct those that oppose themselves; if God peradventure will give them repentance to the acknowledging of the truth; that they may recover themselves out of the snares of the devil, who are taken captive by him at his will. Beloved, let us love one another; for love is of God, and whosoever loveth is born of God and knoweth God." [12]

O Divine love! the sweet harmony of souls! the music of angels! the joy of God's own heart! the very darling of his bosom! the source of true happiness! the pure quintessence of heaven! that which reconciles the jarring principles of the world, and makes them all chime together! that which melts men's hearts into one another! See how St. Paul describes it, and it cannot choose but enamor your affections towards it: "Love envieth not, . . . it is not puffed up, it doth not behave itself unseemly, seeketh not her own, is not easily provoked, thinketh no evil, rejoiceth not in iniquity . . . ; beareth all things, believeth all things, hopeth all things, endureth all things" [1 Cor. 13:4–7]. I may add, in a word, it is the best-natured thing, the best-complexioned thing in the world. Let us express this sweet harmonious affection in these jarring times, that so, if it be possible, we may tune the world at last into better music. Especially in matters of religion, let us strive with all meekness to instruct and convince one another. Let us endeavor to promote the Gospel of peace, the dove-like Gospel, with a dove-like spirit. This was the way by which the Gospel at first was propagated in the world: Christ did not cry, nor lift up his

12. [ED.] This is a composite passage: Jn. 15:12,17; Heb. 12:14; Col. 3:12–14; 2 Tim. 2:25–26; 1 Jn. 4:7.

voice in the streets; a bruised reed he did not break, and the smoking flax he did not quench, and yet he brought "forth judgment unto victory" [Is. 42:3; Mt. 12:20]. He whispered the Gospel to us from mount Sion, in a still voice; and yet the sound thereof went out quickly throughout all the earth. The Gospel at first came down upon the world gently and softly like the dew upon Gideon's fleece, and yet it quickly soaked quite through it [cf. Judg. 6:37]. And doubtless this is still the most effectual way to promote it farther. Sweetness and ingenuity will more powerfully command men's minds than passion, sourness and severity; as the soft pillow sooner breaks the flint, than the hardest marble. Let us ἀληθεύειν ἐν ἀγάπῃ, "follow truth in love" [cf. Eph. 4:15]—and of the two, indeed, be contented rather to miss of the conveying of a speculative truth, than to part with love. When we would convince men of any error by the strength of truth, let us withal pour the sweet balm of love upon their heads. Truth and love are two of the most powerful things in the world; and when they both go together, they cannot easily be withstood. The golden beams of truth and the silken cords of love, twisted together, will draw men on with a sweet violence, whether they will or no.

Let us take heed we do not sometimes call that zeal for God and his Gospel, which is nothing else but our own tempestuous and stormy passion. True zeal is a sweet, heavenly and gentle flame, which maketh us active for God, but always within the sphere of love. It never calls for fire from heaven to consume those that differ a little from us in their apprehensions [cf. Lk. 9:54]. It is like that kind of lightning (which the philosophers speak of) that melts the sword within, but singeth not the scabbard: it strives to save the soul, but hurteth not the body. True zeal is a loving thing, and makes us always active to edification and not to destruction. If we keep the fire of zeal within the chimney, in its own proper place, it never doth any hurt; it only warmeth, quickeneth and enliveneth us; but if once we let it break out, and catch hold of the thatch of our flesh, and kindle our corrupt nature, and set the house of our body on fire, it is no longer zeal, it is no heavenly fire, it is a most destructive and devouring thing. True zeal is an *ignis lambens*, a soft and gentle flame, that will not scorch one's hand; it is no predatory or voracious thing; but carnal and fleshly zeal is like the spirit of gunpowder set on fire, that tears and blows up all that stands before it. True zeal is like the vital heat in us, that we live upon, which we never feel to be angry or troublesome; but though it gently feed upon the radical oil within us, that sweet balsam of our natural moisture, yet it lives lovingly with it, and maintains that by which is it fed. But that other furious and distempered zeal is nothing but a fever in the soul. To conclude, we may learn what kind of zeal it is that we should make use of in promoting the Gospel, by an emblem of God's own, given us in the Scriptures, those fiery tongues, that, upon the day of Pentecost, sat upon the apostles, which sure were harmless flames, for we cannot read that they did any hurt or that they did so much as singe a hair of their heads [cf. Acts 2:3].

I will therefore shut up this with that of the apostle: "Let us keep the unity of the Spirit in the bond of peace" [cf. Eph. 4:3]. Let this soft and silken knot of love tie our hearts together though our heads and apprehensions cannot meet, as indeed they never will, but always stand at some distance off from one another. Our zeal, if it be heavenly, if it be true vestal fire kindled from above, will not delight to tarry here below, burning up straw and stubble and such combustible things, and sending up nothing but gross earthy fumes to heaven. But it will rise up and return back pure as it came down, and will be ever striving to carry up men's hearts to God along with it. It will be only occupied about the promoting of those things which are unquestionably good; and when it moves in the irascible way, it will quarrel with nothing but sin. Here let our zeal busy and exercise itself, every one of us beginning first at our own hearts. Let us be more zealous than ever we have yet been in fighting against our lusts, in pulling down these strongholds of sin and Satan in our hearts. Here let us exercise all our courage and resolution, our manhood and magnanimity.

Let us trust in the almighty arm of our God, and doubt not but he will as well deliver us from the power of sin in our hearts, as preserve us from the wrath to come. Let us go out against these uncircumcised Philistines, I mean our lusts, not with shield or spear, not in any confidence of our own strength, but in the name of the Lord of hosts; and we shall prevail, we shall overcome our lusts: "For greater is he that is in us, than he that is in them.—The eternal God is our refuge, and underneath are the everlasting arms; he shall thrust out these enemies from before us; and he shall say, Destroy them" [cf. 2 Kings 6:16; Deut. 33:27].We shall enter the true Canaan, the good land of promise, "that floweth with milk and honey" [Num. 13:27], the land of truth and holiness. "Wherefore take unto you the whole armor of God, that you may be able to withstand. Let your loins be girt about with truth; have on the breast-plate of righteousness; and let your feet be shod with the preparation of the gospel of peace. Above all take the shield of faith, whereby ye shall be able to quench all the fiery darts of the wicked; and take the helmet of salvation, and the sword of the Spirit, which is the word of God" [cf. Eph. 6:13–17]. And lastly, be sure of this, that ye "be strong only in the Lord, and in the power of his might" [cf. Eph. 6:10].

There be some that dishearten us in this spiritual warfare and would make us let our weapons fall out of our hands by working in us a despair of victory. There be some evil spies that weaken the hands and the hearts of the children of Israel and bring an ill report upon that land, that we are to conquer, telling of nothing but strange giants, the sons of Anak, there, that we shall never be able to overcome. "The Amalekites (say they) dwell in the south, the Hittites, Jebusites, Amorites in the mountains, and the Canaanites by the sea-coast"; huge armies of tall invincible lusts: "We shall never be able to go against this people"; we shall never be able to prevail against our corruptions. Hearken not unto them, I beseech you, but hear what Caleb and Joshua say: "Let us go up at once and possess it, for we are able to overcome them"; not by our own strength, but by the power of the Lord of hosts [Num. 13:26–30]. There are indeed sons of Anak there, there are mighty giant-like lusts that we are to grapple with; nay, there are principalities and powers too that we are to oppose. But the great Michael, the Captain of the Lord's host, is with us; he commands in chief for us and we need not be dismayed. "Understand therefore this day, that the Lord thy God is he which goeth before thee as a consuming fire; he shall destroy these enemies, and bring them down before thy face" [Deut. 9:3]. If thou wilt be faithful to him, and put thy trust in him, as the fire consumeth the stubble and as the flame burneth up the chaff, so will he destroy thy lusts in thee; their root shall be rottenness, and their blossom shall go up as dust [Is. 5:24].

But let us take heed that we be not discouraged, and before we begin to fight despair of victory. But to believe and hope well in the power of our God and his strength will be half a conquest. Let us not think holiness in the hearts of men here in the world is a forlorn, forsaken and outcast thing from God, that he hath no regard of. Holiness, wherever it is, though never so small, if it be but hearty and sincere, it can no more be cut off and discontinued from God, than a sunbeam here upon earth can be broken off from its intercourse with the sun and be left alone amidst the mire and dirt of this world. The sun may as well discard its own rays and banish them from itself into some region of darkness far remote from it, where they shall have no dependence at all upon it, as God can forsake and abandon holiness in the world, and leave it a poor orphan thing that shall have no influence at all from him to preserve and keep it. Holiness is something of God, wherever it is; it is an efflux from him that always hangs upon him and lives in him: as the sunbeams, though they gild this lower world and spread their golden wings over us, yet they are not so much here, where they shine, as in the sun, from whence they flow. God cannot draw a curtain betwixt himself and holiness, which is nothing but the splendor and shining of himself; he cannot hide his face from it, he cannot desert it in the world. He that is once born of God, shall overcome the world [cf. 1 Jn. 5:4], and the prince of this world too, by the power of God in him. Holiness is no solitary neglected thing; it hath stronger confederacies, greater alliances than sin and wickedness. It is in league with God and the whole universe; the whole creation smiles upon it. There is something of God in it, and therefore it must needs be a victorious and triumphant thing.

Wickedness is a weak, cowardly and guilty thing, a fearful and trembling shadow. It is the child of ignorance and darkness; it is afraid of light, and cannot possibly withstand the power of it, nor endure the sight of its glittering armor. It is allianced to none but wretched, forlorn and apostate spirits, that do what they can to support their own weak and tottering kingdom of darkness, but are only strong in weakness and impotency. The whole polity and commonwealth of devils is not so powerful as one child of light, one babe in Christ; they are not all able to quench the least smoking flax, to extinguish one spark of grace [cf. Mt. 12:20]. Darkness is not able to make resistance against light, but ever, as it comes, flies before it. But if wickedness invite the society of devils to it (as we learn by the sad experience of these present times, in many examples of those that were possessed with malice, revengefulness and lust), so that those cursed fiends do most readily apply themselves to it, and offer their service to feed and encourage it, because it is their own life and nature, their own kingdom of darkness, which they strive to enlarge and to spread the dominions of; shall we then think that holiness, which is so nearly allied unto God, hath no good genius at all in the world to attend upon it, to help it and encourage it? Shall not the kingdom of light be as true to its own interest, and as vigilant for the enlarging of itself, as the kingdom of darkness? Holiness is never alone in the world, but God is always with it, and his loving Spirit doth ever associate and join itself to it. He that sent it into the world is with it as Christ speaketh of himself: "The Father hath not left me alone, because I do always those things that please him" [Jn. 8:29]. Holiness is the life of God, which he cannot but feed and maintain wheresoever it is; and as the devils are always active to encourage evil, so we cannot imagine but that the heavenly host of blessed angels above are as busily employed in the promoting of that which they love best, that which is dearest to God, whom they serve, the life and nature of God. "There is joy in Heaven at the conversion of one sinner" [Lk. 15:7]; Heaven takes notice of it; there is a choir of angels, that sweetly sings the epithalamium of a soul divorced from sin and Satan, and espoused unto Christ. What therefore the wise man speaks concerning wisdom, I shall apply to holiness: "Take fast hold of holiness, let her not go, keep her, for she is thy life; keep thy heart with all diligence, for out of it are the issues of life," and of death too [cf. Prov. 4:13,23]. Let nothing be esteemed of greater consequence and concernment to thee than what thou doest and actest, how thou livest. Nothing without us can make us either happy or miserable; nothing can either defile us, or hurt us, but what goeth out from us, what springeth and bubbleth up out of our own hearts [cf. Mk. 7:15]. We have dreadful apprehensions of the flames of Hell without us; we tremble and are afraid when we hear of fire and brimstone, whilst in the meantime we securely nourish within our own hearts a true and living Hell, . . . "et caeco carpimur igni [and we are in the grip of a flame without light]." The dark fire of our lusts consumeth our bowels within, and miserably scorcheth our souls, and we are not troubled at it. We do not perceive how Hell steals upon us whilst we live here. And as for Heaven, we only gaze abroad, expecting that it should come in to us from without, but never look for the beginnings of it to arise within, in our own hearts.

But lest there should yet haply remain any prejudice against that which I have all this while heartily commended to you, true holiness and the keeping of Christ's commandment, as if it were a legal and servile thing that would subject us to a state of bondage, I must here needs add a word or two either for the prevention or removal of it. I do not therefore mean by holiness, the mere performance of outward duties of religion, coldly acted over as a task; nor our habitual prayings, hearings, fastings, multiplied one upon another (though these be all good, as subservient to a higher end); but I mean an inward soul and principle of divine life, that spiriteth all these that enliveneth and quickeneth the dead carcass of all our outward performances whatsoever. I do not here urge the "dead law of outward works," which indeed, if it be alone, subjects us to a "state of bondage"; but the inward law of the Gospel, the "law of the Spirit of life" [Rom. 8:2], than which nothing can be more free and ingenuous. For it doth not act us by principles without us, but is an inward self-moving principle living in our hearts. I do not urge the law written upon tables of stone without us (though there is still a good use of that too) but the law of holiness written within, "upon the fleshly tables of our hearts" [Cf. 2 Cor. 3:3].

The first, though it work us into some outward conformity to God's commandments, and so hath a good effect upon the world, yet we are all this while but like dead instruments of music, that sound sweetly and harmoniously, when they are only struck and played upon from without by the musician's hand, who hath the theory and law of music living within himself.

But the second, the living law of the Gospel, the "law of the Spirit of life" within us, is as if the soul of music should incorporate itself with the instrument and live in the strings, and make them of their own accord, without any touch or impulse from without, dance up and down, and warble out their harmonies.

They that are acted only by an outward law are but like *neurospasts*, or those little puppets that skip nimbly up and down, and seem to be full of quick and sprightly motion; whereas they are all the while moved artificially by certain wires and strings from without, and not by any principle of motion from themselves within; or else like clocks and watches, that go pretty regularly for a while, but are moved by weights and plummets, or some other artificial springs, that must be ever now and then wound up, or else they cease.

But they that are acted by the new law of the Gospel, by the "law of the Spirit," they have an inward principle of life in them, that from the center of itself puts forth itself freely and constantly into all obedience to the will of Christ. This new law of the Gospel is a kind of musical soul, informing the dead organ of our hearts, that makes them of their own accord delight to act harmoniously according to the rule of God's word.

The law that I speak of is a law of love, which is the most powerful law in the world. And yet it freeth us in a manner from all law without us, because it maketh us become a law unto ourselves. The more it prevaileth in us, the more it eateth up and devoureth all other laws without us; just as Aaron's living rod did swallow up those rods of the magicians, that were made only to counterfeit a little life [Ex. 7:10].

> Quis legem det amantibus?
> Major lex amor est sibi.[13]

---

13. [ED.] "Who should lay down the law to lovers? Love is its own overriding law." —Boethius, *The Consolation of Philosophy*, Bk. III, Ch. XII (verse), lines 47–48.

Love is at once a freedom from all law, a state of purest liberty, and yet a law too of the most constraining and indispensable necessity.

The worst law in the world is the "law of sin, which is in our members" [Rom. 7:23]; which keeps us in a condition of most absolute slavery, when we are wholly under the tyrannical commands of our lusts. This is a cruel Pharaoh indeed, that sets his hard task-masters over us, and maketh us wretchedly drudge in mire and clay [cf. Ex. 5:13].

The law of the letter without us sets us in a condition of a little more liberty, by restraining us from many outward acts of sin; but yet it doth not disenthral us from the power of sin in our hearts.

But the "law of the spirit of life," the Gospel law of love, it puts us into a condition of most pure and perfect liberty; and whosoever really entertains this law, he hath "thrust out Hagar" quite, he hath "cast out the bond-woman and her children"; from henceforth Sarah, the free-woman, shall live for ever with him, and she shall be to him a mother of many children; her seed shall be "as the sand of the sea-shore for number," and "as the stars of heaven" [cf. Gal. 4:30; Gen. 22:17; 15:5]. Here is evangelical liberty, here is Gospel freedom, when "the law of the Spirit of life in Christ Jesus hath made us free from the law of sin and death" [Rom. 8:2]; when we have a liberty from sin, and not a liberty to sin: for our dear Lord and Master hath told us, that "whosoever committeth sin, he is the servant of it" [Jn. 8:34].

He that lies under the power and vassalage of his base lusts, and yet talks of Gospel freedom, he is but like a poor condemned prisoner, that in his sleep dreams of being set at liberty and of walking up and down wheresoever he pleaseth, whilst his legs are all the while locked fast in fetters and irons. To please ourselves with a notion of Gospel liberty, whilst we have not a Gospel principle of holiness within us to free us from the power of sin, is nothing else but to gild over our bonds and fetters and to fancy ourselves to be in a golden cage. There is a straitness, slavery and narrowness in all sin. Sin crowds and crumples up our souls, which, if they were freely spread abroad, would be as wide and as large as the whole universe.

No man is truly free but he that hath his will enlarged to the extent of God's own will, by loving whatsoever God loves, and nothing else. Such an one doth not fondly hug this and that particular created good thing, and envassal himself unto it; but he loveth everything that is lovely, beginning at God, and descending down to all his creatures, according to the several degrees of perfection in them. He enjoys a boundless liberty and a boundless sweetness, according to his boundless love. He enclaspeth the whole world within his outstretched arms; his soul is as wide as the whole universe, as big as "yesterday, to-day and forever." Whosoever is once acquainted with this disposition of spirit, he never desires anything else, and he loves the life of God in himself dearer than his own life. To conclude this, therefore; if we love Christ, and keep his commandments, his commandments will not be grievous to us; his yoke will be easy, and his burden light; it will not put us into a state of bondage, but of perfect liberty [cf. 1 Jn. 5:3; Mt. 11:29; Rom. 8:21]. For it is most true of evangelical obedience what the wise man speaketh of wisdom, "Her ways are ways of pleasantness, and all her paths are peace; she is a tree of life to those that lay hold upon her, and happy are all they that retain her" [Prov. 3:17,18].

I will now shut up all with one or two considerations, to persuade you farther to the keeping of Christ's commandments.

First, from the desire which we all have of knowledge. If we would indeed know Divine truths, the only way to come to this is by keeping of Christ's commandments. The grossness of our apprehensions in spiritual things and our many mistakes that we have about them proceed from nothing but those dull and foggy steams which rise up from our foul hearts and becloud our understandings. If we did but heartily comply with Christ's commandments, and purge our hearts from all gross and sensual affections, we should not then look about for truth wholly without ourselves, and enslave ourselves to the dictates of this and that teacher, and hang upon the lips of men; but we should find the great eternal God inwardly teaching our souls, and continually instructing us more and more in the mysteries of his will; and "out of our bellies should flow rivers of living waters" [Jn. 7:38]. Nothing puts a stop and hindrance to the passage of truth in the world but the carnality of our hearts, the corruption of our lives.

It is not wrangling disputes and syllogistical reasonings that are the mighty pillars that underprop truth in the world. If we would but underset it with the holiness of our hearts and lives, it should never fail. Truth is a prevailing and conquering thing and would quickly overcome the world, did not the earthiness of our dispositions and the darkness of our false hearts hinder it. Our Savior Christ bids the blind man wash off the clay that was upon his eyes in the pool of Siloam, and then he should see clearly [Jn. 9:7]; intimating this to us, that it is the earthiness of men's affections that darkens the eye of their understandings in spiritual things.

Truth is always ready and near at hand, if our eyes were not closed up with mud, that we could but open them to look upon it. Truth always waits upon our souls and offers itself freely to us, as the sun offers its beams to every eye that will but open and let them shine in upon it. If we could but purge our hearts from that filth and defilement which hangeth about them, there would be no doubt at all of truth's prevailing in the world. For truth is great, and stronger than all things. All the earth calleth upon truth and the heaven blesseth it; all works shake and tremble at it. The truth endureth and is always strong; it liveth and conquereth for evermore. She is the strength, kingdom, power and majesty of all ages. Blessed be the God of truth.

Last of all, if we desire a true reformation, as we seem to do, let us begin here in reforming our hearts and lives, in keeping of Christ's commandments. All outward forms and models of reformation, though they be never so good in their kind, yet they are of little worth to us without this inward reformation of the heart. Tin, or lead, or any other baser metal, if it be cast into never so good a mold and made up into never so elegant a figure, yet it is but tin or lead still; it is the same metal that it was before. And if we be molded into never so good a form of outward government, unless we new mold our hearts within too, we are but a little better than we were before. If adulterate silver, that hath much alloy or dross in it, have never so current a stamp put upon it, yet it will not pass notwithstanding, when the touchstone trieth it. We must be reformed within, with a spirit of fire and a spirit of burning, to purge us from the dross and corruption of our hearts and refine us as gold and silver; and then we shall be reformed truly, and not before. When this once comes to pass, then shall Christ be set upon his throne indeed, then "the glory of the Lord shall overflow the land"; then we shall be a people acceptable unto him, and as mount Sion, which he dearly loved.

✤ ✤ ✤ ✤ ✤ ✤ ✤ ✤

BENJAMIN WHICHCOTE

Whatsoever Things are True

(DISCOURSE I)

Editor's Introduction. This sermon is the first of a notable series of thirteen preached by Whichcote on the passage in Philippians on the things we ought "to think about." It affords a good example of Whichcote's style of preaching. What is more important, it illustrates a characteristic approach on the part of the Cambridge Platonists to the essential elements in a religious understanding of truth.[1]

✤ ✤ ✤ ✤

Philippians 4:8. "Finally, brethren, whatsoever things are true . . ."

A weightier scripture, more summary and comprehensive of all perfection, more matter of greater weight I do not find contracted anywhere. This text shows how complete and well-furnished the man of God should be; one who professes himself a Christian, and names Christ and pretends to the faith of the Gospel; whatsoever is good in its nature and quality should be well known to him, should be his ornament and accomplishment, should be that which may endow his mind and qualify his spirit; for see how deeply the man of God, or a Christian, is here charged. There are no fewer than eight heads of which I shall give you a full account.

    I. Whatsoever is right, sincere and true.

    II. Whatsoever is comely, grave and venerable.

    III. Whatsoever is fair, just and equal.

    IV. Whatsoever is sacred, pure and holy.

    V. Whatsoever is generous, noble and lovely.

    VI. Whatsoever is of credit, value or esteem among persons competent to judge, viz., persons of well-informed understandings and well-refined

1. [ED.] The text is to be found in *The Works of the learned Benjamin Whichcote,* D.D., 4 vols. (Aberdeen, 1751), III, 368ff.

morals; for other persons are no more competent to judge what is of value or worth than a blind men of colors, or a deaf man of sounds.

VII. Whatsoever is of singular use, or particular virtue.

VIII. Whatsoever may recommend a man's person, or gain him advantage.

Whatsoever is such as this upon any of these accounts, it is to be the exercise and employment of every man that calls himself a Christian; and by these he is to make himself known to the world: in all these cases he ought to think it worthy of himself and becoming him, to discharge himself fully. "Think on these things"; that is, in the use of your reason, mind and understanding, in the exercise of your rational faculties, charge yourselves with these things. It is not barely, have these things in your thoughts; but, in the use of your reason recommend all these things to yourself; think that you do not acquit yourself, that you do not do that which becomes you, that you do not raise a connatural superstructure to the foundation of nature, that you do not do that which is suitable to a Christian, that you have your reason to little purpose; if you do not in the reason of your mind think all these things worthy of you. This is the sum of the words; "finally, brethren, whatsoever things are true, whatsoever things are honest," &c. And this for the general; I now come to particulars.

I. "Whatsoever things are true." And here we must take up Pilate's question, "What is truth?" John 18:38. I will choose to give you an account only in things practical; but yet you must give me leave a little; and the better to give you an account of this particular, I shall digest what I have to say into this following method.

First, declare the difference of truth; for truth is first in things, then in our apprehensions.

Secondly, the truth of things is considerable either *in foro naturae*, or *genere morum*; that is, upon a natural account, or as it is the concernment of an intelligent and voluntary agent.

Thirdly, I shall shew whence ariseth our obligation to truth.

Fourthly, by what rules we shall find out truth.

Fifthly, the evidences and assurances we have of truth.

Sixthly, clear all, by shewing all this in particular instances.

Seventhly, and lastly, make certain inferences.

For the *first; the truth of things* lies in this: that things do exist of their own principles, as a man is a true man, because he doth consist of such a body and an immortal soul. Things are true, as they do exist of their principles and as they are answerable to the idea of them in the divine mind preexistent to them; for this is the manner of working of an intelligent agent, to do things according to a preconceived apprehension of his mind. Now this truth of things is no charge of ours. It is God's charge; it is the effect of God's creation, for he hath made all things true, and therefore things must be true. For God cannot fail either through impotency, or want of power, or through error of judgment. And if anything be monstrous, it ariseth either from some gross matter, or from impediment; if there be any redundant or defective matter, or if the effect be hindered, then the thing must be monstrous, but otherwise we are to take it for granted that things are true, because they are God's workmanship. This is truth, *metaphysically* but then that which we are concerned in, is *the truth of our apprehensions:* and our apprehensions are *then* true, *when* they agree with the truth and existence of things; when we conceive of things as they are; and if we think otherwise, then there is a lie in our understandings. And here is the occasion of all the evil that breaks in upon mortals, that we do not conceive of things as they are, but that all men (except some few) either worship the idol of some particular imagination, or the idol of popular superstition; they either follow private imagination of their own, or general mistakes; and he is a man of a thousand that can rise up and quit himself of these two idols. By false imagination a man deprives himself of good; for it is a true rule, that imagination makes the case within, though not without; for as a man conceives, so is the case within; and Solomon observes, that the simple or the fool believes everything that is represented. But the state of things is determined; this is fixed by God in the moment of creation, and our judgment and apprehension are to be conformable to the reality and existence of things; and when our affections and actions are suitable to such a judgment and sense of our minds, we are then in the truth, and never else. The first belongs to a man's understanding, and that speaks him an able man, a man of judgment, a man of sense and experience; and the latter speaks him a good man. And indeed if men's actions comply not with the sense of their judgments, there will be self-condemnation and no peace at all within; and this is a great and mighty distinction; *the truth of things.* And there it is first; and that is *God's* charge. God made things to exist as they do. God made all things true. God made all our faculties true, and we may be assured our faculties are true, because God gave them us; and we may believe our faculties, because they came out of the hands of God. Our faculties are the tools that God gave us to work by, and by them we receive whatsoever God offers to our consideration. If our faculties are not true, we are not charge-

able for not understanding God, or not receiving from him. And this is
the first, *truth in things*. But then the second is our charge, *truth in our
apprehensions*. And the truth in our apprehensions lies in their conformity
to the truth of things. If we think otherwise than the truth of things, we
live in a lie.

Secondly, the second distinction is the truth of things, either upon a
natural consideration, to know things in their natures and qualities. This is
natural philosophy; and this is of great use in the life of man, and tends to
the enlarging man's understanding. But this is not the concernment of
religion and conscience. Or else it is *in genere morum*, truth upon moral
consideration. This only is the concernment of conscience, and here we do
enquire whether things be right or wrong, good or evil, and accordingly
charge ourselves (if we be persons of conscience). We are to be in reconciliation with things that are good, and to have a displacency against things
that are impure, unholy and contrary to the mind and will of God. This is
the concernment of conscience and the business of religion, and is every
body's charge; for both a good state here and a future good state hereafter depend upon it.

Thirdly, how then come we to be under the *obligation* to truth? Now
man's obligation to truth (that is, that truth should be in all his actions and
apprehensions) is grounded upon the state and principles of his creation;
which I explicate in four particulars. 1. Man's *capacity*. 2. Man's *proper
employment*. 3. Man's *true end*. 4. Man's *relation*.

1. Man's *capacity;* and thereby he is under an obligation of duty to God,
because God hath made him capable to know that he is, and to know that
he himself arises from other causes greater and more good than himself.
For the spirit of a man is the candle of the Lord; and no man hath mind
and understanding, but he may as naturally know, that there is a God
upon whom he depends, as he may know there is a sun in the firmament—
if he will open his eyes. By the power of his understanding he is made
apprehensive of God. Then by that prerogative and privilege of liberty
and freedom, he is able to sacrifice to God, and to bring God the free
consent of his mind: to offer up himself to God, an offering of a sweet-
smelling savor. He may know, according to the rule of righteousness, what
he ought to do, and what to forbear; that he ought to do righteously and
live soberly; and to live in regard and observance of God, and to avoid the
contrary; and this is grounded upon man's *capacity*. 2. Man's *proper employment*. The natural employment and proper business of mind and
understanding, is to attend upon God, to be employed about him, to ob-

serve him, to receive from him, to comply with him and obey him. And if men do not do thus, neither have God in their thoughts, but employ mind and understanding to drudge to worldly ends and purposes, at the day of judgment it will appear to be sacrilege. 3. Man's *true end*. God is a man's ultimate end, and the center in whom he doth rest. God is as properly the end of souls as anything is the end of another. It is as proper for a man's soul to make towards God, as it is for anything in the world to make to its center, as it is for heavy things to fall downwards, or light things to fly upwards. That God that is original to me, I ought to make him final to me; and if I receive all from God, I ought to refer to him, and rest in him. 4. Man's *relation*. And that is treble: to *God*, to his *fellow-creatures* and to *himself*. Now see what things are founded in a man's relation. (i) His relation to *God*, doth import all dependence upon God, all observance of God, all submission to God, all high apprehensions of God, faith and affiance in him; that he adore and reverence him, love and honor him, rejoice and delight in him, make acknowledgment to him, and give him thanks for his free communication and influence, by and through which we live and enjoy all things. (ii) His relation to his *fellow-creatures*. And that lays a foundation of equity and righteousness, and requires a man to do as he would be done by, and to live in love and good-will, wishing well to others, taking delight to do courtesies, to injure none, to offend none, but to have his mind discharged from all spite, fury, malignity, mischief, &c. Then, (iii) in the relation he standeth in to *himself*, as he doth consist of an immortal soul, and a corruptible body, this engageth him to use a proportionable care of his soul in competition with his body, according to the excellency of his soul above his body. The truth of things requires that the soul have the predominance over the body and that the body be subordinate to it, for in all reason the worse must be subordinate to the better.

Upon all these considerations man is obliged to abide in the truth, and to perform all acts of sobriety as to *himself*, all acts of righteousness as in conjunction with *others*, all acts of duty and piety to *God* as his sovereign and his maker. And thus have I showed you the ground of man's being under the *obligation* to truth.

The fourth particular is to give you an account of the *rule* and *measure* of truth; and this is a notion worth every man's carrying away. I will give you but two measures or rules whereby you may find out or judge of truths. 1. According to the nature of God; or (which is the same) according to the reason of things. 2. According to the mind and will of God, or (which concurs with this) according to the resolution of him that hath right; and there is a double right, the right of power and authority, and the right of property. And truth is to be determined by one of these measures.

The first is the *measure*, where the matter is unchangeable and unalterable, where it is so and it cannot be otherwise, and it doth not depend upon the will and pleasure of any agent whatsoever, but the things are necessary in themselves, and they are certainly and constantly so; as all ways of goodness, righteousness, mercy, clemency, benignity, compassion, &c., that which is fit, that which is comely, that which is right, just, honest, pure; these are not to be controlled by any power whatsoever, for these are *suo jure*.

2. But when there are things that are of an indifferent nature; and then the measure is according to the pleasure of God—good, while God appoints them, as the *Mosaical* institution, but after God deserted it, it was the contrary; or else, according to the determination of him that hath right to state, constitute, determine and appoint. And two sorts of persons have this. There is either the right of authority, and so the magistrate may make laws and require obedience, and he ought to have it. For every man, where he hath power, he may make use of it, and he doth not offend if he doth not exceed his bounds. So the magistrate resolves in things that are matters of order; and he that will live in any country, he must observe the rules and laws of that country. Or else, there is the right of property as an owner; every owner hath a right of property to dispose of his own, and no man can invade upon that which is another man's property, unless he be permitted upon terms of bargain or treaty; and so the property of things goes from one to another. These are the rules and measures of truth.

Fifthly, I am to shew you the *evidences* and *assurances* that we have of truth. And they are one of these two: either we know things by the light of God's creation, or some after-revelation from God. By the light of God's creation, I am assured there is a God, and that he is righteous and holy, and just and good. I have as great assurance of this, as I have assurance there is a creature by a creator's make. By the use of my reason I as certainly know the divine being and perfections, as I know anything in the world. Then there is the light of after-revelation for such doctrines as these: who Christ was, what he came into the world for, how he was used in the world, &c. Now the light of these is the light of after-revelation from God. So we are assured of truth by the light of God's creation, that is the principles of reason and natural understanding, together with divine assistance and after-revelation. But,

Sixthly, because generals may prove ineffectual in that they do not so easily enter into particular men's minds and understandings, therefore I will give you certain *instances*. Therefore,

First, I will shew you when there is truth on our part respectively to God. And here, if I discover when we are said to lie to *God*, I shall by the same shew you when there is truth towards God. Now we put a lie upon God in these five ways. 1st. To profess and not to believe. This is high dissimulation and a horrible indignity put upon God: to progress and not to be persuaded in a man's mind, this represents God, as if he might be mistaken or imposed upon. 2dly. To believe and not to do. And this is to "hold the truth in unrighteousness" (Rom. 1:18) which in Scripture is looked upon to be an act of the greatest violence, deformity and malignity. 3dly. To begin and not to persevere. He is remarkably unfit for the kingdom of God, who having put his hand to the plow, looks back. We disparage God extremely when we leave him. 4thly. To pretend God, and to mean a man's self or the world. To make God a *mean*, and the world an *end*. I dread to have to do with any man that will make use of his religion to gain him credit and to make a bargain. Of such a man one had need to take double security. These things are certain, and if a man do examine his conscience, he may find out whether he be treacherous or false, or sincere and true. 5thly. To name the name of God, and not to depart from evil. In these five cases we do not abide in the truth, but we put a lie upon God, which is a great provocation of him.

In the second place, as there is a lie to God, so a man may put a lie upon *himself*, and that five ways too. First, to gratify one's lusts, be the color and pretence what it will. For lust is a false principle; lusts are exorbitances and irregularities, they are false births, they have no true existence. Therefore for a man to gratify his lusts is to put a lie upon himself. Second, to give way to fond imaginations. This is to lie to one's self. For not the bubblings of particular fancy, but the resolutions and determinations of universal, sober and impartial reason, are realities; these only are rules and principles. Thirdly, it is also to put a lie upon a man's self, to live after a mere temper. For this is below reason, and short of virtue; and hence it is that every petty astrologer pretends to tell fools their fortune. There is no man that is wise, but he is more than temper. A man by wisdom doth govern himself and overrule all fate and destiny whatsoever. For man, under God, hath a kind of sovereignty over himself. A man hath power to use diligence, that he may attain to right apprehensions of things; and then he hath power to execute and perform, according to his apprehensions. Fourthly. This also is for a man to put a lie upon himself, to persuade himself in anything without warrant of reason or Scripture. This is Solomon's fool, that believes everything that is said, Proverbs 14:15. To settle in an opinion without warrant of reason or Scripture or credible testimony is a foolish thing, is impotency and fondness. Credulity is a stranger to wisdom, and the very nurse of superstition. Also fifthly, a man puts a lie upon himself, if he have his will for a rule. For will is no rule at all. Will signifies nothing, unless it be that will that is in conjunction with infallible understanding, which is the will of God. Some will, because they will; which is not fit. For will is no rule, if there be reason in the **case**; will is nothing, but right and reason is to over-rule will. Some men think it the highest perfection to be arbitrary; but really, if they do consider, it is a piece of the greatest impotency and foulest deformity. In these five cases a man puts a lie upon himself.

In the third place, I must give you an account of truth between man and man. In which particular if you will abide in the truth, then you must observe these rules. First, all our expressions must answer to our intentions: when we treat one with another, we are not in the truth, unless we speak what we mean. Secondly, it is necessary to truth of a treaty, that the materials which make the case, be fully declared. For it is no agreement if any part of the matter be unknown. For a case is made up of all circumstances; do but diversify one circumstance, and it is another thing. Therefore it is necessary that the materials be fully declared. Thirdly, the parties that treat together, are to take care that they understand and mean the same things; and not make it a practice for one that is more comprehensive than another, to make use of his wit to over-reach, and if they find they did not mean the same things, they are to release one another; for no man is obliged further than he did mean. Fourthly, what is meant in the treaty, is ever after to be stood to: no after-shifts; men must not after use wit, or practise upon the doubtfulness of uncertainty of words and phrases, thereby to make an escape; but what was meant in the treaty, must be stood to. Fifthly, engagements entered into are to be performed. What we have engaged, we must perform, unless we can obtain a release from the party with whom we engage; though it prove inconvenient and worse to us than we imagined. This is truth between man and man; and whosoever faileth in these, forfeiteth his truth. And thus I have shewed you wherein a man may put a lie upon God, upon himself, upon his neighbor. I shall superadd in

The fourth place: if any man resolve to be a good man, he must observe these seven particulars. 1. I will begin with the lowest; but truly it is worthy human nature to take notice of it. That there be from us mercy and fair usage to the beasts that serve us; and undoubtedly he is horridly apostate from God, and degenerate from his own species, that can abuse the beast that serves him. Solomon observes (Prov. 12:10) that whosoever can abuse a beast that readily serves him, he doth show himself to be sunk and degenerate below the principle of human reason. A man may without breach of charity say he is neglective of God, takes no notice of God, and is degenerated from his species, who can abuse the beast that readily serves him. Here is no provocation, no wrong; and his property and title obliges him to preserve it. We ought not to abuse the creation below us, but to use everything according to its nature. 2. Ingenuous education and instruction of all rationals. It is not fit that any one should be born into a Christian commonwealth, nay, not into the world, but that he have ingenuous education and instruction. This Solomon likewise observes (Prov. 22:6), "Train up a child in the way that he should go," &c. It is as much due to human nature, to every man that is born, to have education, information and instruction, to the polishing and improving his rational faculties, as it is due to give him meat for his belly, and clothes for his back; and it is as monstrous and unnatural to bring up a child without mental instruction, as to turn him out of doors to starve in the streets. 3. There ought to be no usurpation, cruelty or oppression anywhere. Where any man happens to have the advantage (for here we are in several forms and orders), they that have the advantage over others, ought not to shew their power or privilege by oppression, usurpation or cruelty; for it cannot be that human nature should be dispossessed of the inherent right that belongs to human nature. 4. There ought to be no inordinancy of spirit, but to think of ourselves according as we ought. 5. No excess in bodily conveniencies. It is a horrible thing for a man when he pretends to eat and drink to continue his life, to exceed so, that instead of preserving his health, he lays up matter of sickness and disease. 6. No displeasure to lodge in any man's breast. And the truth is, a man is certainly injurious to the person of whom he thinks amiss; and he doth himself harm; for he carries that in him, which corrodes and disturbs his mind; and the serenity of a man's mind is his choice and best enjoyment. 7. Use the same measure to others, that we ourselves expect. For undoubtedly every man is as much to himself as we are to ourselves; and this is the glorious rule of Christianity, and hath represented Christianity a lovely and amiable institution in the very sight of the heathen.

Thus have I in several instances declared to you what I mean by abiding in the truth; and by this you may understand this charge of the apostle, "whatsoever things are true." Judge that it becomes you in all transactions of life, to acknowledge, and to abide in, and to be found in them.

Seventhly. Now I come to make some inferences.

First, I shall improve this as a rule of life. If a man would make himself worthy and valuable, then he is to charge himself that his apprehension of things be according to the reality of things, and then that his election and choice and affections be guided by such apprehension, and that he should worship none of those two great idols, neither err in the way of his own particular fancy, nor be led along by any common error, but let truth guide, govern and overrule him, in the whole course of his life.

Secondly, upon this account of truth three things are wholly to be discharged: 1. All falsehood and lying. 2. All dissimulation and hypocrisy. 3. All deceit in every kind. We should strictly adhere to right and truth: we ought to be open-hearted and deal with all simplicity. It is not enough to avoid gross lying, but a man must take care that all his expressions answer the intentions of his mind. Communication one with another is a turning the inside outward, opening your breasts one to another, and if a man pretend to do this and do it not, is he not a cheat? Is not this to lie? We should intend what we say, and do what we intend.

Thirdly, here we have a discovery of the false measures of truth, which do obtain in the world where truth doth not take place; and they are the longest sword, the loudest lungs, and the most voices. 1. The longest sword; and then the Mahometans must have it; and before them the great disturbers of mankind, whom we call conquerors, as Alexander and Caesar. 2. If the loudest lungs must carry it, then the Baal-worshippers must have it from Elijah; for he had but one still voice, but they cry from morning to night. 3. If the most voices; then the condemners of our Savior must have it: for they all cry, "Crucify, crucify." Therefore these are false measures.[2]

In the next place, take notice of the horrid and desperate principles of the Church of Rome. For they tell us that faith is not to be kept with heretics; and the heretic is he whom they determine to be so. For they have the infallibility; and so the power of faith and truth is in their hands. And why then may not Mahometans say, no faith to be kept with Christians? And why may not Christians and Mahometans say, no faith to be

2. [ED.] The same thought occurs in more condensed form in Whichcote's *Aphorisms*, No. 500.

kept with pagans? and so faith and truth shall be banished the world. So you see what work will be made; and there is as good reason for the one as for the other. And,

Lastly, by my opinion, no contempt shall be cast upon honest poverty. Where the accurate observation of right and truth keeps men low in their estates, when they will not prevaricate and transgress in point of conscience, there the person is more admirable and commendable because of his honesty, than his condition can be despicable or contemptible because of his poverty. Such a man is better than he that is rich in an unconscionable way.

And this may serve for an account of this *first* perfection; *whatsoever things are true.*

PART TEN

❖

Epilogue

* * * * * * * *

BENJAMIN WHICHCOTE

Moral and Religious Aphorisms

Editor's Introduction. Whichcote's happy gift of compressing his thought into terse and vivid epigrams heightened the effect of his preaching, and makes his published sermons lively reading. But initially his memorable sayings were buried among his own brief notes and in the stenographic reports of those who had listened to his preaching. When his sermons began to appear in print, they were sometimes published in ill-edited and unauthorized editions. To ensure a better text, his literary remains were entrusted to Archdeacon Jeffery. Among other tasks, Jeffery collected from Whichcote's papers a large number of striking sayings. The five thousand extracts which he originally chose were pruned to ten "centuries" of a hundred each, and were published in 1703. Fifty years later, Samuel Salter deleted some of the original selections, substituted others culled from the printed works, added still others, and so brought the total to twelve hundred.[1]

The task was skillfully done; the *Aphorisms* were popular during the eighteenth century, and were the form in which Whichcote's work was most widely known. The material chosen naturally stressed certain points (e.g., the place of reason in religion) which were particularly congenial to the eighteenth-century mind; but in spite of this slight distortion the selection is essentially a faithful reflection of the man and his mind, and it has seemed right to have it represented in this volume.

Jeffery numbered the items in the *Aphorisms;* so did Salter. For ease of reference the numbers used in the 1753 edition have been retained.

* * * *

5. Knowledge alone doth not amount to virtue, but certainly there is no virtue without knowledge. Knowledge is the first step to virtue and goodness; but goodness is not without delight and choice.

6. It is a great deal easier to commit a second sin than it was to commit

1. [ED.] Salter's edition of 1753 was republished in 1930, with an introduction by W. R. Inge.

the first; and a great deal harder to repent of a second than it was to repent of the first.

9. What is perfected hereafter must be begun here.

11. It is base and unworthy to live below the dignity of our nature.

14. If we consider what is becoming reasonable nature, we shall have a rule to guide us as to good and evil.

17. Man is made for better purposes than for the drugery of the world; much more than for the slavery of sin.

19. That which is not original to itself cannot be final to itself. But to whom it belongs to be the first cause, to the same it belongs to be the last end; so God should be to us, by our own act. He that is original to us, by himself, should be final to us, by our choice.

22. By these two things religion is recommended to us, above all other things whatsoever: 1, by satisfaction we thereby enjoy in life; and 2, by expectation we have thereby at death.

24. There is a natural propension in everything to return to its true state, if by violence it has been disturbed. Should it not be so in grace, in the divine life? Virtue is the health, true state, natural complexion of the soul. He that is vicious in his practice is diseased in his mind.

25. It is the work and business of religion and of our lives to reconcile the temper of our spirits to the rule of righteousness and to incorporate the principles of our religion into the complexion of our minds.

This is to be done, 1, by searching into the nature of things, and the reason of our duty, that our judgment may be such as to approve the laws of our religion; 2, by practising according to our right apprehensions of things, till it becomes easy and delightful to us; 3, by persisting in this course all our days, ever designing and meaning righteousness and ever retracting and correcting what is unrighteous.

26. The whole world is governed by the perfection of truth, righteousness and goodness, in conjunction with the perfections of wisdom and power; and nothing is done by God, but what these perfections do.

28. When the principles of our religion become the temper of our spirits, then we are truly religious; and the only way to make them become so is to reason ourselves into an approbation of them; for nothing which is the reason of things, can be refused by the reason of man, when understood.

29. The natural knowledge of religion is as spiritual as any knowledge that belongs to us. The moral part of religion is the knowledge of God's

nature; the positive part of religion is the knowledge of his will, concerning expiation and pardon.

33. The rule of right is the reason of things; the judgment of right is the reason of our minds, perceiving the reason of things.

34. Right and truth are greater than any power, and all power is limited by right.

35. Everyone that is honestly disposed may find direction for what he is to do from right reason and plain Scripture—the only ways by which men are taught of God; nor is any other teaching necessary.

40. A man has as much right to use his own understanding in judging of truth as he has a right to use his own eyes to see his way. Therefore it is no offence to another that any man uses his own right.

42. Man, as man, is averse to what is evil and wicked; for evil is unnatural, and good is connatural, to man.

43. Only madmen and fools are pleased with themselves; no wise man is good enough for his own satisfaction

44. The soul does contemplate and worship God, when it is not disturbed by the body or disaffected through vice.

45. In the search after God and contemplation of him, our wisdom doth consist; in our worship of God and our obedience to him, our religion doth consist; in both of them, our happiness doth consist.

48. There is no solid satisfaction but in a mental reconciliation with the nature of God and the law of righteousness.

51. That which is the *best* employment here will be the *only* employment in eternity, and with great improvement and advantage. There we shall have none but good company, and they will be better than they now are. We shall have neither guilt *within* us, nor enemies *about* us, nor death *before* us.

52. There is no better way to learn than to teach.

53. He that never changed any of his opinions, never corrected any of his mistakes; and he who was never wise enough to find out any mistakes in himself will not be charitable enough to excuse what he reckons mistakes in others.

55. We are only so free, that others may be free as well as we.

58. Those that differ upon reason may come together by reason.

62. The government of our spirits is the greatest freedom.

65. Conscience without judgment is superstition; judgment without conscience is self-condemnation.

67. No man is wise enough for his own direction, powerful enough for his own defence, or good enough for his own satisfaction.

69. Let not anyone use that severity in the case of another, which his own case will not bear. For a man may condemn himself in the person of another.

71. There is nothing proper and peculiar to man but the use of reason and exercise of virtue.

78. Let no man condemn another for such things as he desires God would pardon in himself.

80. Every misgovernment of ourselves is a punishment of ourselves.

81. Sins of the mind have less infamy than those of the body, but not less malignity.

85. God imposeth no law of righteousness upon us which he doth not observe himself.

94. When the doctrine of the Gospel becomes the reason of our mind, it will be the principle of our life.

97. Religion is unity and love. Therefore it is not religion that makes separation and disaffection.

99. Reason discovers what is natural, and reason receives what is supernatural.

100. Both Heaven and Hell have their foundation within us. Heaven primarily lies in a refined temper, in an internal reconciliation to the nature of God and to the rule of righteousness. The guilt of conscience and the enmity to righteousness is the inward state of Hell. The guilt of conscience is the fuel of Hell.

103. Those who are united by religion should be united by charity.

109. God hath set up two lights to enlighten us in our way: the light of reason, which is the light of his creation; and the light of Scripture, which is after-revelation from him. Let us make use of these two lights and suffer neither to be put out.

114. Nothing spoils human nature more than false zeal. The good nature of an heathen is more God-like than the furious zeal of a Christian.

121. In the use of reason and the exercise of virtue we enjoy God.

129. For contradiction to his reason, a man is challenged now and will be condemned at the great day of judgment. It is the reason of things and of our minds, not the power of God only, which condemns. Fear thyself, for thou art in more danger of being condemned by the reason of thy mind than of any power whatsoever, of God or man.

130. Our fallibility and the shortness of our knowledge should make us peaceable and gentle. Because I *may* be mistaken, I *must* not be dogmatical and confident, peremptory and imperious. I will not break the certain laws of charity for a doubtful doctrine or of uncertain truth.

138. Certainly our Savior accepts of no other separation of his Church from the other part of the world than what is made by truth, virtue, innocency and holiness of life.

170. Ignorance of that will not destroy another, the knowledge of which will not save me.

187. The application of ourselves to God, according to God's manifestation of himself to us, is the only thing necessary to salvation.

200. There is nothing desperate in the state of good men, where there is a right principle within them and God's superintendency over them.

216. It is impossible for a man to be made happy by putting him into a happy place, unless he be first in a happy state.

220. Religion is intelligible, rational and accountable. It is not our burden, but our privilege. It is not for our harm, but given us for our good. There is no one thing in all that religion, which is of God's making (whether that of creation, or Christian) of which any sober man, in the true use of his reason, would say, "Pardon me in this" (as 2 Kings 5:18), or from which he would be released, though he might have his pardon or release under the seal of Heaven.

245. He that commands others is not so much as free, as if he doth not govern himself. The greatest performance in the life of man is the government of his spirit.

246. If, through the help of God, we do not alienate ourselves from the things of the world, the things of the world will certainly alienate us from God.

247. A man hath his religion to little purpose if he doth not mend his nature and refine his spirit by it.

248. We worship God best when we resemble him most.

271. This is the security of us creatures who live under an irresistible and uncontrollable power, that all the ways and proceedings of that power are in loving-kindness, righteousness and judgment.

285. Men of holy hearts and lives best understand holy doctrines and things. Those who have not the temper of religion are not competent judges of the things of religion.

288. Religion begets in us a rational confidence and a transcendent pleasure.

289. Will, without reason, is a blind man's motion; will, against reason, is a mad man's motion.

294. Good men, under power of reason and religion, are free, in the worst condition. Bad men, under power of lust and vice, are slaves, in the best condition.

295. He that useth his reason doth acknowledge God.

296. The perfection of the happiness of human nature consists in the right use of our rational faculties, in the vigorous and intense exercise of them about their proper and proportionable object, which is God.

299. Religion teaches less than we desire to know, and requires more than we are willing to practise.

302. Unless a man takes himself sometimes out of the world by retirement and self-reflection, he will be in danger of losing himself in the world.

311. Punishment is not an arbitrary act according to will but a reasonable act directed by wisdom and limited by goodness.

315. It is not worth the name of religion to charge our consciences with that which we have not reconciled to the reason and judgment of our minds, to the frame and temper of our souls.

316. Sin is a defiance to the authority of God, a contradiction to the law of righteousness, a disturbance to the society of men, and a distraction to the soul of the sinner.

325. Wicked men shake off the government of reason as if it were tyranny and usurpation.

327. We should not have been voluntary in the second place if we had not been intelligent in the first place. The right order is when things, in respect of operation, do imitate the constitution of nature; and nature's order is that men should first understand and be informed and find out the reason of things, and after that determine and resolve accordingly in the use of their liberty.

336. Where the reason of the thing doth not require or determine, where the necessity of the end doth not claim and enforce, where there is no positive prohibition or injunction to the contrary from God—there, under God, we have liberty.

337. The spirit in us is the reason of our minds illuminated by the written word. The spirit now teaches by these writings.

343. Religion does not operate like a charm or spell, but ingenuously by way of mind and understanding.

349. Enthusiasm is the confounder both of reason and religion; therefore

nothing is more necessary to the interest of religion than the prevention of enthusiasm.[2]

357. The Church of Christ hath not two more choice things than the simplicity of her faith and the sincerity of her love.

360. Defamation—evil report—we should be extremely careful in this particular because an injury of this sort is without after-recompence. We cannot follow a lie at the heels, to recover credit taken away, as we can follow a thief to recover goods taken away.

381. Religion is the highest accomplishment of human nature, and human nature is deformed and depraved without religion.

384. The improvement of a little time may be gain to all eternity, and the loss of a little time may be the greatest loss that can be.

393. I have always found that such preaching of others hath most commanded my heart which hath most illuminated my head.

398. It is a more difficult work to reconcile men to God than to reconcile God to men.

406. When a man has a principle in his mind that will work him to repentance, then he is purified. Such an argument is the death of Christ.

407. Christ, who was innocent, was dealt withal as if he were faulty, that we, who are faulty, might be dealt with as if we were innocent.

408. Christian religion is but imaginary if it doth not attain to the reconciliation of our spirits to the rule of righteousness and the nature of God.

425. The truly zealous serve religion in a religious temper; in zeal there is nothing tending to provocation or exasperation. Zeal for God and truth appears to others in fair persuasion and strength of argument.

429. He that doth not govern himself can neither do right to men nor honor to God.

434. Modesty and humility are the sobriety of the mind; temperance and chastity are the sobriety of the body.

436. A benefactor is a representative of God.

444. The truths of God are connatural to the soul of man; and the soul of man makes no more resistance to them than the air does to light.

451. Neither God nor man doth alter anyone's mind, otherwise than by reason, persuasion and satisfaction; for intellectual nature is commanded by nothing but by reason and consideration.

457. There is nothing so intrinsically rational as religion is, nothing that

2. [ED.] In the seventeenth and eighteenth centuries, "enthusiasm" meant fancied inspiration, ill-regulated religious emotion, or fanaticism.

can so justify itself, nothing that hath so pure reason to recommend itself as religion hath.

459. The reason of our mind is the best instrument we have to work withal.

462. The religion of the creation requires the true and full use of reason; as first, to the discerning the differences of things in their own nature, good or evil; then, to the observing such difference in life and action. It is wisdom to find out; it is righteousness to will and do this.

463. God is as good as the perfection of goodness; God is far better than we can conceive him to be.

464. Heaven is first a temper and then a place.

476. They that have not the effect of religion have not the comfort of it.

485. He is not fit to speak in company that has not considered by himself; and he that has done nothing but studied alone is not fit to come into company. A man is nobody where he hath not thought and considered; yet often, what was hid from men while they thought apart by themselves, is manifested while they are communicating with others.

487. I know nothing forbidden by the Gospel, which one of true reason would desire to have liberty to do.

500. The longest sword, the strongest lungs, the most voices are false measures of truth.

506. Great evil is introduced by a little departure from our right judgment. It is harder to return judgment than to have stood out with it, and every vicious act weakens a right judgment.

512. It is a very great evil to make God a means, and the world an end; to name God, and to intend the world.

513. To alienate ourselves from God is the greatest and truest sacrilege.

514. Moral evil is the greatest of all evils, for it has the worst malignity and the worst consequences.

516. When God commands the sinner to repent, this supposes either that he is able or that God will make him so.

517. It does not follow that God doth not enforce, therefore he doth not enable. That God should force, agrees neither with the nature of God nor with the nature of man; but that God should enable agrees with both, as he is creator and we creatures.

535. Reconciliation looks rather forward than backward, at what may be, in time to come, than what has been, in time past.

537. Who will think a man does believe, that does things contrary to what he says he believeth?

547. Let all uncertainties lie by themselves in the catalogue of disputables, matters of farther inquiry; let the certainties of religion settle into constitution and issue in life and practice.

554. The several virtues of religion are connatural to the frame of man; they are according to his nature and agreeable to his reason, which is the superior and governing principle.

571. Sin hardens the hearts of men, spoils the modesty of intellectual nature, and disposes men for evil.

578. In doctrines of supernatural revelation we shall do well to direct our apprehensions and to regulate our expressions by words of Scripture.

581. Where there is only a show of religion there is only an imagination of happiness.

586. There are but two things in religion: morals and institutions. Morals may be known by the reason of the thing; morals are owned as soon as spoken, and they are nineteen parts in twenty of all religion. Institutions depend upon Scripture; and no one institution depends upon one text of Scripture only. That institution which has but one text for it has never a one.

590. Morality is the congruity and proportion that is between the actions of rational beings and the objects of those actions.

599. Though the speaker be a fool the hearer should be a wise man.

612. The effect of Christ's death in us is our death to sin.

617. It is hard to get rid of an error; therefore take heed of admitting it.

618. He is not likely to learn who is not willing to be taught, for the learner has something to do as well as the teacher.

619. It is otherwise than God would have it, where the least of our time is spent in contemplation, for the better informing the mind and for the farther refining the spirit.

624. The laws of Christianity are restorative to our nature, satisfactory to our reason, pacificatory to our conscience, which make up our great concernment.

625. The spirit of God in us is a living law, informing the soul; not constrained by a law without, that enlivens not; but we act in the power of an inward principle of life, which enables, inclines, facilitates, determines. Our nature is reconciled to the law of heaven, the rule of everlasting righteousness, goodness and truth.

640. Men are not so weak (save only in religion) to think anyone is in earnest, if he do no more than talk.

641. The nearer we approach to the God of truth, the farther we are from the danger of error.

643. There is, by the doctrine of Christianity, a restoration of true religion; and, by the practice of Christianity, a restoration of human nature.

644. True reason is so far from being an enemy to any matter of faith that a man is disposed and qualified by reason for the entertaining those matters of faith that are proposed by God.

646. The ways and dealings of God with his creatures are all accountable in a way of reason; but sinners vary from the reason of things, and take upon them to overrule what is settled and established from eternity.

647. If the passions be not under the government of reason, the man is under the government of his passions and lives as if he had no reason. Passion ungoverned by reason is madness.

655. Principles of reason and religion are recommended as things fit to govern in the life of man, as sovereign to nature, and the rule of our actions.

660. We never do anything so secretly but that it is in the presence of two witnesses: God and our own conscience.

675. He that is full of himself goes out of company as wise as he came in.

678. Man, as a sociable creature, is made for converse with those that are his equals; to receive from then, and to communicate to them; to be the better for them, and to make them the better for him.

681. Virtue is in our power, though praise be not: we may deserve honor, though we cannot command it

682. Sin is an attempt to control the immutable and unalterable laws of everlasting righteousness, goodness and truth upon which the universe depends.

692. It is monstrous and horrid for a man to be better in the reason of his mind than he is in the choice of his actions.

695. When men unduly practise[3] upon truth, they are forced into the absurdities of error. So it befalls factions in religion.

697. The benefits of the Gospel are the renovation of our natures and the reconciliation of our persons.

711. Zeal for truth and conscience of duty are high titles, things of great name; but the greatest mischief follows where passion and interest are so clothed.

712. Religion, which is a bond of union, ought not to be a ground of division, but is in an unnatural use when it doth disunite. Men cannot

3. [ED.] I.e., perform tricks or artifices.

differ by true religion, because it is true religion to agree. The spirit of religion is a reconciling spirit.

720. Religion makes us live as those who represent God in the world.

725. It is not liberty to do what is not fit to be done; for this cannot be said of God, who has all true liberty. He is least of all free—nay, he is the veriest slave in the world—who hath either will or power to vary from the law of right.

733. Virtue cannot be forced upon a man's practice, nor happiness be forced into a man's enjoyment.

734. Man, that is a moral agent, must be morally dealt withal.

735. It is easier to bear the scorn of the irreligious than the insolence of the hypocrite.

736. Shall I justify that sin by my life, which Christ condemned by his death?

737. Natural truths are truths of God's creation; supernatural truths are truths of God's revelation. Nothing is more knowable than natural truth; nothing is more credible than revealed truth.

738. Moderation is abating of our own right, to comply with other men's necessities.

743. Morality is not a means to anything, but to happiness; everything else is a means to morality.

753. Expect no greater happiness in eternity than to rejoice in God.

756. There is nothing more unnatural to religion than contentions about it.

757. To insist upon antiquated and unnecessary things or to be contentious about private and particular apprehensions hinders the advancement of truth, the increase of knowledge, and the exercise of charity.

762. Worship of God in spirit, i.e., in the motion of the mind and understanding, is the free, full, noble, ingenuous use of a man's highest powers and faculties. To serve God with the determination of the understanding, and the freeness of choice; first, to judge, and then to choose— this is the immutable religion of God's creation; the service of angels and men, self-established, not depending upon institution, indispensable; the religion of the state of innocency. And there is nothing beyond this, in the state of glory, but as perfected there.

777. When a man obstructs the reason of his mind by the gratifications of the body, or when he subordinates the reason of his mind to the desires of the body, then he sins against sobriety.

788. No man is true to himself if he be ill employed.

798. Reverence God in thyself; for God is more in the mind of man than in any part of this world besides; for we (and we only here) are made after the image of God.

799. He that doth wrong to himself, to whom will he do right?

808. Give me a religion that is grounded upon right reason and divine authority; such as, when it does attain its effect, the world is the better for it.

819. He that takes himself out of God's hands into his own, by-and-by will not know what to do with himself.

828. In acknowledgment of what Christ hath done and suffered, take up this resolution: that it shall be better for everyone with whom thou hast to do because Christ hath died for thee and him.

841. The more you are offended at your evil thoughts, the less they are yours; the more they are your burden, the less they are your guilt. The knowledge or thought of evil is not evil; it is not what you know, but what you consent to.

860. God created man with a vast capacity of receiving, and (answerably hereunto) with a restless desire of, greater good than the creature can afford.

878. They are therefore greatly mistaken who in religion oppose points of reason and matters of faith, as if nature went one way and the author of nature went another.

880. Nothing without reason is to be proposed; nothing against reason is to be believed. Scripture is to be taken in a rational sense.

909. God desires no man's salvation, without his return; and God desires no man's return, without his consent.

929. True religion hath done only good in the world; but superstition, which is the counterfeit of religion, hath done the worst and greatest mischiefs.

948. Religion is a true friend to human nature. In the first instance, it doth uphold and conserve; in the next, it doth repair and recover and restore the principles of God's creation, lost in man by ill-use or neglect of himself.

969. Nothing is more spiritual than that which is moral.

982. When the love of truth rules in the heart, the light of truth will guide the practice.

987. None so empty as those who are full of themselves.

1140. When anger goes before, matter of repentance commonly follows after.

1142. He that repents is angry with himself; I need not be angry with him.

1148. We must not take religion upon us as a task, not bear it as a burden.

1161. Nothing is of faith that is not in Scripture; nothing is necessary, as otherwise expressed; nothing is certain, as farther made out. We may live in Christian love and union without consent and agreement in non-Scriptural expressions and forms of words.

1186. It is not good to live in jest, since we must die in earnest.

❖ ❖ ❖ ❖ ❖ ❖ ❖ ❖ ❖

BENJAMIN WHICHCOTE

A Prayer for Morning or Evening

Editor's Introduction. It has seemed appropriate to conclude this edition of the writings of the Cambridge Platonists with a prayer exemplifying what they understood by the life of piety. To a remarkable degree it epitomizes many of their characteristic convictions; both its form and content convey something of the atmosphere which pervades so many of their writings.

The prayer appears as the final item in Samuel Salter's edition of Whichcote's *Moral and Religious Aphorisms* (1753). As with most of Whichcote's work, its history is very difficult to trace. In 1697 there was published, in Whichcote's name, a book entitled *A Treatise of Devotion; with Morning and Evening Prayer, for all the Days of the Week;* but Salter had not seen it, and it is now extremely rare. The prayer must have been transmitted to Salter along with what remained of Whichcote's papers in the collection of Dr. John Jeffery, Archdeacon of Norwich.

❖ ❖ ❖ ❖

Most blessed God, the Creator and Governor of the world, the only true God and Father of our Lord Jesus Christ, we thy creatures were made to seek and find, to know and reverence, to serve and obey, to honor and glorify, to imitate and enjoy thee, who art the original of our beings and the center of our rest. Our reasonable nature hath a peculiar reservation for thee, and our happiness consists in our assimilation to and employment about thee. The nearer we approach unto thee, the more free we are from error, sin and misery; and the farther off we are from thee, the farther off we are from truth, holiness and felicity. Without thee we are sure of nothing; we are not sure of ourselves. But through thee there is self-enjoyment in the mind, when there is nothing but confusion and no enjoyment of the world.

We could not conceive thee to be perfectly good, if we did not look upon thee as the detester of everything that is unjust, wicked and impious. We should misrepresent thee unto the world, if we should say that will

434

and power alone govern in the disposure of the affairs and states of thy creatures; for thou, O God, dost all things with the greatest reason, in exactest righteousness, in the fullest equity that is possible.

We acknowledge that the law of our nature and of our religion as men results necessarily from our relation to thee, as our Creator and God; and that it cannot be that we should be disobliged from our obedience which is the moral necessity and high privilege of our being. Bring back therefore our minds, by just and wise reflections, to center themselves in thee; that through repentance and pardon our sins may be as if they had never been; and our souls may be in perfect reconciliation with thy nature and will and law; and with the measures of everlasting righteousness, goodness and truth; that our minds may be in love and goodwill, in concord and agreement with the whole creation of God, with whatsoever derives from God, holds of God, and acknowledges him. We know thou canst not vary from the perfections of thy nature and therefore we cannot promise ourselves that thou wilt pardon without repentance, or fear that thou wilt condemn those who do repent. But when we sin against thee, we wrong our own souls, and wickedness makes us enemies to our happiness and to our beings.

Let us always live in the fear and apprehension of God, without whom we cannot live at all. Let the light of truth and the help of grace be vital principles of action in us; that we may, in the time of life, attain the ends for which we live; and that our religion, which begins in knowledge may proceed in action, settle in temper and end in happiness; that we may make it the work and business of our lives to reconcile the temper of our spirits to the rule of righteousness and to incorporate the principles of our religion into the complexion of our minds; that what we attribute to God, as his moral excellencies and perfections, we may propose to ourselves as matter of practice and imitation; and that what is our best employment in this world and will be our only employment in the next may be our free choice and our transcendent pleasure.

Let us not put off that repentance and reformation to our last hours which is a business of difficulty and leisure; as the working out all vicious habits, established by frequent acts and long custom, and the working in of religious dispositions by contrary practice and slow degrees must needs be. Free us timely, by conformity unto the gospel of Christ, from that rancor and malignity with which our former practice of sin had poisoned and depraved our nature.

Help us to shun the beginnings of sin which are modest and to dread the issues of sin, which are impudent because, wherever we begin to miscarry, we know not where we shall end; and to keep ourselves within the measures of reason and nature; and never to subordinate religion, conscience, justice or anything that is holy, to sensual pleasure, worldly gain or popular reputation.

Establish in us a God-like temper and make us sensible of it in ourselves, that we may the more easily part with this world, to go to God by death whenever thou callest us thereunto; and may not be without foundation of hope and future expectation, and so run from death or be in bondage to it, as a prevailing enemy; that we may have in our consciences none of the fuel of Hell and so not fear the kindling of those fires upon us; that we may not, at last, be abandoned from God, upon any unpardonable provocation, inwardly self-condemned by a guilty and awakened conscience, which would render us extremely and eternally miserable. But grant that our religious knowledge being digested into true goodness before we die, we may depart hence to an estate agreeable and happy, natural and proper to that holy and heavenly temper in which we have settled ourselves here, by religious use, practice and custom; and that this divine constitution, which was recommended to our souls by the excellency of its nature, may be perpetuated and consummated in us, when we are gone from hence; and we be for ever with thee, in whose presence is fullness of joy and at whose right hand are pleasures for evermore. All this we humbly beg of thee, O Lord, as we are capable, for ourselves and for all Christian people and for all mankind, through Jesus Christ our Mediator and Redeemer, in whose name we sum up our petitions, saying, *Our Father, &c.*

Selected Bibliography

I. *Primary Works and Contemporary Comments*

(Note: this is not a complete bibliography of the Cambridge Platonists. The works and editions included have been used in compiling the present selection, or are referred to in the introduction and the notes.)

CAMPAGNAC, E. T., ed. *The Cambridge Platonists. Being Selections from the Writings of Benjamin Whichcote, John Smith and Nathanael Culverwel* (Oxford, 1901).

CUDWORTH, RALPH. *The True Intellectual System of the Universe* (London, 1678). Among subsequent editions are *The Works of Ralph Cudworth*, ed. Thomas Birch, 4 vols. (Oxford, 1829); and *True Intellectual System of the Universe*, ed. J. Harrison (with the notes and dissertations of J. L. Mosheim), 3 vols. (London, 1845), which includes most of the other works.

—— *A Sermon Preached Before the Honorable House of Commons March 31, 1647* (London, 1647). Reprinted in the Birch and Harrison editions, and in facsimile (New York, 1930).

—— *A Treatise Concerning Eternal and Immutable Morality*, ed. E. Chandler, Bp. of Durham (London, 1731). Reprinted in the Birch and Harrison editions, and (in abbreviated form) in Selby-Bigge, *British Moralists*.

—— *A Treatise of Freewill*, ed. John Allen (London, 1838).

CULVERWEL, NATHANAEL. *An Elegant and Learned Discourse of the Light of Nature* (London, 1652; reprinted, Oxford, 1669; Edinburgh, 1857).

FOWLER, EDWARD. *The Principles and Practices of certain Moderate Divines of the Church of England Abusively called Latitudinarians* (London, 1670).

MORE, H. *Philosophical Poems* (Cambridge, 1647).

—— *The Immortality of the Soul* (London, 1659).

—— *An Explanation of the Grand Mystery of Godliness* (London, 1660). (As in *Theological Works*.)

—— *An Antidote Against Atheism*, 2d ed., corrected and enlarged (London, 1655); 3d ed. in *A Collection of Several Philosophical Writings of Dr. Henry More* (London, 1662).

—— *A Collection of Several Philosophical Writings* (London, 1662).

—— *Divine Dialogues* (London, 1665).

—— *Enchiridion Ethicum* (London, 1667). English translation: *An Account of Virtue: or Dr. Henry More's Abridgement of Morals,* Put into English [by Edward Southwell] (London, 1690).

—— *Enchiridion Metaphysicum* (London, 1671).

—— *The Theological Works of the Most Pious and Learned Henry More, D.D.* (London, 1708).

NORRIS, JOHN. *Reason and Religion,* in *Treatises upon Several Subjects* (London, 1698).

—— *Cursory Reflections upon a Book call'd, An Essay Concerning Human Understanding* (1699). Appended to *Practical Discourses upon the Beatitudes,* Vol. I, 5th ed. (London, 1707).

—— *An Essay Towards the Theory of the Ideal or Intelligible World,* Vol. I (London, 1701); Vol. II (London, 1704).

—— *An Account of Reason and Faith: in relation to the Mysteries of Christianity.* 13th ed. (London, 1728).

—— "Letters Philosophical and Moral to Dr. Henry More, with the Doctor's Answers," in *The Theory and Regulation of Love* (Oxford, 1688).

PARKER, SAMUEL. *A Free and Impartial Censure of the Platonic Philosophy* (Oxford, 1667).

PATRICK, SIMON. *Autobiography,* ed. Alex Taylor (Oxford, 1839).

"S.P." [Simon Patrick]. *A Brief Account of the New Sect of Latitude men: Together with Some Reflections on the New Philosophy* (London, 1662).

RAY, JOHN. *The Wisdom of God, Manifested in the Works of Creation* (London, 1691).

RUST, GEORGE. *A Discourse of Truth* (London, 1682).

SHERMAN, JOHN. *Commonplaces* (London, 1641).

SMITH, JOHN. *Select Discourses* (1660), 4th ed., corrected and revised, ed. H. G. Williams (Cambridge, 1859).

TILLOTSON. *The Works of the Most Reverend Dr. John Tillotson.* 10th ed. 3 vols. (London, 1735).

TOLAND, JOHN. *Christianity Not Mysterious* (London, 1696).

WARD, RICHARD. *The Life of the Learned and Pious Dr Henry More, Late Fellow of Christ's College in Cambridge.* (London, 1710).

WHICHCOTE, BENJAMIN. *Select Discourses, published by John Jeffery,* 4 vols. (London, 1701–1707).

—— *The Works of the learned Benjamin Whichcote, D.D.* 4 vols (Aberdeen, 1751).

—— *Moral and Religious Aphorisms, To Which are added Eight Letters which passed between Dr Whichcote and Dr Tuckney,* ed. Samuel Salter (London, 1753). Republished (without the *Letters*) in facsimile, with an introduction by W. R. Inge (London, 1730).

WORTHINGTON, JOHN. *Diary and Correspondence,* ed. James Crossby and R. C. Christie (Chetham Society, Vols. XIII, XXXVI, CXIV; Manchester, 1847, 1855, 1886).

II. *Secondary Works*

ANDERSON, P. R. *Science in Defence of Liberal Religion* (New York, 1933).

ASPELIN, G. *Cudworth's Interpretation of Greek Philosophy* (Göteborg, 1943).

AUSTIN, E. M. *The Ethics of the Cambridge Platonists* (Philadelphia, 1935).

BAKER, HERSCHEL C. *The Wars of Truth* (Cambridge, Mass., 1952).

BAKER, J. T. *An Historical and Critical Examination of English Space and Time Theories from Henry More to Bishop Berkeley* (Bronxville, N.Y., 1930).

BREDVOLD, L. I. *The Intellectual Milieu of John Dryden* (Ann Arbor, 1934).

BURNET, GILBERT. *History of My Own Times*, ed. O. Airy. 2 vols. (Oxford, 1897).

BURTT, E. A. *The Metaphysical Foundations of Modern Physical Science* (London, 1925).

CARRÉ, MEYRICK H. *Phases of Thought in England* (Oxford, 1949).

——— "Ralph Cudworth," *The Philosophical Quarterly*, III (1953).

CASSIRER, E. *Die Platonische Renaissance in England und die Schule von Cambridge* (Leipzig. 1932). Translated by James P. Pettigrove as *The Platonic Renaissance in England* (Edinburgh, 1953).

COLERIDGE, S.T. *Notes on the English Divines*, I (London, 1853).

COLIE, ROSALIE L. *Light and Enlightenment: A Study of the Cambridge Platonists and the Dutch Arminians* (Cambridge, England, 1957).

COPLESTON, F. *A History of Philosophy*, Vol. V (London, 1959).

CRAGG, G. R. *From Puritanism to the Age of Reason* (Cambridge, England, 1950).

DEBOER, J. *The Theory of Knowledge of the Cambridge Platonists* (Madras, 1931).

DE PAULEY, W. C. *The Candle of the Lord: Studies in the Cambridge Platonists* (London, 1937).

DILLENBERGER, JOHN. *Protestant Thought and Natural Science* (New York, 1960).

GEORGE, E. A. *Seventeenth Century Men of Latitude* (New York, 1908).

GREENSLET, FERRIS. *Joseph Glanvill* (New York, 1900).

GRIERSON, H. J. C. *Cross Currents in English Literature in the Seventeenth Century* (London, 1929).

GRIFFITHS, O. M. *Religion and Learning* (Cambridge, England, 1935).

GYSI, LYDIA. *Platonism and Cartesianism in the Philosophy of Ralph Cudworth* (Bern, 1962).

JONES, RUFUS M. *Spiritual Reformers in the Sixteenth and Seventeenth Centuries* (New York, 1914).

JORDAN, W. K. *The Development of Religious Toleration in England*, IV (Cambridge, Mass., 1940).

HAZARD, PAUL. *The European Mind, 1680–1715*, trans. J. Lewis May (London, 1953).

HOOD, F. C. *The Divine Politics of Thomas Hobbes* (Oxford, 1964).

HOOPES, ROBERT. *Right Reason in the English Renaissance* (Cambridge, Mass., 1962).

HUNT, J. *Religious Thought in England*. 3 vols. (London, 1870).

INGE, W. R. *Christian Mysticism* (London, 1899).

—— *The Platonic Tradition in English Religious Thought* (London, 1917).

—— *The Philosophy of Plotinus*, 2nd ed. (London, 1923).

KOYRÉ, A. *From Closed World to Infinite Universe* (Baltimore, 1957).

KRISTELLER, P. O. *The Philosophy of Marsilio Ficino* (New York, 1943).

LAMPRECHT, STERLING. "The Role of Descartes in Seventeenth Century England," *Studies in the History of Ideas*, III (1935).

—— "Innate Ideas in the Cambridge Platonists," *Philosophical Review*, XXXV (1926).

LICHTENSTEIN, AHARON. *Henry More: The Rational Theology of a Cambridge Platonist* (Cambridge, Mass., 1962).

LOVEJOY, A. O. "Kant and the English Platonists," in *Essays Philosophical and Psychological in Honor of William James* (New York, 1908).

LOWREY, C. *The Philosophy of Ralph Cudworth* (New York, 1884).

MACKINNON, FLORA I. *Philosophical Writings of Henry More* (New York, 1925).

MARTINEAU, JAMES. *Types of Ethical Theory*, 2 vols. (Oxford, 1886).

MASSON, D. *The Life of John Milton*, VI (London, 1859).

MAYOR, J. E. B. "Henry More," in *Notes and Queries*, Second Series, VII (London, 1859).

McADOO, H. R. *The Spirit of Anglicanism* (London, 1965).

MINTZ, SAMUEL I. *The Hunting of Leviathan* (Cambridge, England, 1962).

MUIRHEAD, J. H. *The Platonic Tradition in Anglo-Saxon Philosophy* (London, 1931).

MULLINGER, J. BASS. *Cambridge Characteristics in the Seventeenth Century* (London, 1867).

—— *History of the University of Cambridge* (London, 1885).

—— "Platonists and Latitudinarians," in *The Cambridge History of English Literature*, VIII (Cambridge, England, 1912).

NAIRNE, A. "The Cambridge Platonists," in *Church Quarterly Review*, CI (1925–1926).

NICHOLSON, MARJORIE H. "Christ's College and the Latitude-Men" *Modern Philology*, XXVII (1929).

——, ed. *The Conway Letters: The Correspondence of Anne, Viscountess Conway, Henry More and their Friends, 1642–1684* (New Haven, 1930).

—— "The Early Stages of Cartesianism in England," *Studies in Philology*, XXVI (1929).

PASSMORE, J. A. *Ralph Cudworth, An Interpretation* (Cambridge, England, 1951).

PAWSON, G. P. H. *The Cambridge Platonists* (London, 1930).

PLOTINUS. *The Enneads*, revised ed., trans. S. Mackenna (London, 1957).

POWICKE, F. J. *The Cambridge Platonists, a Study* (London, 1926).

RAVEN, C. E. *Science, Religion and the Future* (Cambridge, England, 1943).

—— *Natural Religion and Christian Theology*, I (Cambridge, England, 1953).

SELBY-BIGGE, L. A. *British Moralists*, 2 vols. (Oxford, 1897).

SCOTT, W. R. *An Introduction to Cudworth's 'Treatise Concerning Eternal and Immutable Morality,' with Life and a Few Critical Notes* (London, 1891).

SETH, JAMES. *English Philosophers and Schools of Philosophy* (London, 1912).

SORLEY, W. R. *A History of English Philosophy* (Cambridge, England, 1920).

TULLOCH, JOHN. *Rational Theology and Christian Philosophy in England in the Seventeenth Century:* Vol. II, *The Cambridge Platonists* (Edinburgh and London, 1874).

WARRENDER, H. *The Political Philosophy of Hobbes* (Oxford, 1957).

WEBB, C. C. J. *Studies in the History of Natural Theology* (Oxford, 1915).

WESTCOTT, B. F. "Benjamin Whichcote," in *Masters in English Theology*, ed. A. Barry (London, 1877).

—— "Benjamin Whichcote," in *Essays in the History of Religious Thought in the West* (London, 1897).

WHITTAKER, T. *The Neo-Platonists* 2nd ed. (Cambridge, 1928).

WILEY, MARGARET L. *The Subtle Knot* (Cambridge, Mass., 1952).

WILLEY, BASIL. *The Seventeenth Century Background* (London, 1934).

—— *Christianity Past and Present* (Cambridge, England, 1952).

—— *The English Moralists* (London, 1964).

III. *The Contemporary Background of the Cambridge Platonists*

(Note: to understand the Cambridge Platonists, it is necessary to understand their age. The books suggested here are chosen from an immense general literature on the period; many others with a strong claim to inclusion have been omitted.

The best background, of course, is the incomparable literature of the century, and there is no substitute for reading Bacon and Donne, Johnson, Milton, Bunyan, Baxter, Hobbes and Locke. The age was also one of great diarists and writers of memoirs—Ludlow, Fox, Mrs. Hutchinson, Pepys, Evelyn and the Duchess of Newcastle.)

ABBOTT, W. C. *The Writings and Speeches of Oliver Cromwell.* 4 vols. (Cambridge, Mass., 1937–47).

ALLEN, J. W. *English Political Thought, 1603–1644* (London, 1938).

BETHELL, S. L. *The Cultural Revolution of the Seventeenth Century* (London, 1951).

BOAS, MARIE. *Robert Boyle and Seventeenth Century Chemistry* (Cambridge, England, 1958).

BOSHER, R. S. *The Making of the Restoration Settlement* (London, 1951).

BOWLE, JOHN. *Hobbes and His Critics* (London, 1951).

BUSH, DOUGLAS. *English Literature in the Early Seventeenth Century* (Oxford, 1945).

BUTTERFIELD, H. *The Origins of Modern Science* (London, 1949).

BRAITHWAITE, W. C. *The Beginnings of Quakerism,* new ed. (Cambridge, England, 1955).

——— *The Second Period of Quakerism,* new ed. (Cambridge, England, 1961).

CLARENDON, EDWARD HYDE, EARL OF. *History of the Rebellion,* ed. W. D. Macray; 6 vols. (Oxford, 1888).

——— *The Life of Edward, Earl of Clarendon, written by Himself.* 2 vols. (Oxford, 1857).

CLARK, G. N. *Science and Social Welfare in the Age of Newton* (Oxford, 1937).

——— *The Seventeenth Century,* 2nd ed. (Oxford, 1947).

——— *The Later Stuarts,* 2nd ed. (Oxford, 1955).

CRAGG, G. R. *Puritanism in the Period of the Great Persecution* (Cambridge, England, 1957).

CRANSTON, M. *John Locke* (London, 1957).

CURTIS, M. H. *Oxford and Cambridge in Transition, 1558–1643* (Oxford, 1959).

DAVIES, G. *The Early Stuarts,* 2nd ed. (Oxford, 1959).

——— *The Restoration of Charles II* (San Marino, 1955).

FIRTH, C. H. *The Last Years of the Protectorate* (London, 1909).

——— *Oliver Cromwell* (London, 1901).

FULLER, THOMAS. *Church History of Britain* (1655).

——— *Worthies of England* (London, 1662).

GARDINER, S. R. *History of England, 1603–1642*, new ed. (London, 1895).

—— *A History of the Great Civil War, 1642–1649*, new ed. (London, 1897).

—— *A History of the Commonwealth and Protectorate* (London, 1899).

—— *The Constitutional Documents of the Puritan Revolution*, 3rd ed. (Oxford, 1906).

GOOCH, G. P. *The History of English Democratic Ideas in the Seventeenth Century*, ed. H. J. Laski (Cambridge, England, 1927).

HALLER, W. *The Rise of Puritanism* (New York, 1938).

—— *Liberty and Reformation in the Puritan Revolution* (New York, 1955).

HILL, CHRISTOPHER. *Economic Problems of the Church* (Oxford, 1956).

—— *Puritanism and Revolution* (London, 1958).

—— *The Age of Revolution* (Edinburgh, 1961).

—— *Society and Puritanism in Pre-Revolutionary England* (London, 1964).

—— *The Intellectual Origins of the English Revolution* (London, 1966).

HUTTON, W. H. *A History of the English Church from the Accession of Charles I to the Death of Anne* (London, 1903).

JAMES, M. *Social Policy during the Puritan Revolution* (London, 1930).

JONES, I. D. *The English Revolution* (London, 1931).

JONES, J. R. *Britain and Europe in the Seventeenth Century* (London, 1966).

JUDSON, MARGARET. *The Crisis of the Constitution* (New Brunswick, N.J., 1949).

KENYON, J. P. *The Stuarts* (London, 1958)

—— *The Stuart Constitution* (Cambridge, England, 1966).

KNIGHTS, L. C. *Drama and Society in the Age of Jonson* (London, 1937).

LOCKYER, R. *Tudor and Stuart Britain, 1471–1714* (New York, 1964).

LYON, T. *Religious Liberty in England* (Cambridge, England, 1937).

MACPHERSON, C. B. *The Political Thought of Possessive Individualism* (Oxford, 1962).

MASSON, DAVID. *The Life of John Milton;* 6 vols. (London, 1859).

MATTHEWS, A. G. *Calamy Revised* (Oxford, 1934).

—— *Walker Revised* (Oxford, 1948).

NEW, J. F. H. *Anglican and Puritan* (Stanford, 1964).

NOTESTEIN, W. *The English People on the Eve of Colonization* (New York, 1954).

NUTTALL, G. F. *Visible Saints* (London, 1957).

OGG, DAVID. *England in the Reign of Charles II*, 2nd ed; 2 vols. (Oxford, 1955).

PAUL, R. S. *The Lord Protector* (London, 1955).

PORTER, H. C. *Reformation and Reaction in Tudor Cambridge* (Cambridge, England, 1958).

PROTHERO, G. W. *Select Statutes and other Constitutional Documents, 1558–1625* (Oxford, 1894).

RAVEN, C. E. *John Ray, Naturalist* (Cambridge, England, 1942).

RERESBY, SIR JOHN. *Memoirs,* ed. A. Browning (Glasgow, 1936).

SCHLATTER, R. B. *Social Ideas of Religious Leaders, 1660–1688* (Oxford, 1940).

SIMPSON, ALAN. *Puritanism in Old and New England* (Chicago, 1955).

SHAW, W. A. *A History of the English Church, 1640–60,* 2 vols. (London, 1900).

SYKES, NORMAN. *From Sheldon to Secker* (Cambridge, England, 1959).

TANNER, J. R. *English Constitutional Conflicts of the Seventeenth Century* (Cambridge, England, 1928).

THOMSON, G. S. *Life in a Noble Household, 1641–1700* (London, 1937).

TILLYARD, E. M. W. *The Elizabethan World Picture* (London, 1943).

TREVELYAN, G. M. *England Under the Stuarts* (London, 1904).

—— *English Social History* (London, 1942).

TREVOR-ROPER, H. R. *Archbishop Laud,* 2nd ed. (London, 1962).

WEDGWOOD, C. V. *Poetry and Politics under the Stuarts* (Cambridge, England, 1960).

—— *The King's Peace* (London, 1955).

—— *The King's War* (London, 1958).

WHITING, C. E. *Studies in Puritanism, 1660–1688* (London, 1931).

WOODFALL, R. S. *Science and Religion in Seventeenth Century England* (New Haven, 1958).

WOODHOUSE, A. S. P., ed. *Puritanism and Liberty* (London, 1938).

WORMALD, B. H. G. *Clarendon: Politics, History and Religion* (Cambridge, England, 1951).

WRIGHT, LOUIS B. *Religion and Empire* (Chapel Hill, N.C., 1943).

YULE, G. *The Independents in the English Civil War* (Cambridge, England, 1958).

Index